India: The Ancient Past

'Burjor Avari's balanced and well-researched book is a most reliable guide to the period of Indian history that it covers. It displays considerable mastery of primary and secondary literature and distils it into a wonderfully lucid exposition. This book should be of interest to both lay readers and academic experts.'

Lord Bhikhu Parekh, *University of Westminster*

A clear and systematic introduction to the rich story of the Indian past from early pre-history up until the beginning of the second millennium, this survey provides a fascinating account of the early development of Indian culture and civilisation.

The study covers topics such as the Harappan Civilisation, the rise of Hindu culture, the influx of Islam from the eighth to the twelfth century, and key empires, states and dynasties. Through such topics and their historiographies, the book engages with methodological and controversial issues.

Features of this richly illustrated guide also include a range of maps to illustrate different time periods and geographical regions. Selected source extracts for review and reflection can be found at the end of every chapter, together with questions for discussion.

India: The Ancient Past provides comprehensive coverage of the political, spiritual, cultural and geographical history of India in a uniquely accessible manner that will appeal both to students and to those with a general interest in Indian history.

Burjor Avari was born in India in 1938, spent his childhood in Kenya and Zanzibar, graduated in history at Manchester University and was trained as a teacher at the Oxford University Institute of Education. He taught history in Kenyan and British schools for twenty-two years, from 1962 to 1984; and he gained experience as team leader for developing multicultural education in the schools of the English borough of Tameside from 1984 to 1987. He was appointed in 1988 as Principal Lecturer at the Manchester Metropolitan University, where he now coordinates multicultural education and teaches Indian history (part time). He received an MBE in 1988 in recognition of his work in multicultural education.

India: The Ancient Past

A history of the Indian sub-continent
from *c.* 7000 BC to AD 1200

Burjor Avari

Routledge
Taylor & Francis Group

LONDON AND NEW YORK

First published 2007
by Routledge
2 Park Square, Milton Park, Abingdon, Oxon OX14 4RN

Simultaneously published in the USA and Canada
by Routledge
270 Madison Ave, New York, NY 10016

Routledge is an imprint of the Taylor & Francis Group, an informa business

Typeset in Garamond by
Book Now Ltd, London
Printed and bound in Great Britain by
MPG Books, Bodmin

British Library Cataloguing in Publication Data
A catalogue record for this book is available from the British Library

Library of Congress Cataloging in Publication Data
Avari, Burjor.
    India, the ancient past: a history of the Indian sub-continent from
  c. 7000 BC to AD 1200/Burjor Avari.
       p. cm.
    Includes bibliographical references and index.
    1. India–History–To 1500. I. Title.
    DS451.A87 2007
    934–dc22   2006030369

ISBN10: 0–415–35615–6 (hbk)
ISBN10: 0–415–35616–4 (pbk)

ISBN13: 978–0–415–35615–2 (hbk)
ISBN13: 978–0–415–35616–9 (pbk)

Dedicated to the memory of my dear parents, teachers
and good friend David Melling

A vision for India

Where the mind is without fear and the head is held high;
Where knowledge is free;
Where the world has not been broken up into fragments by
   narrow domestic walls; . . .
Where the clear stream of reason has not lost its way into the
   dreary desert sand of dead habit; . . .
Into that heaven of freedom, my Father, let my country awake.

(From Gitanjali, by Rabindranath Tagore,
Nobel Laureate, 1913)

Contents

Extracts

Illustrations

Figures

Maps

While every effort has been made to trace and acknowledge ownership of copyright material used in this volume, the publishers will be glad to make suitable arrangements with any copyright holders whom it has not been possible to contact.

Preface

There has been a profound change in the study of ancient Indian history within the last six or seven decades. Influential cadres of historians, archaeologists, anthropologists and environmentalists have rejuvenated earlier scholarship in this vast area, opening up unfamiliar lines of investigation, and contributing new insights for our deeper understanding of the multi-faceted aspects of ancient India.

This book is a modest attempt at bringing together some of the recent researches of committed scholars such as Professors D.K. Chakrabarti, R. Champakalakshmi, Brijadulal Chattopadhyaya, François Jarrige, R.S. Sharma, Romila Thapar, André Wink and several others. The book's twofold aim is to generate fresh interest in the culture and history of ancient India among undergraduates qualifying in South Asian history in the colleges and universities of the English-speaking world, as well as those who come under the category of serious-minded enquirers – some perhaps with long-held Eurocentric viewpoints. There are also those, globally dispersed, of Indian and South Asian origin, born and educated in the lands of the sub-continent's diaspora, whose knowledge of their *madar vatan* – the Motherland – is often limited to current issues, but who could benefit from an enduring realisation of their wider cultural antecedents.

Ancient India evolved in many stages, and her development is analysed and explained over the eleven chapters presented here. They are chronologically arranged, from the earliest known human settlements and the examination of their societies from 7000 BC, through to the commencement of the Turco-Afghan military forays into northern India in the eleventh and twelfth centuries AD. Wherever pertinent, the chapters contain the essential details concerning rulers and dynasties; but their critical thrust is to highlight the chief lines of politico-economic, socio-cultural and intellectual developments within each distinct period. The chapters are sectioned and sub-sectioned for detailed information, followed by select extracts linked to the text for review and revisiting, raising relevant questions for reappraisal and discussion. Also included are select glossaries of the most frequently met Indic terms and ancient place-names, a classification of ancient Indian texts by subjects, simplified maps with topographical and historico-geographical relevance to the subject matter of the chapters, and several illustrations which, it is hoped, will convey some immediacy to the book's topicality and heighten the reader's appreciation of the greatness that was ancient India.

Here I take the opportunity to express my gratitude to a number of people who have helped me in this project. Some of them have inspired and encouraged me all along. Professor Lord Bhikhu Parekh is one such person whose wisdom and insights have been constantly stimulating and thought-provoking. I am also very thankful to Mr C.B. Patel, the editor of the London-based newspaper *Asian Voice* and a pioneer of ethnic journalism in Britain, who kindly offered me space in his journal to write twenty-three short historical pieces on ancient India, giving me the confidence to embark on producing a book. Among many other friends, Dr Ajit Halder, formerly of Salford University, Mr Mohammed Ibrahim and Drs Mahesh and Shabani Godbole have over many years been my well-wishers. To my wife, Zarin, and daughters Rushna and Anahita, I owe all the comfort and happiness of a rich family life, within which writing became a joyful exercise. To Anahita I also owe special thanks for helping me cope with the pitfalls and hazards of computer technology. All the fine line drawings are the work of a highly creative Manchester-based artist, Mrs Pat Baker, who has spent many hours at this task.

My sincere thanks are also due to seven colleagues who have spent a great deal of their time reading my chapters. Dr Daud Ali, Senior Lecturer and Research Fellow in Ancient Indian History at the School of Oriental and African Studies, University of London, a scholar steeped in knowledge of his field, has rescued me from a huge number of errors and made me aware of ideas and concepts critical to a balanced understanding of the subject. I owe him a great amount of gratitude. Dr George Gheverghese Joseph, an internationally renowned historian of non-European mathematics, and a treasured friend for the last forty-four years, has enriched the book by his perceptive comments on the intellectual history of ancient India. Mr Farrokh Vajifdar, Fellow of the Royal Asiatic Society of Britain, and a specialist in Indo-Iranian studies, has not only given me advice over many controversial issues and ideas in the early history of India but has gone through the drafts with a fine tooth-comb, bringing polish to my grammar and style of writing, without which the book would be less than perfect. Professor Robin Coningham, Professor of Archaeology at Durham University, has made a number of useful suggestions in the field of pre-history and the Harappan archaeology, for which I sincerely thank him. Dr Ram Prasad, of Lancaster University, and a rising star in the philosophical circles of Britain and India, has kindly read the whole draft. Two colleagues – Dr Leela Joseph, a medical specialist, and Professor Ian Steedman, Professor of Economics at Manchester Metropolitan University – provided critical and thought-provoking comments on some of the chapters from a non-historian's point of view, which I have greatly valued.

The book is a result of many years of teaching Indian history and promoting extra-mural Indian studies at Manchester Metropolitan University. I would like to thank the university authorities, and particularly the Department of

History and Economic History, for allowing me time and space to carry on with my research and teaching in a relaxed and friendly atmosphere.

Finally, my sincere thanks are due to my publishers, Routledge, and Victoria Peters, the history editor, for reposing confidence in me to write the book and submit it on time.

Burjor Avari
Manchester, 2006

A note on spellings and the use of italics

For the reader's convenience diacritics and accents have been omitted. The vast majority of Indic names in the text are spelt as widely pronounced today. Indic terms and toponyms no longer in current use, along with the titles of ancient texts, are given in italics.

Four major eras of ancient Indian history

A summary of key themes

1 Pre-historic era: until *c.* 2000 BC

- We are all Africans. South Asians are descendants of those who first migrated from Africa.
- The first South Asians were hunter-gatherers who made stone tools during the Old and Middle Stone Ages – from 500,000 BC to 11,000 BC, and drew the cave paintings at Bhimbetka.
- South Asian farming first began at Merhgarh, in Baluchistan, during the New Stone Age – 11,000 BC to *c.* 3000 BC.
- The great cities of Mohenjo Daro and Harappa – from 2500 BC to 1900 BC – provide us with much archaeological evidence of a refined, indigenous Indian civilisation.

2 Vedic and post-Vedic era: 2000 BC to 300 BC

- There was no Aryan invasion, but there was a migration of an Indo-European speaking group of nomadic people from Iran and Afghanistan, who called themselves *Arya*, or the noble. The Indo-Aryan culture has developed uniquely within India herself over the last four millennia, but its origins lie in the fusion of values and heritages of the *Arya* and the indigenous peoples of India.
- The *Rig-Veda* is the oldest text of the Indo-European language family. It, along with three other Vedas and much complementary Vedic literature, is a key text of Vedic Hinduism.
- The Indo-Aryans expanded from the Punjab to the Ganga basin, cut down the forests and created conditions for the vast agricultural infrastructure of north India that we have today.
- The Vedic polity was consolidated in sixteen *mahajanapadas* (great states), of which Magadha was the dominant state. Both the Persians and the Greeks invaded north west India during the later part of this period.
- Vedic Hinduism was strongly challenged by the religious dissenters, such as Ajivakas, Buddhists and Jains, who objected to the caste system, animal sacrifices, *brahman* dominance and the Vedas.

3 The era of the Great Empires: from *c.* 300 BC to *c.* AD 500

- The Mauryan Empire, founded from Magadha by Chandragupta Maurya in 321 BC, was a highly centralised pan-Indian political authority, the principles of which may be understood from Kautalya's *Arthashastra*, a great manual of political economy. The empire was humanised by Emperor Ashoka who propagated Buddha's principles in many rock and pillar inscriptions.
- The smaller Shaka, Kushan and Satavahana kingdoms followed the Mauryan Empire. Indian prosperity greatly increased during this era, owing to flourishing agriculture and trade, both internal and external. China and Rome were India's great trading partners.
- The Gupta Empire followed a model of decentralised power, based on the *samanta* principle of tolerant neighbourliness. Under the Guptas the Hindu–Buddhist–Jain civilisation reached the heights of elitist excellence. That is called the Classical culture of India.
- Buddhism remained popular but changed into *Mahayana* Buddhism, with its emphasis on the *Bodhisattavas*. Sanskrit literature, mathematics and Buddhist architecture, as at Ajanta, all flourished during this era.

4 The feudal era: from *c.* AD 500 to *c.* AD 1200 (and beyond)

- Among the post-Gupta regional and feudal kingdoms the most distinguished were those of King Harsha, the early Chalukyas and the Pallavas. The kings maintained their power by making large land grants and creating feudatory systems of power and patronage.
- The inter-Indian wars of the ninth and the tenth centuries, waged by the Gurjara–Pratihara, Pala and the Rashtrakuta kingdoms, exhausted India, thereby making it easier for the aggressive and iconoclastic Turco-Afghans to invade India during the eleventh and twelfth centuries.
- Under the Pallavas and the Cholas the deep south remained highly dynamic and very Hindu in character.
- Vedic Hinduism gradually gave way to Puranic and devotional Hinduism, while Buddhism was fast disappearing from India.
- From 1206 onwards Muslim power, in the form of the Slave dynasty of Qutb-ud-Din Aybak, entrenched itself in north India, clearing the way for the future development of the Indo-Islamic culture.

1 Introduction

Three terms in context: 'India', 'ancient', 'Hindu'

Modern India came into existence in 1947 on the eve of the partition of British India. This is the Republic of India of familiar renown – the largest democracy in the world today, and an increasingly powerful political and economic force in the globalised twenty-first-century world. Before 1947, and well into the ancient period, however, India geographically embraced all the Indian sub-continent, which included the areas covered by the modern states of Pakistan and Bangladesh. In fact, the earliest roots of Indian civilisation can only be understood through study of what has been recovered from excavations and field-work mainly inside Pakistan. Nepal and Sri Lanka too have always had close links with the Indian cultural world. And, during varied periods of ancient history, Afghanistan and India had enjoyed a lasting symbiotic relationship.

The etymological roots of the term 'India' lie in a Sanskrit word, *sindhu*, meaning river frontier. The earliest sacred text of India, the *Rig-Veda*, speaks of a land called *Sapta-Sindhava*, which can be identified as the province of Punjab, formerly the land of seven rivers. Today, five rivers flow through it – the Indus, Jhelum, Chenab, Ravi and Sutlej/Beas – but it is believed that some 4,000 years ago there were two other rivers, called the *Saraswati* and the *Drasadvati*, which have long since dried up. When the Persians began to penetrate Indian lands in the sixth century BC, they referred to the modern River Indus, the most westerly of the seven rivers, and the peoples living in the region, by the term *Hindhu* in Old Persian, the cognate of the Indic *sindhu*.[1] When the Macedonians, under Alexander the Great, invaded the same region in the fourth century BC, they used the Greek *Indos* to refer to the river, and *India* to refer to the land around and beyond the river. So 'India' is actually a Greek expression: no native in ancient India would have thought of using this term. They used Sanskritic proper nouns such as *Bharat* (a descendant of the ancient Puru clan), *Madhyadesha* (the Middle Country), *Aryavarta* (the land of the Aryans) and *Jambudvipa* (the shape of a *Jambu* tree, broad at the top and narrow-ing at its base, like the map of India) to describe the vast terrain with which they became familiar. Even today the constitution of the Republic of India recognises the official name of the country as 'India that is *Bharat*'.

The term 'ancient' refers to times long past. But how long ago? And at what point does 'ancient' turn to modern or pre-modern? Histories of Europe frequently begin with a section called 'The Ancient World', rather than 'Ancient Europe'. This basically means Greek and Roman history, but also includes brief references to Egypt and Mesopotamia, because the European historians have always acknowledged, and rightly so, that the genesis of European civilisation lay in the histories of those two ancient lands beyond Europe. And, for them, that ancient world normally ends with the fall of the Western Roman Empire in AD 476. Although this book begins with our remotest ancestors in the Stone Age period, we place our starting point for ancient India at approximately 7000 BC, with the emergence of the first farming community at Mehrgarh in Baluchistan. All civilisations began with farming, and it is one of the most objective criteria to determine the antiquity of a civilisation. The date of 7000 BC has been arrived at through systematic archaeological research.[2] It is not based on an interpretation drawn from an ancient text or mythology. We end the story at around AD 1200. This book is therefore a broad survey of 8,200 years of ancient Indian history. The choice of AD 1200 as the end point may be legitimately contested, and earlier or later dates have been proposed for differing reasons.[3] Here, the rationale for this date is based on the fact that after it the Indian civilisation came under intense pressure from two other major world civilisations, the Islamic and the West European. Before AD 1200 India had, to be sure, been attacked by outside forces and absorbed many foreign influences; but, apart from relatively minor Persian and Greek control on the periphery of northwest India for a few centuries, the occasional Central Asian conquerors such as the Kushans or the Hunas, and Arab and Turkish intruders, the Indian rulers, whether imperial or regional, had managed to remain the masters of their own lands. After AD 1200, however, their autonomy and capacity for independent action came to be increasingly compromised, firstly by the Turco[4] – Afghan/Mogul rulers who, in due course, came to consider India as their only home, and then by the British, for most of whom India existed only for Britain's aggrandisement and enrichment. Before AD 1200 the Indian civilisation was already a composite civilisation, but one that was deeply anchored in its native soil; after AD 1200 foreign concepts and practices profoundly modified its character. Fortunately, the new fusion – whether Indo-Islamic or Indo-Western – enhanced rather than diminished the cultures of the sub-continent. Nevertheless, the date of AD 1200 was a turning point in India's political and cultural fortunes; and, in this sense only, the period before 1200 may be described as 'ancient'.

Originally coined by the Persians to refer to the people who lived beyond the River Indus, the term 'Hindu' actually came into popular usage with the arrival of the Arabs and the Turks.[5] At first they called all the people of India Hindu, but later, with their increased understanding of Indian social structures, they became discerning enough to distinguish the Hindus from the non-Hindu Buddhist or Jain religious groups. It was even later in history that the Hindus called themselves by that name. In ancient India they had used the names of their particular sects or castes for self-description. They were always a highly diverse group, although their caste system, along with certain ritual practices and the teachings of their religious texts, legends and epics, provided them with the resource of an underlying unity. Despite their numerical preponderance, it would be a mistake to regard the ancient period as the 'Hindu period'. There is very little archaeological evidence of Hindu culture during the first 4,000 years of ancient Indian history, from 7000 BC to 3000 BC. Some precocious signs of this culture are traceable, in the northwest, through the artefacts of the following thousand years. What is generally known as Vedic Hindu culture began from around 2000 BC, and flourished for some 1,500 years, until about 500 BC. Then, pervasive Buddhist and Jain influences began strongly to make their impact for a thousand years and more, amid a plethora of sectarian dissents. From about AD 500 onwards, however, we find the evidence of a resurgent, and rebranded, Hinduism known as the Puranic and devotional Hinduism, which has endured ever since. The greatest and the finest monuments of India nevertheless testify to the fact that the classical civilisation of India was the result of a partnership of architects, designers, craftsmen, masons and labourers who could have been Hindus, Buddhists, Jains, dissenters or atheists. This also holds true for the intellectual progress of India in the ancient period.

Why study ancient India?

A most unsatisfactory reason for studying ancient India would be for the purpose of glorifying India and proclaiming the quite unproven achievements of ancient Indians. This unfortunate tendency, prevalent among some modern Indians, is a defensive reaction in the face of the progress that has been made in the West during the last 200 years. It has also been encouraged by excessively lavish praises showered on India by some foreign intellectuals and philosophers (see Extract 1.1). Another dubious reason for studying ancient India is for the purpose of drawing attention to the so-called decline of India after the arrival of Islam in the country and comparing, unfavourably, the course of events in India post-AD 1200 with the achievements of the pre-AD 1200 period. For a large number of people in the West it is religion that seems to have mostly excited their interest in ancient India. Both the Hindu and the Buddhist traditions have been intensively studied and popularised in the West over the last 150 years or so. Scholars and thinkers such as Sir William Jones (1746–94), Professor Max Muller (1823–1900), Sir Edwin Arnold (1832–1904) and Swami Vivekananda (1863–1902), among many, have made accessible to Western people the profound wisdom and deep spirituality contained in the two religions. Without their pioneering work, many Western peoples would have remained spiritually impoverished within the narrow confines of their Judaeo-Christian edifice.

An interest, bordering on the obsessive, in the religions of India has led to a major Western bias in its perception of the sub-continent. A large number of stereotypes have grown up in the West, the most oft-repeated of which are that the Indians are a highly spiritual people who do not care for material goods or that they have a fatalistic approach which entrusts everything to their gods. This imbalance in the thinking about India can be corrected by attending to other valuable legacies from ancient India. One such heritage, which needs deeper exploration, is its intellectual patrimony. The Indians composed learned texts long before the Europeans; they were the first great grammarians; their epics dealt with issues of eternal significance, which makes them so popular with millions of people in India to this day. Among ancient Indians there were also great mathematicians and astronomers, whose work eventually passed into the mainstream studies.[6] Without the ancient Indians we would not have had our number system upon which all modern science and technologies are based. Some ancient Indians were also great dissenters, and quite disputatious.[7] They were accustomed to debating issues both in a passionate and an icily logical style long before such experiments evolved within the European civilisation. Another major heritage of ancient India is the artistic and aesthetic. The craftsman has a distinct place in Indian society.[8] From the very first civilisation of India, the Harappan, archaeologists have retrieved beautiful and stylistic women's jewellery and children's toys, indicating a sophisticated lifestyle of its people. The bronze and copper works of Indian craftsmen have always been in demand throughout the ages. Ancient Indian textile designs are still avidly sought after by international fashion houses, and the temples of ancient India draw tourists in their millions. Indian trade and trading skills show a people as concerned with material goods as any others. The third great heritage from ancient India is that of a vision of a morally ordered society,[9] busy at its work and generally at peace with itself. Of course there was violence and disorder at many junctures of her history; but essentially ancient India evolved gradually and, compared with many other countries, peacefully over the long period of 8,200 years. Internationally, India did not engage in rapacious warfare or humiliate foreign peoples, as did so many ancient and modern nations to their own, their neighbours and peoples abroad. Indian warfare was always constrained by clear ethical guidelines.[10] From the earliest times the Indians have borne a strong moral responsibility of promoting international amity and goodwill. In modern times, distinguished Indians such as Mahatma Gandhi (1869–1948), Rabindranath Tagore (1861–1941) and Pandit Jawaharlal Nehru (1889–1964) have much emphasised this particularly affirmative and attractive feature of India and her peoples.

It is clear that there are many positive reasons why we should study ancient Indian history. At the same time we need to be critical and comparative in our approach. In certain aspects of public life ancient India lagged behind such civilisations as Mesopotamia, Egypt, China, Greece and Rome, and its shortcomings should be recognised. It does not behove modern Indians to boast about ancient Indian technology, when it is manifest that China was far more advanced in this area than any other nation. The Indians were also slower in developing intelligible scripts than the ancient Egyptians and Mesopotamians.

The early Indians paid scant attention to precise documentation and systematic recording of events in their country, whereas other ancient civilisations, particularly the Chinese and the Roman, were scrupulous with their historiography. The ancient Indians showed abysmal disregard for issues of inequality and poverty that have disfigured the face of India throughout its history.[11] Many Indian texts lament the conditions of poverty and inequality, but in none do we find any effusion of outrage or passion. The caste system had much to do with this passivity, and it remains perhaps the greatest moral blot on the record of ancient India.

Time, space and people

Chronological signposts

Although the ancient Indians were great calculators of time,[12] they did not standardise the dates of important events in a uniform manner. This is because ancient India, except for the two relatively brief imperial periods of the Mauryans and the Guptas, 321 BC to 185 BC and AD 320 to AD 467, was largely both politically and culturally fragmented and regionalised. There were numerous ancient Indian calendars, each with its own commencement year, used by different dynasties or religious communities. The early scholars and historians who systematised ancient Indian studies performed a most valuable service in establishing the credibility of certain dates and then synchronising them with the modern European system of dating events before and after Christ (BC and AD). Part of the success of synchronisation is owed to foreign sources or mathematical calculations from ancient India itself, as the following three examples demonstrate. From the Greek sources, for example, we learn that Alexander the Great invaded India in 327 BC; this, along with the information about the Buddha's dates from Sanskritic and Pali sources, enabled the scholars to work out the accession date of the first Mauryan emperor, Chandragupta Maurya.[13] Again, the famous astronomer Aryabhatta wrote his definitive mathematical work in AD 499, which was the year that, through his astronomical calculations, he claimed to complete 3,600 years of the *Kali Yuga*, the latest of the time-periods of the main Hindu religious calendar that began in 3101 BC. This means that, when the third Christian millennium began in AD 2000–01, the Hindus had just completed the first century of their sixth millennium. Finally, Islamic historiography, being more systematic in its approach than the ancient Indian, also developed a more reliable dating system: calculating the dates from the start-year of the Islamic lunar calendar (AD 622) against the modern solar reckoning, we are on firm ground with Islamic chronology. That is why we can be confident of the veracity of a date such as AD 1000 when Mahmud of Ghazni attacked India. The modern European system of dating is inaccurate, because Christ was born at least four years before what we consider to be its start-year of AD 1, supposedly the year of his birth; and there have also been both slippages of days and days added artificially by the

Church authorities at different times in European history. Nevertheless it is now a well-established universal dating system; compared with many Indian calendars, it is more meaningful to the modern researcher. It is, of course, worth bearing in mind that all dates of ancient Indian history are somewhat fluid, and in the dating of some events one has to agree a certain 'give and take' of a few years.

Physical geography and its impact on history

Geography plays a crucial part in shaping a country's history, and so it was with ancient India. One of the earliest references to the geographical configuration of the sub-continent comes from Kalidasa, the great dramatist and poet of the fourth century AD. In his work *Kumarasambhavam*, he correctly observed that 'along the north ... stretches the ... lord of all mountains, which bears the name Himalaya [the abode of snow]; dipping [his two arms] into the eastern and western seas he stands as the measuring rod [as it were] of the earth.'[14] The physical geography of the sub-continent provides four main landscape profiles, each involved in the shaping of ancient India (see Map 1.1). Firstly, there is the great chain of northern mountains, stretching from the Sulaiman, Hindu Kush and Chitral valley in the northwest to the Karakorams (see Figure 1.1) and the Himalayas in the north-centre. This chain may appear to be impenetrable but, in fact, numerous mountain passes are dotted along its continuity. The most famous passes are those of the Bolan (see Figure 1.2), Gomal and Khyber in the northwest. It was through these passes that the earliest humans from eastern Africa and, later, such Indo-European waves as the Aryans and other Central and West Asiatics must have entered the sub-continent over different periods. The passes along the north, through Chitral and Karakoram, established communications with central Asia; and certain remote high passes linked India directly to Tibet. Buddhism spread from India into Central Asia along these passes. The mountains of the northeast, however, with far fewer passes, acted as a barrier between India and China.

The great northern mountains are the source of some of the northern sub-continent's greatest rivers, and the melting of the glaciers in spring and summer fill the rivers with more than enough water to bring to the parched plains below. Three great river systems arise from the Tibetan and the Indian Himalayas. The Indus, later joined by its tributaries, begins its long course from Tibet, flows towards the northwest and then drops down south, flowing through Kashmir and Punjab and emptying into the Arabian Sea. The Brahmaputra also starts from Tibet, flows east for hundreds of miles, and then turns southwest into India, progressing through the Garo Hills and confluent with the Padma, a tributary of the River Ganga, and finally ending up in the Bay of Bengal. From the Indian Himalayas spring two parallel rivers, the Ganga (the Ganges) and the Yamuna, which first flow to the southeast, meeting at the modern city of Allahabad, and then progress directly east, and also finish in the Bay of Bengal. It is in the vast plains and river valleys of these three great

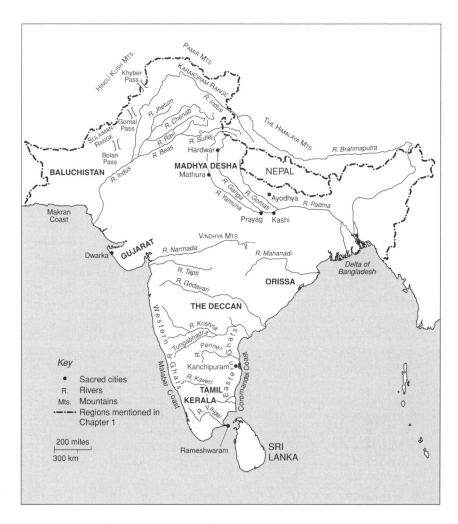

Map 1.1 Physical geography and sacred cities.

northern river systems – the Indus, the Brahmaputra and the Ganga–Yamuna – that the greatest concentration of the sub-continent's population lived, farmed and built cities in the ancient period. And they still do. Ample water, from the glaciers and the monsoon rains, has been the life-blood of the entire plains terrain. Farming first began in the relatively fertile areas of Baluchistan and the Indus region. The first of the Indian civilisations, the Harappan, also developed there. It was only after the most systematic felling of forests, by the Aryans during the second millennium BC, that the Ganga–Yamuna plain was cleared for farming; it was on this plain that Vedic culture and some of the great cities of the historic period became established and flourished.

Figure 1.1 Karakoram mountains (by permission of the Robert Harding Picture
Library: RHPL).

South of the plains lie the Vindhya Mountains which, in ancient times,
acted as great barriers to communication between the north and the south.
However, they too were never entirely impenetrable. Passages on the two sides
of the Vindhyas, rather than through them, allowed access between the two
natural divisions; and it was through these corridors that the *brahman* priests of
the north were able to migrate to the south for settlement and missionary work
in the promotion of Vedic Hinduism. With the crossing of the Vindhyas, one
enters the rather inhospitable plateau of the Deccan or the south, located in the

Figure 1.2 The Bolan Pass (by permission of RHPL).

rain shadow of the monsoon winds. This thirsty land suffers from the fact that its main water supply comes from the rains limited to their monsoon season and that the rivers carry little water in comparison with those of the north. The three rivers with their source in the Vindhyas – the Narmada, the Tapti and the Mahanadi – bring a sparse sufficiency of water to Gujarat and Orissa; but the other five rivers – the Godavari, the Krishna, the Tungabhadra, the Penner and the Kaveri – are poor in flow to that of the northern rivers. Four of these latter easterly rivers have their origin in the Western Ghats, which are fairly low mountains running along the western coast of the peninsula. There are no glaciers, and therefore the quantity of water brought down by these rivers is extremely limited. In the dry, scorching summer they become mere trickling streams. On the eastern coast there are the parallel Eastern Ghats, but not a single major river rises from them. The peninsula has a major water problem, which is why the southern peoples practised irrigation from the earliest times in ancient history. Irrigation and commerce, both trans-Indian and inter-national, gave the Deccan its importance. For many centuries in the ancient world great regional kingdoms arose and fell in this area: the kingdoms of the Satavahanas, the Chalukyas, the Rashtrakutas and, outside our period, the Hoysalas and the Vijaynagar empire. Some of the finest rock-cut temples, monuments and palaces, hewn out of the volcanic rock of the Deccan, testify today to the wealth and glory of these polities. Far in the deep south, below the Deccan, and along the Malabar and the Coromandel coasts, there grew up the ancient kingdoms of the Kerala and Tamil people. The lusher terrain, the irrigation skills and international trade created the prosperity of these lands from as early as the first millennium AD.

The fourth important feature of the sub-continent's landscape lies along its coastline. Although not indented enough and, therefore, devoid of the natural harbours and ports on a highly indented coastline, such as that of Britain, the sub-continent's coastline is very extensive, stretching from the Makran coast in the west to the Bangladesh delta. It was to the ports of the western coastline, running from the Indus delta to the southern tip of India, that traders and travellers from countries such as Mesopotamia, Arabia, Persia, Egypt, Ethiopia and those of the Roman Empire and East Africa came, traded, exchanged ideas and sometimes settled. Similarly, on the east coast, trade and traffic flowed between India and Southeast Asia. In the ancient world India was the hub of the sea routes to everywhere.

Myths and sacred geography

The idea of geographical sacred space has deeply permeated the Hindu religion and mythology. This space, for the vast majority of the Hindus, is the sub-continent of India itself. This, to them, is the land sanctified by saints and sages who left their footprints on its soils and sands over many millennia. The politically inspired modern Hindu revivalist organisations sometimes success-fully tap into this most emotive of Hindu sentiments, leading to pointless conflict with other religious communities. This does not, however, detract from the fact that the fascination of India lies in the continuity of the myths and legends that the Hindu religious authorities treasure, augment and communicate to the masses. The Hindu myths consist of everything encompassed within human, divine and cosmic universes: nature, creation, planets, the earth, gods, animals, birds, reincarnation of the soul, heroism, morality, lifestyle and countless themes besides. These myths have been transmitted, in India, by word of mouth over four millennia; but the public appetite for them has never waned or been fully sated, because the great storehouses of myth and legend, such as the *Ramayana* and *Mahabharata* epics or the ancient texts of the *Puranas*, are interwoven in Indian life through folklore, festivals, literature, music, dance, drama, and now the cinema, TV and the Internet. They are reflections of human experience and aspiration, constantly reworked through thriving media outlets. They occupy an inner sacred space. Geography has its boundaries, but the human 'inscape' is limitless and infinite.

India is a land of pilgrims and saints. Peoples from various religious communities – Hindus, Muslims, Sikhs, Jains, Buddhists, Parsis, Christians and others – are imbued with the idea of pilgrimage, but the most ancient and hallowed of the sites visited by pilgrims are those that are venerated by the Hindus.[15] The Hindu pilgrims visit sacred mountains, rivers, lakes and cities, in order to perform rituals and ceremonies and heighten their efficacy. The high peaks of the Himalayas are worshipped because they are considered to be the abode of gods and a repository of their heroic deeds. The mythical mountain *Meru*, also somewhere among the Himalayan ranges, is envisioned as the centre of the universe.[16] Most mountains are endowed with strength and life-giving properties. Rivers are also considered as sources of life. In early Vedic sources we read about the seven rivers of the Punjab, the *Sapta Sindhu*, but among them the one that is specially revered is the invisible river, *Saraswati*, associated with the goddess of learning. From Vedic times onwards the river that has held an unwavering sacred place in the hearts and minds of the Hindus is the Ganga (the Ganges). Bathing in the waters of the Ganga is a requisite for every devout Hindu; for many of them, the filthy and polluted water of the modern river is no deterrent whatsoever to drinking it, because for them it is water made holy. Such is the ineffable power of sacred geography in the Hindu psyche (see Extract 1.2). As with rivers, lakes too are associated with the deities and therefore become part of the 'sacred space'. Many city sites are sacred too. The Hindus assign a particular significance to six city-sites in north India and three in the south.[17] The northern ones are Ayodhya, the birthplace of the Hindu god Rama; Mathura, the birthplace of Krishna, the eighth incarnation of the god Vishnu; Hardwar, a city renowned for its great river festival of Kumbh Mela and a staging-post for the Hindu pilgrims who make arduous treks to the Gangotri glacier, the source of the Ganga, which then flows into the plains; *Kashi* (Varanasi/Benares), where the embankments of the River Ganga are the last stopping points, in this world, for the dying Hindu; *Prayag* (Allahabad), where the rivers Ganga, Yamuna and the invisible *Saraswati* meet in a mystical threefold confluence, and where also the festival of Kumbh Mela takes place every twelve years; and Dwarka, on the Gujarat coast, where Krishna came from Mathura for his safety. Most of these northern sites are located in *Madhyadesha*, the spiritual heartland of Hindu, Aryan and Brahmanic culture. The three important southern sites are Madurai, Kanchipuram and Rameshwaram. These sites came to be added to the list of sacred cities only after the south conformed to the Vedic/Brahmanic mainstream religion.

Social and cultural diversity

Ancient Indians were as diverse as their modern descendants. Older history books, influenced by the nineteenth-century obsession with race and racial classification, adopted such terms as Negrito, Proto-Australoid, Mongoloid, Mediterranean, Alpinoic and Nordic-Aryan to identify the peoples of India, mostly by pigmentation of the skin.[18] This type of racial classification, on the basis of physical features, has now been found to be not only irrelevant but also irresponsibly dangerous. A more meaningful concept than racial classification is that of ethnic diversity. There is but one human race, but history, geography and culture have divided it into ethnic groups. By that criterion India was, and still is, a nation of many ethnic groups. Some of these groups have lived in India for countless millennia. Sometimes they are called the aborigines or Adivasis. In the Stone Age they were the nomadic hunter-gatherers or forest-dwellers, and constituted the majority of the very small population that existed then in India. In the course of history, different ethnic groups separately developed their particular historical cultures in the diverse geographical terrains, such as mountain regions, river valleys and plains, deserts, coasts or forests. Ethnic groups also came from abroad, such as the Aryans, Iranians, Turco-Afghans, Graeco-Macedonians and Tibeto-Burmans, and to be absorbed in the ethnic admixture. Another strand of diversity was occupational. Hunter-gatherers and forest-dwellers dominated the land, excepting the Indus region, almost until the beginning of the first millennium BC. After that, major farming activities in the Ganga–Yamuna plains began with the felling of forests and, in the south, with the acquisition of irrigation skills. In time, the farmers and the pastoralists displaced the hunter-gatherers and the forest-dwellers, thereby constituting the majority of the people. Surplus crops enabled farming communities to form the core of the first towns and cities of ancient India; that was how town-dwellers, craftsmen and traders came to fulfil their respective crucial roles.[19] The bards and priests of ancient India also remind us of the religious diversity of ancient India. Most aborigines were animistic nature-worshippers, but the people of the first civilisation of India, the Harappans, were perhaps beginning to develop some rituals and practices that formally metamorphosed into a more sophisticated religious structure known later as Vedic Hinduism. This new structure was the result of a cultural fusion between the ancient Indians and the incoming Indo-Iranian Aryans. The hierarchical and ritually ordered caste system became a prominent feature of Vedic Hinduism.[20] Although a large number of people adhered to Vedic Hinduism, many remained outside its fold, belonging to either the animistic or the dissenting tradition. Buddhism and Jainism were major challengers to Vedic Hinduism. Ancient India was therefore evolving into a diverse multi-faith society. By AD 1200 at least four non-Indic religions – Islam, Christianity, Judaism and Zoroastrianism – had also become familiar to some of the Indians. Lastly, the linguistic diversity of ancient India should not be forgotten. We have no clear idea of what language the ancient Indians spoke. The language and the scripts of the first Indian civilisation, the Harappan, remain a mystery (Chapter 3). We can, however, draw some deductions from the current language map of South Asia. Leaving aside minor languages spoken by the remaining aboriginals or by those living in the peripheral border areas, the two main language families are known as the Indo-Aryan and the Dravidian. It is believed that the Dravidian family is indigenous to India; and Tamil, the premier Dravidian language, is perhaps the oldest Indian language in use today. Sanskrit, the mother language of the Indo-Aryan family, evolved out of a fusion of proto-Sanskrit, brought from Iran and Central Asia, and native Dravidian. It flourished in ancient India as a classical language of both the north and, later, the south; but the ordinary people in the north came to use such vernacular and non-standard languages known as Prakrits and the Apabrahmashas, from which the regional languages of the north have developed. Tamil has remained the predominant language of the Dravidian family throughout the ages, although it has been enriched by Sanskrit since ancient times. At least two other Dravidian languages – Telugu and Kannada – also developed during the ancient period.

Primary sources and the historians

The contents of this book are drawn from the writings of some of the eminent historians of ancient India. This means that the evidence presented here is secondary; but the writers themselves drew their evidence from primary sources. In the context of ancient India, there are three valid forms of primary historical evidence: literary texts, archaeological finds and modern multidisciplinary research findings. The literary corpus can be divided into two sections: religious and secular. The religious texts relate to the spiritual heritage of the Hindus, Buddhists and Jains. These scriptures, composed in Sanskrit, Pali, Tamil or Prakrit languages, include such works as the *Vedas* and the related Vedic literature (see Chapter 4), the *Mahabharata* and the *Ramayana* epics (Chapter 5), the great Buddhist works of the *Tripitakas*, the *Nikayas* and the *Dipavamsa* (Chapter 5), the *Agam* texts of the Jains (Chapter 5), the manuals of religious law such as the *Dharmashastras* and *Dharmasutras* (Chapter 7), the devotional texts of the *Puranas* (Chapter 8) and the devotional songs and hymns composed by saints who propagated the worship of the gods Vishnu and Shiva (Chapters 9 and 11). The secular literary texts include a major work of political economy known as the *Arthashastra* (Chapter 6), mathematical and astronomical treatises (Chapters 4, 8, 9, 10), writings on medicine and surgery (Chapter 7), grammatical works and lexicons (Chapters 5, 7, 9), volumes on architecture (Chapters 7, 8, 9, 10,11) and works of music, and dance and drama (Chapters 4, 7, 8, 9, 10 and 11). No systematic historical works by ancient Indians are available, in the way historians such as Herodotus (485–425 BC), Livy (59 BC to AD 17), Ssu-Ma-Chien (*c*. 145–87 BC) or the Venerable Bede (*c*. AD 673–735) composed histories of early Greece, Rome, China and England. There are, however, two particular works of value. One is a biography of a famous seventh-century king, Harsha, written by a courtier named Banabhatta, or Bana for short (Chapter 9), and the other is a fairly coherent account of the history of Kashmir called *Rajatarangini*, by Kalhana, a scholar and courtier in the Kashmiri kingdom (Chapter 11). Among the secular works we include the accounts of India left by Greek (Chapters 5 and 6), Chinese (Chapters 8 and 9), Tibetan (Chapter 9), Roman (Chapter 7) and Islamic writers such as Al-Biruni (Chapter 11). Despite the paucity of the specifically historical texts written by the ancient Indians themselves, historians have been able to extract a huge amount of material from both the religious and the secular literary texts.[21] Both the religious and the secular texts, many of which remain to be translated into English, are absolutely fundamental to understanding the richness of life that existed in ancient India. The challenge for the historians is to be able to distinguish the historical from the non-historical evidence.

The second form of primary historical evidence is archaeological.[22] There have been three strands of archaeological work in India. The first, and the earliest, has been that of discovering, recording, restoring, renovating and cata-loguing of thousands of material remains that stand 'above the ground'. The most important of these remains, for the historian, have been the inscriptions engraved on rocks, stones, pillars, temple walls and wells, and copper or metallic plates. The inscriptions, written in a variety of Indic scripts, serve different purposes. They consist of declarations of religious piety and worldly advice, such as those of King Ashoka (Chapter 6); commemorative inscriptions, such as birth registers, records of deaths or visits of kings and famous people; dedicative inscriptions, recording grants of land by the kings to *brahman* priests, Buddhist and Jainist monks, or to temples and monasteries (Chapters 8, 9, 10, 11); and commercial inscriptions issued by guilds of merchants, monarchs or town councils (Chapters 10 and 11). Many inscriptions also carry lengthy panegyrics eulogies, known as *prasastis*, glorifying the kings and pro-claiming their administrative prowess. Whatever their weaknesses as reliable sources, it is through the inscriptions that our knowledge of ancient history has both widened and deepened.[23] The care of the buildings and monuments on which inscriptions have been found are the prime responsibility of the Department of Archaeology of the government of India. By the early twentieth century many of the structures had fallen into disrepair, but the position was remedied by Lord Curzon, the British viceroy, who provided sufficient funding for repair work and the training of specialists.

A second strand of archaeological work consisted of recovering materials 'under the ground'. This obviously included the sequence of ancient coins from hoards and finds, which particularly enhance our chronological knowledge of dynasties, etc. (Chapters 6 and 7). But the most significant discoveries in this field were made in the excavation of pre-historic fossils and tools and, from the 1920s onwards, the uncovering of the Harappan culture and civilisation (Chapters 2 and 3). The last of the archaeological strands consists of selected recent diggings at famous religious, urban or commercial sites in order to corroborate some of the available textual and epigraphic evidence.

Apart from archaeology and the literary texts, another form of primary evidence consists of data collated through multi-disciplinary researches. Since the mid-twentieth century our understanding of the history of India has been greatly facilitated by some exciting developments in areas as varied as anthropology, ethnography, geology, meteorology, genetics, biology and botany. They have provided the historians with valuable data and insights. Genetics, for example, gives us clues to the origins of South Asian people, while anthropology guides us towards oral history, which is valuable in piecing together the history of the marginalised subaltern groups of people who exist in large numbers in India.

Reconstructing the history of ancient India

Two important developments took place in India in the middle of the eighteenth century. One was the political ascendancy of the British East India Company, particularly after a victorious battle at Plessey in Bengal. From then on the British control over India tightened until India eventually became a virtual colony of Britain. The second development concerned the rise of Indology, the study of India through European eyes and mindsets.[24] Until the mid-eighteenth century most Europeans in India, particularly the British, had been interested primarily in trade; a mere handful among them were curious travellers who kept diaries and journals. However, after the mid-eighteenth century the British and European interest in India was accelerated through the dispassionate endeavours of some empathetic and committed scholars, administrators and intellectuals who came to be known as the orientalists. The two developments – that of British domination and the rise of Indology – came to be inextricably linked but, as we shall see, with varying consequences over the course of time.

There was little achieved by way of systematic historiography of ancient India until the mid-eighteenth century. This developed only through the rise of Indology, but the manner and rate of its progress depended on how scholars responded to the nature and character of British political domination. We can identify four separate phases in this intellectual activity. In the first phase, during the late eighteenth century, there was a uniquely fruitful interaction between power and scholarship. The central political character in this phase was Warren Hastings, the governor-general of Bengal, who held India and her culture in great esteem. He offered his patronage to a group of empathetic orientalists including Sir William Jones (1746–94), Nathaniel Halhead, Charles Wilkins (1749–1836) and Henry Colebrook (1765–1837). These men sought out suitable Indian tutors for studying Sanskrit, without which they realised they could never access ancient texts concerning early religion, laws and customs. Persisting through many difficulties they mastered Sanskrit as well as other Indian languages and then translated complex works such as the *Bhagavadgita*, the *Manusmriti* and various *Dharmashastras*, the collection of fables called the *Hitopadesha* and the famous dramatic work of *Shakuntala*. From the translations came the interpretations and the wider understanding of a society with ancient cultural roots over which the British ruled.[25] However, a major weakness of the orientalists' approach was that, because they had been tutored mainly by *brahman* Sanskritists, they interpreted the Indian past mostly through the Sanskrit texts, which narrowed their horizons.

During the second phase the work of the orientalists came to be challenged and threatened. By the end of the eighteenth century the balance of power between the British and the Indians was shifting dramatically in favour of the former. In 1799 British military might finally vanquished the one great and dangerous Indian challenger in the person of Tipu Sultan of Mysore (1750–99), who had been trained in military tactics by French officers, and from then onwards until the great rebellion of 1857 there was nothing to stop the British exercising overwhelming authority over India. The rise of such social and economic movements in Britain as utilitarianism, evangelism and free trade also exercised a profound impact in India. The arrogant British men who carried the gospel of these movements to India were imbued with an overweening sense of pride, convinced that they alone had both the superiority and the therapy to cure India of all her ancient maladies. The iconic figure of Indian historiography in this category was James Mill (1773–1836), the father of the famous philosopher John Stuart Mill (1806–73). James Mill's multi-volume book is titled *The History of British India*, but the author ventured far deeper into ancient history as well. He unwisely partitioned Indian history into three periods – Hindu, Muslim and British – and argued that India had been gripped by the terror of oriental despotism during the first two periods, but had a redemptive opportunity to benefit from the wisdom and enlightenment of British rule.[26] A great statesman of the period, Lord Macaulay (1800–59), also displayed a patronising attitude towards the country and her culture, and he felt that Westernisation would revitalise India. He is best remembered for his famous Minutes on Indian Education, in which he castigated both the Hindu and Islamic system of education in India and proposed the replacement of Sanskrit and Urdu by English in the state schools[27] (see extracts 1.3 and 1.4).

The influence of Mill and Macaulay pervaded most of the nineteenth-century British writings on India. Today we label such writings by the pejora-tively used term orientalism. The concept of orientalism has been profoundly analysed by the late Palestinian writer Edward Said, who has shown, in numerous writings, how the official British and European colonial mentality of arrogance and pejorative perceptions of the subject people permeated the works of famous nineteenth-century novelists, poets, historians and travel writers.[28] Said's analysis does not wholly apply to the orientalists of the first phase referred to above or to those others who dedicated themselves to uncovering the truth about India's past even when British officialdom was unsympathetic towards their researches. It would be unjust to class such British historians and archaeologists as Sir Alexander Cunningham (1814–93), James Prinsep (1799–1840), James Fergusson, Vincent Smith (1848–1920) and Sir John Marshall (1876–1958), who did so much to expose India's past, as among those tainted by Said's orientalism.

Despite much good work done by the British and European historians, it was only to be a matter of time before the Indians bestirred themselves and reacted against the foreigners' monopoly over the reconstruction of India's ancient past. This falls into the third phase. The Indian response came in two forms. Highly politicised Hindus, with extreme facility in the use of English, and bursting with pride over the evaluations and translations of ancient texts that were increasingly made in the nineteenth century, adopted a nationalistic fervour with regard to their past.[29] This is to be seen in the works and speeches of B.G. Tilak (1856–1920), Dayanand Saraswati (1824–83), Bankim Chandra Chatterjee (1838–94) and V.D. Savarkar (1883–1966). However, they uncritically examined and glorified Hinduism and the Hindu past. The works of two particular Europeans, Madame Blavatsky (1831–91) and Mrs Annie Besant (1847–1933), also betray the same tendency. But there were other Indians who adopted a more measured approach in their understanding and interpretation of ancient India. Most were academics and historians who had closely studied the historical criteria and refrained from reading too much into the available evidence. They included people such as R.G. Bhandarkar (1837–1925), H.C. Raychaudhuri (1892–1957), R.C. Majumdar and Humayun Kabir. They followed, and even improved on, the high standards set by Vincent Smith in his nine books on Indian history.

The period since independence from British rule is the fourth phase. There has been a sea change in the attitude of those British and European historians who specialise in India. Gone are some of their predecessors' Victorian assertive declarations. More humble in their approach, they have produced some outstanding works in their specialist fields. Perhaps the most magnificent of these works is *The Wonder that was India*, written by A.L. Basham. Among the Indian historians the most important and influential name is that of D.D. Kosambi. With his mathematician's logic, ethnologist's acute observation and scholar's incisive interpretation of the Indian texts, Kosambi was the pioneer of a Marxist approach to historiography.[30] Marx himself was not knowledgeable about India, but the Marxist method of studying the present by asking relevant social and economic questions from the past is one of the soundest ways of studying history. Kosambi took this to heart and introduced new concepts and methodologies in his *An Introduction to the Study of Indian History* (1956) and *The Culture and Civilisation of Ancient India in Historical Outline* (1965). Eminent contemporary historians, such as professors Romila Thapar and Irfan Habib, have appreciated the new pathways opened up by Kosambi's work, and their books reflect a new richness and diversity. Ancient India continues to remain a fertile ground for vast fields of investigative and forensic work from the primary sources.

SELECT EXTRACTS FOR REVIEW AND REFLECTION

Extract 1.1 The use of hyperbole in praise of India

The following extract is an example of exaggerated admiration for India as displayed by Will Durant, the eminent American thinker and historian. Some statements in the extract are historically accurate; others are just the writer's reflections of his love for India.

> India was the motherland of our race, and Sanskrit the mother of Europe's languages: she was the mother of our philosophy; mother, through the Arabs, of much of our mathematics; mother, through the Buddha, of the ideals embodied in Christianity; mother through the village community, of self-government and democracy. Mother India is in many ways the mother of us all.

Source: Will Durant, *The Case for India*, New York: Simon & Schuster, 1931; and quoted in Vivekananda Kendra Prakashan, *Imprints of Indian Thought and Culture Abroad*, Madras, 1980, p. 9.

Extract 1.2 Sacred geography in the Hindu imagination

Pandit Nehru, the first prime minister of independent India, was a thoroughly modern man. He had little time for religious rituals and conventions. Nevertheless he made clear in his last will and testament that he wanted part of his ashes to be immersed in the waters of the River Ganga. In the following extract his feelings betray a deep sense of appreciation as to why the Indian people stand in awe of the Ganga, a mere river to those without a sense of the history of India.

> The Ganga is the river of India, beloved of her people, round which are intertwined her racial memories, her hopes and fears, her songs of triumph, her victories and her defeats. She has been a symbol of India's age-long culture and civilization, ever-changing, ever-flowing, and yet ever the same Ganga ... Smiling and dancing in the morning sunlight, and dark and gloomy and full of mystery as the evening shadows fall ... the Ganga has been to me a symbol and a memory of the past of India, running with the present and flowing on to the great ocean of the future. And although I have discarded much of the past

tradition and custom ... I do not wish to cut myself off from that past completely ... And as witness of this desire of mine and as my last homage to India's cultural inheritance, I am making this request that a handful of my ashes be thrown into the Ganga at Allahabad to be carried to the great ocean that washes India's shore.

Source: Dorothy Norman, *Nehru: The First Sixty Years*, London: Bodley Head, 1965, pp. 574–5.

Extract 1.3 The Macaulay Minutes

The main proposal in the Macaulay Minutes was the adoption of English as the medium of instruction in all state schools. This, in his opinion, would create knowledgeable Westernised Indians, who would then be able to help to uplift native education and culture.

> We must at present do our best to form a class who may be interpreters between us and the millions whom we govern; a class of persons, Indian in blood and colour, but English in taste, in opinions, in morals, and in intellect. To that class we may leave it to refine the vernacular dialects of the country, to enrich these dialects with terms of science borrowed from the western nomenclature, and to render them by degrees fit vehicles for conveying knowledge to the great mass of the population.

Source: Macaulay's Minutes on Indian Education, printed in John Clive and Thomas Pinney (eds), *Thomas Babington Macaulay: Selected Writings*, Chicago: University of Chicago Press, 1972, p. 249.

Extract 1.4 An example of tampering with historical evidence

The following extract has recently been propagated in the political circles of India as having been spoken or written by Lord Macaulay.

> I have travelled across the length and breadth of India and I have not seen one person who is a beggar, who is a thief. Such wealth I have seen in this country, such high moral values, such calibre, that I do not think we would ever conquer this country, unless we break the very backbone of this nation, which is her spiritual and cultural heritage and, therefore, I propose that we replace her old and ancient education system, her culture, for if the Indians think that all that is foreign and English is good and greater than their own, they will lose their self-esteem, their native self-culture and they will become what we want them, a truly dominated nation.

No proof of this statement has been found in any of the volumes containing the writings and speeches of Macaulay. In a journal in which the extract appeared, the writer did not actually reproduce the exact wording of the Minutes, but merely paraphrased them, using the qualifying phrase: 'His words were to this effect'. This is extremely mischievous, as numerous interpretations can be drawn from the Minutes. The Belgian historian Koenraad Elst has analysed this mischief in a brilliant piece on his Internet site.

Source: 'The Merits of Lord Macaulay', http://koenraadelst.bharatvani. org/articles/hinduism.macaulay.html.

RELEVANT QUESTIONS FOR DISCUSSION

1 What intellectual issues would the ancient Indians have argued about?
2 How would global warming affect the livelihood of the sub-continent's people?
3 Why would anyone want to ascribe to Lord Macaulay a statement that cannot be found in any of his works?

Notes

1 Basham 1954: 1.
2 Jarrige and Meadow 1980; Coningham 2005: 520.
3 A number of historians end the ancient period at around AD 600, with the rise of feudalism from then on.
4 Turco is to specify Central Asian tribal entities; Turk(o) – for West Asiatic national affiliates, but Turkic for languages.
5 Thapar 2002: 439–40.
6 Joseph 2000: 10, 14.
7 Sen 2005: 3–33; Melling 1993: 1–16.
8 Kramrisch 1959.
9 Basham 1964: 57–71.
10 Date 1929: 80–81.
11 Ramesh 2006.
12 For a clear understanding of the modern Hindu calendar, see Prinja 1996: 120–23.
13 Allen 2002: 71–2.
14 Ray *et al.* 2000: 360.
15 Bhardwaj 1973: 1–13.
16 Patil 2004: 66, 71–6.
17 Ibid.: 145–54.
18 E.g. Rapson 1922: 37–50.
19 Thapar 2002: 55–62.
20 Ibid.: 62–8.

21 Majumdar 1961a.
22 Allchin 1961.
23 Ali 2000: 225–9.
24 Thapar 2002: 7–15.
25 Rocher 1993.
26 Philips 1961; Breckenridge and Veer 1993: 263–5.
27 Minutes of 2 February 1835, in Clive and Pinney 1972: 240–51; read also Das Gupta 1961.
28 Said 1994: 1–35; 73–95.
29 Thapar 2002: 15–22; Majumdar 1961b.
30 Thapar 1993: 89–113.

2 From Africa to Mehrgarh

The early pre-history of India

(Time-span: before the third millennium BC)

In the absence of contemporary written records, the skills and methods of archaeology are our principal assistants in the study of the pre-history of any region in the world.[1] The archaeologist can now also call upon the services of specialists in such diverse fields as cultural anthropology,[2] geology,[3] and climatic[4] and genetic studies[5] to shed further light on the interpretation of his available data. The cumulative results of archaeological and other researches over the last two centuries have been highly impressive; and, while controversies over the significance of this or that piece of evidence will always continue, we now at least possess a great amount of scientific evidence to probe into questions relating to pre-history. Among such questions that arise while studying the pre-history of India and South Asia, the following are of particular interest: When did the first humans emerge in those regions? What tools did they make? What was their socio-economic lifestyle? At what stage did they take up farming? When do we get the first pointers to urban civilisation in the sub-continent? The answers are frequently unclear because research in this area is still much in progress. On the basis of what is available, however, this chapter attempts to address the questions in three settlement phases.

Earliest phases of human settlement and activity

A critical stage in human evolution took place some 6 million years ago when our remotest ancestors, acquiring skills of bipedal locomotion (walking on two feet), emerged in Africa, descended from primates. Palaeontologists (students of animal and human fossils) and archaeologists call them by the term *hominin*. Different species of hominins co-existed for the next 3.5 million years, but around 2.5 million years ago we find evidence of the first tool-using members from their lineage in eastern and southern Africa.[6] These tool-using hominins continued to evolve inside Africa, and developed into three branches, known as *Homo habilis*, *Homo ergaster* and *Homo erectus*.[7] The more enterprising members of the last two began to issue out of Africa just over 1 million years ago, reaching as far as Europe, West Asia, East Asia and the Indonesian islands.[8] It would, however, be wrong to conclude that there were no tool-using hominins in places outside Africa before 1 million years ago; the fossil remains of hominins such as *Sivapithecus* and *Ramapithecus* have been discovered in the northern regions of the sub-continent; also, the recent discovery, in northwest Pakistan, of a chopping tool that is 2 million years old suggests that the dating of human ancestry is an evolving subject;[9] it would be imprudent to be too categorical with the dates.

The culmination of the long period of evolution, adaptation and diffusion by the pre-human species such as the *Australopithecines* and the three hominin branches was reached when our own species, *Homo sapiens*, modern humans biologically similar to us, emerged around 400,000 years ago.[10] There are two conflicting hypotheses for the origin of *Homo sapiens*. One holds to the multi-regional model of human origin, which asserts that *Homo sapiens* arose gradually from the *Homo erectus* populations in different regions of the world.[11] The other model, known as the Out of Africa hypothesis, asserts that over thousands of years the African humanity, in the form of *Homo erectus* and later *Homo sapiens*, spread to other parts of the world and dominated all other species[12] (see Extract 2.1). Both theories have their champions, but the relative abundance of the African fossil remains and sophisticated research into the history of human genes[13] increasingly point to an African origin for modern humans, including South Asians.[14] Most probably, *Homo erectus* might have moved, in significant numbers, from Africa to South Asia via West Asia around 500,000 years ago. *Homo sapiens*, on the other hand, arrived much later in the sub-continent from two directions and over two different time-sequences. One was the traditional route through West Asia, around 30,000 years ago; but an earlier group could have landed around 50,000 years ago on the shores of south India while on their sea journey towards the Andaman Islands, Indonesia and the Australasian archipelagos.[15] The entire subject of the first settlements of *Homo sapiens* in different parts of the world is wholly fascinating, but new theories, particularly from genetic studies, will undoubtedly help us to obtain further insights. We are, of course, still undecided about the sequence of the peopling of India and South Asia, but there can be no doubt that the South Asian *Homo sapiens* has truly flourished and multiplied in the region. The Indian sub-continent holds the largest areal concentrations of humanity in the world today.

By 100,000 years ago, the *Homo sapiens* species had shown its dominance throughout the known world, replacing all other *Homo* genera. Archaeology comes into its own when, from the later hominins onwards, we see signs of the advancing material culture of stone tools. In time, the artefacts become more complex, as with pottery. In their search and analysis of fossils, human or animal, tools and artefacts, whether of the most primitive kind or of a sophisticated design, archaeologists generally employ three recognised procedures. One is known as typological classification, by which the similarities and differences among the tools and artefacts are analysed.[16] Another is stratigraphy, by which the layers and strata of the ground are studied.[17] Materials found at deeper levels below the ground, for example, could indicate the remains of an older chronological period, as the levels get covered by the debris of successive generations. Each layer is numbered in relation to a chronological period, and the deepest level, containing the oldest of materials, is treated as Period I. The third important procedure concerns dating, of which there are a variety of methods, such as spectrometric dating of the materials earlier than 10,000 years ago[18] and radio-carbon dating,[19] dendro-chronology[20] and thermo-luminescence[21] for dating objects from the last 10,000 years. Archaeological procedures and the researches from other sciences have combined, over the last 150 years, to shed much light on the earliest humans and their activities.

The Palaeolithic era

The pre-historic period for all regions of the world is characterised by the gradual increase in the human ability to shape tools from stone, which is why most of the pre-historic period, from the time of the first tool-making hominins 2.5 million years ago, is called the Stone Age. Owing to the difficulties posed in studying such a long period, archaeologists have divided it into three parts: Old (or Palaeolithic), Middle (or Mesolithic) and New (Neolithic) Stone Ages. The Palaeolithic, being the longest of the three, is itself further sub-divided into three sub-periods, Lower Palaeolithic (or the earliest period of the Old Stone Age), Middle Palaeolithic and Upper Palaeolithic (the most recent period of the Old Stone Age). The period divisions do not apply uniformly to all parts of the world because, owing to factors such as time lag, climatic vagaries, great distances or numerous geographical and physical barriers, the peoples in different regions of the world progressed at varying paces. We can affirm that Africa was the first region in the world to display characteristics of the Lower Palaeolithic; but that approximates the limits of our chronology. Even today there are isolated groups of people whose skills lie essentially in working with stone artefacts and who are considered as still living in the Stone Age. The Stone Age, theoretically, comes to an end when human beings start working with metals such as copper, tin and iron.

In the context of Indian and South Asian history, we may be justified in saying that the Stone Age began around 500,000 years ago, assuming that the tool-making members of *Homo erectus* had then arrived, and that it lasted until at least the third millennium BC, when we come across copper objects from the Harappan Civilisation. The remains of the earliest *homo* species yet found in the sub-continent, Narmada Man, are actually only about 250,000 years old,[22] while those of the earliest *Homo sapiens*, found in Sri Lanka, date to 34,000 years.[23] The Palaeolithic era of the Stone Age lasted the longest, stretching until about 26,000 BC.[24] Although we have very little evidence of human remains from most of the Palaeolithic era,[25] the remains of fauna fossils have been recovered in great numbers, giving vital clues to researchers about climatic conditions and their effects on landscapes; we also have a variety of stone implements from all the sub-periods of the Palaeolithic era, unearthed from different sites in South Asia (see Map 2.1). The two predominant utensils of the Lower Palaeolithic era were pebble tools and hand axes. Extensive deposits of pebble tools and choppers were discovered in the Soan river valley in

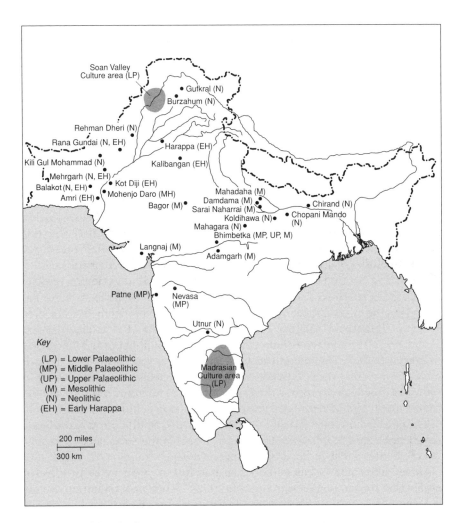

Map 2.1 Pre-historic sites.

Pakistan, and the hoards found there and at other sites are known as the Soan Culture.[26] The hand axes were first discovered near Chennai (Madras) by a British archaeologist, Robert Bruce-Foote, in 1863, and so the hand-axe assemblage is generally known as Madrasian Culture.[27] From the Middle Palaeolithic era we have many flake tools, cores, scrapers and borers; despite regional variations, they constitute a tool culture known as Nevasan Culture, named after the Nevasa site in the valley of the Godavari river in the Deccan.[28] The skills of giving a sharper cutting edge to all the various stone tools, resulting in finer blades and burins, were perfected later in the Upper Palaeolithic era. A collection of these later tools was found at the site of Patne in Maharashtra.[29]

The evidence of tools and fossils suggests clearly, however, that the Palaeolithic people remained essentially hunter-gatherers throughout that long period. They hunted and scavenged, collecting berries, roots and fruits of all kinds that grew in the wild. Mostly they lived in nomadic fashion in open spaces, but also used caves for shelter and protection. There is one remote piece of evidence that may help us to reconstruct a picture of their social life in the Upper Palaeolithic age.[30] This consists of a few of the earliest cave paintings at Bhimbetka on the bank of the Narmada river in central India, depicting scenes of hunting and fertility symbols. Otherwise there is nothing except fossils, pebble tools and hand axes.

The Mesolithic era

The transition from the Palaeolithic to the Mesolithic witnessed the emergence of a new type of stone tool known as the microlith. Although small in size, this was a superior implement. A typical microlith kit would consist of tiny micro-blades, triangles, trapezes, crescents and arrowheads, all extremely sharp at their cutting face and truly effective weapons.[31] The earliest evidence of these microliths in South Asia comes from sites in Sri Lanka dating back to 26,000 BC.[32] The sites on the Indian mainland that have been explored in detail include Bagor in Rajasthan, Langnaj in Gujarat, Sarai Nahar Rai, Mahadaha and Damdama in the Gangetic plains, and Adamgarh, Bhimbetka and Ghagharia in central India.[33] The microliths, found at all these sites, date from a much more recent period than 26,000 BC. The microlith helps us to interpret life in the Mesolithic as an advance on the Palaeolithic. The microlith was functionally a more useful tool than a large stone pebble because it could be hafted to many other tools, for instance to make knives or scissors. By the use of arrowheads too animals could be killed from a distance, reducing the chance of their attacking the hunter.[34] The production of microliths depended upon the availability of stones that could be easily flaked, such as quartz, chert, or other types of chalcedony (precious stones). As pebble stones became less important, a shift in habitat, from river sites to hills and forests, can be detected.[35] Seasonal mobility has also been noticed in relation to the movement of people between the Gangetic plains and the Vindhya escarpments in central India. Animals generally moved during the winter from the plains to the hills, and the people followed game, taking shelter in hill caves. The reverse movement occurred during the hot season, when the people would be able to augment their subsistence with the plant resources of the plains.[36] The discovery of many querns and stone rings at different sites attest to a primitive form of cultivation. Ring stones were probably used as weights on the ends of digging sticks. Animal bones of cows, sheep and goats found in the habitation areas indicate the domestication of animals; but the bones of such other animals as deer, boar and ostrich have also been found among adjacent debris. Within a number of habitation areas are burial sites containing skeletal remains as well as grave goods such as microliths, shells and even an ivory pendant. This suggests a belief in an afterlife or some form of status consciousness.[37] We cannot be sure. Human remains have been studied, and some of them show signs of osteoarthritis.[38] There were, however, some burial sites which were just in middens with rubbish, as in Sri Lanka. Good examples of rock art, accurately depicting animal bodies and human figures, have been discovered across a wide extent of the Indian landscape, at cave sites as far afield as Kerala and Kashmir. At Bhimbetka, in central India, however, a unique continuity of rock-art tradition can be noticed from the Palaeolithic period onwards, and there is greater sophistication demonstrated during the Mesolithic and the Neolithic periods.[39]

The Neolithic Revolution and the rise of agriculture

Although there was no clear-cut shift from hunter-gathering to farming, a transition was gradually but clearly occurring in four or five regions of the world around 8000 BC. This happened after the end of what is known as the Pleistocene era or the Last Ice Age. The retreat of the ice ushered in post-glacial times, the most recent of climatic eras, known as the Holocene epoch. From the archaeological perspective, it was in the Holocene period that the New Stone Age began. The new venture of farming is sometimes referred to as the Neolithic Revolution, a major landmark in human history, when men and women in Egypt, Mesopotamia, Mesoamerica, China and parts of South Asia began to domesticate plants and animals and learn about crops and seasons.[40] The stone tools of the New Stone Age, such as polished ground-stone axes, stone sickles, hammer stones and stone blades, were also far more varied and efficient than those of the earlier periods. The evidence from the Neolithic sites, however, suggests that farming, pastoralism and the establishment of settlements did not all emerge simultaneously; developments occurred gradually and, at some times, the old and the new co-existed for a very long period before the new supplanted the old.[41] In the Indian and South Asian context the earliest archaeological evidence of the Neolithic period dates back to almost 11,000 BC, the end of the Ice Age; but the evidence for farming and domestication of animals ranges between 7000 BC and 1000 BC at different sites. It is, arguably, also believed that the very first farmers of South Asia, in Baluchistan, might have come from Mesopotamia and the Fertile Crescent.[42]

Main Neolithic regional concentrations

The Neolithic sites are spread out across the sub-continent, but there are four particular concentrations of sites that help us identify regional similarities and dissimilarities.[43] The first concentration of Neolithic farming villages is found in Baluchistan, in the vicinity of the Bolan river and its pass that links the uplands with the plains of the River Indus. The remains of mud-built structures, chert blades, barley and wheat seeds, and bones of sheep, goats and cattle provide the clearest evidence of the development of a farming and pastoral community in this part of the sub-continent. The key site is that of the village of Mehrgarh, where, since the 1970s, extensive archaeological excavations have unearthed some of the earliest strata dating back to 7000 BC.[44] The other linked sites are those of Kili Gul Mohammad and Rana Ghundai. The second concentration of sites is to be found in the Kashmir and Swat valleys of Pakistan. At sites such as Burzahom and Gufkral there is evidence present of Neolithic farming settlements, consisting of the usual Neolithic implements, ceramics and faunal remains. Additionally, there have been discovered peculiar bell-shaped pits, nearly 15 feet in diameter and 13 feet in depth. It has been suggested that these pits served as underground dwellings for humans or as burial hoard sites, and that the people here might have had links with the Central Asian Neolithic communities that dug similar pits.[45] This is still a subject of speculation among the excavators, some of whom think that the pits could have been grain stores or merely gigantic refuse dumps.[46] The third concentration of sites is located in a very wide area covering the Gangetic basin and stretching into eastern India. Here some of the Neolithic remains are pre-farming sites, indicating a continuity of the Mesolithic and the Neolithic eras. At certain sites, however, such as Chopani Mando, Mahagara, Koldihawa and Chirand, we have distinct evidence of farming and domestication of animals taking place around the fourth millennium BC. The remains of rice grains have been found, but there is continuing debate as to whether rice cultivation was an indigenous development or whether it entered the sub-continent from East and Southeast Asia sometime during the second millennium BC[47] (see Extract 2.2). The fourth regional concentration of Neolithic sites is south India. There, at such a site as Utnur, huge deposited ash-mounds have been found. Most probably, there were stockades where cattle were seasonally brought and tamed, and the ash-mounds could be the result of the burning of successive phases of stockades or pens. In the many open-air settlements of south India traditional Neolithic tools such as polished stone axes and stone blades, along with the remains of pulses, millets and local tubers, provide evidence of a distinct regional farming and pastoral culture.[48]

The socio-economic consequences of agriculture

Some of the consequences of the rise of agriculture applied universally. One of them was a sharper divergence between the nomadic ways of the hunter-gatherers and the sedentary lifestyle of the cultivators of land. The latter became increasingly dominant in all areas as, compared with the efforts of the hunter-gatherers, they garnered greater rewards for themselves by more intensive use of a limited amount of land.[49] Technological innovations too, such as irrigation, ploughing and, much later on in India, terracing in hill regions, helped produce sizeable surpluses of food; and this, with the general predictability of food supplies, resulted in the increase of the agricultural population. Yet it would take many millennia after 7000 BC before the hunter-gatherers became truly marginal figures in the Indian landscape.[50] For a long time the farmers and hunter-gatherers maintained contacts, because the former needed forest produce and honey. As agriculture involved both cultivation of land and the nurturing of domesticated animals, the cultivators co-laboured seasonally with the settled and semi-nomadic pastoralists. After the harvest the herders brought their cattle, sheep and goats to feed on the stubble, and the animal manure helped to fertilise the land. The barter of essential items normally took place between the cultivators and the pastoralists. Both materially benefited through the exchange of surplus cereals, milk, meat and animal skins.[51] In time, the surplus came to be exchanged with the artefacts and produce of those who were neither peasants nor pastoralists but craftsmen. And eventually the process of exchange came to be increasingly facilitated by another class of people, the traders. While the hunter-gatherers lived a day-to-day existence, the agriculturists could enjoy incremental levels of prosperity. The remains of pots and pans, beads, shells and assorted jewellery that have been discovered in Baluchistan and the Indus basin, the very first areas of farming in South Asia, testify to this diversity from at least the sixth millennium BC.[52] Agriculture helped to establish permanent habitations and settlements that, in turn, became identified with the founding of communities. The concepts of identity, ethnicity and ancestry became meaningful in the context of agricultural communities.[53] Within such communities family kinship became a unifying factor among groups bound by marriage ties; and within families there emerged gifted or powerful personalities, on whom the task of leadership devolved. The development of hereditary leadership could also be traced to this stage. The social complexity became more marked with status-seeking by particular families within a community. The remains of grave goods are an indication of this particular trend. A negative element of the social complexity engendered by settled agricultural communities was warfare.[54] The main contentious issue was land. In contrast to the hunter-gatherers, who roamed over vast tracts of land that belonged to no particular clans, the agriculturists had to be protective of their land, or risk losing it to raiding parties of nomadic pastoralists or other enemy clans. The remains of defensive enclosures or skeletons of bodies impaled with weapons indicate degrees of violent conflict among both Neolithic and post-Neolithic agricultural people.

The Early Harappan phase: proto-urban settlements of the late Neolithic period

While Neolithic farming communities and villages have been found in four different regions of the sub-continent, as noted above, their transformation into proto-urban dwellers took place essentially in the northwest, particularly in the Indus region. This process takes us into the first phase of the Harappan Civilisation: the Early Harappan phase, also called the Era of Regionalisation, which was a prelude to its mature phase. The term 'Harappan', referring to the great city-settlement of Harappa in the Punjab, is frequently used to describe collectively the styles and features of monuments and artefacts from the entire Harappan/Indus Civilisation to which the city belonged. Since the antecedents of this civilisation go back into the late Neolithic times, the development of village settlements into proto-urban forms may be said to be part of the story of the Early Harappan period. It was believed, almost until the mid-twentieth century, that the urban civilisation of the Indus could not have developed indigenously; and that it must have had foreign origins, probably Mesopotamian. The archaeological researches since the 1970s have disproved this thesis.[55] The early archaeologists had paid little attention to the varying ecological and geographical conditions of many different sites in the entire northwest zone, and the focus of their research was very much on the metropolitan cities themselves rather than on the evolution of human occupation before the rise of the cities. Many post-war archaeologists, however, excavated at different and remote sites and, after uncovering layer after layer of habitation levels, have provided us with a unique understanding of the historical sequences of the evolution of human societies before mature urbanism took place. They have shown how, at a number of sites throughout the area, the people of the northwest of the Indian sub-continent ultimately progressed from a Neolithic state of existence to a fine urban cultural lifestyle of the Copper/Bronze Chalcolithic Age. The roots of the Indus cities lie, therefore, not outside the sub-continent but within.

Within the northwest the relevant areas for understanding the rural to urban transition are Baluchistan (key sites being Mehrgarh, Kili Gul Mohammad, Rana Ghundai and Balakot), Sind (key sites being Amri and Kot Diji), the plains of western Punjab (key site of Harappa), the Gomal valley (key site of Rehman Dheri) and the Ghaggar–Hakra valley (key site of Kalibangan) that runs through the states of Rajasthan and Haryana in modern India. These sites were more than villages, and the clues to their incipient urbanism lie in the relative sizes of their ground plans, the remains of foundations of their houses and streets, and the varied types of pottery manufactures (see Figure 2.1), household effects, tools and valuable grave goods. These sites most often lay on or near agriculturally fertile land and along the trade routes. Chronologically speaking, they vary in antiquity. There is a general consensus among the archaeologists that the Mature Harappan period lasted from about 2600 to 1900 BC, and that the development phase before 2600 BC should be designated as Early Harappan, not pre-Harappan, because of the continuity of the tradition.[56] On the other hand, it would be too simplistic to call the very early farming phase in the sixth millennium as Early Harappan. A compromise could be that the time-span of about 7000 to 4500 BC should be called the Baluchistan phase, because of the importance of Mehrgarh; that the years 4500 to 3500 BC be considered an age of transition; and that the years from about 3500 to 2600 BC be called the Early Harappan phase[57] or, according to the American historian Jim Shaffer, an Era of Regionalisation.[58] Although an increasing amount of data are available from many sites, chosen here are four sites – Amri, Kot Diji, Kalibangan and Mehrgarh – which provide differential evidence of proto-urban features in the Early Harappan period (*c.* 3500–2600 BC).

Figure 2.1   Early Harappan pottery fragments (Pat Baker: line drawings adapted from Gregory Possehl, *The Indus Age*, Philadelphia: University of Pennsylvania Press, 1999, pp. 500–1, 577, 641).

Evidence from three proto-urban sites: Amri, Kot Diji and Kalibangan

Amri, the first of these four sites, is situated about 160 kilometres to the south of Mohenjo Daro on the west bank of the Indus. It was excavated throughout the 1960s, and four clear periods were distinguished from the diggings. Period I (*c.* 3500 to 3000 BC), the earliest phase, is known as the Amri Culture.[59] Among the ruins of very rough, low-level rectangular houses with mud flooring, which were just a few inches higher than the outside level, have been found red earthenware jars, black and red hand-moulded pottery and a few scraps of copper, blades, bangles and stone tools. Definite advances in pottery styles and the design of houses are noticeable from Period II (3000 to 2700 BC). Period III was when Amri was part of the Indus Civilisation, during the Mature Harappan age, lasting from about 2700 to 2400 BC, when it reached its high point of urbanism. It was the time when larger houses, constructed from adobe bricks of standardised design, were built and wheel-turned pottery, with strong individualistic design styles, was popular.[60] The rise of Mohenjo Daro, however, was bound to lead to the eclipse of sites like Amri, and in Period IV, or the Late Harappan period, the evidence points to an overall decline. From the four archaeological periods of Amri we can trace a sequence of styles, skills and developments that document for us the pointers towards the Indus Civilisation.

The site of Kot Diji in Sindh also provides us with unique examples of a culture developing into an urban form. Here firstly, between about 3200 and 2600 BC, a major ceramic industry developed, and the Kot Diji ceramic style reached sites as far apart as Rehman Dheri, Amri and Kalibangan. The conspicuous feature of this style was the wheel-thrown globular jar of red ware with such decorative motifs as fish-scales and *pipal* leaves.[61] The plain and painted terracotta bangles, cattle figurines, cones, beads of semi-precious stones, and many objects of shell and bone testify to a standard of living far advanced from that of the people who inhabited the early Neolithic villages. Kot Diji possessed an important feature of urbanism that both Amri and Mehrgarh lacked: a fortified citadel complex, along with a lower town.[62] This pattern of layout in the central area of a settlement was a key pointer to similar planning at the metropolitan sites of Mohenjo Daro and Harappa.

Kalibangan, in Rajasthan, nearly 300 kilometres northwest of Delhi, was a key site on the banks of the now dry *Ghaggar–Hakra* river which once flowed through Rajasthan and Haryana. Its maximum area would have covered approximately 20 hectares, or 50 acres, of land.[63] At no other site do we notice the continuity between the late Neolithic proto-urban phase and the Indus Civilisation more clearly than at Kalibangan. In its Mature Harappan phase, as in Mohenjo Daro, the site possessed both a citadel mound and the lower town; but archaeologists have also uncovered an Early Harappan settlement under the citadel mound that indicates a similar ground plan.[64] During this early phase, which lasted from about 3000 to 2700 BC, the fortification wall was made of mass-produced mud bricks of standard size and proportion. Both the inner and the outer faces of this wall were plastered with mud. From the foundation remains of houses it may be surmised that each house had three or four rooms. Many useful household items such as ovens and storage pits have been excavated. Some of the antiquities discovered include chalcedony blades, carnelian, faience, gold and silver beads and pottery of various designs. The predominant pottery was red or pink with black and white painting, and on some of the pottery there was also non-scriptural graffiti that may be seen to anticipate the Mature Harappan script.[65]

Evidence from Mehrgarh

Even more important than the above three locations is the site of Mehrgarh in Baluchistan. Owing to the findings of major excavations there, in 1974, under Jean-François Jarrige and his Franco-Pakistani team, Mehrgarh furnishes us with a perfect example of a site that links Neolithic society to the Mature Harappan culture.[66] Nowhere in the Indian sub-continent does a site exist which allows us this unique glimpse into the previous 4,500 years before 2500 BC when Mohenjo Daro was at its zenith. The geographical position of Mehrgarh is particularly worth examining. The site lies at the foot of the Bolan Pass on the River Bolan, a tributary of the Indus, at a distance of 250 kilometres northwest of Mohenjo Daro. This means that it belongs to the Indus drainage system, although it is located within the Kachi plain of Baluchistan. The alluvium and floodwaters of the Bolan river and Indus basin made the Mehrgarh site suitable for farming. And since the Bolan Pass is, like the Khyber Pass, one of the important access points between India and Afghanistan, Mehrgarh was strategically located on a historical route that links the Indus valley with the Iranian plateau, leading on to Central and West Asia.[67] It is worth noting that the discovery of some very early beadware of precious stone such as lapis lazuli would indicate that the people of Mehrgarh were trading even during the earliest period of their history.[68] The Mehrgarh site consists of six mounds spread over an area of approximately 500 acres. This was a large site, but as the habitation focus shifted over time each period covered only a small section of that. Archaeologists have named the oldest mound MR3, where they have uncovered evidence of continuous human occupation from about 7000 to 4700 BC.[69] The greater antiquity of Mehrgarh's Period I can be appreciated by comparing it with that of Amri, whose Period I begins only at 3500 BC. After Period I there were six other periods, bringing the chronology down to 2300 BC.[70] During their seven periods of history, until 2300 BC, the Mehrgarhians were improving their skills and arts to a level that eventually matched that of the Mature Harappa society. Their pottery, copper ware, figurines and various other ornaments show a people striving towards a state of advancement and perfection, by experimenting, innovating and improvising rather than by imitating foreign models. Some of the oldest cotton seeds have been recovered from the mounds of Mehrgarh, again raising the possibility of the first cotton-manufacturing processes occurring in the Indus zone.[71] A recent report from the Human Biology Department of the University of Rome also credits the people of Mehrgarh with the skills of dentistry.[72]

SELECT EXTRACTS FOR REVIEW AND REFLECTION

Extract 2.1 The African origins of human beings

Until the 1960s, the multi-regional model of human origins long held sway among scientists and anthropologists. Racial differences are perhaps more easily explainable under the hypothesis of this model. It was also argued that gene flow, or the introduction of new genes into regional populations, helped to ensure that the evolving regional populations were similar in reproductive and anatomical character and that they all belonged to a single *Homo sapiens* type. From the 1960s onwards, however, researchers have become more convinced by the hypothesis of Africa being the geographical cradle of human origins, as the following two extracts explain.

The rise of modern humans is a recent drama that played out against a long and complex backdrop of evolutionary diversification among the hominids, but the fossil record shows that from the earliest times Africa was consistently the centre from which new lineages of hominids sprang. Clearly, interesting evolutionary developments occurred in both Europe and eastern Asia, but they involved populations that were not only derived from but also eventually supplanted by emigrants from Africa. In Africa our lineage was born and, ever since its hominids were first emancipated from the forest edges, that continent has pumped out successive waves of emigrants to all parts of the Old World.

Source: Ian Tattersall, 'Out of Africa Again ... and Again', *Scientific American*, 276, April 1997, pp. 60–67.

... all the genetic data shows the greatest number of polymorphisms in Africa; there is simply far more variation in that continent than anywhere else. You are more likely to sample extremely divergent genetic lineages within a single African village than you are in the whole of the rest of the world ... Why does diversity indicate greater age? [Taking the example of a hypothetical Provençal village, we can ask] why do the bouillabaisse recipes change? Because in each generation, a daughter decides to modify her soup in a minor way. Over time, these small variations add up to an extraordinary amount of diversity in the village's kitchens. And – critically – the longer the village has been accumulating these changes, the more diverse it is. It is like a clock, ticking away in units of rosemary and thyme – the longer it has been ticking, the more differences we see ... when we see greater genetic diversity in a particular population, we can infer that the population is older – and this makes Africa the oldest of all.

Source: Spencer Wells, *The Journey of Man: A Genetic Odyssey*, New York: Random House, 2003, p. 39 – a most illuminating book in this field.

Read also Chris Scarre (ed.), *The Human Past: World Prehistory and the Development of Human Societies*, London: Thames & Hudson, 2005, pp. 14–73; and Brian Fagan, *World Prehistory: A Brief Introduction*, New York: Longman, 1999, pp. 62–88.

Extract 2.2 Major crop types: native or foreign?

The controversy among botanists and plant agricultural specialists about whether rice was a native Indian plant or was imported from China is further fuelled by the evidence provided by the great American physiologist and biologist Jared Diamond, who says that all the main cereals consumed by the Indians were first domesticated elsewhere. They include wheat, barley, rice, sorghum and millet. Most probably, apart from rice, these cereals arrived from the Fertile Crescent (Mesopotamia). Diamond agrees that pulses such as hyacinth beans and black and green gram, along with cucumber, cotton and flax, are Indian domesticates. In the case of cotton, Diamond's evidence confirms Jarrige's conclusions about the earliest cotton seeds being found at Mehrgarh. Diamond, however, is quite categorical about the importance of the Fertile Crescent when he writes that:

> ... even for those crops whose wild ancestor does occur outside of Southwest Asia, we can be confident that the crops of Europe and India were mostly obtained from Southwest Asia and were not local domesticates.

Source: Jared Diamond, *Guns, Germs and Steel: A Short History of Everybody for the Last 13,000 Years*, London: Vintage, 1998, p. 182; see also pp. 126–7, 181–2.

RELEVANT QUESTIONS FOR DISCUSSION

1 How will genetics help us to understand the origins of the subcontinent's people?
2 What are the qualities required of a good archaeologist?
3 In the context of world history, what is the significance of the 1974 Mehrgarh excavations carried out by François Jarrige and his team?

Notes

1 Renfrew and Bahn: 49–52, 89–116.
2 Sounderarajan 1981: 3–7.
3 Scarre 2005: 50–51.
4 Ibid.: 55–7, 177–83.
5 Wells 2003: iii–xvi.
6 Scarre 2005: 25.
7 Toth and Schick 2005: 47–83.
8 Klein 2005: 101–3.
9 Coningham 2005: 522.

10 Toth and Schick 2005: 62.
11 Pettitt 2005: 127–8, 130–31; Wells 2003: 33.
12 Pettitt 2005: 128, 132–7.
13 Fagan 1999: 85–6.
14 Ibid.: 88.
15 Wells 2003: 182–3; Klein 2005: 102.
16 Renfrew and Bahn: 120–24.
17 Ibid.: 118–20; Scarre 2005: 30.
18 Thapar 2002: 70; Toth and Schick 2005: 74–5; Fagan 1999: 126.
19 Scarre 2005: 33–4; Pettitt 2005: 157; Bahn 1996: 222–6; Thapar 2002: 70.
20 Renfrew and Bahn: 133–7; Fagan 1999: 164.
21 Renfrew and Bahn: 151–2.
22 Coningham 2005: 522; Thapar 2002: 72.
23 Coningham 2005: 522.
24 Ibid.
25 Wells 2003: 77.
26 Allchin and Allchin 1982: 15–16, 36.
27 Ibid.: 36; Narasimhiah 1981.
28 Ray *et al*. 2000: 143–7; Allchin and Allchin 1982: 47–50.
29 Kachroo 2000: 73.
30 Thapar 2002: 74; Jha 2004: 26.
31 Ray *et al*. 2000: 142–3.
32 Coningham 2005: 523.
33 Ibid.: 522–3; Chakrabarti 1999: 100–10.
34 Thapar 2002: 72.
35 Ibid.: 72–3.
36 Coningham 2005: 523.
37 Thapar 2002: 73; Coningham 2005: 523.
38 Thapar 2002: 73.
39 Chakrabarti 1999: 110–16.
40 Fagan 1999: 115–53; Kochhar 2000: 58.
41 Thapar 2002: 74–6; Coningham 2005: 524.
42 Diamond 1998: 101, 181.
43 Coningham 2005: 525–8.
44 Ray *et al*. 2000: 560–61; Jarrige and Meadow: 1980; Jarrige 1982.
45 Bahn 1996: 252.
46 Coningham 2005: 526.
47 Ibid.: 527; Chakrabarti 2004: 18; Allchin and Allchin 1982: 118.
48 Coningham 2005: 527–8; Kachroo 2000: 80.
49 Thapar 2002: 59–60; Diamond 1998: 88.
50 Thapar 2002: 57.
51 Ibid.: 58–9.
52 Chakrabarti 2004: 24.
53 Scarre 2005: 190–91.
54 Ibid.: 192.
55 Coningham 2005: 529; Chakrabarti 2004: 8–9.
56 Thapar 2002: 80.
57 Kochhar 2000: 193.
58 Coningham 2005: 528.
59 Kochhar 2000: 66; Chakrabarti 2004: 25; Allchin and Allchin 1982: 141–3; Khan 1964: 55–9.
60 Ray *et al*. 2000: 169–71.
61 Coningham 2005: 529–30; Khan 1964: 41–4, 49–55.
62 Chakrabarti 2004: 26.

63 Coningham 2005: 533.
64 Bala 2004: 35–6; Coningham 2005: 531; Chakrabarti 1998.
65 Bala 2004: 39.
66 Coningham 2005: 524–5, 528–30; Chakrabarti 1999: 120–26.
67 Chakrabarti 2004: 24.
68 Ray *et al.* 2000: 560–63.
69 Kochhar 2000: 60–65.
70 Ibid.: 65.
71 Ibid.: 63.
72 McMahon 2006.

3 The Harappan Civilisation

(*Time-span:* c. *2600 to 1700 BC*)

The Harappan Civilisation, also known as the Indus Civilisation, was the culmination of a long and sustained cultural evolution that took place in the plains, valleys, and surrounding regions of a mighty river in the northwest of India: the Indus. This river, with its many tributaries, is still the lifeline of Punjab and Sind – being the basis of their agricultural prosperity; but its importance in world history cannot be overstated. Just as three of the world's oldest civilisations grew along the banks of their great rivers – the Egyptian on the Nile, the Mesopotamian on the Tigris–Euphrates, and the Chinese on the Yangtse – similarly, along the banks of the Indus developed the first major civilisation of the Indian sub-continent. Substantial human settlements also existed along the banks of other nearby rivers, the now dried up *Ghaggar–Hakra*, the *Saraswati* and the *Drasadvati*. Our evidence of these settlements is drawn from the earliest of the Old Indian Vedic literature and from the various modern geological and archaeological surveys.[1] The area covered by the culture and tradition based on the Indus and other rivers was vast, embracing practically the whole of modern Pakistan and northwest India, along with modern Gujarat (see Map 3.1). The mature phase of the Harappan Civilisation, the specifically urban phase, lasted between about 2600 and 1900, BC but, as noted in Chapter 2, the antecedent of this phase, the Early Harappan, was in the making at least a thousand years before 2600 BC. Indeed, the very first roots of this civilisation go back even farther, to 7000 BC, the earliest date assigned to the findings at Mehrgarh. Although the great cities had markedly declined by 1900 BC, the cultural influence of this civilisation continued for another few centuries after that date.

From the hindsight of history one would like to think that the legacy of this civilisation would have been acknowledged, remembered and cherished by at least the thinking and literate section of the Indian population during the subsequent four millennia. Unfortunately, apart from the sparse clues that one may seek in the early Vedic texts, no one seemed to have remembered, or cared to remember, anything about the culture or achievements of the Harappans until the twentieth century. The change came only after the groundbreaking discoveries of the ruins at Mohenjo Daro (see Figure 3.1) and Harappa in the 1920s. Historians then radically revised their interpretation of early Indian

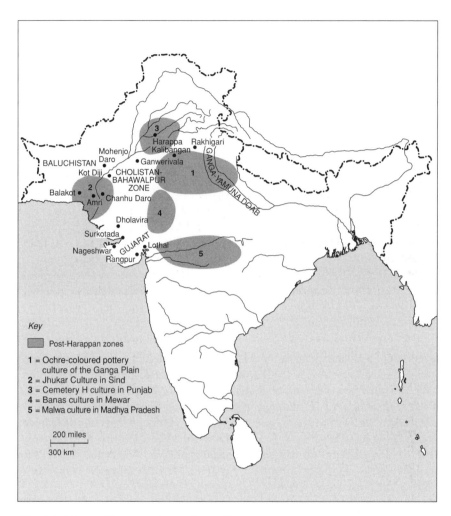

Map 3.1 Mature Harappan sites and post-Harappan zones.

history in two stages. During the first stage, in the 1920s and the 1930s, they acknowledged that the history of India was much older than they had expected. The belief that Indian civilisation started with the Aryans sometime around 1500 BC had to be discarded, and the new consensus was that it went back to at least 3000 BC. Although historians confirmed the revised chronology, there was nevertheless a certain amount of doubt nurtured concerning the origins of the Harappan Civilisation, and some wondered whether it was an imported model from Mesopotamia.[2] These doubts were put to rest by research from the 1970s.[3] As noted in Chapter 2, this research has clearly indicated that the roots of the Harappan Civilisation go back to the Neolithic villages of Baluchistan,

Figure 3.1 Mohenjo Daro perspective (by permission of RHPL).

as at Mehrgarh, and there is no evidence of the Mesopotamian or any other foreign influence at least in the shaping of the mature phase of this civilisation. This did not, however, imply that the Harappan Civilisation was built on Vedic culture – actually the next phase in Indian history – as some modern revisionists are keen to claim[4] (see Extract 3.1). Although some of the features of the Harappan Culture can be detected within Vedic Culture,[5] there can be little doubt that the former was essentially pre-Vedic and non-Vedic, but indigenous, as the pioneer-explorer Sir John Marshall affirmed.[6] Chapter 4 takes up this discussion further.

Phases of progress in Harappan archaeology

The story of Harappan archaeology, although perhaps not as romantic or nostalgic as those of Egypt and Mesopotamia, is a remarkable story of scholarly and persevering endeavour in the task of uncovering the forgotten past. A large number of sites, of varying extent, have been excavated in the geographical and cultural zone of the northwest of the sub-continent. The excavations and the unearthing of some astonishing finds have taken place in three major phases, and each phase is distinguished by the remarkable work of one or more archaeologists at one or more specific sites.

The first phase covered the nineteenth century.[7] The earliest pioneer was Charles Masson, whose real name was James Lewis. He was actually an English soldier who deserted from the East India Company's army. In his new guise he travelled in the 1820s to the Punjab, where he first encountered the remains of Harappa. He described the site as a 'ruinous brick castle'[8] with high walls and towers, and noticed a large number of fine and standard-size bricks there. He was followed, some years later, by Lieutenant Alexander Burns who, while making a historic journey up the River Indus, also visited Harappa. Burns described its ruins as extensive and calculated that the place was 3 miles in circumference. He too noted that there were a large number of bricks, but that there was not an entire building standing. Earlier on his journey he had also visited an Indus site called Amri, which was to provide crucial evidence for future archaeologists. When the findings of Masson and Burns came to the attention of Sir Alexander Cunningham, the first director general of the Archaeological Survey of India, he decided to visit Harappa himself. He made three expeditions, two in the 1850s and a third in 1873. During the first two visits he could corroborate the evidence of Masson and Burns, but during the 1873 visit he was much disappointed to witness the depletion of huge quantities of bricks. This was because the British engineers who were building the railway line between Lahore and Multan had been utilising the bricks as ballast under the tracks. Cunningham decided to conduct an archaeological survey of Harappa before all the bricks disappeared. One of the first objects that he discovered was a seal made of unpolished but smooth black stone, on which was deeply engraved a bull, without hump, with two stars under the neck, along with an inscription in six characters. This seal, which is now in the British Museum, is the first of hundreds that are inextricably associated with the Harappan Culture.[9]

The second phase began with the appointment in 1902 of a young and brilliant archaeologist, John Marshall, as the new director general of the Archaeological Survey of India.[10] Marshall owed his appointment to Lord Curzon, the viceroy, who aimed to keep India in subjugation to the British crown, but who also greatly loved and admired her historical monuments and wished to restore them to their ancient glory. He helped Marshall to make his mark by authorising extra funding for the Archaeological Survey. Marshall's interest in Harappa and other similar sites had been aroused not only by the work of Cunningham but also by that of an Italian scholar, Luigi Pio Tessitori, who had written about a place called Kalibangan.[11] Marshall ordered a systematic excavation of Harappa in 1914, but the onset of the First World War delayed it. It was only in 1920 that one of his deputies, Dahya Ram Sahni, embarked on it. His work continued until 1925. The results were not encouraging, as there had been much plundering by the railroad authorities, but Sahni found three more seals with further curious pictographic legends.

The first man to see and write about the other prime site, Mohenjo Daro, was D.R. Bhandarkar. After his visit there in 1911 he wrote the following words, something that he must have long regretted afterwards: 'According to the local tradition, these are the ruins of a town only 200 years old ... This seems to be not incorrect, because the bricks here found ... are of the modern type, and there is a total lack of terra-cottas amidst the whole ruins.'[12]

Fortunately, his pessimistic assessment of the finds at Mohenjo Daro was not universally accepted; and in 1919 R.D. Banerji began excavating there. He came to the conclusion that the site was very ancient and that it would yield many treasures. To start with, he came across three soapstone seals, similar to those found at Harappa. When both the Harappa and Mohenjo Daro seals and other materials were compared, Marshall and his deputies, Sahni and Banerji, became increasingly certain that the two cities were sites from a common historical civilisation that flourished nearly 4,500 years ago. From 1925 to 1927 Marshall, in collaboration with a team of brilliant Indian deputies, such as M.S. Vats and K.N. Dikshit, worked indefatigably with hundreds of labourers on the Mohenjo Daro site. The results of his efforts were astonishing and stupendous.[13] The interpretations of his findings were to have a monumental impact upon the study of Indian history. It has been said that Marshall 'left India two thousand years older than he found it'; and a distinguished archaeologist, Robin Coningham, thinks that 'Marshall's museums and newspaper coverage of the Indus Civilisation played an important part in the road to self-determination – it provided a civilised backdrop'.[14] New excavations continued during the 1930s. At one particular settlement, Chanhu Daro, east of the Indus, an American team led by Norman Brown was given permission to dig and to be able to send some of the artefacts to their sponsor, the Museum of Fine Arts at Boston.[15] Another great archaeologist, Sir Aurel Stein, toured around the region of the dried-up Ghaggar–Hakra river system and listed nearly sixty different sites.[16] The 1930s were the years of economic depression, with little funding available for the archaeologists. The effects of this on the training of new staff and many other administrative problems were investigated by the world-renowned Sir Leonard Woolley, on the orders of the viceroy, Lord Linlithgow; but the Woolley Report of 1939 was savagely attacked, particularly by the Indian archaeologists, for adopting an unduly negative tone.

The third major phase opened in 1944 with the appointment of Mortimer Wheeler as director general of the Archaeological Survey[17] (see Extract 3.2). Wheeler brought new methods of controlled stratigraphic excavation and recording – methods which are still used today. He trained a whole new generation of South Asian archaeologists in his methods and expounded new theories about the demise of the Harappan Culture. Some of his theories are now rejected, but there can be no doubt that he brought new skills to the archaeological projects of the Indus basin and prepared the groundwork for post-independence Indian and Pakistani archaeologists. Wheeler became an adviser after partition, and both Indian and Pakistani archaeologists broke new ground in the region. Fresh discoveries are continually being reported, such as the one about a 3,500-year-old stone axe engraved with the Harappan script being recently found in Tamil Nadu, indicating a much broader span of Harappan influence in the sub-continent and a closer historical link between the regions of India.[18] A world-class Museum and Centre of Study for Indus Civilisation has also been established at the University of Vadodara in India.

These developments will offer new insights into the various phases of the Harappan Culture and Civilisation. The most critical excavation of the post-war period took place at Mehrgarh in Baluchistan in 1974–5, under the super-vision of Jean-François Jarrige, who led a joint Franco-Pakistani team.[19] It was the work of this team that demonstrated the thread of archaeological continuity from the earliest foundations of Mehrgarh in the seventh millennium BC to the great cities of the Indus.

Understanding the Mature Harappan phase

The mature phase is essentially the high urban phase. The rich material evidence dug out from the ground by dedicated teams of specialists and labourers and systematically studied and interpreted by the above-mentioned names helps us to reconstruct this urban civilisation and gain an insight into the lives and customs of the Harappans. The evidence from the mature period covers a time-span of some 700 years, but at any particular site one may discover finds from different epochs. The finds are fascinating in themselves, and each has to be examined in a particular way. Some can speak for themselves, for example the brick walls or children's toys. There is little argument as to their purpose. Other finds need to be interpreted for their especial significance, such as a piece of sculpture, a terracotta seal or a recognisable seal motif. These on their own do not describe themselves, but may provide valuable clues to understanding the art, trade and religion of the Harappans. There are also finds which tell us nothing, such as the Harappan script or the peculiarly shaped figurines and strange animals on seals: it is very difficult to investigate them. The problem of the script is particularly frustrating, because our understanding of the Harappans would be so much more enhanced if it could be deciphered. Despite these difficulties, there is sufficient material evidence for us to discuss the characteristics of the mature urban phase of the Harappan Civilisation.

The extent and hierarchy of settlements

Numerous Harappan settlements have been identified in Sind, Baluchistan, the Cholistan desert in the Bahawalpur district of Pakistan, Haryana, Rajasthan, Gujarat and the upper areas of the Ganga–Yamuna *doab*, the land between the two rivers. A similar settlement has also been found at Shortughai, near the river Oxus, in north Afghanistan.[20] Owing to the variability of their size and importance, a four-tier hierarchy of settlement forms has been proposed.[21] The first tier consists of five very large sites, at Harappa (west Punjab), Mohenjo Daro (Sind), Dholavira (Gujarat), Rakhigari (Haryana) and Ganveriwala (Bahawalpur). Three of these sites each cover an area of 100 hectares, or 250 acres, while each of the other two is 80 hectares, or 200 acres. The discoveries at Harappa and Mohenjo Daro have been like benchmarks against which the relative urbanism of other sites can be judged. The second tier consists of thirty-two sites, each of which has an area of about 20 hectares, or 50 acres.

Although smaller in size, they have walled enclosures and other architectural features similar to the first-tier sites. The two prominent sites in this tier are Kalibangan (Haryana) and Lothal (Gujarat). A third tier of settlements, more numerous than those of the second, consists of such sites as Surkotada and Kuntasi (both in Gujarat), which cover on average 3 hectares, or 7.5 acres. Aspects of these sites, such as fortifications and their ceramics, provide evidence of a distinct Mature Harappan style. The fourth and lowest tier consists of nearly 15,000 settlements, each covering about 1 hectare, or 2.5 acres. These were either villages or centres for specialised crafts. Balakot (Sind) and Nageshwar (Gujarat) are typical sites. Whether collectively all the settlements were part of an empire, perhaps run from large sites such as Harappa or Mohenjo Daro, is a question that has preoccupied historians and archaeologists alike. Rather than thinking in terms of an empire, we should imagine a particular pattern of culture and a certain type of organisation that covered a very large area. In the absence of substantial archaeological evidence of a central political authority, one can only conclude that there was a great deal of cultural but not political uniformity.[22]

Civic planning and great structures

Even before any digging had begun at the two cities of Harappa and Mohenjo Daro, the first archaeologists were already being introduced to the urban splendours of the Indus people through the hundreds and thousands of bricks that they saw stacked or scattered about on the ground. While the brick stocks of Harappa were much depleted owing to railway depredation, those in Mohenjo Daro were massive.[23] There were many mud bricks that belonged to the period before the middle of the third millennium BC, but the ones that truly fascinated the archaeologists were those from about 2600 BC onwards. They were bricks baked in kilns fired with charcoal from the wood of the dense forests which, at that time, must have been plentiful throughout the Indus valley. These perfectly shaped baked kiln bricks were all of a standard size, measuring 7 x 14 x 28 cm, with the ratio of thickness to width and to length being 1 : 2 : 4. After the top layers of debris and overgrowth had been cleared, what emerged at Mohenjo Daro, particularly, was nothing short of spectacular.[24] There appeared, from below, the ruins of an entire city, extremely well planned and divided into sectors or mounds. In the west there was a high citadel mound with strong fortifications, and in the east was the lower city with smaller mounds. On the citadel mound there were the ruins of two or three large public buildings, of which the Great Bath is the best known today (see Extract 3.3). Another building looks like a granary, although archaeologists are not entirely sure; and a third building could possibly be a great hall. In the lower city, the streets were arranged in grid patterns, with major north–south and east–west streets intersecting each other, while numerous smaller streets and alleyways criss-crossed them. In between them were constructed blocks of houses, none of which opened onto the main streets. A feature of houses, public buildings and streets that fascinates the modern observer or tourist was a system of clean water supply to the inhabitants, along with latrine facilities by which the waste was channelled off without coming into contact with clean water.[25] Each house had its own well, and one authority has calculated that there were nearly 700 wells in the city.[26] These, along with the cisterns and reservoirs, would have ensured that the citizenry had sufficient water for drinking, cooking, bathing and cleaning. Today, millions of people in poverty-stricken Third World cities suffer from an acute shortage of water, with disastrous consequences for their quality of life; the people of Mohenjo Daro did not encounter this problem 4,500 years ago. The skills of their engineers and plumbers in laying out separate inflows and drains under the streets and buildings deserve admiration.

What has been discovered at Mohenjo Daro is also noticed at other major sites. With a few exceptions, most of these sites possess a raised citadel sector in the west and a lower town in the east, burnt-brick or mud-brick houses, a drainage system and fairly straight wide streets intersecting narrow lanes. One particular structure of Mohenjo Daro, however, was unique to that city: it is not found elsewhere and, moreover, there is nothing like it in the entire ancient world – the Great Bath. However, in other Harappan settlements we do some-times notice other architectural features. Harappa, for example, does not have a citadel mound, but has a unique set of circular brick platforms, supposedly for threshing grain.[27] The remains at Lothal reveal an artificial platform with streets and houses along with, arguably, either a unique brick dockyard con-nected by a channel leading to the Gulf of Cambay,[28] or a bath or a fresh water reservoir. One of the most interesting sites, Dholavira, contained three sectors: the castle and bailey sector, the middle sector and the lower town.[29] It was built of stone, not brick. The citadel there uniquely contained features such as gateways, stairs, corridors, ceremonial routes and guard chambers, none of which has been found at Mohenjo Daro or Harappa. Large reservoirs of water were also integrated into the civic planning at Dholavira.[30]

Food security, occupations and trading systems

The absence of evidence indicating a unified empire or city-states in the Harappan system does not imply an absence of organisation. The complex civic planning of the settlements of the first three tiers and the standard of living of the people, superior by far to the semi-rural level of the Early Harappan phase, suggest to us a high degree of competency in management and administration by those in authority. The western citadel area was, generally speaking, the headquarters of the elite, although large public buildings have been identified in different parts of the metropolitan cities.[31] All major civic affairs were probably organised from there. The paramount concern of those in charge of the large settlements was to ensure a continuous food supply for the inhabitants; this was less than difficult because the larger sites were in prox-imity to varied geographical zones with rich farming plains, river and coastal fisheries, grazing lands for domestic animals, and dense forests.[32] Sufficient food was brought into the cities by farmers, who sold them to the state officials overseeing the great granaries. The seeds of wheat, barley, peas, melons, sesame and mustard have all been found,[33] with a number of them dated. There is disagreement among the archaeologists as to the identification of the actual granaries,[34] but there can be no doubt that storage depots and food warehouses existed. There is a high probability that there were granaries at both Mohenjo Daro and Harappa, although the two structures were built on different plans. Standardised weights and measures, in graduated sizes and calculated by decimal increments, were used in commercial exchanges between the farmers and the granary officials.[35] There were also stringent trading regulations.[36] Animal husbandry was an important aspect of farming, with the faunal bone remains and terracotta animal images indicating the Harappan familiarity with varied types of domesticated and wild animals.[37] We are unsure of the proportion of the meat-consuming classes.[38]

From the number of artefacts and finds available, we must visualise Mohenjo Daro and other large centres to be very busy settlements. A variety of craftsmen, traders and workmen were occupied everywhere, particularly in the lower city. The most important crafts were in the fields of textiles, ceramic manufacturing, stone carving, household artefacts such as razors, bowls, cups, vases and spindles, and the production of jewellery, statuettes, figurines and children's toys, some of which were mechanical in function. This last category of goods is perhaps the most reliable evidence of the sophistication of this society.[39] The processes employed in the making of these articles demonstrate the best of the Indus valley technology. The Harappans knew how to manufacture bronze by mixing copper and tin, but both metals were difficult to obtain; so, although the Harappans were the first Bronze Age people of Indian history, there are few remains of bronze tools.[40] Gold and silver were widely used in the manufacture of pendants, armlets, beads and other decorative ornaments.[41] Brick manufacture and masonry engaged many workers, and a large number of artisans were engaged in the potter's trade.[42] Most Harappan pottery was wheel-turned and produced in large quantities. The most captivating of the smaller material finds from the ruins of Mohenjo Daro and Harappa are the nearly 2,000 inscribed steatite or soapstone seals, which indicate that the making of seals and seal-cutting were extremely important occupations; a specialised class of people were engaged in their production.[43] All traders had their stalls full of consumer goods related to the various crafts; food and drinks were sold by both farmers and city people. Unskilled labourers would have worked in street cleaning, garbage collecting,[44] well-digging, masonry and transporting people in ox-drawn wagons.[45] Compared with the cities of mediaeval Europe or modern India, Harappa and Mohenjo Daro were much cleaner. There were also entertainers, musicians, drummers and jugglers, who would have provided recreation for the leisured citizens.[46]

The craft and manufacturing activities in the settlements depended for their prosperity on the internal and external trade networks.[47] Raw materials from across the region were imported by the middlemen who employed craftsmen and skilled workers to manufacture the finished products to satisfy the consumer market. Certain places, particularly ports such as Lothal, acted as *entrepôts* or warehouse depots.[48] Copper ore was imported from a number of sites for making sharp-edged bronze saws that could efficiently cut through hard shells, collected from a number of coastal sites and passed on to the jewellers who fashioned bracelets and bangles from them.[49] Precious stones were used for making ornaments and utensils. Agate and jasper, the hard stones imported from Kutch and Gujarat, were much valued as they long retained their brightness and polish. The softer varieties, such as turquoise, lapis lazuli or carnelian, were used in the manufacture of assortments of much prized beads[50] (see Figure 3.2). Raw materials such as stones, marine shells and precious metals were bulk-transported across land by bullocks and buffalo-drawn carts and, on the River Indus and its tributaries, and between coastal ports, by boats, sometimes depicted on the Harappan seals.[51] Although the Indus economic zone is generally self-sufficient, its people have throughout history been enterprising traders who pioneered commercial links with foreign countries. We have evidence of such links made during the Mature Harappan phase. The countries involved were Afghanistan, Turkmenistan, Iran, Mesopotamia and Oman. The only Mature Harappan site outside the sub-continent was at Shortugai in Afghanistan, and it has been argued that its position as a transit point for many routes in that region encouraged a settlement of Indus traders engaged in the exchange of goods. They sought tin and lapis lazuli in return for the Indus products such as textiles, combs, beads, dice, etc.[52] Objects from the Indus region

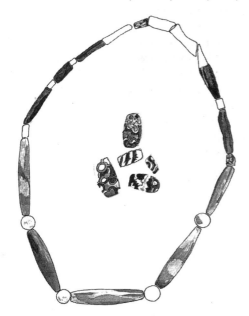

Figure 3.2 A necklace of Harappan beads (Pat Baker: line drawing).

have been found in both Turkmenistan and Iran, the latter country providing the main land route to Mesopotamia.[53] A flourishing sea trade linked the Indus settlements with Oman and southern Mesopotamia.[54] From Oman came copper and shells primarily, and also dates, honey, incense and salt fish. The exports to Oman included various foodstuffs, boats, livestock and utility arte- facts. Beads, bangles, hard woods, pearls, ivory and numerous exotic animals reached Mesopotamia by boat from the Indus region, and the Indus valley seals have also been found there. A Mesopotamian text from the reign of King Sargon of Akkad refers to boats bringing the cargo from a place called Meluhha, now identified as the Indus valley; these boats probably sailed from the port of Lothal on the Gujarat–Kathiawar coast.[55] In the absence of reliable trade figures it is difficult to find out whether the balance of trade worked in favour of the Indus zone or the foreign countries. However, far more Indus valley products have been retrieved in regions outside India than foreign products within the Indus zone.[56]

Secular power and religion

It is difficult for archaeologists to obtain a picture of the elites who held power in the cities of the Indus: most probably, there was a coalition of rich merchants, priests and bureaucrats. While no palaces or rich tombs have been found, there can be no doubt that, without someone exercising power in a systematic way, Mohenjo Daro's period of glory would have been much shorter than the estimated 700 years during which the city flourished. A powerful piece of sculpture, retrieved from Mohenjo Daro and now in the National Museum in Karachi, is that of a personage who has been described as a priest-king. His gravitas definitely conveys the impression of a person of influence and auth- ority, of which, unfortunately, he is the sole representative. It has been suggested that the power of the elite may be discerned from the images on soapstone seals,[57] which may symbolise political, economic or ecclesiastical power. Apart from the script, the seals carry depictions of ten different animals: these are the mythical unicorn, the zebu, elephant, rhinoceros, water buffalo, short-horned humpless bull, goat, antelope, crocodile and hare (see Figure 3.3). It may even be that the animal images acted as symbols of authority of certain officers or of dominant lineages and clan families.[58] Since the unicorn appears on the largest number of seals it might be the power symbol of the most numerous clan.[59] Rich merchants too might have used the seals as their personal or official insignia for goods to be traded.[60]

It is unwise to conjecture as to the organised religion of the inhabitants of the Indus cities. However, we can deduce certain aspects of their religiosity and spirituality from some of the archaeological finds and from the living traditions of India today. Some of them may even be linked to Hinduism itself. The water in the Great Bath on the higher citadel of Mohenjo Daro was, most probably, considered holy and was perhaps reserved for ritual washing by groups of priests;[61] and ritual washing has been one of the immemorial customs

Figure 3.3 Harappan seals (Pat Baker: line drawings adapted from Possehl, op. cit., pp. 50, 53, 80).

of Hindu India. Some interesting symbols of religious art, with close Hindu associations, can be seen on seals and tablets. On some are found images of a male with horned headdress seated in the Yoga posture of *padmasana*.[62] Yoga is one of the great keys to understanding Hinduism. The pipal and the banyan trees, very common trees of India used as symbols of fertility, protection and death in Hindu mythology, are also depicted in the Indus script as well as on ornaments.[63] Other religious art symbols, also in common with the Hindu tradition, include garlands, arches, bangles, figurines of fertility goddesses, etc. In addition to religious and ritual art symbols, there are many abstract symbols and geometric designs. The endless-knot, the swastika, the circle, the ring – all have their motifs etched, engraved or carved into seals, pottery, copper and ivory objects.[64]

Sculpture, script and mathematics

All the material evidence that we have referred to thus far – the ruins of the great monuments, the standardised bricks and the terracotta seals, along with a great variety of craft goods and tools – adds up to a considerable treasure; but in its overall grandeur and magnificence the entire collection pales in

comparison with, say, the treasures of ancient Egypt. This is even more noticeable when we compare the achievement of the two civilisations in the art of
sculpture. The Harappan heritage is indeed very undistinguished. A recent
scholarly publication has listed just eight major items of true Harappan
sculpture.[65] The most well known of the eight are a solid figure of a robed
priest-king (only 17.8 cm high), mentioned earlier, and the figurine of the so-
called Dancing Girl of Mohenjo Daro, in her graceful and elegant pose, quite
nude except for her bangles and a necklace (see Figure 3.4). What is interesting,
however, is that there is 'a difference in conceptualisation, form and technique'[66]
between the two works. The first one is wonderfully crafted in stone and fore-
shadows the great stone art of India in the historic period. The Dancing Girl,
on the other hand, is a bronze product, made by the lost-wax process, and it too
provides a model for the later copper and bronze objects made in the sub-
continent. The two examples, along with the fact that a Harappan motif has
been identified as the 'inter-circling motif' on the Bodhi stone of Bodh Gaya,
suggest to us a degree of Harappan precedence to the future sculptural tradition
in India.[67]

The Harappans possessed a script which they used for inscribing on a variety
of objects: soapstone or steatite seals, impressible materials such as clay or soft
metal, and objects such as stone or copper tablets, bracelets, marble, ivory,
shells and bangles. Nearly 4,200 inscribed objects have been recovered, with
Mohenjo Daro and Harappa accounting for some 85 per cent.[68] The script

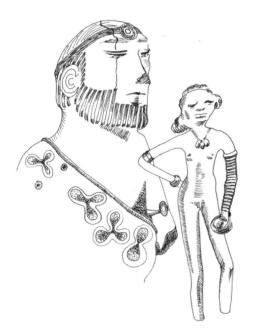

Figure 3.4 Dancing girl and priest-king (Pat Baker: line drawings adapted from
Possehl, op. cit., p. 75 and plate 2:28).

contains 419 signs, of which 113 occur once only, 47 twice, 59 fewer than five times and 200 every so often.[69] These signs are far too many to constitute an alphabetic or syllabic script; they are mostly logo-syllabic characters. Only eight texts longer than fifteen signs have been found.[70] The average length of an inscription is five signs, although the longest inscription is made up of twenty-six signs. The script was written from right to left, but started from the left when it carried on to the second line.[71] Perhaps the most striking Harappan inscription – containing nine signs, each 37 cm high and 25 to 27 cm broad, and each made by joining crystalline pieces and engraved on a wooden board – has been found at Dholavira.[72] Were it a signboard, it would indicate a certain degree of literacy among the people. Writing is the key to understanding the mind of a society; and history begins with the written word. We should become more knowledgeable about the Harappans if we were able to read their script or see some clear links between their script and the innumerable scripts used in the sub-continent today. Three great scholars – Professors Mahadevan of the Archaeological Survey of India, Asko Parpola of the University of Helsinki and Walter Fairservis Jr. of Vassar College, New York – spent years attempting to understand the mysteries of the script; but they too have been unable to decipher it. Nor are we able to state definitively whether their language belonged to the Indo-Aryan or the Dravidian family of languages. In this sense, the Harappan Civilisation must, therefore, be classed as pre-historic. The script remains undeciphered and cannot provide help, despite assertions made to the contrary.[73] If, however, a bilingual text, one using the Harappan script against another, already understood, were to be found on a single seal or some object, then the mystery might unravel, in the same way as the decryption of the Rosetta Stone in Egypt, containing the same text in three languages, solved the puzzle of the hieroglyphs. Most archaeologists, however, seem to be in general agreement that, since the majority of inscriptions are found on seals, and since the seals were an important symbol of authority or an exchange mechanism in trade relations, it is likely that the script must have something useful to say in terms of administration, trade or perhaps spirituality. Up to the present, we can judge the Harappan Civilisation only from its material remains.

While mathematical problems were inscribed on the Sumerian and other Mesopotamian clay tablets, there is nothing similar to be found in the Indus region. One should not conclude that the Harappans lacked mathematical insights or knowledge. As with all aspects of this civilisation, the clues to understanding lie in its ruins and artefacts. We have already referred to the standard ratio of $1:2:4$ in brick technology; and many skills of measuring and computational techniques can be easily discerned from the architectural and town-planning profiles. Weighing scales and instruments for measuring length have also been found. Part of a shell recovered at Mohenjo Daro, measuring 6.62 cm, or 2.6 in, is divided into nine equally spaced parallel lines cut with a fine saw. One of these lines is marked by a circle, and the sixth line from it by a dot. The distance between the circle and the dot has been calculated as 1.32 in, and is known as the Indus inch.[74] As this Indus inch is equal to two Sumerian equivalent measures called *shushi*, we may rightly conclude on the exchange of computational or commercial information between the Harappans and the Mesopotamians.[75] Two other measuring scales, with very finely graduated divisions, have also been discovered at Lothal and Harappa.[76] All three scales indicate a certain uniformity in establishing ratios and in modes of division and measurement. In addition the Harappans possessed a highly standardised system of cubical stone weights. A red seed, called 'gunja', equivalent to two grains of barley, constituted the base weight, and three different series of stone weight ratios have been calculated. The first series of seven weights doubled in size from $1:2:4:8:16:32:64$, while in the second and third series of weights we find a ratio of 160, 320 and 640, and then moving up from 1,600, 3,200, 6,400 to 12,800. The average 'gunja' seed weighed 0.109 grams; and the largest weight found at Mohenjo Daro, weighing 10,865 gm, or 25 lb, is nearly 100,000 times the weight of the 'gunja' seed.[77] From the various weight details gained from such tools as the plumb-line balls used by masons, mathematicians have constructed frequency charts which show that the weights were fractions or multiples of a standard weight known as *uncia*. This weight was 27.2 gm, and weights on the multiples of 5 uncia (136 gm) or one-sixteenth uncia (1.7 gm) have been found, once again suggesting a decimal system of calculation.[78] Finally, we must acknowledge that the Harappan farmers, like their Egyptian and Mesopotamian peers, must have relied upon their practical mathematical knowledge and intuition in order to control the flood cycles of their great river with sluices and irrigation channels, and to maximise crop yields by systematic sequencing of sowing and harvesting of spring wheat and barley and autumn crops such as cotton and sesame.[79]

The eclipse of the Harappan Civilisation

A decline set in around 1900 BC in the dynamics of the Harappan system, and there is little doubt that after 1700 BC little remained of the Harappan Civilisation. It did not, however, come to an abrupt end within a particular period of decades or during a particular century. Until quite recently it was believed that the Indus cities were destroyed by the Aryans who entered India from Iran and Afghanistan through northwestern passes such as the Bolan and the Khyber. This theory was based on two sets of evidence. One was the reference in the *Rig-Veda*, the premier Vedic text, that the Aryan god Indra destroyed a hostile people called the Dasas or Dasyus who lived in fortified places called *pur*.[80] The other concerned the discovery of some skeletons of men, women and children from the lower city of Mohenjo Daro, killed during the so-called last massacre.[81] The archaeologist who was most vehement in putting forward this theory of an Aryan onslaught on the Indus cities was Sir Mortimer Wheeler who, after admittedly considering and rejecting other theories, had no doubt that 'on circumstantial evidence, Indra stands accused'.[82] Wheeler later admitted the validity of other reasons for the Harappan decline, but nevertheless stuck to his claim about the massacre.[83] Most literary scholars and archaeologists today dismiss Wheeler's theory as too simplistic.[84] For example, the Rig-Vedic *pur* was nothing like an Indus city; it was just a structure of flimsy ramparts and stockades.[85] If the *purs* that Indra is supposed to have destroyed were the Indus cities, it is most curious that the first great sacred text of Hinduism, the *Rig-Veda*, does not mention anything about such recognisable features of the Harappan cities as the well-laid-out streets, houses, wells, drains, granaries and seals. Again, the skeletons of some people in the lower city of Mohenjo Daro are considered a wholly insufficient evidence of an attack on such a large system of authority and government as represented by the Indus Civilisation. The Aryan invasion theory will be discussed further in Chapter 4.

Scholars now consider a combination of natural and socio-economic factors to be the most likely reason for the decline of the Indus cities. Two of the natural factors could be the geological and the climatic.[86] It is presumed that the Indus region experienced severe tectonic disturbances brought about by earthquakes at the beginning of the second millennium BC.[87] These upheavals not only affected the normal course of the Indus and its tributaries but also helped dry up the nearby Ghaggar–Hakra river. Modern satellite imagery confirms the theory that the dramatic shifts in the river courses might have created great floods that could have cut off the food-producing areas from the cities themselves.[88] The quantities of silt layers in the upper levels of Mohenjo Daro, which are today many feet above the river course, are also a witness to those floods. Without the surrounding food-producing areas the cities themselves could have been left isolated. And with the frequent uncertainty of regular food supplies, the city populace prudently decided to migrate before starvation overtook them. Research into the history of rainfall patterns brings out the climatic factor of the decline. During the Mature Harappan period, about 2500 BC, there was a great rise in the amount of rainfall, but by the beginning of the second millennium BC it had dropped markedly.[89] This too would have had a damaging effect on food production, further resulting in depopulation of the cities. One of the reasons for the rainfall's unpredictability was the extreme deforestation and loss of trees caused by the burning of charcoal in brick-baking kilns. With the rivers shifting their courses, the rainfall declining and sufficient food failing to arrive from the countryside, we have to recognise a slow but inevitable collapse of the Indus system.[90] This collapse, it should be re-emphasised, cannot be explained by any one particular cause; we must think in terms of a 'combination of factors'.[91] The final outcome was catastrophic for the Mature Harappan phase. The Indus cities no longer had surplus produce for trade, and the ensuing loss of revenue would have affected all classes of people. The city authorities became powerless to prevent civil unrest or brigandage, and groups of people were continually leaving the cities for their own safety and survival. As the cities became poorer, their services declined dramatically. The drains and sewers of Mohenjo Daro, kept in good and clean working order for centuries, clogged up with waste and excreta, resulting in disease and pestilence. By about 1700 BC the desolated Mohenjo Daro had become a ghost town. Thirty-seven centuries would pass before its former grandeur was revealed to a world hitherto ignorant of it.

Civilisations continually rise and fall, but they rarely disappear without trace. It became so with the Harappan Civilisation. The collapse of the Indus system was really a collapse of its urban features.[92] Its culture did not cease to exist wholesale. The sophisticated lifestyle of the Indus people had certainly ended, but their folk culture continued at the village level.[93] Several of the beliefs and rituals, and the simple crafts and skills for making various utensils and artefacts, along with many rural features, survived and developed into proto-historic cultures in the surrounding regions.[94] The two important migrations of people, caused particularly by the accelerated drying up of the Ghaggar–Hakra river during the later phase, were in the direction of the Ganga–Yamuna *doab* and Gujarat, leading towards the Deccan.[95] Apart from these two big inter-regional movements, local migrations from the urban settlements into the rural areas similarly occurred. Archaeologically speaking, the cultures that resulted were relatively quite advanced, in the sense that they evolved as part of the Chalcolithic/Bronze Age, and did not regress to the skills level of the Stone Age. Different names have been assigned to these lesser regional cultures, such as the Ochre-Coloured Pottery Culture in the Ganges plain,[96] the Jhukar Culture in Sind,[97] the Cemetery H Culture in the Punjab,[98] the Banas Culture in Mewar in Rajasthan[99] or the Malwa Culture of Madhya Pradesh.[100] Historians identify these cultures on the basis of their pottery styles, grave goods and burial patterns and the quality of ornaments and tools, particularly those of copper. Some of these cultures survived for many centuries, thus continuing many of the non-urban Harappan traditions. The peoples of these cultures, in course of time, came into contact with other nomadic foreign groups, such as the Aryans, some of whom began to enter India from 1700 BC onwards; and a new Indo-Aryan civilisation would come to shape India's history for the next thousand years and more. Even today, however, a historically conscious traveller, making a journey of exploration in Punjab, Sind and Baluchistan, will certainly notice the imprints of the glorious Harappan past.

SELECT EXTRACTS FOR REVIEW AND REFLECTION

Extract 3.1 The claim of the Indus Civilisation being a Vedic Civilisation

This claim is made by some Indian historians essentially on the basis of the *Puranas* (see Chapter 8) being accepted as a credible source of Indian chronology. The *Puranas* provide long lists of ancient dynasties, and the so-called Uttanapada Dynasty of Manu Swayambhuba of the tenth millennium BC is considered as the first of the dynasties that continue for thousands of years. The *Puranas* are certainly a valuable source of general knowledge for the historians but, as there is no archaeological or any other type of evidence for claiming a continuity of Indian kingship from such an early period, we need to treat it with scepticism. The claim is also based on the false belief that no waves of migrants entered India after the tenth millennium BC. Despite its intellectual weaknesses, this claim has much resonance among a large number of Hindu religious nationalists imbued with the idea of *Hindutva*. The following passage gives a flavour of this revisionist version of history.

> The Indus Civilisation was essentially a Vedic Civilisation ... That since in India there was a continuity of Kingship from Manu onwards to Candragupta there could have been no 'Aryan' invasion or migration, at least unknown to the closest neighbours, the Persians. Since the majority of the people of this part of the world belonged to the eastern branch of the Mediterranean race from about the 9th or 10th millennium BC, the people of the Indus cities also belonged to the same race, as also the Vedic Indians and, consequently, there can be no question of 'pre-Aryan' or 'non-Aryan' orientation of this civilisation. The Indus people belonged to one of the Vedic tribes or 'Janas' and were essentially Indian with Vedic culture. In the circumstances, there could have been no invasion 'Aryans' or 'Indo-Europeans' into India as professed by occidental orientalists. Hence the Indic Civilisation was Rig-Vedic Civilisation.

Source: A.N. Chandra, *The Rig-Vedic Culture and the Indus Civilisation*, Calcutta: Ratna Prakashan, 1980, p. 218.

Extract 3.2 Mortimer Wheeler as director general of the Archaeological Survey of India

Sir Mortimer Wheeler was one of the greatest archaeologists of the twentieth century. His energy and dedication to work were legendary. As soon as his ship arrived at Bombay in 1944 he took a train to Delhi and then to Simla, where his headquarters were established. The efficiency that he generated among his staff can serve as an example to the many complacent officials and bureaucrats who today man the government departments in India. In the following passage he recalls his first day at work.

> On the top floor of the gaunt Railway Board building where the Archaeological Survey was then housed at Simla, I stepped over the recumbent forms of peons, past office windows revealing little clusters of idle clerks and hangers-on, to the office which I had taken over that morning ... As I opened my door I turned and looked back. The

sleepers had not stirred, and only a wavering murmur like the distant drone of bees indicated the presence of drowsy human organisms within. I emitted a bull-like roar, and the place leapt to anxious life … One after another my headquarters staff was ushered in, and within an hour the purge was complete. Bowed shoulders and apprehensive glances showed an office working as it had not worked for many a long day. That evening one of the peons (who later became my most admirable Headquarters Jemadar) said tremulously to my deputy's Irish wife, 'Oh, memsahib, a terrible thing has happened to us this day.'

Source: Sir Mortimer Wheeler, *Still Digging*, New York: E.P. Dutton, 1955, p. 186.

Extract 3.3   The Great Bath at Mohenjo Daro

The Great Bath at Mohenjo Daro is a monumental structure that came to be revealed to the world through the excavations carried out under Sir John Marshall. The following extract provides clear evidence of the excellence of the architecture of the Great Bath, and it is also a good example of Marshall's precision in his description of this wondrous treasure of the ancient world.

The Great Bath … was part of what appears to have been a vast hydropathic establishment and the most imposing of all the remains unearthed at Mohenjo Daro. Its plan is simple: in the centre, an open quadrangle with verandahs on its four sides, and at the back of three of the verandahs various galleries and rooms; on the south, a long gallery with a small chamber in each corner; on the east, a single range of small chambers, including one with a well; on the north, a group of several halls and fair-sized rooms. In the midst of the open quadrangle is a large swimming bath, some 39 feet long by 23 feet broad and sunk about 8 feet below the paving of the court, with a flight of steps at either end, and at the foot of each a low platform for the convenience of bathers, who might otherwise have found the water too deep. The bath was filled from the well in Chamber 16 and possibly from other wells besides, and the waste water was carried off through a covered drain near the S.W. corner, the corbelled roof of which is some 6 ft 6 in. in height … for careful and massive construction the Great Bath could hardly have been improved upon. From N. to S. its overall measurement is 180 ft, from E. to W. 108 ft. The outer walls were between 7 and 8 ft in thickness at the base, with a batter on the outside of about 6 ft; the inner walls for the most part about half as much … the actual lining of the tank was made of finely dressed brick laid in gypsum mortar, between 3 and 4 ft in thickness. Backing this was an inch thick damp-proof course of bitumen, which was kept in place and prevented from creeping by another thin wall of burnt brick behind it. Then came a packing of crude brick and behind this again another solid rectangle of burnt brick encompassing the whole, with short cross-walls between it and the verandah foundations in order to counteract any outward pressure . . . .

A more effective method of construction with the materials then available would hardly have been possible, and how well it has stood the test of time is sufficiently apparent from the present state of the tank which, after 5000 years, is still astonishingly well preserved.

Source: Sir John Marshall (ed.), *Mohenjo Daro and the Indus Civilization*, Vol. 1, London: Arthur Probsthain, London, pp. 24–5.

RELEVANT QUESTIONS FOR DISCUSSION

1 What is the rationale for describing the Harappan Civilisation as the Saraswati Civilisation? To what extent is it a credible rationale?

2 Why did the ancient cities of Mohenjo Daro and Harappa never enter into the Indian consciousness until the early twentieth century?

3 In what ways did the post-Harappans continue the Harappan traditions?

Notes

1 Chakrabarti 2004: 9.
2 Gadd and Smith [1924] 1979: 109–10; Dales [1968] 1979: 138–44.
3 Jarrige 1982.
4 E.g. Frawley and Rajaram 1995, or Mishra 2004.
5 Sastri 1957: 15–24; Sastri 1965: 92–147.
6 Chakrabarti 2004: 8; Kochhar 2000: 198ff.
7 Pande 1982: 395; Possehl 1982: 406–8.
8 Pande 1982: 395; Time-Life Books 1994: 9.
9 Cunningham [1872/3] 1979.
10 Time-Life Books 1994: 10–14; Bahn 1996: 170–72, 253–8.
11 Dolcini and Freschi 1999: 155–63.
12 Possehl 1982: 405.
13 Ibid.: 408–11; Marshall [1924] 1979.
14 From a note sent by Professor Robin Coningham, University of Durham, to the author.
15 Thapar 1984: 3.
16 Ibid.; Pande 1982: 397.
17 Time-Life Books 1994: 16; Bahn 1996: 256–7.
18 Associated Press 2006.
19 Time-Life Books 1994: 32–5; Jarrige 1982.
20 Chakrabarti 2004: 10.

21 Coningham 2005: 533–5.
22 Thapar 2002: 83–4.
23 Time-Life Books 1994: 12.
24 Marshall [1923/4] 1979.
25 Kenoyer 1998: 58–62.
26 Ibid.: 59.
27 Time-Life Books 1994: 19.
28 Chakrabarti 2004: 15; Leshnik [1968] 1979: 203–10; Time-Life Books 1994: 28.
29 Chakrabarti 1998: 103–6; Chakrabarti 2004: 15–16; Ray *et al.* 2000: 567–9.
30 Chakrabarti 1999: 175–6.
31 Kenoyer 1998: 52.
32 Ibid.: 40, 168.
33 Ibid.: 163.
34 Ibid.: 64–5.
35 Ibid.: 98–9.
36 Mackay 1948: 103.
37 Kenoyer 1998: 164–7.
38 Mackay 1948: 141–2; Jha 2004: 34.
39 Kenoyer 1998: 130–33.
40 Jha 2004: 35.
41 Kenoyer 1998: 75, 138, 146.
42 Ibid.: 151–6.
43 Ibid.: 73–4, 83–9; Chakrabarti 2004: 19.
44 Kenoyer 1998: 127.
45 Ibid.: 89; Jaggi 1969: 81–3.
46 Kenoyer 1998: 130, 133.
47 Chakrabarti 2004: 29–33.
48 Possehl [1976] 1979.
49 Kenoyer 1998: 91–6.
50 Jyotsna 2000: 6–7; Kenoyer 1998: 160–62.
51 Kenoyer 1998: 90.
52 Francfort 1984; Chakrabarti 2004: 31; Bahn 1996: 252.
53 Chakrabarti 2004: 31–2; Heskel 1984.
54 Oppenheim [1954] 1979; Lamberg-Karlovsky [1972] 1979; Chakrabarti 2004: 32.
55 Kenoyer 1998: 98; Rao [1968] 1979.
56 Chakrabarti 2004: 33.
57 Kenoyer 1998: 83–4.
58 Ibid.: 84–6.
59 Ibid.: 87; Time-Life Books 1994: 25–6.
60 Lamberg-Karlovsky [1972] 1979: 132.
61 Kenoyer 1998: 64.
62 Ibid.: 112.
63 Ibid.: 105–6.
64 Ibid.: 108–10.
65 Chakrabarti 2004: 20.
66 Ibid.
67 Ibid.
68 Fischer 2005: 60; Kochhar 2000: 73; Coningham 2005: 532.
69 Kochhar 2000: 73–4.
70 Ibid.: 74.
71 Boustrophedon fashion = as the ox turns in ploughing; Fischer 2005: 62.
72 Chakrabarti 2004: 19.
73 Witzel and Farmer 2000; Witzel 2006: 53–4.

74 Joseph 2000: 222.
75 Bose *et al*. 1989: 138.
76 Mainkar 1984: 146.
77 Kenoyer 1998: 98; Mainkar 1984: 142–3.
78 Bose *et al*. 1989: 137; Mainkar 1984: 145–6.
79 Joseph 2000: 223.
80 Wheeler [1947] 1979; Kochhar 2000: 76–8.
81 Dales [1964] 1979.
82 Quoted in Kochhar 2000: 77.
83 Wheeler 1966: 72–83.
84 Dales [1964] 1979; Raikes [1964] 1979: 298–9; Dales [1966] 1979: 308;
    Srivastava 1984.
85 Kochhar 2000: 78–9.
86 Allchin 1984.
87 Agrawal and Sood 1982: 226–9.
88 Kochhar 2000: 123–5.
89 Ibid.: 136.
90 Allchin 1995: 27–9; Fairservis 1971: 296–306.
91 Coningham 2005: 538.
92 Chakrabarti 1998: 138–40; Ghosh 1982.
93 Allchin 1982: 329–33.
94 Coningham 2005: 539–40.
95 Chakrabarti 2004: 9.
96 Kochhar 2000: 80–81.
97 Allchin 1995: 31; Kochhar 2000: 188–90.
98 Kochhar 2000: 190–92, 221–2; Allchin 1995: 33–4.
99 Kochhar 2000: 81–2.
100 Chakrabarti 1998: 148–50.

4 The Indo-Aryans in the Vedic Age

(*Time-span:* c. *1700* BC *to* c. *600* BC)

The 6,000 or so languages spoken in the world today are classified by scholars into major language family groups. The dominant language family of the northern part of the Indian sub-continent is the Indo-Aryan. This family is also considered to have a sister branch in the Iranian family; and both branches are said to belong to a much larger family of families, which is known as Indo-European.[1] The longest established language of this entire family is Sanskrit; and it is from the progressive evolution of Sanskrit, over many millennia, that the other present-day Indo-Aryan languages of India developed.

Apart from being a modern-day label for a family of languages, the term 'Indo-Aryan' can serve to describe the evolution of Indian culture, over more than 1,000 years, following the demise of the Harappan Civilisation. Groups of nomadic tribal people from eastern and southern Afghanistan started migrating to the Indian sub-continent around 1700 BC; and their movement gained momentum with the arrival, about 1400 BC, of a particular group which called itself *Arya*, or noble. We sometimes call them the Rig-Vedic Aryans, because they brought with them the earliest portion of a collection of hymns, known as the *Rig-Veda*, which was composed by their bards and seers in a very early form of Sanskrit or Old Indic.[2] Other tribal groups of that period, who did not call themselves *Arya*, also tend to be included by historians under the generic label of Aryans.[3] In the new society that was born out of the mix of the pre-Aryan and Aryan cultural elements, the Rig-Vedic Aryans increasingly came to occupy a central position. The Indo-Aryan culture that eventually emerged, more commonly known as the Vedic Culture, is still with us in India, forming the essential core of Hindu religion and society. The word 'Vedic' is the adjective of the noun 'Veda', which refers to the *Rig-Veda* and other collections of sacred hymns and chants.

This chapter will examine different aspects of the Indo-Aryan society and its culture; but before we do that we need to explore a little deeper the origins of the Aryans. This is a fascinating story in itself, but it is also necessary to understand it for two particular reasons. One has to do with the consequence of the abuse of the term 'Aryan' in the twentieth century; and the second with the controversy provoked through the denial, by some revisionist writers, of the non-Indian origins of the Aryans.

The Aryan background

The first thing to understand about the Aryans is that they were not some sort of innately superior race of people. The Nazis misappropriated the term 'Aryan' for a wholly sinister purpose. In Hitler's Germany the populace was segregated on the basis of whether they were Aryans, the supposedly superior race, or inferiors such as the Jews and Gypsies. On the basis of pseudo-scientific and racialised systems of classification of human beings, the 'Aryan' race of Germanic stock was presumed to be endowed with extraordinary powers of mind, spirit and beauty. While this racist connotation of the term Aryan has no basis in historical truth, it was a distorted legacy derived from the writings of nineteenth-century European scholars of ethnology.[4] Their 'fascination with the "Aryans" was ... very much part of the intellectual environment of the nineteenth and early twentieth centuries.'[5] These scholars lived at a time when European imperialism dominated the world.[6] Obsessed with a desire to explain the intellectual superiority of European peoples and their scientific prowess, they obviously sought answers in some particular roots and origins of the Europeans. They, then, overstated the significance of some important linguistic research that had actually begun in India during the late eighteenth century and eventually arrived at the misconception of the racial superiority of the so-called Aryan Germanic race. The Holocaust of the Jews and Gypsies by the Nazis is a reminder to us of the power of poisonous intellectual ideas of a misguided generation.

A number of scholars in Victorian India too, both Europeans and Indians, were preoccupied by the idea of the glory of the Aryan race.[7] It was presumed that India had only a primitive culture before the arrival of the Aryans around 2000 BC, and that the Aryans destroyed the dark-skinned, uncivilised natives by enslaving, killing or driving them down into south India. The Indian civilisation, it was asserted, only began with the Aryans. This facile theory was rudely shattered when the impressive ruins of Mohenjo Daro and Harappa came to light in the early 1920s. The dating of various artefacts and materials confirmed their age to be older than 2000 BC. This meant that Indian culture was much older than the second millennium BC and that there was at least one truly glorious civilisation pre-dating the Aryans. Mistakes multiplied, as when it was asserted that the Aryans destroyed the Harappan Civilisation.[8] With advancing research, however, the Aryans came to be seen for what they really were: nomadic and pastoral migrants from Afghanistan, some with an inflated sense of self-esteem, who brought with them an early form of a spoken language which later evolved into what became classical Sanskrit.

The Indo-European dimension

To understand the term 'Aryan' in the context of Indian history, we must first explore the study of the history of languages. Our starting point has to be with Sanskrit, which can be described as the mother language of almost all the languages of north India. After studying it over many years, the great eighteenth-century linguist and lawyer Sir William Jones concluded thus:

> Sanskrit language, whatever be its antiquity, is of a wonderful structure, more perfect than the Greek, more copious than the Latin, and more exquisitely refined than either; yet bearing to both of them a stronger affinity, both in the roots of verbs and in the roots of grammar, than could possibly have been produced by accident; so strong, indeed, that no philologer could examine them all three, without believing them to have sprung from some common source, which, perhaps, no longer exists.[9]

Over the two hundred years since Jones's time, linguists, philologists and grammarians have been carefully studying the various inter-connections that link the world's languages and some of their structures. It is through the findings of their research that the languages of Europe, Iran, Afghanistan and the northern part of the Indian sub-continent have come to be collectively called the Indo-European family.[10]

There are, of course, enormous differences among the Indo-European languages; but Jones and his successors have identified certain very striking similarities in terms of grammar, syntax and vocabulary. These similarities have led the researchers to assume that in the distant past a group of people might have spoken a language that was the common ancestor of the modern Indo-European languages. They call this language proto-Indo-European. Much study has also gone into whether there was an ancestral homeland in which this postulated language was spoken.[11] The evidence uncovered by linguists and philologists, so far, suggests that this homeland covered a far smaller area than that in which the spread of modern Indo-European language speakers live; the general consensus is that it was in the Eurasian steppe lands north and east of the Black Sea, and extending towards the Caspian Sea.[12]

We have no hard and fast knowledge of the proto-Indo-European language, and we have no direct proof of the existence of proto-Indo-European speakers. What we do know is that, sometime during the third millennium BC, owing to climatic and environmental changes, differentiated groups of people from the Eurasian steppe lands were migrating to a variety of zones outside their smaller original homeland. We know this partly through archaeology and partly through examination of oral traditions. The people who were migrating had domesticated the horse and developed wheeled vehicles, thereby making their migration process much easier. We should not assume, however, that they came out in one mighty torrent and spread out over Eurasia with force of arms. Migrations in ancient times were always slow, gradual and mostly peaceful. The migrants spoke a variety of dialects and languages. Eventually they came to occupy areas with a natural environment vastly different from their homeland. This meant that their language must also have changed, since many words and expressions peculiar to the requirements of their homeland would not have been useful in their new surroundings. Their original vocabulary would have been augmented and modified by their encounters with settled groups of people they came to assimilate or displace.[13]

Of the many branches of the Indo-European languages of those early migrants the oldest is called the Indo-Iranian family. It is comprised of two main sub-groups – Indo-Aryan and Iranian – along with two related languages – Romani of the Gypsies and Nuristani of the Hindu Kush region of Afghanistan and Pakistan. A number of undifferentiated Indo-Iranian speaking groups, mainly pastoralists with their cattle, had migrated southwards on foot from the Eurasian steppe lands about 2000 BC and spread over Central Asia, Iran and Afghanistan. One branch, speaking a type of Aryan language, possibly a very early form of Sanskrit, might have reached as far as the River Indus as early as 1700 BC. They would be the first of the Indo-European or Aryan pastoralists speaking some early form of Sanskrit which would in time fuse with the indigenous languages. The first of the appropriate contexts, therefore, in which the word 'Aryan' may be used is in that of language families.

The Indo-Iranian dimension

A deeper understanding of the term 'Aryan' can be gained by studying the religious customs and traditions that were prevalent among two particular groups of Indo-Iranians in eastern Iran and Afghanistan. Between 1700 BC and 1400 BC there co-existed, in that area, two peoples: the Avestan and the Rig-Vedic.[14] They represent the two most important arms of the Indo-Iranian tradition as a whole. Common ties of language,[15] culture, mythology and rituals developed between them before they ultimately separated. In their religious beliefs and practices they worshipped a number of gods together. They both shared a tradition of composing hymns in praise of their gods. In both traditions the descriptions of such nature gods as those of wind and sun, for example, are similar in tone and feeling. Some of their earliest prayers are also very similar. Sanskrit is very close to the language of the *Yashts*, the earliest hymns of the *Avesta*, the sacred text of the present-day Zoroastrians of Iran and India. The Iranian prayers are part of the *Avesta* collection. Some sections of the *Avesta* resemble, not only in language but in content as well, the Rig-Vedic hymns that were composed by the Indian bards.[16] The two groups also shared a common practice of drinking the juice of a fertility plant, called *soma* in the *Rig-Veda* and *haoma* in the *Avesta*, for strength, virility and awakefulness. This plant has now been identified as a species of *ephedra*, and its main habitat is the area around eastern Iran and south Afghanistan.[17] The symbolic importance of fire in the rituals of worship for both groups should also be noted. In the words of a noted Sanskrit scholar:

> taking into account the similarities in mythology, language, religious practice and beliefs, we may safely conclude that the traditions of the *Avesta* and that of the *Rig-Veda* have emerged from a single common source.[18]

What is striking, also, is that among the Indo-Iranian speakers only the Avestan and the Rig-Vedic people called themselves Aryans, or the noble ones.[19] So, while historians somewhat loosely call most of the Indo-Iranian speakers Aryans, and while Iranians particularly use the word Aryan in an ethnic sense, in that they call their country, Iran, the land of the Aryans, strictly speaking the precise self-ascription of the word 'Aryan' applied only to the Avestan and Rig-Vedic people, because they alone claimed a special status of nobility among all the other related and neighbouring tribes of the original settled people of the territories they inhabited.

Around 1400 BC, nearly 300 years after their other Indo-Iranian compatriots had reached the Indus, the Rig-Vedic people also left Afghanistan and moved into the Indian sub-continent. They carried with them their collection of sacred hymns and chants that they had been composing for centuries during their Iranian and Afghan sojourn. That collection is the earliest section of the *Rig-Veda*. The original form of Sanskrit which they took with them would have been more complex and sophisticated than that of their predecessors, but their proto-Sanskrit too would have had to adjust to the then existing languages of India. The Rig-Vedic people were, culturally speaking, the most influential of the Aryans, and it was their great literary and spiritual opus, the *Rig-Veda*, that provides useful insights into the Vedic Culture of India.

The Avestan people continued to follow the old Indo-Iranian religion that the Rig-Vedic people had shared; but, about 1000 BC, a visionary and philosopher called Zarathushtra carried out a religious revolution in eastern Iran and Afghanistan by dethroning most of the Indo-Iranian gods and charting out a new ethic and religious philosophy for his followers.[20] The hymns that he composed are known as the *Gathas*. Although the contents of the *Rig-Veda* and the *Gathas* are different in character, nevertheless the similarities of the Gathic language and the early Vedic Sanskrit are very striking indeed[21] (see Extract 4.1). Despite his quarrel with the older Indo-Iranian tradition, Zarathushtra nevertheless retained fire as the supreme symbol for the Aryan people of Iran. Even today, the one common element in the rituals of the Hindus and of the Zoroastrians of Iran and India is fire.[22]

Some revisionist arguments and counter-arguments

Although there is considerable evidence, from research in both linguistics in general and the Indo-Iranian studies in particular, that the Aryans were originally migrants to India, an aggressive campaign of revisionism has been launched by writers who are of the *Hindutva* political persuasion.[23] These writers, viewing the Indian civilisation from a purely Hindu religious perspective, have advanced a number of arguments, which have aroused some robust counter-arguments.

The first contention is that the Indus Valley Culture and the Vedic Aryan Culture are one and the same; and central to that culture was the River *Saraswati*, not the Indus. The Indus Valley Culture, according to the revisionists, was really the *Saraswati* Culture, and the foundations of some settlements, discovered along the direction of the now dried-up *Saraswati*, are cited as proofs. The argument against this view is that the Indus Valley Culture could not be the same as the Vedic Culture, because otherwise it would have been celebrated in the extensive Indo-Aryan literature and remembered, in the oral tradition, by posterity. Nowhere in the texts are the cities of the Indus (or *Saraswati*) mentioned,[24] or even remembered with pride and affection. This seems very curious for a people who recited, and passed down the generations, thousands of hymns and verses in the oral tradition. The fact of the matter is that the Indus Valley Culture came to light only in the nineteenth century, and it was not recognised in India until then. The *Saraswati* river was drying up even at the time the Aryans were first settling in India; most likely, the *Saraswati* that is glowingly described in the Vedic texts could actually be the River Harahvaiti in Afghanistan.[25]

The second contention is that the Vedic texts make no mention at all of the foreign lands to the west, in the Afghanistan region, from where the Aryans were supposed to have come. Most linguistic experts, however, are of the opinion that the *Rig-Veda* was first composed in the Afghanistan area; the early parts of the text include references at least obliquely to places, rivers, animals, etc., of that land.[26] Also, the *Rig-Veda* was composed over a long period: by the time of its completion (*c.* 900 BC) the Rig-Vedic Aryans had been in India for 500 years, while the non-Rig-Vedic Indic speakers had been there for some 800 years. Their integration into Indian society had been so long-established and complete that the composers would have had no need to remember the dim past of their earliest origins.[27]

The third contention is that whatever is composed in the Vedic texts is uniquely Indian. While this has a specious validity, it has been pointed out that three of the oldest written documents containing any reference to Aryan names come not from Iran or India but from Mesopotamia.[28] From the documents of the Kassite rulers of Babylon (*c.* 1750 BC–1170 BC) we learn of three names: two gods, Suriya (the sun god) and Marutta (the god of war), and a king, Abirattas, or Abhi-ratha ('facing the war chariots'). Northwest of Babylon there lay the Mittani kingdom (*c.* 1500 BC–1300 BC), from where the cuneiform documents in the Akkadian language list the various princes and noblemen whose names are very strikingly Aryan, e.g. Sutarana, Sauksatra, Purusa, Subandhu, Indrota, etc. The final, clinching evidence comes from the cuneiform tablets discovered at Boghazkoi in eastern Turkey. These tablets record the details of a treaty signed in about 1350 BC between the losers, the Mittani, and their victors, the Hittites. Both sides list their gods, but among the Mittani gods are those who are distinctly Rig-Vedic: Indra, Nasatya, Varuna, Mitra. In the *Rig-Veda* itself these gods are assigned the task of overseeing the treaties between warring peoples. Apart from some of the seal images from the Indus Valley Culture, no documents about the Aryan gods earlier than these Mesopotamian records have been found in India; it therefore makes sense that some of the earliest of the Rig-Vedic concepts were developed 'in a central area, from where they travelled towards the west as well as the east'.[29]

The fourth contention has already been alluded to. The argument is that the entire theory of Aryan invasion/migration was very much a nineteenth-century construct of the European scholars who strove to justify British rule in India in an oblique way by reminding their reading public about how a glorious civilisation had once come into India from somewhere near Europe. This argument assumes a uniform attitude among imperial historians of that era. There were those who held to that attitude, but there were many others who simply wished to study the past in the light of the hard evidence obtained. A great scholar, Professor Max Muller, has been particularly reviled over this matter; but even he changed his position on a number of occasions, showing that he was quite open to new evidence and fresh interpretations.[30]

The Aryan expansion

There were two main regions in the Afghanistan area where the Aryans had been settled since 2000 BC. One was the area around modern Kabul, stretching in the east towards modern Peshawar. The Kabul–Peshawar enclave might have been the initial area from where migration towards the Swat valley began in about 1700 BC. Another equally important zone was the area around Kandahar, with links to Quetta via the Bolan Pass. It is believed that the Rig-Vedic Aryans moved from there about 1400 BC, crossing the various rivers and then proceeding towards either the Swat valley or the Punjab. The entire region, including eastern Afghanistan, the Swat valley, Punjab and the Indo-Gangetic watershed is referred to, just once in the *Rig-Veda*, as *Sapta Sindhava*, the land of the seven rivers. Although the *Rig-Veda* does not dwell at any length on the pre-Indian past of the Aryans, there are some hymns in which the newcomers vaguely remember and reminisce about the Iranian, Afghan and Central Asian localities, tribes and animals.

Among the many sites and regions in the northwest of the sub-continent, scholars and archaeologists have identified the Swat valley of northern Pakistan as possibly the first area of intrusion by the Aryans into the sub-continent[31] (see Map 4.1). The valley's extensive layers of settlement from 3000 BC to 300 BC have made it possible to examine the continuities in, and interruptions to, the local culture. From the surveys undertaken, it has been found that from 1700 BC onwards a change occurred in the burial rites of the people. Inside the cemeteries the archaeologists have found both flexed inhumation in a pit and cremation burial in an urn. This dual practice was not common among the contemporary cultures of the same region, but the early Vedic literature indicates that both inhumation and cremation burial were practised among the early Indo-Aryans. Another indication of change is the ceramic style. A new type of grey ware, that was handmade and decorated with incisions, is much in evidence during this period. On the basis of the change noticed in burial rites and ceramics, the archaeologists call the new culture of the valley the Gandhara

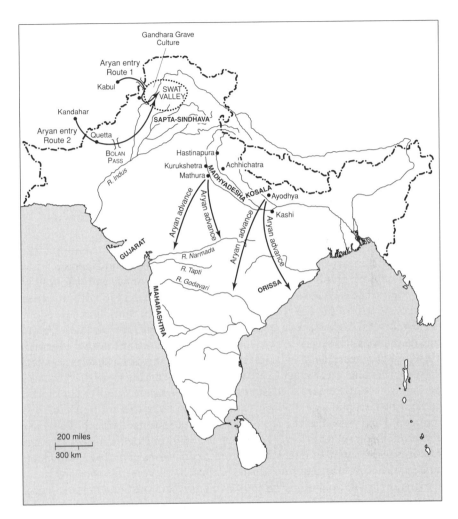

Map 4.1 India in the Vedic Age.

Grave Culture. Another argument in favour of the Swat valley being the original area of the Aryan reception in the sub-continent is also the fact that the natural features and scenes depicted in the Rig-Vedic hymns match the geographical reality of the valley.[32]

The Aryans lived in the Punjab for many centuries, and from the *Rig-Veda* we learn that they were confronted by an indigenous people, called by them *dasas*, *dasyus* or *panis*, and by many pejorative names such as blacks, demons or cattle-thieves.[33] The Aryans, helped by Indra, the war god, vanquish these people. It is important to stress that these defeated people were not the Harappans. Another piece of information concerns the organisation of the

Aryans into tribes and clans. It is thought that the term 'fivefold race' of people refers to five clans: Yadu, Turvasa, Anu, Druhyu and Puru.[34] Through both inter-tribal fighting and alliance-building the Puru had come to occupy a central position for themselves on one of the seven rivers of the *Sapta Sidhava*. In due course, one of their branch clans, the Bharata, subdued them, and eventually became the dominant group in the Punjab. This was achieved at the famous Battle of Ten Kings in which Sudas, king of the Bharata, defeated a confederacy of ten Aryan tribes. Various dates, going far back into time, have been proposed for this battle, but most historical opinion has settled on about 900 BC as its date.[35] The third vital piece of information that the *Rig-Veda* provides us about the Aryans in the Punjab concerns their transition from a semi-nomadic life to settled agriculture. After centuries of nomadic life in not very fertile terrain the Aryans found themselves in a land blessed with great rivers and innumerable streams. They had much to learn about the skills of irrigating and harnessing the rivers. In this process too there would be scope for rivalries and inter-clan fighting over land and resources. More importantly, they would come to learn much from the skills of the indigenous people.

From 900 BC onwards the centre of gravity of the Aryan world shifted to what is called *Madhyadesha*, the Middle Country. This land extended from east of the *Saraswati* to the Ganga plains. The events of this land form part of the setting of the *Mahabharata*, a post-Vedic epic. New clan formations and amalgamations took place at this time, and two dominant lineages emerged: the Kuru and Panchala. The centre of Kuru power was at Kurukshetra, while the Panchala base was further east. With the steady drying up of the *Saraswati* and its sister river, *Drsadvati*, the Kuru had to move their base from Kurukshetra to Hastinapura; and a new centre, called *Indraprashtha* (the future Delhi) was founded. This meant a certain amount of tension and warfare with the Panchala. From the post Rig-Vedic texts and the epics we learn that there were two sets of wars going on: Aryan versus Aryan, and Aryan versus non-Aryan. However, despite constant warfare, the Kuru and Panchala came together at crucial periods, and their hold on power in *Madhyadesha* later inspired many rulers of India to possess this region and make it the centre of their influence.[36]

From now on, it becomes somewhat simplistic to talk just of the Aryan advance. It was more an Indo-Aryan advance, because the pre-Aryans were as much involved in the building of a new society as the Aryans (see Extract 4.2). We are no longer talking about simple migrant folks from Afghanistan, entering India through the passes in small groups. We now have a new situation, with the Indo-Aryans becoming colonisers. From 900 BC onwards the further Aryan expansion both eastwards and southwards continued inexorably. The lands of modern Bihar and Bengal were colonised. From the later epic of the *Ramayana* we also learn about the expansion to the south, into modern Madhya Pradesh, Gujarat, Maharashtra and Orissa. A particular clan, called Yadu, might have been forced by the Kuru–Panchala to migrate southwards from their base at Mathura; another Aryan group from *Kosala* penetrated the Deccan by establishing a kingdom on the River Godavari. The literary sources give us information about the tools and accoutrements that the Indo-Aryans carried with their herds. Chariots and carts, pulled by horses and oxen, and laden with weapons made of bronze and iron, bore the Indo-Aryan warriors towards new horizons. The cutting down and the burning of forests were particularly onerous tasks, but they became easier in due course with the use of iron technology. Iron weapons must have had a demoralising effect on the rebellious or uncooperative non-Aryans. The Aryanisation of the entire Gangetic basin was in full swing between 900 BC and 600 BC, and powerful warrior-clan settlements became established throughout the area.[37] With the forest clearances came farming; the village no longer meant a band of itinerant warriors and travellers with their wagons but small farmsteads and craftsmen living in huts and simple houses.

The Vedic world

We describe the world of the Indo-Aryans as Vedic, because it is essentially through the Vedic literature that we know so much about them. A significant portion of this extensive literature has been translated into English. The literature that is contemporary with the chronological period of this chapter consists of the four *Vedas*, the three great commentaries of the *Brahmanas*, the *Aranyakas* and the *Upanishads*, and the *Vedanga* and *Upaveda* texts. There is also much literature after 600 BC, consisting of such great epics as the *Mahabharata* and the *Ramayana*, and they too are useful for learning about this period. While religious and spiritual themes do dominate this literature, there are many references to a host of other subjects. This literature, however, does not provide a body of systematic historiography from which we can trace and outline a chronological sequence. Also, some of the most abstract as well as abstruse ideas, composed in a highly cryptic form, cannot be easily grasped without the scholarly interpretations of those who are learned in Vedic Sanskrit. The second useful tool in our understanding is archaeology. However, while its indications have been absolutely central to the study of the Indus Valley Culture, its role in uncovering the Indo-Aryan world is somewhat limited. Nothing as exciting as the Great Bath or the grid-planned streets of Mohenjo Daro has been discovered elsewhere from the rubble of the Vedic Age. What archaeology can do is to corroborate, or confound, textual evidence. Yet another way of studying the Indo-Aryan world is by looking around modern India today and observing the living traditions of the people. These traditions are varied and heterogeneous, but some of them go back to Vedic times. Here, in this section, we present six selected aspects of Vedic life.[38]

Pastoralism, farming and trades

The Aryan migrants were essentially a pastoral people, and for a long time, in India too, their main occupation remained cattle-rearing.[39] Cattle were the most valued of their possessions, their protection being considered almost a religious duty. As in Iran, cattle raiders and thieves were considered as evil people who needed to be destroyed. The Sanskrit term *gavishthi* could mean searching for cows that were stolen or fighting battles with the raiders.[40] In the very early Vedic period cattle might have been owned collectively. Those who herded their cows in the same cowshed belonged to the same *gotra*, a term which later became part of caste terminology, meaning a descent from a common ancestor.[41] The relative importance of the pastoral economy can be gauged by the fact that the *Rig-Veda* carries more references to pastoralism than to agriculture. Such details as the marking of the ears of cattle for ownership, the accessibility of pasture lands and the daily tasks of the herdsmen are mentioned there. Large quantities of charred bones of cattle and other animals, found at various archaeological sites, also testify to the pre-eminent role the pastoral economy played in the daily life of the early Aryans. From their original Iranian and Afghan backgrounds the early Aryans were familiar with seasons and their role in the promotion of agriculture; but the farming and husbanding of crops was something that they had to learn from the indigenous people. The latter had, after all, been perfecting these skills in Baluchistan and the Indus region since 7000 BC, and the plough itself was a pre-Harappan tool.[42] It was in the lush terrain of Punjab that the Aryans first appreciated the advantages of farming crops; but it was after the dense forests of the Ganga plain were burnt and felled systematically that agriculture overtook pastoralism as the main daily activity of most people, and rice rather than wheat became the main crop of cultivation. The *Rig-Veda* contains much information about farming in general. There are references to ploughs and plough teams drawn by a number of oxen; to the cutting, bundling and thresh-ing of grain; to irrigation canals and wells; and to such foods as milk, butter, rice cakes, cereals, lentils and vegetables. A copious number of Vedic hymns invoke the blessings of gods for plenty of crops, rains and the welfare of the cattle. While a number of terms describing various types of fields and the prac-tice of measuring land are mentioned, there is no reference to any transaction of land that can be carried out by an individual.[43] Most probably, therefore, there was some form of common ownership of land. In the villages and larger settlements there were people practising a variety of crafts and trades – carpenters, weavers, metal workers, tanners, potters, goldsmiths, bow makers, chariot makers and many others – and a lively trade in their products and a large number of building projects[44] created a hub of activity throughout the countryside, particularly in the later Vedic period, from 1000 BC to 600 BC.

Pottery and iron: the material base as evinced from archaeology

Over the last six decades or so extensive archaeological excavations have been carried out in the areas of north India where the Aryans first settled or where they later moved. The excavations of the Indian archaeologist B.B. Lal at Hastinapura in 1954–5 were the most remarkable; but many other famous sites, such as *Ahicchatra* and *Indraprashtha* (the site of the Purana Qila mound of Delhi), Mathura and *Kausambi* have also been extensively dug and closely inspected.[45] The archaeologists were particularly keen to find material evidence that would, for example, confirm on the ground poetic descriptions of cities such as Ayodhya in the later epic of the *Ramayana*, but they have been unsuccessful (see Extract 4.3). The most valuable information they have gathered concerns varieties of pottery and the transition, within certain cultures, from the Chalcolithic to the Iron Age.

Pottery provides clues to the quality of life in the ancient world. It was a status symbol of the people in India too. The crudest form of post-Harappan pottery, known as Ochre-Coloured Pottery (OCP), was generally found in the lowest levels of the major sites. It was so-called because, on rubbing, it produced a yellow-brown stain on the finger; its worn-out condition was due to poor firing techniques. At all ground levels that contained materials dating pre-900 BC the most common form of pottery was the OCP.[46] This pottery could therefore have belonged to the early Rig-Vedic Aryans. From 900 BC, with the Aryans branching out from beyond the *Sapta-Sindhava* region to the Ganga basin, a new style of pottery came into fashion. This was the Painted Grey Ware (PGW), the name given to fine, wheel-made, well-fired grey pottery with linear patterns and dots in black. With an imaginative mixture of painted designs, involving various shapes, the PGW was the most excellent form of pottery product available to well-off people of that era. It would, however, be a mistake to believe that the Aryans were particularly involved in the creation of the PGW. Practically all of it would have been produced by the local indigenous pre-Aryans who occupied the bottom rung of the Indo-Aryan social ladder. It is reckoned that PGW formed only between 10 and 15 per cent of the total pottery.[47] From the PGW sites of the period 900 BC to 600 BC the materials unearthed include various animal skeletons, several cereal grains, burnt bricks, glass fragments, semi-precious stones, gambling dices and some iron. Of a poorer quality than the PGW but superior to OCP was the vast mass of pottery known as Black-and-Red Ware (BRW). Only after the end of our period, about 600 BC, do we see the emergence of the most excellent variety of pottery called Northern Black Polished Ware (NBPW).[48]

Apart from pottery, another product of importance with which Indo-Aryan archaeology is much concerned is iron. A cheaper and more accessible material than copper, iron came to be used widely by a number of communities within India during the last four centuries of our period, 1000 BC to 600 BC. The earliest Iron Age sites of India were located in three main regions: the Ganga plains, the central regions of Malwa and the Tapti valley, and the megalithic sites in south India. Many of the sites in the Ganga plains are the very ones that are connected to the PGW potteries and the Aryan expansion. From the evidence found, some important conclusions have been arrived at. Firstly, the Iron Age did not succeed the Chalcolithic Age uniformly throughout India at a particular point of time; the progression and transition between the two ages remained extremely uneven in different parts of India. Secondly, iron technology was not brought by the Aryans; it developed gradually from about

1000 BC onwards, long after the Aryans had metamorphosed into Indo-Aryans. It is also not particularly useful to start searching for one original site where this technology first developed. Rather, we should think of such a technological advance developing at different places and at different paces. Thirdly, the first iron tools were not axes and ploughshares, but weapons; and so the clearing of forests in the Ganga basin is more likely to have taken place in the later centuries of this period, that is after 1000 BC, than before.[49]

The patriarchal family

The Vedic family, the *kula*, was highly patriarchal. Extended families of three generations or more were the norm. The senior male, the father or sometimes the grandfather, was the head of the household.[50] The sons lived with the parents for both economic and religious reasons. The sons helped the fathers with the daily chores of farming or any trade and thus increased the general prosperity of the family;[51] they also had a valuable role to play in the performance of various ceremonies. For example, when cremation displaced burial in later Vedic times, the eldest son was made the chief torch-bearer for the funeral pyre of the dead parent.[52] It is more than likely that younger sons were pampered and spoilt by their parents, a phenomenon still noticeable in many Indian homes. It was a different story with girls. In a patriarchal home their freedom of action and movement was constrained. They might have enjoyed greater freedom in the clan situation of the early Rig-Vedic period, but with caste rectitude and other proprieties assuming greater importance in the later Vedic period their position worsened.[53] They were honoured and feted as queens of their households, but outside the household their conduct was monitored in a subtle manner. Any form of overt deviance could put them in trouble. A sensitive traveller, with his eyes open, should be able to observe this ancient phenomenon in modern India even today. One of the most barbaric customs within sections of Hindu India until the early nineteenth century, that of a widow becoming a *sati* through self-immolation on her husband's death, also had its origins in the later Vedic period.[54] There were, however, positive features of the patriarchy that we must not ignore. The homesteads and households provided comfort and warmth for the whole family. Various rituals and ceremonies, both at home and in the public arena, kept the family bonds tight; and the giving and receiving of gifts (*dana*) would have made individuals feel good about themselves.[55] The staple diet within the average household included milk, clarified butter, vegetables, fruit, wheat, rice and, on auspicious occasions, meat: a healthy fare for any human being. The very small population of the entire country, probably about 20 million at the end of the Vedic age,[56] helped to reduce the strains and stresses of living in congested spaces such as the cities of India today; but, on the other hand, diseases must have been rampant too. The texts give us a diverse picture of the life of the Vedic people. While the poor, the humble and all manner of working people carried on unobtrusively with their daily life, the rich dressed ostentatiously and their women wore much jewellery. A variety of amusements are mentioned in the *Rig-Veda*, such as chariot-racing, horse-racing, dancing and music; but gambling is rightly condemned as an activity leading to ruin.[57] Despite the rigours of the patriarchy, the Vedic family lived in a society that seemed to be at ease with itself.

Political power and social differentiation

While attempts have been made to construct lists of kings and dynastic lines, based mostly on correlating the Vedic texts with accounts from the *Puranas*, the semi-religious texts of the mid-first millennium AD, and the great epics of the *Mahabharata* and *Ramayana*, we need to be more circumspect about this methodology. The *Puranas* contain a good amount of credible history, but it is mixed in with much non-historical or unhistorical material; and the epics are, after all, great works of imagination, not of history as such. It is only from the fifth century BC onwards, after the end of the Vedic period, and with the corroboration of the Buddhist sources, that we can be more certain about the chronology of dynasties and monarchs. This does not, of course, mean that there were no states or monarchs in the Vedic period. There definitely were; we just do not know enough about them. What we do know, however, is that side by side with facts lie a large number of ideas in the Vedic texts, and idealisations of power are but one example.

As we have mentioned, the basic unit of power lay within the patriarchal family (*kula*); a number of families lived in a village (*grama*), controlled by a headman (*gramani*); groups of villages belonged to the clan (*vis*); and many clans made a community (*jana*). In the early Vedic period there was no real state structure. There were no kings as such but clan chieftains. Raiding and extraction of war booty was a way of life and an important way of redistributing wealth. There was also no regularised system of taxation. In the later Vedic period groups of communities became part of a region or a state (*janapada*). The idea of kingship evolved gradually from clan chieftainship, but there was at first a control exercised on the king (*raja*) by assemblies (*vidatha, parishad, sabha, samiti*). By the end of the Vedic period the king's authority was beginning to derive less from the support of such assemblies than from his own success in the struggle for power among his warrior-nobles. The hereditary element crept in with the further consolidation of power by the *rajas*, and from that point onwards the role of the courtiers or officers became critical. The main offices within the palace of a *raja* of the late Vedic period would be held by the chief priest (*purohit*), the commander-in-chief (*senani*), the treasurer (*samagrahitri*), the collector of taxes (*bhagadugha*) and the keeper of the king's household (*kshata*).[58] The legitimisation of the king's power was confirmed by lengthy and elaborate rituals of sacrifice (*yajna*) conducted by the priests, to be examined in the next sub-section. The alliance between priest and king, a fundamental feature of Indian polity, became a key element in the maintenance of the hierarchical balance within the caste system.

The legendary caste system of India is the result of social differentiation developing into social stratification. Social divisions must have existed among the Harappans; it is also known that the Iranian Aryans, closely associated with the Rig-Vedic Aryans, practised a threefold division of society, consisting of priests, rulers and producers. What happened in the Indo-Aryan society, however, was something quite novel, extraordinary and most negative in its social impact.[59] During the Vedic period the priests (*brahmans*) and the rulers (*kshatriyas*) consolidated their positions. The producers came to be split into two groups. Free peasants and traders became the third group, called *vaishya*, while slaves, labourers and artisans were degraded into the fourth group, the *shudra*. Within a relatively small population, the groups came to be rigidly compartmentalised on the basis of a religiously inculcated system of colour bar, known as *Varnashrama Dharma*. This had little to do with the division between the Aryan and the pre-Aryan. The two higher castes were not necessarily dominated by the Aryans, with the pre-Aryans consigned to the lower rungs. The main reason why many pre-Aryans would have been on the bottom rungs was that they were the main craftsmen and workers with skills; but those very skills of menial and manual work were derided on grounds of ritual impurity by the learned and the powerful, who could be either Aryan or pre-Aryan. The greatest stigma was attached to pollution of the upper castes by the lower. The Vedic texts not only contain elaborate rationalisations for the fourfold caste system based on colour, or *varna*, but they also describe the specific privileges and disabilities of each group. Many modern Hindus therefore tend to justify the caste system on the basis of the *Vedas*. However, since all Vedic texts were revised by the learned *brahmans*, who were in close alliance with the *kshatriyas*, there is a danger that the inviolate caste system as explained in the texts is a particular form of ideological construct. Apart from the Vedic strictures, there are other ways of understanding the caste system – for example, by studying changes in kinship patterns or the way in which economic resources came to be distributed.[60] There are also more acceptable social reasons in defence of the caste system than the explanations set out in the scriptures. One's caste can, for example, provide a secure psychological umbrella for someone with no friends or relations settling in a large town.[61]

The religion of the sacrifice

Essentially the religion that the Aryans had brought with them was that of the Indo-European sense of awe and wonder about the forces of nature and the worship of nature's powerful gods. For the simple and untutored people of the early Vedic period the most common way of keeping the great gods, such as Indra (the warrior god), Agni (fire) and Varuna (supreme judge), happy and mollified was through a sacrifice (*yajna*) within the household.[62] A *brahman* priest would be called to perform the ceremony in front of a fire lit in the sacrificial altar, into which were placed various foods such as milk, butter, barley and meat.[63] As the Aryans had learnt from the pre-Aryans the skills of making fire altars with bricks in a particular mystico-geometric formation, different types of altars were made available for specific sacrificial rituals. Square or circular-shaped altars were generally used for household rituals. The priest normally recited the Rig-Vedic hymns for dedication not just to the gods but also to sacrificial objects such as the altar or *soma*, the plant of fertility.[64] The chanting of hymns, the placing of foods into the fire, the gifts to the priest, the exchange of gifts among the members of the household, and the consumption of some of the consecrated food were all supposed to bring prosperity and happiness to the family or the clan. This simple ceremony of sacrifice, common in some aspects even today among the Hindus and the Zoroastrians of Iran and India (see Figures 4.1, 4.2), became a much more spectacular affair in the later Vedic period. The purpose of the sacrifice was transformed from being an offering to the gods to a celebration of the power of the kings.[65] The kings used the sacrifice to confirm their legitimacy. Loyal *brahman* priests were drafted in by the *purohit*, the chief priest, for prayers and chants in front of massive fire altars. Elaborate altars, in the shape of rectangles, triangles and trapeziums, were built to hold the fire. One such altar, particularly

Figure 4.1 A modern Hindu Yajna ceremony (courtesy of Dr N. Prinja).

Figure 4.2 A modern Zoroastrian fire ceremony (private family photo).

impressive in its geometry, was built in the shape of a falcon, as it was believed that the falcon would carry the soul of the supplicant straight to heaven[66] (see Figure 4.3). Vast numbers of animals, particularly cattle, were slaughtered; large donations of gifts were made to the *brahmans* by the grateful kings; the people were fed well, and the richer among them gave expensive gifts to the kings. Some kings of the post-Vedic age engaged in even more ostentatious sacrifices, and thereby the original purpose and the modest scale of the sacrifice were both subverted, for the glory of men rather than gods.

Vedic literature and learning

The crowning glory of the Indo-Aryans lies essentially in their literature. The Vedic texts were composed, and orally transmitted, in Sanskrit for many hundreds of years before they were written down. The earliest parts of the *Rig-Veda*, the oldest of the *Vedas*, may have been composed as early as, or even earlier than, 1700 BC, but was written down only after 500 BC. For forty generations and more it was handed down by word of mouth by bards and poets, who chanted the sacred hymns and the ritual prayers (see Extract 4.4). Even today the oral tradition is continued. During the transition from the oral to the written it is natural that both the language and the ideas to be conveyed by the language would have evolved; and linguists have also noted certain differences

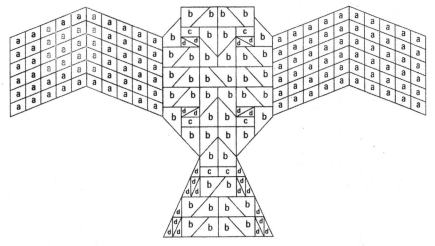

The first layer of a Vedic sacrificial altar in the shape of a falcon; the wings are each made from 60 bricks of type a, and the body from 46 type b, 6 type c, and 24 type d bricks (after Thibaut, 1875).

Figure 4.3 A falcon altar (by permission of Dr George Joseph).

between what is known as the earlier Vedic Sanskrit from the later Classical Sanskrit.

The *Vedas* constitute the very heart of the Indo-Aryan literature of this period. The word *veda* simply means 'knowledge' – the best of all knowledge in Hindu eyes. There are four main *Vedas* – *Rig-Veda*, *Sama-Veda*, *Yajur-Veda* and *Atharva-Veda* – and each has a core, called *Samhita*, which is a collection of metrical hymns and prayers, spells and exorcisms, mixed in some cases with prose passages. The principal *Veda* is the *Rig-Veda*, which, until the Harappan script is deciphered, must be considered as the oldest significant extant Indian text. It is also the first major composition in any Indo-European tongue. It has ten books or *mandalas*, with 1,028 hymns and 10,600 verses in all. The books were composed by sages and poets from different priestly families over a period of at least 500 years (1400 BC to 900 BC), if not earlier. The sacred hymns were addressed, in the sacrificial ceremonies of nature worship, to the principal Aryan gods such as Agni and Indra, and to gods such as Varuna and Surya. In the other three *Vedas* we see the first of the changes affecting the Indo-Aryan religion. The *Sama-Veda* is a rearranged version of some of the hymns of the *Rig-Veda*, but set to music. It is the first Indian treatise on music and chants, so essential in most Hindu worship. The *Yajur-Veda*, which is divided into two versions, known as Black and White *Yajur*, is the manual of the priest. One of the key duties of a Vedic priest, as we have already mentioned, was to perform a sacrificial ceremony for the glory of the king. As has also been mentioned, this was done around a fire altar, and the geometry involved in the construction of the altars is alluded to in the texts attached to the *Yajur-Veda* and known as *Sulvasutra*.[67] In fact, one way of understanding all the *Vedas* is to imagine them as 'a vast and complex instruction manual for the sacrifice ... rather than as sacred books. Sacrifice preceded the *Vedas*, not vice-versa.'[68] The *Atharva-Veda* consists of material of a more popular character; and it includes references to plants, herbs and diseases; it may be described as the first Indian treatise on medicine.[69]

Attached to the *Samhitas* of the *Vedas* are the *Brahmanas*, which interpret the rituals. They form a manual of worship and provide explanations of the *Samhitas*. In many ways they Hinduise the Indo-European aspects of the *Vedas* by emphasising the role of the priest in the great sacrifices. Some of the best *Brahmanas* are *Aitareya Brahmana* attached to the *Rig-Veda*, the *Jaiminiya Brahmana* attached to the *Sama-Veda*, and the *Taittiriya* and *Satapatha Brahmana* attached to the *Yajur-Veda*. The *Taittiriya* and *Satapatha Brahmana* provide information about astronomy and geometry. Both subjects were vital to the work of the priests and the learned interpreters. Astronomical calculations helped with the forecasting of seasons and the construction of calendars for determining the auspicious occasions for the great sacrifices. Geometry served a religious function because its noblest use was in the designing of fire altars. It is worth pointing out that the technical results in these subjects can only be elucidated by understanding the meaning of precisely expressed concepts in Sanskrit aphorisms. Hindus consider the *Vedas* and the *Brahmanas* as knowledge born out of *Shruti*, which means inspired revelation, as against the later classical and traditional knowledge, which they term *Smriti*, or what might simply be called man-made transmitted knowledge. The *Aranyakas*, or the forest-books, are the concluding portions of the *Brahmanas*; they are concerned not with ritual, but with mysticism. A class of texts constituting the last stage or the end of *Veda*, *Vedanta*, is known as the *Upanishads*. These are normally embedded in the *Aranyakas* or form their supplements. It is in the *Upanishads* that some of the deeper questions of cosmological and personal significance are raised. It has been argued that both the *Aranyakas* and the *Upanishads* represent the thoughts and speculations of intellectually and spiritually advanced thinkers who were less interested in the ritualism of Vedic sacrifices; they foreshadowed the dissenting tradition that emerged after 600 BC[70] (see Extract 4.5).

We can obtain a flavour of what was meant by learning in ancient India by studying the *Upanishads*. There are over a hundred of them, and each *Upanishad* is concerned with the student sitting at the master's feet and receiving instruction. Most of the instruction concerned the main religious concepts of Hinduism, such as the Universal Soul, or *Brahman*, and the Universal Self, or *Atman*, and how ordinary mortals can reach union with the Divine through meditation and *yoga*. The teaching style was not didactic but discursive and intellectual and, channelled through a variety of pedagogical tools, such as Socratic dialogue, or posing questions in the form of riddles and paradoxes, the teacher stimulated the student's imagination and thinking. At the same time, the skills of memorisation were highly esteemed, and students were encouraged to learn by rote the main verses.[71] This intense guru–student interaction and relationship is one of ancient India's greatest but largely unacknowledged contributions to the theory of learning.

Learning was not just about religion in the abstract. The students had to combine that with the study of the *Sutras*, or traditional learning, concerned with ritual and customary law. Then there were certain texts called the *Vedangas*, which concentrated on such skills as phonetics and pronunciation (*Siksha*); metres (*Chhandas*); grammar (*Vyakrana*); etymology, or understanding roots of words (*Mirukti*); religious practice (*Kalpa*); and astronomy and astrology (*Jyotisha*). Another group of texts, the *Upa-Vedas*, contain information on secular subjects, such as medicine (*Ayur-Veda*), war or, literally, archery (*Dhanur-Veda*), architecture (*Sthapathya-Veda*) and music and arts (*Gandharva-Veda*). These works clearly demonstrate a wide range of interest shown by the Indo-Aryan intellectuals, professionals and practitioners in theoretical and practical studies.

SELECT EXTRACTS FOR REVIEW AND REFLECTION

Extract 4.1 Pertinent Sanskrit/Avestan equivalents of some random words

The very close similarity between Vedic Sanskrit and Avestan provides one indication of the common origins of the Aryans of India and Iran.

yo vo apo vasvish yajate asuranish asurasya vashishthabyo hotrabhyo
(Sanskrit)
yo vo apo vanguhish yazaite ahuranish ahurahe vahishtabyo zaothrabyo
(Avestan)
he who worships you, the good waters, the Ahurian wives of Ahura, with best libations (English)

English	Sanskrit	Avestan
horse	asva-	aspa-
cattle	pasu-	pasu-
pasture	gavyuti-	gaoyaoti-
cow	go-	gav-
earth	bhumi-	bumi-
plough	krs-	karsh-
(to) bind	bandh-	band-
(to) believe	sraddha-	zrazda-
(to) know	vid-	vid-

English	Sanskrit	Avestan
man	nar-	nar-
woman	jani-/nari-	jani-/nairi-
brother	bhratar-	bratar-
son	putra-	puthra-
daughter	duhitar-	dugedar-
intelligence	buddhi-	baodha-
full	purna-	perena-
part	bhaga-	bagha-
army	sena-	haena-
worship	yajna-	yasna-

Source: from a note communicated to the author by Mr Farrokh Vajifdar, Fellow of the Royal Asiatic Society of Great Britain.

Extract 4.2 The pre-Aryan legacy

The Aryan advance through north India did not result in the elimination of the pre-Aryan people or culture. Both the Aryan and the pre-Aryan learnt to co-exist. The Aryan might have become more dominant, but the native Indians' influence and usefulness in the new Indo-Aryan society remained pervasive. For example, in the event of the union of Aryan men and non-Aryan women, the children were greatly influenced by their mothers in matters of custom and attitude. The migrant Aryans also learnt from the pre-Aryans a great deal about the Indian landscape and the semi-medical esoteric knowledge concerning herbal drugs and charms. One aspect of the Vedic religion in which both the Aryan and the pre-Aryan rituals were brought together was the ceremony of worship. While the Aryans made their ritual of *homa*, associated with fire-worship, an act of thanks to the gods for favours bestowed by them, the pre-Aryans used a ceremony called the *puja* as a way of invoking the supreme Spirit into an object and then meditating upon that object. In an act of compromise, the Aryan and the pre-Aryan combined the two rituals by introducing the fire-cult into the *puja* ceremony.

There are not many definitive works on this subject, but interesting ideas may be found in Alain Daniélou, *A Brief History of India*, Rochester, VT: Inner Traditions, 2003, pp. 11–38; the multi-volume *Cultural Heritage of India*, published by the Ramakrishna Mission Institute of Culture (Calcutta, 1970); A.L. Basham, *Studies in Indian History and Culture*, Calcutta: Sambodhi, 1964, pp. 20–29; and John R Marr, 'The Early Dravidians', in A.L. Basham (ed.), *A Cultural History of India*, Oxford: Clarendon Press, 1975, pp. 30–37.

Extract 4.3 Description of Ayodhya in the *Ramayana*

Since Ayodhya is a place of great significance for both the Hindus and the Jains, archaeologists have undertaken a number of excavations in the city, in order to retrieve some of the ancient glory in the form of impressive ruins or monuments. Alas, apart from a burnt brick fortification wall, a ditch and some indifferent structures, nothing much of archaeological value has come to light that can directly corroborate the contents of the following beautiful passage from the *Ramayana*. The reason for this could be that Ayodhya has been such an established site for so many centuries that it is just too difficult for archaeologists to dig really deeply in the central populated area. Or was Valmiki just imagining rather than describing?

On Sarju's bank of ample size,
The happy realm of Kosal lies
With fertile length of fair champaign
And flocks and herds and wealth of grain . . .
There, famous in her old renown,
Ayodhya stands[,] the royal town,
In bygone ages built and planned
By sainted Manu's princely hand
Imperial seat[,] and her walls extend
Twelve measured leagues from end to end,
And three in width from side to side,
With square and palace beautified.
Her gates at even distance stand;
Her ample roads are wisely planned.
Right glorious is her royal street,
Where streams allay the dust and heat,
On level ground and even row
Her house[s] rise in goodly show:
Terrace and palace, arch and gate
The queenly city decorate.
High are her ramparts, strong and vast,
By ways at even distance passed
With circling moat, both deep and wide,
And store of weapons fortified . . .
She seems a painted city, fair
With chess-board line and even square.

Source: Ralph Griffith, from *The Ramayana of Valmiki*, Benares, 1915, Book 1, canto 5; quoted in Niharranjan Ray *et al.*, *A Sourcebook of Indian Civilization*, Hyderabad: Orient Longman, 2000, pp. 222–3. Read also

F.R. Allchin, *Archaeology of Early Historic South Asia*, Cambridge: CUP, 1995, and D.K. Chakrabarti, *The Archaeology of Ancient Indian Cities*, Oxford: OUP, 1998.

Extract 4.4   Verses from two well-known hymns of the *Rig-Veda*

1   *The hymn of creation:* Rig-Veda *Book X, 129.6 and 129.7*

The last line from verse 7 is an indication of the early Indian thinkers' doubts and uncertainty about creation. This is in marked contrast to the definitive positions on this issue taken up by some modern-day dogmatists and fundamentalists.

(6): Who verily knows and who can here declare it, whence it
     was born and whence comes this creation?
     The Gods are later than this world's production. Who knows
     then whence it first came into being?

(7): He, the first origin of this creation, whether he formed it all
     or did not form it,
     Whose eye controls this world in the highest heaven, he verily
     knows it, or perhaps he knows not.

2   *The hymn of the sacrifice of Purusha, the first man:* Rig-Veda *Book X, 90.11–12*

The hymn itself was a later addition to the *Rig-Veda*, but the two verses have been quoted, time and again, by the orthodox in support of the caste system. This is a pity, because caste is thereby legitimised by so-called religious sanction.

(11): When they divided Purusha how many portions did they make?
      What do they call his mouth, his arms? What do they call
      his thighs and feet?

(12): The Brahman was his mouth, of both his arms was the Rajanya
      made.
      His thighs became the Vaisya, from his feet the Sudra was
      produced.

Source: Ralph T.H. Griffith, *The Hymns of the Rig-Veda*, Vol. 2, Benares: E.J. Lazarus, 1920, pp. 519 and 576.

Extract 4.5 An early example of dissent against the idea of Vedic sacrifice

... The fools who delight in [the] sacrificial ritual as the highest spiritual good go again and again through the cycle of old age and death.

Abiding in the midst of ignorance, wise only according to their own estimate, thinking themselves to be learned, but really obtuse, these fools go round in a circle like blind men led by one who is himself blind.

Regarding sacrifice and merit as most important, the deluded ones do not know of any other higher spiritual good. ...

Source: *Mundaka Upanishad*; quoted in Ainslee Embree (ed.), *Sources of Indian Tradition*, Vol. 1, London: Penguin, 1992, p. 31.

RELEVANT QUESTIONS FOR DISCUSSION

1 What is the difference between racial prejudice and racism? What are the origins of European racism?
2 Why are the writers subscribing to Hindutva ideology so reluctant to accept the large quantity of conventional research findings about the origins of the Aryans?
3 What were the positive and negative aspects of Vedic culture?

Notes

1 Mallory 1989: chapter 1; Crystal 1997: 298–305; Gamkrelidze and Ivanov 1990.
2 Mallory 1989: 35–6; Renfrew 1987: 178.
3 Varied viewpoints on the Aryans can be read in Frawley and Rajaram 1995, Kak (n.d.), Kochhar 2000, Mallory 1989, Renfrew 1987, Thapar 1993, Thapar 2002.
4 Riencourt 1986: 254–68.
5 Mallory 1989: 266.
6 Thapar 2002: 4–5; Mallory 1989: 266–70.
7 Thapar 2002: 12–15; Trautmann 1997: 1ff, 172–87, 194–8.
8 Kochhar 2000: 76–80.
9 Quoted in Mallory 1989: 12.
10 Thapar 2002: 12–13; Renfrew 1987: 9–19.
11 Mallory 1989: 144–51, 186–8.
12 For two interesting but differing perspectives, compare Mallory 1989: 9–23, with Renfrew 1987: 9–19.
13 Mallory 1989: 257–61; Renfrew 1987: 77–86; Gamkrelidze and Ivanov 1990: 85–6.
14 Kochhar 2000: 89–117.

15 The indication of a strong co-occurrence of Indic and Iranian words is referred to in Renfrew 1987: 193.
16 Dange 2002.
17 Kochhar 2000: 104–12.
18 Dange 2002: 191.
19 Kochhar 2000: 37.
20 Boyce 2002c.
21 Hinnells 1985: 30–33; Boyce 1984: 8–11.
22 Jamkhedkar 2002.
23 See, particularly, Frawley and Rajaram 1995, Jain 2004, Kak (n.d.), and Venkat (n.d.).
24 Thapar 2002: 110.
25 For a clear discussion on these issues, see Kochhar 2000: 120–36.
26 Witzel 1995: 321–4.
27 Kochhar 2000: 94.
28 Mallory 1989: 37–9; Thapar 2002: 107–9.
29 Kochhar 2000: 117.
30 Thapar 2002: 12–13.
31 Kochhar 2000: 180–85; Mallory 1989: 47.
32 Mallory 1989: 47.
33 Griffith 1920: I, 101.5, 104.2; V, 29.10.
34 Griffith 1920: I, 7.9.
35 Kochhar 2000: 49–53.
36 Rapson 1922: 77–108.
37 For another interesting perspective on the Aryanisation of the Indus Culture, see Bhan 2002.
38 For a succinct summary, read Parpola 2006.
39 Thapar 2002: 112–14; Sengupta 1950: 34.
40 Thapar 2002: 115.
41 Jha 2004: 48.
42 Thapar 2002: 116.
43 Jha 2004: 48–9.
44 Sarkar 1928: 1–46.
45 Chakrabarti 1998: 186–8.
46 Kochhar 2000: 80–81.
47 Ibid.: 84.
48 Ratnagar 1995: 25–6; Thapar 1995: 89–91; Kochhar 2000: 80–88.
49 Ratnagar 1995: 20–24; Ray *et al.* 2000: 196–214; Schwartzberg 1992: 155–60.
50 Thapar 2002: 117.
51 For an interesting discussion on the ideals of the Hindu family life, read Prinja 1996: 166–70.
52 On the Hindu philosophy of life after death, etc., see Prinja 1996: 170–71.
53 Thapar 2002: 118; but also see Sarkar 1928: 103–12 for another point of view.
54 Sarkar 1928: 82–4; Thapar 2002: 118.
55 Prinja 1996: 173–4.
56 Thapar 2002: 53.
57 Griffith 1920: X, 34.
58 For later Vedic kingship, see Spellman 1964: 26–42.
59 Thapar 2002: 122–6.
60 Thapar 1995: 101–2.
61 For a balanced summary of the caste system, see Prinja 1996: 69–72.
62 Walker 1968: Vol. 2, 316–21.
63 Aspects of the modern *Yajna* ceremony are clearly explained in Prinja 1996: 102–4.

64 Thapar 2002: 128.
65 Jha 2004: 60–61.
66 Joseph 2000: 226.
67 Ibid.: 225–8, 400.
68 A note to the author from Dr Daud Ali, School of Oriental and African Studies, University of London.
69 Bose *et al.* 1989: 216.
70 Walker 1968: Vol. 2, 531.
71 Roebuck 2000: xix–xxiv.

5 Formative centuries of the pre-Mauryan era

(*Time-span:* c. 600 BC to c. 320 BC)

Two sets of developments were to change the face of most of north India during the three centuries after 600 BC. Firstly, a complex state system encompassing princely kingdoms and clan states emerged out of the petty polities of the Vedic period. This led to a hierarchy of states through warfare, duplicity and alliances; and this in turn resulted in the emergence of a single most powerful state, *Magadha*, which would eventually become the heartland of a great pan-Indian Mauryan empire, the subject of our next chapter. From a very early stage, the newly emerged state system came to be challenged by two foreign intrusions and influences, those of the Achaemenid rulers of Persia and the Macedonians/Greeks, the results of which affected India to a certain extent. Secondly, the systemic power wielded by the rulers, along with the benefits of iron technology, created huge agricultural surpluses for supporting non-agricultural populations in the new urban centres that developed during this period. This new phase of urbanism engendered much dynamism in the socio-economic life of north India. The urban people, however, were less receptive to the Brahmanic hegemony, and many came to be influenced by various dissenting traditions, particularly Jainism and Buddhism. Despite all the turmoil of change, Indian intellectual life remained as vigorous as ever, with new literatures being added to the enormous stock of knowledge compiled by Vedic teachers during the previous thousand years.

Politics and the geography of power

By 600 BC the geography of India was understood by its learned people in terms of five large regions.[1] These were: *Madhyadesha*, the Middle Country; *Praticya*, the western lands; *Pracya*, the east; *Uttarapatha*, the northern route; and *Dakshinapatha*, the southern route (see Map 5.1).

The *Madhyadesha* was the original core land around the *Kurukshetra* plain, which gradually encompassed the Ganga–Yamuna *doab* and the lands west of *Prayag*. Southwards, it tended to extend towards the Vindhya and Aravalli ranges; in future centuries, the entire area came to be called *Aryavarta*. The western lands of *Praticya* encompassed all the territory from eastern Afghanistan to the Aravalli hills. Two routes were already known then: one through the

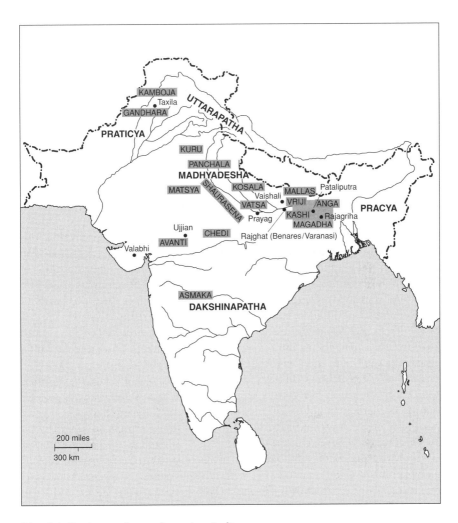

Map 5.1 Regions and states in ancient India.

Bolan Pass and the other along the sea coast. Since the Persians considered the plain of the River Indus as their eastern frontier and the Indians regarded eastern Afghanistan as part of their sphere of influence, there was much warfare between the two. The east, *Pracya*, meant all lands between *Prayag* and the Ganga delta. It would be the east that would decide the destiny of India for the next thousand years, because that was where the ascendancy of the Magadhan state was established. *Uttarapatha*, the northern route, led to the north and northwest beyond the Pamirs and the Himalayas and towards Central Asia. Here, in this rugged mountainous terrain, lived (and still live) hardy and self-sufficient ethnic and tribal groups who looked both towards Afghanistan and

Central Asia on the one hand, and towards the *Madhyadesha* on the other. In contrast to these four regions during this period, there was much less certainty about the boundaries of *Dakshinapatha*. At first, the south began beyond the gates of the Middle Country; but, as the Middle Country itself expanded southwards and pushed towards the Vindhya range, the northern limits of the south came to be revised. The Aryanisation process accompanied the northern expansion, and the first three south-lying regions to be heavily influenced by the colonisers from *Madhyadesha* were Karnataka, Andhra and *Kalinga*.

Clan states and kingdoms

Around the eighth century BC the *janapadas*, or the territories of the *janas*, the peoples, became more clearly marked.[2] There must have been numerous *janapadas*; in a unique grammatical compendium, the *Ashtadhyayi* of Panini, sixty-nine polities of various sizes are named.[3] There were many amalgamations that eventually created sixteen *mahajanapadas*, or the greater states (see Map 5.1). Their geographical spread provides us with a clearer understanding of how human settlement patterns in the northern part of South Asia evolved up to 600 BC. The focus of settlement in the Harappan era was the Indus basin; in the early Vedic period it was Punjab; then it moved eastwards, and by the end of the Vedic age the entire Gangetic basin consisted of eleven of the sixteen *mahajanapadas* and their capital cities. Central and peninsular India had only three between them, and there were two in the northwest.

As for their political structures, both the *janapadas* and the *mahajanapadas* can be classified into two groups: a smaller one of clan states, and the greater one of numerous kingdoms. The clan states were situated mostly on the periphery of the heartland kingdoms, in the Himalayan foothills, northwest India, Punjab, Sind, and central and western India. The people of the clan states, hardy and independent-minded hill people, continued with the ancient clan traditions of working together with others whom they regarded of as part of a bigger family, which was the clan. Two *mahajanapadas*, *Mallas* and *Vriji*, became the most important clan states.[4] Historians have variously described the clan states as democracies, republics or oligarchies,[5] and each designation has a definable element of truth in it. The clan states practised democracy to the extent that there were great assemblies in which people expressed heterodox ideas; but, since the lowest orders were excluded from the consultative process, it was an imperfect sort of democracy. The states were republican in the sense that they did not subscribe to the institution of monarchy, with the accompanying panoply of ritual ceremonial and sacrifices; but a number of clan states produced powerful personalities who called themselves *rajas*, or kings, and who came to dominate the discussions and assembly proceedings. Generally speaking, an oligarchy of a few strong men obtained a dominant voice in the governance of the clan states. Although 'kingship was dissolved and republics were set up, the class divided patriarchal society, bureaucracy, taxation system and an army for the coercion of people remained.'[6]

In whichever way we understand the clan states, there were two aspects that were common to all of them. One was their corporate style of government. The heads of clan families met in an assembly, or *sangha*, which was ordinarily convened in the main town, and the proceedings were conducted by someone who was recognised as the most senior. The role of the leader was not hereditary but highly honoured; the debates were rigorous, and a vote was taken in the absence of unanimity.[7] The second aspect common to the clan states was a great degree of anti-Brahmanic tendency among their citizenry. The Vedic orthodoxy of the caste system based on *varna-ashrama* was rejected, and the alliance of the *brahmans* and the *kshatriya*, which underpinned the structure of authority in the kingdoms, did not hold well in the clan states. The powerful *kshatriya* families in these states accorded little awe or respect for their *brahman* peers, and this was why the orthodox of the Vedic tradition called these *kshatriyas* 'degenerate'.[8] Although it is perhaps coincidental, it is worth noting that most of the dissenting traditions arose within the clan states.

In contrast to the clan states there were the kingdoms, great and small, ruled by the monarchs. Two millennia and a half later, with the end of British rule in 1947, and the adoption of a republican constitution in 1950, the institution of monarchy in India was to become obsolete. The king of England then ceased to be the emperor of India, and nearly 600 Indian princes lost their authority. The fundamental principles and styles of government that had operated in Indian political life for at least 2,700 years were thus destroyed. The early history of the *jana* kingship began around the eighth century BC, during the later Vedic age, when the *rajas* belonging to elite lineages, called *rajanyas*, within the *kshatriya* caste, came to dominate the military–nobility nexus within the Indian context.[9] The word *kshatra* means power. The authority of the *rajas* derived partly from stories of righteous heroism in the great epics of the *Mahabharata* and the *Ramayana*, which bestowed upon them the legitimacy of a sacred right to rule. As what unfolded in the epics has such great resonance within the Hindu psyche, it is to be expected that many Indians even now regard the divine origin of kingship very seriously. There was also a long tradition in India of people trusting their monarchs to do what was right and just. This sense of an unwritten code of conduct was derived from all the religious traditions to which the various monarchs subscribed. They enjoined a monarch to be strong, wise, decisive, kind and a concerned protector of his people; and the king's power was to be matched 'by his obligations to his subjects, as is made clear in relation to his right to levy taxes ... The king who takes his sixth share as tribute and fails to protect his subjects commits a sin.'[10] But alas, with a few exceptions, the Indian monarchs turned out to be no less violent and cruel, or vain and stupid, than their many counterparts in various parts of the world in different epochs.

Continuing with the late Vedic tradition, the post-Vedic kings used to hold major ceremonies of sacrifice in order to bolster their authority. Among the main ceremonies was the royal sacrifice, called the *rajasuya*. At this annual ceremony, the king honoured his patrons and courtiers with the title of *ratnin*, the jewels, and would make offerings to them, as a way of protecting his patrimony and winning the loyalty of the men closest to him. The king also gave *dana* (gift) to the chief priest (the *purohit*).[11] There were many royal rituals in ancient India. They involved such activities as cattle raids, games of dice and chariot races, but perhaps the most crucial rite was that of the horse sacrifice, called the *ashvamedha*. In a semi-settled society which was not yet fully agricultural and where the territorial boundaries were very fluid, the acquisition of land was a marker of status for any aspiring *raja*. Initially, ambitious *rajas* tested the limits of their rivals' territories by allowing a white stallion to wander at will for a year, monitored by soldiers who, when the horse was challenged, would either fight if they sensed a weaker enemy or prudently withdraw in the face of a stronger one. At the end of the year the *raja* would claim all the territory over which the horse had wandered freely. Then, at a huge sacrificial rite attended by vast crowds, the horse would be consecrated. There then followed a symbolic mating ceremony involving the *raja*'s chief wife and the sacred horse. The horse was then sacrificed by the *brahman* priests. Sex and magic, religion and superstition, were combined in this ceremony, with the aim of symbolically demonstrating the mystical authority of royal power.[12]

The supremacy of Magadha

The greatest of all the kingdoms was to be *Magadha*. Its location demonstrates an interesting aspect of the historical geography of India. Although the entire Gangetic basin is generally considered as the region where the north Indian civilisation has grown and flourished since 600 BC, the political heart of that civilisation for the first thousand years, until about the sixth century AD, was in an area southeast of that basin. This area is today covered by the Patna and Gaya districts of Bihar. This is the area where the *mahajanapada* of *Magadha* developed into a great state and then into an empire. Certain key advantages gave it an edge over all its rivals. Even today Bihar is rich in iron-ore deposits. Iron was the key resource that gave the Magadhans supremacy in both agricultural and military technology.[13] *Magadha* also controlled the main trade route of the Gangetic basin leading to the Bay of Bengal, which brought in substantial revenues to the state.[14] The two great cities of *Magadha*, first *Rajagriha* and later *Pataliputra*, were both massive fortress-cities, which were impervious to attacks from outside.[15] *Magadha*'s supremacy was, at first, challenged by such kingdoms as *Kosala* and *Kashi* and the clan state of *Vriji*,[16] but her kings proved to be brilliant both at strategy and at tactics in warding off their threats.

Three major dynasties guided *Magadha* between the middle of the sixth century BC and 321 BC, when the empire of the Mauryas was proclaimed from *Pataliputra*, by then the capital of *Magadha*. The first two kings, Bimbisara (544–493 BC) and Ajatsatru (492–462 BC), belonged to the Haryanka dynasty.[17] Under them the *mahajanapadas* of *Anga*, *Kosala* and *Kashi* were defeated, and the long war with the *Vriji* Confederacy was begun. Both kings were men of immense energy and talent. Bimbisara, the first great Indian monarch about whom we have some considerable certainty of knowledge, streamlined his administration by instituting four grades of officer class, known as *mahamatras*. Through them it became easier to collect tax revenues. He allowed a degree of autonomy through a system of sub-kings, or *mandalika-rajas*, and yet was able to keep in check the centrifugal tendencies of the system. He was murdered by his own son, Ajatsatru, who proved to be an outstandingly energetic ruler. The latter greatly increased the military capabilities of *Magadha*, strengthened the fortifications at *Rajagriha*, the then capital, and started building a new stronghold at *Pataligrama* which, later, came to be known as *Pataliputra*. The victories over all his enemies were celebrated in great style with horse sacrifices.

Just as he had done, the successors of Ajatsatru all killed their parents to gain the throne. The Haryankas were finally overthrown in 413 BC by the founders of the dynasty of Shishunaga. The Shishunaga ruled for half a century, from 413 BC to 364 BC, and annexed the strategically important *mahajanapada* of *Avanti* in central India, overwhelming its capital, Ujjain. The last of the three dynasties before the Mauryas was that of the Nandas, who ruled between 364 BC and 321 BC.[18] The dynasty started with a brilliant usurper, Mahapadma, whose mother was a *shudra* and who disliked the *kshatriyas* intensely. With his reign we see the beginnings of non-*kshatriya* involvement in the control of power in different parts of north India.[19] Mahapadma Nanda was succeeded one after the other by his eight sons, each ruling only very briefly. Although the nine Nandas ruled altogether for just forty-three years, they are still remembered as the most powerful pre-Mauryan monarchs of India.

Two foreign intrusions

The first important foreign intrusion to challenge the emerging state system of India was that of the Persians. They became a power to be reckoned with after the establishment in the sixth century BC of the Achaemenid dynasty by Cyrus II (550–529 BC). Although it is not clear how much of the northwest of India he actually controlled, a number of ancient Greek sources have confirmed that his empire included *Gandhara*, i.e. western Punjab, one of the sixteen *mahajanapadas*.[20] From the reign of Darius I (521–486 BC), the third Achaemenid ruler, we have more substantial evidence, from his own inscriptions about the Persian stake in northwest India. The famous Behistun Rock Inscription (520–518 BC), engraved on a cliff 100 metres off the ground along the road between Hamadan in Iran and Baghdad in Iraq, contains Darius's political testament and autobiographical details; and among the twenty-three lands of the Persian Empire are mentioned *Gandhara*, *Arachosia* (southern Afghanistan) and *Maka* (the Makran coast of Baluchistan).[21] Two other inscriptions, one in Old Persian block tablets sunk in the wall of the platform at the royal palace of Persepolis (518–515 BC) and another chiselled around the tomb entrance of Darius at Naqsh-i-Rustam (just after 515 BC), expressly mention Hi(n)dush – i.e. the Indus basin – as Persian controlled.[22] This could mean that Darius had not fully conquered the Indus area by the time the Behistun rock inscription was carved.

Darius's fame rests principally on the efficient ways he ruled the empire and the manner in which he added more territories. He divided it into twenty satrapies (or provincial governments) and judiciously balanced central authority with decentralisation within each territory.[23] His Indian possessions were well integrated into his empire by means of highways. The wealth of his empire was legendary, since resources and tributes flowed into Persia from all directions. The well-known Greek historian Herodotus stated that India (Hi(n)dush or the Indus basin) counted as the twentieth satrapy of the empire, and yet it contributed a third of all the revenues, mostly gold, that came from the Asiatic provinces (i.e. nearly 80 per cent of the empire).[24] *Gandhara*, Sind, the Indus basin, Baluchistan and Afghanistan were the geographical limits of the Persian Empire in the east. The Persians did not enter the Gangetic basin or Rajasthan.[25]

By the middle of the fourth century BC, a new force came to dominate all the Greek city-states: the kingdom of Macedon. Its ruler, Philip II, created a formidable military structure, which was based on phalanxes backed by armoured cavalry and siege trains of catapults. He left this formidable inheritance to his son, Alexander, who became king in 336 BC. Alexander first destroyed the continuing Persian hold over the Greek cities of Asia Minor by his victory over them at the battle of Issus in 333 BC. Two years later, at Gaugamela, Persian power was decisively broken when the last Achaemenid, Darius III, fled to Bactria, where he was murdered. After burning Persepolis (330 BC), Alexander marched through the heart of Iran towards the eastern Persian satrapies of Drangiana, Arachosia, Bactria and Sogdiana. The news of his victories and cruelties preceded him, creating great panic and fear among those who awaited his arrival. In the spring of 327 BC he had nearly reached the western banks of the River Indus.

The first group of people that Alexander met on South Asian soil were those whom the Greeks called the Assakenois, who lived on the present borders of the North West Frontier province and Kashmir in Pakistan. They resisted him, in the way the frontier people have done throughout history, but in vain. Alexander proved much too strong for them. Next was the turn of the *Gandhara* satrapy, with its capital of *Pushkalavati* taken. In this case, overwhelming force was unnecessary because of Indian collaboration. The most significant collaboration was offered by the new king of Taxila, Ambhi, whose forces dominated the lands between the rivers Indus and Jhelum. Taxila was an ancient city where Vedic culture had flourished for centuries, and to a certain extent Ambhi's collaboration made sense. His reward came with the confirmation of his kingdom within the Alexandrine world empire. The next stage in Alexander's conquest was the encounter with Porus, the Paurava king, who ruled the lands between the rivers Jhelum and Chenab. Porus has been 'portrayed as a figure of heroic grandeur' and 'a worthy opponent of Alexander'.[26] The Porus of history nowhere actually matched Alexander in might and power. He did fight bravely, but his army was massacred and he was decisively beaten. Legend has it that he refused to cringe or be obsequious to Alexander, but the reality was that he had become a subaltern to Alexander. The latter awarded him with an extension of territories beyond the Chenab almost to the Ravi, but with the strategic aim of protecting his own larger stake in the Indus basin.

Alexander moved yet further east to the River Beas, which joins up with the Sutlej to become a mighty tributary of the Indus basin. Reaching the Beas was the high point of Alexander's military adventure; but however further east he wished to go, both he and his men realised that it would be a journey without end in the vast Indian landscape that spread before them. Finally, in July 326 BC, his pride and ambition gave way before the demands of his armies to turn back. Alexander may have intruded into India but, in a sense, India had conquered him. He turned back up to the Jhelum river and, with great forces and accoutrements, sailed south towards the open sea. On his way he met ferocious resistance from the Mallavas, a hardy and free-spirited people, and from the *brahman* clans who considered it a part of their *dharma* or religious duty to fight him. With overwhelming force and some good fortune he saved himself and his crew.[27] After sailing through the confluence of the Indus tributaries, he devised a three-pronged exit strategy. One army, under a general called Craterus, was to return through Arachosia. Then, at the mouth of the Indus, Alexander ordered his navy, under Nearchus, to proceed through the Arabian Sea towards the Perso-Arabian Gulf, while he himself proceeded to Iran through the scorching desert of Baluchistan. He never reached his Macedonian homeland, dying in Babylon in 323 BC (see Map 5.2).

Volumes have been written about the character and personality of Alexander; nevertheless he remains difficult to evaluate (see Extract 5.1). For the Persian Zoroastrians he was 'the accursed';[28] for the Indians he was remembered only as a ruthless aggressor who came and went, allegedly leaving no lasting imprint on their imagination; while for most Europeans he still is the 'heroic ideal'.[29] All three assessments are seemingly correct and yet false. In the context of India, Alexander's intrusion was only a minuscule event; 'India was not Hellenised . . . and soon forgot the passing of the Macedonian storm.'[30] However, the settlement of many of his soldiers all along the northwest of India, within a number of succeeding Indo-Greek kingdoms, influenced the politics, art, religion and trade of India in later centuries. The intellectual worlds of both Greece and India also came to know each other better.[31] Alexander himself became fond of a naked Indian ascetic, Kalanos (*Kalyana*, or 'lucky'), whose wisdom and eccentricity were both instructive and amusing for him and his soldiers.[32]

Second urbanisation and the rise of heterodoxy

The political power of the rulers of various states, whether clan-based or monarchic, was greatly underpinned by the new economic prosperity that emerged

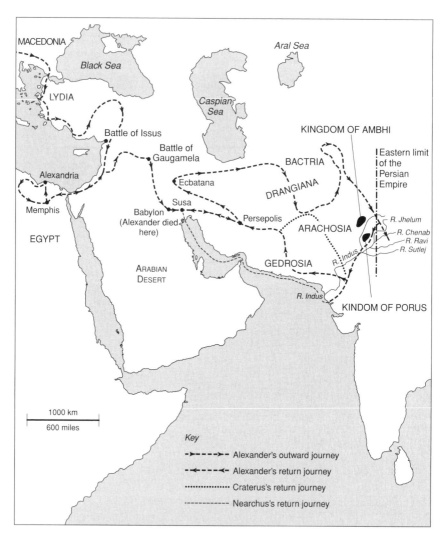

Map 5.2 Marathon march of Alexander the Great.

after 600 BC. This prosperity was based on the surplus produce from land that the rulers came increasingly to enjoy. Large-scale clearances of forests were taking place in the upper and middle Ganga valley, and the newly developing iron technology helped in the process.[33] Iron axes, hoes, ploughshares and nails were the crucial artefacts in increasing farm efficiency. Large areas of marshland were also being drained through inundation channels;[34] these complemented the terrain that relied on wells and water-lifting devices. Another important factor was the efficient deployment of labour on the farms.[35] The rulers and nobles of the new states acquired enormous power over labour through such means as the caste system, the clan organisation and, in the case of the kingdoms, the political legitimacy acquired through the alliance between the royal and Brahmanic authorities. From now on, the vast use of labour, either by state authorities or under the patronage of the rural nobility, came to be an enduring feature of Indian agriculture. Through a variety of taxes, in the nature of either voluntary offerings or royal entitlements, collected by special tax collectors, the *gramabhojaka*, the royal treasuries were greatly augmented.[36]

The growth of towns

The agricultural surplus had a positive effect on the growth of towns during this period. It was this surplus that enabled the rulers of states to encourage relatively large numbers of non-agricultural people to live in towns and pursue their crafts and skills. This development was most marked in the Ganga valley, and hence historians have described this area as the home of the second phase of urbanisation in Indian history. The first phase had come to an end nearly a thousand years before in the Indus valley with the collapse of such cities as Mohenjo Daro and Harappa. The agricultural surplus fed the townspeople at prices they could afford, which might be monetary-based or through barter. There congregated in the towns all manner of craftsmen: masons, bricklayers, plumbers, carpenters and general labourers for building work; metal workers for producing weapons and tools from copper and iron; and a host of specialist craftsmen who manufactured trade commodities, such as glass, ivory objects, ceramics, beads and textile fabrics. The towns were the principal centres of trade and exchange; and into the towns poured huge amounts of revenue in the form of both agricultural surplus and the profits of trade. They therefore housed the principal treasuries, of grain, silver and gold, which the rich and the powerful commandeered. The secure guarding and the defence of these treasuries set the town apart from the village.[37] Villages do not constitute centres of power and wealth in the way towns do; and that is why so many types of defensive structures are mentioned in the various texts in relation to the newly developing towns. The gateways, bastions, moats and ramparts were some of the main features of urban defence. With secure defences, the rulers and the nobility embarked on prestigious architectural projects, of which the ruler's palace would have been the chief attraction. Built generally at the intersection of two principal highways, which could be as broad as 25 to 30 feet, the palace was the building around which all the bureaucratic and mercantile operations would be housed.[38] Certain towns, such as *Kashi* or *Vaishali*, also became centres of religious activity and pilgrimage; and Buddhism, particularly, came to have a strong following among the townsfolk.

Much of our speculation about what the towns in the second phase of urbanisation would have looked like is deduced from such literary sources as the Buddhist *Jataka* stories. Modern archaeology is further able to confirm or question our traditional understanding. Thus, from the excavations carried out at over 100 sites on which important historic cities of South Asia have developed, archaeological evidence can confirm that there are six definite sites where the remains of walls, gateways and ramparts can be dated to the period around 600 BC.[39] These were *Taxila, Rupar, Rajghat, Rajagriha, Kausambi* and Ujjain. These six towns were either the capitals of their *mahajanapadas* or else they straddled 'one of the earliest well-defined trade routes of India';[40] their sites have yielded valuable evidence of the Northern Black Polished Ware pottery (NBPW), the hallmark of the quality of life and prosperity after 600 BC. Other towns also developed during this period; but archaeologists are, as yet, unable to confirm that the growth of the vast majority of the towns of the sub-continent can be dated before the Mauryan period. This does not mean that the textual evidence can be dismissed because, as in the case of the six towns, archaeological and textual evidence quite often complement one another.[41] It is possible that further advances in archaeological methods and techniques will confirm, not dispute, the contents of the texts regarding the towns of the sub-continent.

A particularly crucial contribution of archaeology has been to establish, in spatial terms, the differences between various types of settlement in a 'hierarchy of settlements' at any particular urban site. From the texts we learn of a number of terms, such as *grama* (village), *nagara* (town), *pura* (defensive-cum-administrative structure), *rajdhani* (capital city) or *mahanagara* (metropolitan city). Traditionally, historians and sociologists have used these terms, casually, on the premise that their meaning can be taken for granted. Archaeological rigour has now made it easier for us to grasp the precise significance of these terms, by carefully mapping out and delineating the clusters of settlement spaces at a particular site and, with the help of the evidence found at actual sites, calculating the concentration of population and the constellation of power which would have been the likely factors determining the evolution of a settlement, from a *grama* to a *mahanagara*. Pottery findings are also significant for the archaeologists. Homogeneous pottery types across distances and settlements imply a sharing of technology and material culture. Such archaeological work that has been carried out at *Kausambi*, the capital of *Vatsa mahajanapada*, in the modern Allahabad district, furnishes us with the best documented evidence of how a hierarchy of settlements can be archaeologically determined at a historic site.[42]

Dissent and heterodoxy

The sixth century BC was a period that was 'a watershed in the history of speculative ideas'.[43] By this time, at one level, Vedic society had become highly stratified, with gross inequality pervading its structure. There was a feeling of injustice and grievance among the ordinary populace. At the same time, as we have seen, a number of developments were taking place in the political and economic sphere throughout northern India, and impacting upon the mind-set of social classes and groups. The stage was set for a greater fluidity and mobility within the social pyramid. The position of the large majority of the lower caste *shudras* and the untouchables remained as depressed and subservient as ever, although increased prosperity might have trickled down to some of their artisans.[44] The *brahmans* retained their monopoly of priestly functions and religious scholarship, while the more enterprising among them were prepared to assume greater political responsibilities, thereby reaping yet more power and prestige. The *kshatriyas*, or the secular ruling elites, benefited greatly as their kingdoms or republics thrived and became richer, but it was the innumerable trading groups, part of the *vaishya* caste, that assumed the role of the bourgeoisie of the Gangetic basin. The *vaishyas* originally controlled land, but were able to convert surplus from land into more mobile forms of wealth production, such as trade. Their newly found wealth gave them the confidence to ignore any humiliation attached to their third place in the ritual ranking within the caste system. They were irked by obsolete restrictions not just in trade but in religion too. Over one particular Vedic practice, the ritual sacrifice of animals, most of them, along with the more liberal of the *kshatriyas*, were opposed to the meaningless cruelty and extravagance displayed by the Brahmanic authorities (see Extract 5.2). As far as they were concerned, it was a senseless practice that needed to be disbanded.[45]

Religious ferment was particularly widespread in the towns of the sixth century BC. A variety of atheistic, amoralist and materialist doctrines were being preached by philosophers, ascetics and hermits, in opposition to Vedic beliefs and rituals, in one form or another. Collectively speaking, the movement that was to bind various heterodoxies came to be known as Shramanism. The *shramanas* were the voices of dissent, opposed to Brahmanism.[46] Thus, the sect of Ajivakas, led by Makkhali Goshala, did not believe that good deeds could affect the transmigration of souls, a key Vedic concept.[47] They believed that all individual fate was entirely predetermined. The sect of Charavakas, led by a leader called Ajita Kesakambala, believed in pure materialism. They did not believe in any form of afterlife; for them, 'when the body dies both fool and wise alike are cut off and perish. They do not survive after death.'[48] There was also a school of extreme sceptics, led by a certain Sanjaya Belatthiputa, who is reputed to have said:

> If you asked me 'is there another world?', and I believed that there was, I should tell you so. But that is not what I say. I do not say that it is so; I do not say that it is otherwise; I do not say that it is not so; nor do I say that it is not not so.[49]

In other words, there is no certainty of any definable knowledge at all. The presence of such sects is growing evidence of a stimulating intellectual atmosphere in India at the time. The greatest amount of dissidence was in the clan states and, particularly, in the areas of the east, such as modern Bihar and in the marginal lands between India and Nepal. While Brahmanism was much too strongly entrenched in places such as the Punjab, the Gangetic *doab* or the middle Ganga valley, in the east and along the Nepalese border it was far more vulnerable to challenges. Among many ethnic groups there was considerable contempt for Brahmanic sacrifices and caste rigidities. Jainism and Buddhism, although now having matured into full-fledged universalist religions, began life as dissident traditions in the areas that were clan states rather than kingdoms.

Mahavira, the twenty-fourth *Tirthankara*, or the teacher of the Jain faith, was born in 599 BC and died in 527 BC. Buddha's dates are more controversial, but conventionally accepted as from 563 BC to 483 BC. Belonging to the noble *kshatriya* families, they both left settled lives of luxury for a period of renunciation. Both Buddhism and Jainism are rooted in the idea of renunciation. The renunciatory movements became stronger, ironically, during this period when urban affluence was increasing, because 'the ideology of renunciation presupposed the affluence of possessions, as renouncers were dependent on those who lived the worldly life.'[50] Each of the two men obtained enlightenment in his own way and then preached for some three decades all over northern India. Both founded monasteries, and were received enthusiastically by kings, merchants and ordinary people. They championed the reform of Vedic Brahmanism by their insistence that people should learn to give up their vices and follies, to adopt right conduct in their daily lives and not be too concerned with rituals and sacrifices; but, at the same time, both of them believed in the key Vedic concept of the transmigration of souls and the process of reincarnation. They both preached not in scholastic Sanskrit, but in a vernacular such as *Ardha Magadhi*, in order to spread widely their message among ordinary people. Above all, they championed non-violence and a sort of primitive/early egalitarianism. The credibility of their personal efforts to improve the life and status of the *shudras* is undoubted; they incessantly conveyed the message to their followers that the *shudras* had every right to be teachers or monks, and there should be no discrimination in their treatment in the monasteries. However, they were not necessarily against the existing socio-economic relations between the classes at that time, and one could conclude that the dissenting heterodoxies were more interested in benign improvements for the depressed classes than in starting a revolution in their favour[51] (see Extract 5.3). Nevertheless, the two most famous Indians of the twentieth century, Mahatma Gandhi and Dr Bhimrao Ambedkar, based their philosophy of life on the spiritual principles of Jainism and Buddhism.

Varieties of literature

We possess a spectacular literary legacy from the three centuries under review. First and foremost is a work that has been described as 'one of the greatest monuments of human intelligence'.[52] This was the *Ashtadhyayi*, written about 500 BC by Panini, a scholar and linguist who lived in Shalatula, in the northwestern *mahajanapada* of *Gandhara*. The *Ashtadhyayi*, which is a systematic grammar of the Sanskrit language, can be considered one of the earliest works of descriptive linguistics. The Sanskrit language and its various dialects had been evolving for more than a millennium, and, as Panini himself acknowledged, a number of attempts had been made by grammarians before him to systematise the language. Panini called it the living language, or the *Bhasa*, and he was the first great and true codifier of Sanskrit. Two other grammarians, Katyayana (*c.* 300 BC) and Patanjali (*c.* 200 BC) carried forward Panini's work. *Ashtadhyayi* itself means eight chapters, and these eight chapters contain, in all, just under 4,000 *sutras* – concise aphorisms – which illustrate the ordered morphological rules that govern the Sanskrit language.[53] From the *Ashtadhyayi* we can also derive a huge amount of geographical and cultural data concerning regions, towns, peoples, rivers, economic products, historical associations with place-names, and so on. The data's value is in the way grammatical rules are explained rather than in expounding geographical knowledge *per se*.[54]

Long before television gave them their current international fame, the two large epics of the *Mahabharata* and the *Ramayana* were known to millions of South and Southeast Asians. Besides the traditional Hindu versions of them, there are Buddhist, Jainist and even Muslim versions. For centuries the children of these regions have not only been entertained by the theatre and puppet shows of these two epic stories, but also have had their value-systems influenced by the moral message of their narratives. The dim origins of these epics lie in the Vedic period when poets and bards recited tales and sang songs in the honour of heroic warriors; the stories of their valorous pride and achievements/feats would have carried on through centuries by word of mouth. The present form in which the two epics are set out took shape during the post-Vedic age, after 600 BC; they were still transmitted orally, and it took a few centuries more before we witness their written form. Scholars believe that a series of recensions (revisions) made it inevitable that the process of completion for both epics might have taken several centuries. The *Mahabharata* is supposed to have been compiled by Vyasa, or the arranger; and one could speculate that, in view of the central heroic narrative of the epic and the plots within plots, there would have been more than one arranger for the entire story. It is worth remembering that the *Mahabharata* has upwards of 100,000 couplets. The *Ramayana*, with its 24,000 *shlokas*, or verses, is a more compact piece of work in terms of its linguistic style and vocabulary, and most of the original composition was the work of one individual genius called Valmiki. The affairs of royalty and warfare are the backdrop to the plots of both epics; the honour of a hero is the *raison d'être* of all the wars and sufferings, and the call to duty and *Dharma*, as interpreted in Vedic Brahmanism, is the core message of the epics. The essential story of the *Mahabharata* is the family war among two sets of cousins in the Indo-Aryan society of the western Gangetic basin, with rulers from different parts of the then known India taking sides. The *Ramayana* story, set in the eastern part of the Gangetic basin, with the main plot centring upon a family jealousy and the conflicts between Aryan and non-Aryan, is a straightforward story of Rama, the hero, who loses his throne through the jealousy of his stepmother, is exiled in the jungle with his wife Sita for fourteen years, fights Ravana to save Sita, and then is besieged by doubts about Sita's fidelity (see Figure 5.1). Both epics raise a plethora of issues of private and

Figure 5.1 A boy playing the part of Sita (by permission of RHPL).

public morality, such as succession rights, the conscience of a king, sexism, the honour of the female sex, the morality of warfare, and so on; they are also a mine of information for geographical, cultural and social details. With successive revisions over many centuries, both epics have become suffused with Hindu religious imageries. This in fact mattered less in connection with the *Mahabharata*, because pious Hindus normally consider its text 'inauspicious' to read or recite in their homes.[55] The *Ramayana* is, however, cherished in every Hindu home, and the gradual evolution of Rama 'from a moral hero to a divine figure'[56] has had dramatic political and social consequences in recent decades in modern India.

   Although much of the great Buddhist literature dates from the middle of the third century BC, it is worth noting that the earliest sections of it are from our period; they contain some valuable historical material.[57] In line with the dissenting tradition, a large amount of the important, and original, Buddhist literature is in Pali, a vernacular language, rather than Sanskrit. The so-called Pali Canon represents the teachings of the oldest Buddhist sect, the *Thera*, or 'ancient', from which is derived the term *Theravadin*. The canon consists of 'three baskets' of knowledge, called *Tripitaka*. The first basket is *Vinayapitaka*, which gives an account of the Buddha's life, his times, his relationship with Ajatsatru, the king of Magadha, and the economic conditions of town and country during the sixth and fifth centuries BC. A section called *Mahavagga* also includes some medical information concerning diseases and their remedies and the importance of hygiene. The second basket, the *Suttapitaka*, contains five collections, or *Nikayas*, which provide inestimable information on economic and social history. Each *Nikaya* has further sub-divisions in the form of whole books. The third basket, the *Abhidhammapitaka*, deals specifically with religious and ethical concepts. Tradition has it that the three *Tripitakas* were compiled by Buddha's followers shortly after his death, in 483 BC, at the first Buddhist Council at *Rajagriha*; but there is doubt as to whether such an extensive work as the Pali Canon could have been closed so early on. It is more likely that the true progress over the formulation of the *Tripitakas* was made at the second Buddhist Council at *Vaishali* in 377 BC.

The Jains believe that their earliest literature goes back to some 250 years before Mahavira, and that it originally consisted of sixty texts.[58] A number of these texts are now lost, but those remaining are classed in five categories: eleven limbs, or *Angas*, twelve secondary limbs, or *Upangas*, ten miscellaneous texts, or *Prakirnakas*, six separate texts, called *Chadasutras*, and two other texts, known as The Blessing, or the *Nandisutra*, and the Door of Inquiry, or *Anuyogadvara*. Although the Jain canon, consisting of these principal texts, was not fully codified until the Council of *Valabhi* in AD 450, some of the earliest parts of it come from our period. Most of this early literature deals with doctrinal matters, rituals, legends, ethics and Jain philosophy in general, but it also contains fragments of scientific material. The Jains, for example, have had a great fascination for enumerating truly large numbers, and two of the earliest *Upangas*, from our period, the *Surya Prajnapti* and the *Jambu Dwipa Prajnapti*, contain mathematical and astronomical information. The *Tamdula Veyaliya*, which is part of the *Prakirnakas*, discusses physiology, anatomy and embryology.[59] It must, however, be acknowledged that most of the Jain philosophical, scientific and technical literature dates from the later centuries of the first millennium AD.

SELECT EXTRACTS FOR REVIEW AND REFLECTION

Extract 5.1   Two accounts of Alexander's conduct at Taxila

Alexander's conduct towards the Indians was consistent with the behaviour one expects of military men with an inflated ego. General brutality softened by conspicuous generosity is the hallmark of such people, and Alexander was no exception. The following two accounts from European classical writers bring this out clearly.

Between the Indus and the Hydaspes is Taxila, a large city and governed by good laws ... The inhabitants and their king, Taxiles, received Alexander with kindness, and in return came by more than they bestowed, so that the Macedonians were jealous, and said it appeared as if Alexander had found none worthy of his bounty until he had crossed the Indus.

(Strabo)

As the Indian mercenary troops, consisting, as they did, of the best soldiers to be found in the country, flocked to the cities which he attacked and defended them with great vigour, he thus incurred serious losses, and accordingly concluded a treaty of peace with them; but afterwards, as they were going away, set upon them while they were on the road, and killed them all. This rests as a foul blot on his martial fame ... The philosophers gave him no less trouble than the mercenaries, because they reviled the princes who declared for him and encouraged the free states to revolt from his authority. On this account he hanged many of them.

(Plutarch)

Source: A.H. Dani, *The Historic City of Taxila*, Paris: UNESCO, 1986, pp. 40, 49–50.

Extract 5.2 Gandhi's comment on animal sacrifices

The most famous *vaishya* of modern times was Mahatma Gandhi, a man deeply influenced by the philosophy of *ahimsa*, non-violence towards all living creatures, which he learnt partly from the Jains. Gandhi was shocked to witness the practice of animal sacrifices in the great Kali Temple in Calcutta. The practice, which must have been carried on in some form or other all through the ages, repulsed him terribly. He describes in his autobiography what he experienced on his trip to India from South Africa in the year 1901.

On the way to the [Kali Temple] I saw a stream of sheep going to be sacrificed to Kali ... I asked [a religious mendicant]: 'Do you regard this sacrifice as religion'?
'Who would regard killing of animals as religion?'
'Then, why don't you preach against it?'
'That's not my business. Our business is to worship God.'
'But could you not find any other place in which to worship God?'
'All places are equally good for us' ...

We did not prolong the discussion, but passed on to the temple. We were greeted by rivers of blood. I could not bear to stand there ... That very evening I had an invitation to dinner. There I spoke to a friend about this cruel form of worship. He said, 'The sheep don't feel anything. The noise and the drum-beating there deaden all sensation of pain.' I could not swallow this. I told him, that if the sheep had speech, they would tell a different tale ... It is my constant prayer that there may be born on earth some great spirit, man or woman, fired with divine pity, who will deliver us from this heinous sin, save the lives of the innocent creatures, and purify the temple.

Source: M.K.Gandhi, *An Autobiography, or The Story of my Experiments with Truth*, Ahmedabad: Navjivan Publishing House, 1940, pp. 171–2.

Extract 5.3   Buddhist emphasis on character rather than birth

While the Indian Buddhists learnt to live with the reality of caste and class, the pristine message of the Buddha is summed up in the Buddhist text of *Sutta Nipata*:

No Brahman is such by birth.
No outcaste is such by birth.
An outcaste is such by his deeds.
A Brahman is such by his deeds.

Source: *Sutta Nipata*, v. 136; quoted from Ainslee Embree (ed.), *Sources of Indian Tradition*, Vol. 1, London: Penguin, 1992, p. 139.

RELEVANT QUESTIONS FOR DISCUSSION

1   To what extent are the ancient texts inadequate as historical sources?
2   What were the significant differences between the Vedic and the post-Vedic worlds?
3   Why are the *Upanishads* so popular in Western religious circles, as compared with the four *Vedas*?

Notes

1 Schwartzberg 1992: 165.
2 Erdosy 1995b: 115–19.
3 Schwartzberg 1992: 167.
4 Raychaudhuri 1996: 105–15.
5 Sharma 1968: 15–80, 85–135.
6 Sharma 1959: 93.
7 Mukherji 1989: 205–13.

8 Thapar 2002: 148.
9 Raychaudhuri 1996: 139–58.
10 Brockington 1998: 401.
11 Sharma 1977: 116–20.
12 Jamison 1996: 65–72.
13 Raychaudhuri 1996: 577.
14 Thapar 2002: 115.
15 For a theoretical analysis of key factors affecting the rise of early states, consult Cohen 1978: 37–69.
16 Raychaudhuri 1996: 113.
17 Ibid.: 181–90.
18 Ibid.: 201–10.
19 Thapar 2002: 155–6.
20 Raychaudhuri 1996: 582–3.
21 Cook 1983: 58–9; Chattopadhyaya 1974: 8–24.
22 Raychaudhuri 1996: 583–6.
23 Cook 1983: 67–76.
24 Herodotus 1972: 243–4.
25 Cook 1983: 188–92.
26 Bosworth 1996: 8.
27 Ibid.: 94–6, 133–46.
28 Jong 2002: 68.
29 Briant 1996 (title of the book).
30 Vincent Smith, quoted ibid.: 157.
31 Narain 1974: 57–65.
32 McCrindle [1901] 1971: 69–74.
33 Thapar 2002: 143–4.
34 Ibid.: 142–3.
35 Ibid.: 149.
36 Sharma 1959: 130–42.
37 Thapar 2002: 141.
38 Chakrabarti 1998: 259.
39 Ibid.: 242–9.
40 Ibid.: 248.
41 Ibid.: 257.
42 Erdosy 1995b: 105–10.
43 Ray *et al.* 2000: 248.
44 Sharma 1958: 101–2.
45 Walker 1968: Vol. 1, 49–50.
46 Warder 2002: 32–41.
47 Embree 1992: 46.
48 Ibid.
49 Ibid.: 47.
50 Ali 1999: 39.
51 Sharma 1958: 133–42.
52 Cardona 1976: 243.
53 Katre 1987: ix–xxv.
54 Schwartzberg 1992: 167–8.
55 Brockington 1998: 1.
56 Brockington 1984: 307.
57 Singh 2003: 53–9.
58 Marett 1985: 82.
59 Bose *et al.* 1989: 44.

6 The paradox of Mauryan imperialism

(Time-span: 321 BC to 184 BC)

For a brief period of less than two centuries, from the early fourth to the late second century BC, an imperial polity held sway over nearly three-quarters of the land mass of the Indian sub-continent and the eastern half of Afghanistan. This was the Mauryan Empire. As with any empire, its genesis lay in the economic and military strength of a heartland state and the ability of its leaders to assert their power beyond its frontiers. From their central state of *Magadha*, the first three Mauryan emperors evinced a capacity, never before witnessed in Indian history, to muster extraordinarily large material resources for maintaining an imperial hegemony in South Asia. This hegemony was exercised by two methods of governance which, paradoxically, were contradictory but which helped weld together the many different peoples of the empire. On the one hand, as under any imperial system, the strong buttresses of bureaucratic institutions and administrative diktats gave the people a sense of security and belonging but also demanded strict obedience to the emperor. This remained the style of governance throughout the period of the empire; but, halfway through its history, a new element was introduced. Under the third emperor, Ashoka, a unique form of cultural coherence based on the moral values of Buddhism came to be bestowed upon the empire, in the shape of moral exhortations inscribed on stone erected in different parts of India. These messages constituted an ideal norm of benignity, civility and humanity in matters of governance: they are benchmarks of progress in Indian political maturity. The relative prosperity of the Mauryan Empire was underwritten by a huge base of agricultural wealth and extensive commercial networks. It would be a long time before India would experience, nay enjoy, such a bold experiment in imperial sovereignty on this scale. The experiment did not last long, and most of the knowledge concerning the empire was lost. However, the painstaking researches of the last two hundred years, along with accidental discoveries, have made it possible for us to appreciate the empire today in a truer perspective.[1] This chapter will review certain essential aspects of this story.

Advising and observing at the court of Chandragupta Maurya

The term 'Maurya' is derived from *moriya* (Skt. *Mayura*), or peacock. According to a Jain tradition, the founder of the empire, Chandragupta, came from a clan of peacock-tamers who owed allegiance to the kingdom of *Magadha*. Until the late eighteenth century there had been much uncertainty about who Chandragupta really was, where and when he ruled, and even whether he ever existed. There were fragments of information about him in the *Puranas*, in the Buddhist *Mahavamsa* and in a drama dating from the middle of the first millennium AD called *Rudra-rakshasa*. There was also mention of a king called Sandrocottos, sometimes known as Sandrokoptos, in the works from the first century AD of the Roman writer Plutarch, who had learnt about him from the writings of Megasthenes, an ambassador representing Seleukos Nicator, one of Alexander the Great's successors, at the Mauryan court. Megasthenes had also referred to a river named Erannoboas, and a city called *Palimbothra*, which lay at the confluence of the rivers Ganga and Erannoboas. The man who made sense of all these disparate references, through his vast knowledge of Greek, Latin and Sanskrit, was Sir William Jones, the Calcutta scholar and judge. In 1793, at the annual meeting of the Asiatic Society of Bengal, he modestly said, 'I cannot help mentioning a discovery which accident threw my way',[2] and went on to explain how he had worked out that Sandrocottos was the same personage as Chandragupta, that the River Erannoboas was in fact the River Son, whose waters merged into the Ganga until as late as the fourteenth century AD, and that *Palimbothra* was the same place as *Pataliputra*. He also clarified the various dates concerning the accession of Chandragupta to the Magadhan throne and his relationship with Seleukos Nicator, Alexander's successor in India. Jones's work credibly established the sequence of events for the beginnings of the Mauryan Empire, and his discovery may therefore be considered as 'one of the great chronological anchors of Indian history'.[3]

Chandragupta was the first true great emperor of India. He is always known as Chandragupta Maurya, to be distinguished from Chandragupta I, the founder of the Gupta kingdom that was established over 600 years later. After defeating the last of the nine Nandas of *Magadha* he assumed power in 321 BC. By the time his reign ended in 297 BC he had, by war, threats of war, and aggressive diplomacy, reduced the kingdoms and republics of north India to impotence. His greatest triumph lay in the northwest. There, after Alexander's death in 323 BC, the Graeco-Macedonian authority over the Indus basin and the areas to the west had significantly declined. In 305 BC Seleukos Nicator, who controlled the eastern or the Syrian part of the old Alexandrine Empire, turned his attention to India to reclaim Alexander's heritage. Chandragupta confronted him with victorious outcome – and forced him to surrender the Indus basin, Baluchistan and all lands east of Kabul. Seleukos made a dignified retreat from India in 302 BC, after giving his daughter in marriage to Chandragupta, establishing diplomatic relations at the Mauryan court in *Pataliputra* and accepting Chandragupta's modest gift of 500 war elephants, which he later used against his western rival Antigonos. The successful campaign in the northwest brought to a close the military career of the emperor; and in his last few years he was much absorbed in the teachings of Jainism. Chandragupta's interest in Jainism is the first significant indication of the influence that the heterodox religions were to have on the future rulers of India for the next few centuries. If a Jain tradition is to be believed, Chandragupta ended his life as a pilgrim and recluse in Karnataka, in the vicinity of Sravana Belgola, a major centre of Jain pilgrimage.[4]

Kautalya and his Arthashastra

The key to Chandragupta's worldly successes lay in the help and advice he received from his chief minister, Kautalya. While, after 1793, Chandragupta became a figure of importance in the pages of world history, Kautalya remained, for a further century and more, a marginal figure. In the old Vedic, Jainist and Buddhist sources, and in the later *Itihasa-Purana*, the genealogical records, he was known as Chanakya, the one who was the chief minister of Chandragupta. This was all that was known, and except for a very strange twist of history the memory of his name would have remained confined within those sources! One day, in 1904, an anonymous *pandit*, a learned man from the Tanjore district, came to the Mysore Government Oriental Library and handed over to the librarian, Dr Shamasastry, a palm-leaf manuscript of an ancient text. This text, which is now known as Kautalya-*Arthashastra*, was translated by the librarian in the pages of the *Indian Antiquary* in 1905. With the encouragement of the Maharaja of Mysore, Dr Shamasastry published the full text as Volume 37 of the Bibliotheca Sanskrita of Mysore in 1909. Thus was resurrected the fame of Chandragupta's adviser, Kautalya, and his great text, the *Arthashastra*[5] (see Extract 6.1).

This work is one of the most important documents concerned with diplomatic skills, political economy and general secular knowledge to come out of ancient India. It is a guidebook for monarchs and a rulebook for citizens. While it is not a text of political philosophy, it deals with the issues of political craftsmanship in great detail. It is also concerned with civil and political institutions and the ways the ruler can operate them. Above all, it is a primer of secular law; after reading the precepts of the *Arthashastra*, no one can claim that ancient India was a lawless place. Dr Shamasastry's translation of the Sanskrit text is laid out in fifteen books, each with a number of chapters. The English text has approximately a quarter of a million words. In addition to the names of people and places, the index to the text lists 430 different items and issues, ranging over a wide spectrum of subjects and experiences in which humanity is involved. Although the entire text is concerned with material and worldly issues and contains very little on religious matters, the philosophical premise of the work is entirely Vedic in outlook. The Vedic ideas of a social hierarchy, for example, along with the dominance of the *brahmans* and *kshatriyas*, are taken for granted. Heterodoxy is shunned, as can be evidenced in the following injunction: 'when a person entertains, in dinner dedicated to god or ancestors, Buddhists, Ajivakas, Sudras and exiled persons, a fine of 100 panas shall be imposed.'[6]

Because of what is written in the *Arthashastra* we can surmise that Kautalya must have advised Chandragupta in the arts of war and peace. There is a great deal of originality in his ideas on the relationship between a monarch and his neighbouring states. For example, he tells us that there are only two forms of policy for a king to choose in his dealings with other kings: war or peace. The operation of these two policies can take six different forms: agreement with pledges is called peace; offensive operation is war; indifference is neutrality; making preparations is marching; seeking the protection of another is alliance; and making peace with one and waging war with another is termed a double policy.[7] Kautalya deals at considerable length with the complexities and duplicities required for a king to pursue his relationships with his peers. The collecting of intelligence was particularly vital. It was the specific task of officially employed spies, informants and secret service agents, and its diligent use was of the utmost importance to the ruler.[8] What is generally termed Machiavellian in the context of historic rivalries of dynasties and ruling elites in European history was very much grounded in Kautalya's thinking eighteen centuries before Machiavelli himself.[9] A large part of the text is also concerned with the duties of a king. Many of the personal qualities recommended for the king would be considered admirable in any age. The king is advised to avoid betaking to others' women, appropriating others' wealth and injuring others; long sleep, fickleness, falsehood, gaudy dress, associates of low character and unrighteous actions are all condemned.[10] This emphasis on the king's personal discipline is part of the wider rule of law that Kautalya prescribes for society in general. A quite harsh and unforgiving environment of rules and regulations is to be maintained by an extremely efficient and organised bureaucracy, whose officers wield great authority over every aspect of the lives and occupations of the people. The legal relationships between husbands and wives, debtors and creditors, employers and workers, masters and servants, traders and customers – in all these relationships a severely retributory regime is invoked as soon as one party is deemed to have broken the contract. The index to the text lists 336 different offences for which fines are to be levied. The offences and fines, in a sense, tell us about one highly placed person's criteria for a well-governed society based on Vedic codes of conduct.

Megasthenes and his Indica

Our understanding of the early Mauryan world in the reign of Chandragupta is further enhanced if we complement the *Arthashastra* with fragments of the contemporary account left behind by the Greek ambassador at the court. Megasthenes was a native of Ionia (modern Turkey) who represented the diplomatic interests of Seleukos Nicator. During his four years in India, from

302 BC to 298 BC, he observed and recorded the varied features of life in India; although his diary, *Indica*, is now lost, its contents were known to the later European classical writers such as Strabo, Arrian and Diodorus Siculus, and it is from their writings that we learn what Megasthenes had earlier described. Considerable doubt was cast on both the veracity and the credibility of Megasthenes' writing even by the ancient historians themselves, particularly Strabo.[11] Megasthenes was certainly wrong on a number of matters. His erroneous calculations of the area of India and the length of the rivers can be excused by the fact that no one could have done better with the sort of instruments they possessed at that time. He also had a most distorted view of India's history before his time, when he wrote that 'the Indians had no cities ... [and] they dressed in the skins of animals and ate the bark of trees'; and that it was only after 'Dionysus came and made himself master of India, he built cities and established laws for them, and he became the giver of wine, for Indians as well as the Greeks, and he taught them to sow the land, furnishing them with seed'[12] (See Extract 6.2).

Notwithstanding such errors, historians are satisfied that on at least some of the matters Megasthenes was correct in his observations. The first is his social picture of India. He observed that its people formed seven estates. At the pinnacle were the philosophers who, according to him, performed public sacrifices, learnt the ancient texts, gave blessings to kings and led a life of abstinence and frugality. Many of them went about naked. In the context of the ritual caste system of India, this class would include the *brahmans* and various groups of sages and mendicants belonging to both Vedic and dissident traditions. The second estate consisted of the majority of the Indian people, the cultivators. Their task was to produce food and remit one-fourth of it to the king who owned all the land. Unlike in mediaeval Europe, they did not have to fight for him, although this was not strictly true. In the third estate were the herdsmen and the hunters who had to bring in a certain proportion of their cattle into the cities as tribute, for which, in return, they received free corn. Traders, artisans and the boatmen constituted the fourth estate. The fifth estate was that of the soldiers, who did nothing else but fight, and were always paid and maintained, thereby constituting a standing professional army. The sixth estate was made up of spies and intelligence officers, whose work is also described at length in the *Arthashastra*. The seventh and the smallest estate was that of those who constituted the political and imperial establishment. This sevenfold division seems to be a more elaborate classification of Indian society than the ritual hierarchy of the traditional caste system.[13]

Another item of interest in Megasthenes' diary was his description of the Magadhan capital, *Pataliputra*, which he called *Palimbothra*. This is especially valuable, as we have relatively little evidence for what the cities and towns of India in the third and fourth centuries BC looked like. While the splendid bricks and the isolation of Mohenjo Daro and Harappa preserved the original layout of those cities for posterity, the cities of the Ganga have suffered from both poor quality materials and periods of great turbulence. That is why

Megasthenes' *Pataliputra* is so evocative. Built at the confluence of the Ganga and the Son, the palisade defences of *Pataliputra* formed a great oblong, 9 miles long and 1.8 miles in width. All along the palisade were 570 towers and sixty-four gates. Outside the palisade ran a ditch, 60 feet deep and 200 yards wide, serving as both defence and public sewer.[14] Megasthenes describes both the hustle and bustle of the streets of the capital and the peace and beauty of the royal park, and he gives a colourful account of the royal palace, which he considered more sumptuous than those of Susa and Ecbatana in Iran.[15] It is also in his accurate understanding of the way in which the municipality of *Pataliputra* was organised by Chandragupta that historians have found Megasthenes most useful. The work of six major committees is described at length. Their duties covered such varied issues as the promotion of arts and crafts in the city, the reception and care of foreigners, the registration of births and deaths, the supervision of weights and measures, the quality control over manufactures and the collection of duties over goods sold. An examination of the departmental details indicates to us not only a high level of bureaucracy but also a certain concern for the quality of life of the ordinary people.[16] The greatest of all the Mogul emperors, Akbar, 'had nothing like it, and it may be doubted if any of the ancient Greek cities were better organised.'[17] When the accounts of Megasthenes are corroborated with the vast number of details in Kautalya's *Arthashastra*, our knowledge of the world of Chandragupta Maurya becomes more complete. It was indeed a highly ordered and well-regulated world.

The *Dhamma* of Ashoka

'*Dhamma*', in *Pali*, is related to the Sanskrit word '*dharma*'. While Sanskrit was the classical language of the learned in Vedic society, Pali became the scriptural language of Buddhism. Pali itself began as *Prakrit*, the vernacular of the common masses of north India. *Dharma*, in Vedic thought, implies a sense of universal law or norm, eternal and unchanging. Many Hindus therefore like to call their religion *Sanatana Dharma*, or the religion of the eternal law. In Buddhism, *Dhamma* has varied meanings. One meaning refers to the teachings of the Buddha himself, while another deals with the philosophical aspects concerning the 'nature of things' or what may be termed as natural. However, a more practical interpretation of *Dhamma* was provided by the emperor Ashoka (c. 269 BC–232 BC). The *Dhamma* of Ashoka, or the law of moral virtues, exhorted people to engage themselves in ethical behaviour and good deeds.

Ashoka's grandfather, Chandragupta, had founded the Mauryan Empire in 321 BC, and under his father, Bindusara, this empire had been consolidated into one of the strongest and most extensive of the political authorities of Asia. Yet one strategic region on the eastern seaboard, *Kalinga*, had escaped Mauryan control. A vigorous attack by Ashoka, in which hundreds of thousands of enemy troops died, finally subdued *Kalinga*. Witnessing death and destruction on this scale, Ashoka felt acute remorse and the imperative of repentance. For him this was a point of catharsis, when he felt he had to purify himself holistically. He now understood that only through the complete attainment of the Buddhist ideal of non-violence could a just and noble society be established on this earth. Although he still remained a strong-minded Mauryan ruler, his main goal from then on was to establish a *Dhamma*.

Before we examine the contents of the *Dhamma*, let us digress briefly to consider how Ashoka's fame came to be established in modern times. The principal method within India that Ashoka adopted in propagating his *Dhamma* was by issuing a set of edicts and having them inscribed on the faces of cliffs and hillocks (rock edicts) and pillars (pillar edicts) in different parts of the empire. With a few exceptions, the language used for the inscriptions at most sites was *Prakrit*, carved in *Brahmi*, the most ancient of the intelligible Indian scripts (See Extract 6.3). Centuries rolled on after Ashoka's death, and Indian history moved along new pathways. The Ashokan pillars and rocks were forgotten, and the memory of Ashoka himself faded. Two millennia later, however, the curiosity and methodicalness of some of the British scholars of India, in their unrelenting search for India's past, led to a recovery of knowledge of this emperor, and a new analysis of his empire could be constructed. The early British scholars had come across the Ashokan pillar and rock edicts, but had been unable to decipher the *Brahmi* script. This could only be possible if a clue were to be discovered from among the characters of the script. The breakthrough came with the efforts of an assiduous scholar called James Prinsep, who deciphered the script and thereby rescued the magnificent work of Emperor Ashoka from obscurity.[18]

In India today Ashoka is considered the greatest of all the kings who have ruled over her. The lion capital of an Ashokan pillar is the official emblem of the Indian republic, and every Indian child is taught about Ashoka at school. Outside India too his name has spread far and wide, and all encyclopaedias of world history list his august name. However, no other book of modern times could have influenced the English-speaking public's awareness of Ashoka more than H.G. Wells's great work *The Outline of History*, first published in London in 1920. *The Outline* became a worldwide bestseller, and remained so well until the 1960s. There is no doubt that Wells's fulsome praise of Ashoka had a powerful impact on the consciousness of world readers.[19]

The Ashokan edicts and their message

The Ashokan edicts can be classified into three separate groups.[20] Firstly, there are the fourteen major rock edicts, in a single corpus or in a partial form, inscribed on rock in *Prakrit* in *Brahmi* script. These are found at sites as varied as Kalsi (Himachal Pradesh), Girnar (Gujarat), Sopara (Maharashtra), Yerragudi (Andhra Pradesh) and Jaugada and Dhauli (Orissa). At the last two sites there are also inscribed two separate edicts, known as the *Kalinga* Edicts, which may be considered as part of the major rock edicts. At two further sites in Pakistan, Shahbazgarhi and Manserah, on the upper Indus, the fourteen edicts are inscribed in another script, known as *Kharoshthi*, derived from the Persian Aramaic. Major rock edicts have also been recently found at a place called Sannathi, in Karnataka, and Kandahar in Afghanistan. Secondly, three minor rock edicts have been found at nearly twenty different places in the sub-continent, covering areas such as the Deccan, the Ganga valley, the lands east of the Yamuna river, and in Afghanistan. A minor rock edict, recently discovered at Kandahar, was inscribed in two scripts, Greek and Aramaic. Thirdly, there are seven pillar edicts in *Prakrit*, again inscribed as a single corpus or in a partial form, in the *Brahmi* script. They can be seen today at Delhi, Allahabad, Buner in Pakistan, Amaravati on the east coast, and at three sites in Bihar: Lauriya-Araraj, Lauriya-Nandangarh and Rampurva. At Delhi there are two pillars, Delhi-Meerut and Delhi-Topra. They were originally brought down to Delhi from Meerut and Topra (both in Uttar Pradesh) by Sultan Firoz Shah Tughluq in the fourteenth century, and given a pride of place in his new mediaeval Delhi. Finally there are two minor pillar edicts, one at Lumbini in Nepal, which is known as the Rummindei Pillar Inscription, and another at *Kausambi*, called the Schism Edict. The geographical spread of the rock and pillar edicts clearly delineates the extent of the Mauryan Empire. The empire's influence spread as far west as Afghanistan but stopped short of penetrating the far south. Also, no rock or pillar edicts have been found in Punjab, Sind, the deserts of Rajasthan or the lands immediately south of the Vindhya hills in central India (see Map 6.1).

Distinguished scholars, from Prinsep onwards, have translated the edicts and pondered over what Ashoka meant to tell his people. A number of versions are available,[21] but here we shall highlight some particular subjects emphasised in them. Firstly, the rock and pillar edicts are a key to understanding the mindset of Ashoka after his conversion. One major rock edict gives us the context of the conversion by describing the trauma of the *Kalinga* war and Ashoka's agony and remorse. He is truly repentant at having caused enormous suffering to all classes of people that, he says, 'weighed heavily on [his] mind'.[22] Despite this weighty confession, it is interesting that this particular major edict was left out among the rock inscriptions found in modern Orissa. The two Kalinga rock edicts emphasise, instead, the king's desire for justice and fairness. The theme of justice is likewise taken up in other edicts. Prisoners, for example, need to be treated humanely.[23] Ashoka wanted his officers, known as *mahamattras* or *rajukas*, to oversee agricultural improvements in villages and promote law and order in the countryside.[24] He went on tours around the empire to monitor their work.[25] The edicts also emphasised the emperor's own sense of self-discipline. He refused to spare himself from the rigours of introspection and self-analysis. In one of the pillar edicts he said that the hardest thing for a human being was to recognise the evil that was within his or her own self; only when that was achieved could a genuine conversion to a humanist path begin; and he was aware that he needed to be strict with himself.[26] For him, the crowning glory lies in his dedication to the service of his people and their welfare. Another major rock edict mentions his effort at securing medical help,

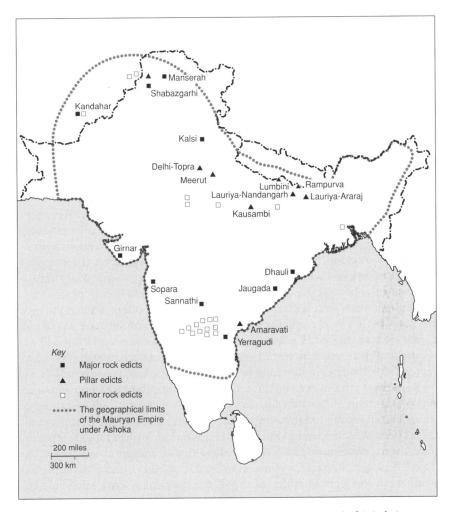

Map 6.1 The Mauryan Empire at its greatest extent and the spread of Ashoka's inscriptions.

from home and abroad, for sick humans and animals, building roads and wells, and planting trees, while a pillar edict mentions the building of rest houses for travellers.[27] Non-violent behaviour by humans towards other humans is emphasised again and again. This may be a result of extreme guilt over the slaughter of the *Kalinga* war; but it would be somewhat churlish to doubt his sincerity, merely because emperors normally do not develop such a consistent philosophy of non-violence. For Ashoka, non-violence extended to humans and animals alike. He exhorted all people to stop killing animals for wanton pleasure at festivals, and he laid down specific days at regular intervals when various classes of animals and fish could not be hunted at all. He had enough knowledge of animal welfare to realise that an animal must not be fed with the meat of other animals.[28] We also need to examine Ashoka's attitude towards religion in general and the religions of others. He appreciated that, on occasions of birth, marriage, illness or long journeys, people needed to perform religious ceremonies, however 'trivial and useless', for their own mental satisfaction; but 'if such ceremonies must be performed they have but small results'.[29] The *Dhamma* was of greater value than ritualistic religion. This did not imply that Ashoka was necessarily anti-Vedic; he desired that all sects might dwell harmoniously everywhere, for all seek self-control and purity of mind.[30] He exhorted his officers to be fair to all, both to the *brahman* priests of the majority Vedic society and to dissenters such as the Buddhists, Jains and Ajivakas.[31] He shows a profound sensitivity towards issues that arise in a multi-faith society when he urges his subjects to honour other sects and not to disparage other religious viewpoints; and 'if there is a cause for criticism [against someone's religious outlook] it should be done in a mild way.'[32] By talking the language of tolerance and understanding, Ashoka makes his *Dhamma* 'the common property of all religions'.[33] It is also the most appropriate way of binding together a vast and variegated society of the empire and providing it with a cultural and spiritual value-system.

Historians have wondered to what extent Ashoka promoted a royal Buddhist government. There is no doubt that, after his conversion, he took Buddhism extremely seriously, and his zeal for this faith increased as he grew old. He was the first king to embody an imperial ideal called *Chakravartin*, the 'wheel turner', which is largely Buddhist in inspiration. The *Chakravartin*, unlike the Vedic warrior king, was to be the promoter of peace and prosperity – leading to a new concept of irenical (peaceful) sovereignty that was later incorporated into Hindu kingship. He was a patron of Buddhist causes and promoted the founding of Buddhist shrines and cities (see Figure 6.1). He also supported the efforts of a renowned Buddhist monk, Moggaliputta Tissa, in summoning the Third Buddhist Council at *Pataliputra* in 250 BC and organising Buddhist missions to the Hellenistic kingdoms, Tibet, Nepal, the deep south of India and Ceylon. His own son, Mahinda (Mahendra), led the mission to Ceylon. Good public relations man that he undoubtedly was, Ashoka encouraged the model for propagating Buddhism by means of peaceful exchange of ideas. Having become a Buddhist, he naturally showed great interest in the pristine tradition that the Buddha himself had bequeathed. For several decades before and after his reign began, the Buddhists had been occupied in much infighting over the nature of their most important institution, the *sangha*; and Ashoka took the opportunity, in one of the minor rock edicts and in the Schism Edict at Allahabad, of proclaiming his belief in the unity of the *sangha* and issuing a threat of expulsion to those who created schisms. In the Rummindei Pillar Inscription, at Lumbini village in Nepal, the birthplace of the Buddha, he exempted the villagers from taxes and fixed their grain due at the liberal rate of one-eighth of their produce.

Figure 6.1 Ashoka's temple at Bodh Gaya (from E.B. Havell, *A Handbook of Indian Art*, London: John Murray, 1920, p. 62).

The Mauryan world

Agriculture

As in all periods in Indian history agriculture remained the central activity of the people in the Mauryan Empire (see Figure 6.2). The key unit in the agricultural landscape was the village, and it was the collective effort of people in each village that buttressed the village economy in the empire. It was in the fields around the village that the bulk of the production of crops and the rearing

Figure 6.2 Farmers worshipping a sacred tree in the Buddhist tradition (Pat Baker: line drawing adapted from a photo in Jeannine Auboyer, *Daily Life in Ancient India*, London: Weidenfeld & Nicolson, 1965, plate 12).

of livestock took place. The ultimate ownership of the land in the village, at the primary level and throughout the empire, depended upon its nature and quality. The state itself owned and controlled, as crown lands, extensive areas of terrain. Some of these were highly fertile and productive, but a great majority were fallow and wastelands. Fertile crown lands were leased to landlords on the payment of both rent and taxable produce, but only for the duration of their lifetime. Some of these landlords, described in Buddhist sources as *gahapati* or *gramabhojakas*, were both rich and powerful in their own right. They would then sub-lease the land to sharecroppers and tenants against paid rent. As regards the wastelands, the state at first organised the large-scale clearing of desolate areas and then usually settled *shudra* cultivators on those newly reclaimed lands. They would be initially exempt from tax, but once the land began to be cleared the tax was imposed. Slaves conquered in wars were also employed as hired labourers. Although the Greek historian Diodorus, echoing Megasthenes, affirmed that slavery did not exist in India,[34] the Indian sources themselves contradict him.[35] Although both the slaves and the *shudras* suffered from prejudice, discrimination and a lack of real freedom, their treatment, as employees of the state or of private landlords, was made more humane in the reign of Ashoka through the work of the *rajukas*, the state officials, who were charged with the task of maintaining harmony and equity in the countryside. The appropriate auditing of the crown lands was in the hands of the superintendent of agriculture who, in addition to holding seed stocks, hired contingents of labourers to private owners of land.[36] That all land in the country did not belong exclusively to the king is evidenced by the fact that there were many estates that were not crown lands. In his *Arthashastra*, Kautalya has numerous references to the idea of the purchase of land and to the kinsmen, relations and neighbours interested in the purchase; he also provides details of how purchases could be secured, including by auctioning; and he gives priority to kinsmen and creditors in the case of lands sold by private owners facing hardships.[37] The concept of private landed property was validated: not only were title, ownership and the purchase and sale of private land recognised as ratified in the eyes of law, but even its mortgage was legalised.[38] In whatever form the ownership of land existed, a range of rural taxes and dues made the Mauryan state a great beneficiary of agricultural production. Taxes included those levied on the area of land cultivated, or on the value of the yield. The assessment was regionally based, and it could range from one-sixth to a quarter of the produce of the land. The arable quality of the land was normally taken into consideration in any assessment. A tax, known as *pindakara*, could also be gathered as a collective sum from an entire village. Shepherds and livestock breeders were taxed depending on the number and produce of the animals. In addition there was a labour tax, which could be provision of labour in lieu of a tax. Sometimes, craftsmen had to provide a stipulated amount of free time to the state. Then there was a charge for the supply of irrigation water by the state to private owners, by means of reservoirs, tanks, canals and dams.[39] Agriculture evidentially enriched the rulers of the empire, but to what extent the ordinary people benefited is uncertain. It may be averred that, while famines, diseases and the lack of advanced medicine and technology would have taken a big toll of the relatively small Mauryan population of 100 million or so,[40] the rural population were probably better fed than during the British rule in India, a period of enormous famines.

Urban life

Cities and urban centres had once been the pride of the Harappan Civilisation, but during the Vedic era, when the Gangetic basin was being opened up, there was only a crude conception of urbanism. In Chapter 5 we observed that, during the three centuries of the pre-Mauryan period, a number of settlements grew and expanded, which we may refer to as towns, but it was really during the Mauryan period that some of these towns developed into cities. From this period onwards we have a clearer idea of the distinctions between the settlements as identified by their sizes. The *grama*, or the village, was, then as now, the most numerous class of settlement, but in size and importance it was being superseded by the town, or the *nigama*, which was a settlement between a village and a city in size but with a specific function, as an administrative or market centre. At the top of the settlement hierarchy was the *nagara*, the city. Cities could be classified into the *mahanagara*, or great city; the *rajadhaniya nagara*, or shortened to *rajdhani*, generally the capital city; and the *sakha nagaraka*, or the branch city.[41] Nearly twenty urban centres which can be credited as *nigama* or *nagara* have been identified. The Mauryan metropolis, *Pataliputra*, covering an area of 2500 hectares, or about 12 square miles, was then the largest city in South Asia. All other urban centres were less than 240 hectares in size, and they included such places as Rajgir, *Kausambi*, *Ahicchatra* and *Sravasti* in the Ganga valley, Vidisa and Ujjain in the centre, Sisupalgarh and Jaugada in Orissa, Taxila and Pushkalavati in Gandhara, Kondapur in Maharashtra, Broacha and Girnar in Gujarat, Sannathi and Maski in Karnataka, and Kandahar in Afghanistan. These cities were political, commercial or monastic centres, all fortified by walls, ditches and ramparts.[42]

The theoretical ground plan of an ideal city described in Kautalya's *Arthashastra* and the description of *Pataliputra* by Megasthenes are a testimony to the vigour of urban life. The ground model in the *Arthashastra* suggests that a typical Mauryan city was built on a grid plan.[43] Along each side of the surrounding wall would be three gates, with the middle one carrying the central entry. The four middle gates would be known by the names of Brahma, Indra, Senapati and Yama. The entire city was divided into sixteen blocks, with central areas taken up by the royal palace and the quarters for the royal functionaries. The *brahman* castes occupied two middle blocks to the north of the palace; the *kshatriya* bureaucrats and officers took up three blocks to the east; the *vaishya* traders and their various guilds were spread out in six blocks, south of the palace; while the *shudras* and other manual workers were confined to three blocks in the west. All crematoria, sanctuaries and quarters for extreme heretics were outside the city moat. The Mauryan city was a hive of activity and industry for craftsmen and traders, who were all organised within guilds and had allotted portions within towns and cities from which to operate. The products were sold not only locally, but regionally and nationally, as well as abroad. A network of trade routes criss-crossed the sub-continent, covering the hinterland centres of trade as well as ports such as Broach in Gujarat or *Tamralipti* on the Bay of Bengal. Coins of varied values, of both copper and punch-marked silver, have been found, and provide clues to internal and external trade.[44] A number of foreign artisans, such as the Persians or even the Greeks, worked alongside the local craftsmen, and some of their skills were copied with avidity. It is difficult for us, after such a long interval, to visualise a Mauryan city, but limited archaeological research testifies to its relatively large size and permanence. Unlike in the Indus cities, however, we cannot be sure what sort of hygiene and sanitation prevailed in the Mauryan city. Very likely these were of a poor standard, with public refuse and disease prevalent. We know that during the post-Mauryan era, when Indian external trade by land and by sea expanded enormously, India exported not only its valuable commodities, which were in great demand everywhere, but also the unwanted dreaded epidemics of plague, tuberculosis, cholera and leprosy.[45]

Administration

The Mauryan administration has been studied in great depth by a large number of scholars; and much has been written about it. As mentioned earlier, Megasthenes himself has left us an account of the administration of *Pataliputra*, the capital; much can be gleaned from the *Arthashastra*; and the Ashokan edicts give us further clues. Here we shall highlight three particular aspects: the degree of administrative control exercised over a vast territory, the hierarchy of control, and the functions of administration. The cultural and economic diversity of the varied areas of the empire meant that a completely uniform degree of control throughout was impossible to operate. Instead, one should treat the empire as consisting of three zones of culture and economy.[46] The first was the heartland, i.e. the state of *Magadha* and the Gangetic plain. Here there had been a long tradition, going back many centuries, of a tight political authority being exercised, almost in the way its concept is described in the *Arthashastra*. This was the zone where power ultimately resided in the royal palace at *Pataliputra*; interestingly, a large number of Ashokan pillars are also found in this zone. The second zone consisted of the conquered areas, such as *Gandhara* in the northwest, Karnataka, *Kalinga* or Saurashtra. These were areas of great potentiality in terms of trade, revenue and strategy, but 'as areas brought into the ambit of the Mauryan system they experienced state formation at second remove.'[47] These were also the places where numerous Ashokan rock edicts are found. As conquered areas, they carried the risk to the Mauryan governors of being volatile regions. A gentler and more sensitive style of governance was therefore needed in this second zone. The third zone consisted of isolated, buffer areas, where lived nomads, forest people or hill tribesmen. From their lands came valuable resources, such as elephants, timber and precious stones. Inside this third zone it was important for the agents of the empire to create conditions in which a plentiful labour supply was able to exploit and marshal the natural resources for the economic benefit of the empire. The Mauryan state attempted to secure maximum compliance and subservience from the people of all three zones, but the means employed naturally varied. The principles of both direct and indirect rule were attempted.

The empire was divided into a number of provinces, which were sub-divided into districts. A prince or a member of the royal family ruled over a province and a hierarchy of officers controlled the bureaucracy. This stratification must have been extremely elaborate and finely graded, and one can see in it the antecedents of the hierarchy at the court of the great Mogul or the British viceroy. Those occupying the top echelons of power and privilege were far removed from those at the lower grades. It has been estimated that the ratio of the clerk's salary to that of the chief minister or of the humble soldier to the commander was approximately 1 : 96.[48] With such a high level of remuneration, it is quite likely that the highest officials of the administrative service would have been required to meticulously oversee a large number of civil and economic tasks and a variety of public works mentioned in contemporary sources. Two of the topmost officers were the treasurer and the collector. The former kept complete accounts for the whole empire, while the latter made the arrangements for the collection of taxes. It was its ability to garner revenues from all classes of people that particularly marks out the special quality of the Mauryan government. The Mauryan taxation bureau scrupulously exacted every *pana* (silver coin of that period) and every *masaka* and *kakini* (copper coins) owed to it, in revenue, from town and country. If the punishments for misdeeds and corruption, as described in the *Arthashastra*, are any indication, it was most unlikely that the Mauryan state could be defrauded by the people or its officials. That is in striking contrast to the taxation regimes prevalent today in South Asian countries.

The large-scale collection of taxes leads us to ask: Where did the revenue go? Most of it must have been spent on maintaining the royal family and replenishing its treasury, the military establishment and administrative services. The Mauryans encouraged a mixed world of state enterprise and private capitalism that was highly regulated; and their desire to control the 'commanding heights of the economy' meant incurring great expense in the staffing of a bloated civil service. What is significantly missing, however, is the notion of public finances being systematically expended on supporting public services, such as health, education, social security or pensions. The notion of the state undertaking such responsibilities is, however, a relatively recent one, arising out of a more varied and enlightened understanding of a government's functions. The Mauryan government would have neither understood nor accepted the public finance implications of the humanistic duties of a government.

Architecture and sculpture

For at least a thousand years after 1700 BC, during most of the Vedic period, there is little evidence of architectural creativity in India. Of course, large wooden palaces, halls and barns must have been constructed, but we cannot really tell how durable they were. From 600 BC, however, with the growth of towns once again, there is a certain change; but it is from the Mauryan period particularly that we first get evidence of the large-scale use of hewn stone as a building material.[49] There is a lively debate among scholars as to whether the beginnings of stone architecture and sculpture in India from 300 BC onwards should be associated with the contacts of the Indians with the Persians from the Achaemenid Empire and the Greeks. Both these peoples had built impressive monuments of stone, such as the palace at Persepolis and the Parthenon on the acropolis of Athens; and both the Persians and the Greeks could be found working in various capacities in India at that time. There were skilled craftsmen in stone who could have been mentors of the Indian workers. Another viewpoint challenges this 'Perso-Hellenistic ... post-Alexandrian' influence altogether and argues for an indigenous evolution of stone architecture from the tradition of wood architecture. Either viewpoint may be correct; the Indians could quite easily have observed and emulated the masonry skills of the foreigners, but what they finally produced was distinctly Indian in both reality and symbolism.[50] The first piece of evidence of both stonework and brickwork of the Mauryan craftsmen relates to secular urban architecture. Archaeologists have now been able to locate solid brick or stone defences and ramparts in such places as *Kausambi*, Taxila, Rajgir and Sisupalgarh. Megasthenes' description of *Pataliputra* and the ideal city plan projected in the *Arthashastra*, both referred to above, have helped archaeologists to identify particular types of ground plans and the layout of domestic houses at places such as Bhita and Taxila.[51] Much effort has also gone into excavating parts of the pillared hall at *Pataliputra*, although here the timber framework had perished. The elements of the urban architecture and planning that developed as a process from the pre-Mauryan to Mauryan times, and later elaborated in texts such as the *Shilpashastras*, persisted for many centuries and gave the cities of India a particular distinctiveness.[52] The Mauryan architects and builders were also the pioneers of a particular strand of religious architecture which was to dominate the Indian landscape for some seven or eight centuries. This was the Buddhist religious architecture, and two of its forms have their roots in the Mauryan period. One was the stupa, a massively built dome, housing the relics of the Buddha and Buddhist preachers, and standing on a square or circular base, with a flattened top and a kiosk. The earliest part of the Stupa I of Sanchi dates from the Mauryan times[53] (see Figure 6.3). The second type of structure was the cave form, hollowed out from the living rock, later developing into what is called a *chaitya* hall (see Figure 6.4). The Buddhist monks used the *chaitya* as their place of retreat, and

Figure 6.3 Stupa of Sanchi (Pat Baker: line drawing adapted from a photo in Philip Rawson, *Indian Asia*, London: Elsevier-Phaidon, 1977, p. 77).

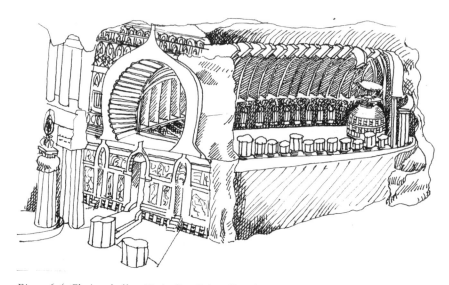

Figure 6.4 Chaitya hall at Karle (Pat Baker: line drawing adapted from Edith Tomory, *A History of Fine Arts in India and the West*, Hyderabad: Orient Longman, 1982, p. 61, and Gordon Johnson, *Cultural Atlas of India*, New York: Facts on File, 1996, p. 77).

the best of the Mauryan caves are Lomas Rishi (see Figure 6.5) and Sudama in the Barabar Hills.[54]

Mauryan art was essentially the art of the sculpture.[55] The Ashokan pillars are beautifully polished monolithic shafts, made from sandstone quarried at Chunar, in Benares, without footings and with carved capitals in the form of lotus flowers with inverted petals, with an animal or animals mounted. The capitals are decorated in relief. The bull capital of Rampurava and the lion capital of Sarnath are the best examples of the animal figured pillars. Another animal sculpture of the Mauryan period, of equal renown, is popularly called the Dhauli Elephant. With its slightly raised right leg and flowing trunk, this massive elephant, carved *in situ* from the living rock at Dhauli in Orissa, is one of the most impressive sculptures in animal studies anywhere in the world. Another achievement of Mauryan sculpture consists of a number of statues of *Yaksha* and *Yakshini*, which are male and female divine spirits. Among them the most polished and sophisticated statue is the *Didarganj Yakshini*, whose beautifully rounded figure with sensuous curves might be called the precursor of the later more famous Mathura *yakshinis*.

The decline of the empire: some causes

A number of causes of Mauryan decline have been identified by historians, but it is difficult to place them in order of importance. One set of issues has to do

SUDĀMA CAVE (LONGITUDINAL SECTION)

Figure 6.5 Lomas Rishi entrance (from Havell, op. cit., p. 24).

with the size of the empire at a time when the means of communication were poor. The outlying areas always had a temptation to pull away from the centre, and there is some evidence of the reassertion of regionalism under the fairly autonomous governors and princes within the empire. This pulling-away process would intensify in areas where the people felt oppressed by the system.

The Mauryan bureaucracy failed to establish long lasting popular institutions through which the local people could participate in their own governance. The state used espionage much too frequently for a true bond of trust to develop among the people. One may rightly suspect that the officers appointed by Ashoka to promote harmony in the countryside were not above using spies to collect information. The large-scale economy of the empire also concealed an underlying stress of raising enormous revenues through a near penal form of taxation. On the other hand, feelings for autonomy grew in some of the conquered areas where substantial development had taken place, such as the provinces of *Kalinga* or *Avanti*. Historians have also suggested that the overtly Buddhist pieties of Ashoka had made a large mass of people subscribing to the Brahmanic traditions antipathetic to the empire, thereby weakening the internal cohesion of the state. This point has been challenged on the grounds that Ashoka dealt fairly towards all in his kingdom. There may be something in another view that holds that Ashoka's non-militarism undermined the strength of the army, leading to disaffection within the ranks. The last Mauryan emperor was stabbed to death by his own commander-in-chief at a military parade: he had been weak and indecisive. All Ashoka's successors lacked force and character, a fact that would certainly have contributed to the decline of the empire. That decline was accelerated by both external and internal threats.

SELECT EXTRACTS FOR REVIEW AND REFLECTION

Extract 6.1 The question of dating and authorship of the *Arthashastra*

There has been much controversy, among scholars, about the dating of the *Arthashastra*. Several believe that the present text is from a later period and that it may also have been written by more than one person. This is an understandable argument, because in ancient India there was quite often multiple authorship of the texts; also, the texts were refined and embellished long after the core sections had been written by the original author. This work would be undertaken with great love and respect for the memory of that original author, and could have happened in the case of the *Arthashastra* too. Indeed, in the very first sentence of Chapter 1 in Book I, we are told that the *Arthashastra* is made as a compendium of almost all the *Arthashastras*, 'which, in view of acquisition and maintenance of the earth, have been composed by ancient teachers'. Kautalya, therefore, modestly eschews the claim of complete originality. At the same time, every chapter and book in the text ends with the phrase 'Thus ends Chapter X from Book Y of the *Arthashastra* of Kautalya'. When the overall message, rather than the technical language, of the text of the *Arthashastra* is closely examined, it is indeed very striking that it greatly confirms the picture of the early Mauryan world and society that is corroborated from other Indian and foreign sources. On the other hand, the name of Chandragupta Maurya is not once mentioned – which, of course, leads to an understandable uncertainty among historians as to whether the *Arthashastra* describes the Mauryan, the pre-Mauryan or the post-Mauryan society.

The translation of the *Kautalya-Arthasastra*, by Dr Shamasastry, is a well-established standard work, published by the Wesleyan Mission Press, Mysore, 1923.

Extract 6.2　European ignorance of non-European geography

The lack of proper geographical knowledge about distant places did not necessarily make the European travellers and observers humble. They sometimes wrote to stimulate the imagination of their compatriots. Thus Megasthenes claimed that there were gold-digging ants in India, that India never suffered famines, that there was a river there on which nothing could float, that winged snakes dropped their urine from above, and that there were men who had no mouths.

We must forgive Megasthenes for these errors because, even after a millennium and more, European writers of the late mediaeval and the early modern world were propagating similar types of nonsensical images of the non-European world. The English satirist Jonathan Swift correctly described the way the mapmakers of the sixteenth and seventeenth centuries solved the problem caused by the lack of hard facts about Africa in the following lines:

Geographers in Afric-Maps
With Savage Pictures fill their Gaps,
And o'er inhabitable Downs
Place Elephants for want of Towns

Source: Jan Nederveen Pieterse, *White on Black: Images of Africa and Blacks in Western Popular Culture*, New Haven, CT: Yale University Press, 1992, p. 18.

Extract 6.3　The early history of writing in the Indian sub-continent

Most literature in ancient India was transmitted orally. Leaving aside the Harappan script, which remains undeciphered and therefore unintelligible, the first written documents of India were the Ashokan edicts of the third century BC. They were carved on rocks and pillars in two principal scripts: *Kharoshthi* and *Brahmi*. By the third century BC *Brahmi* had become the dominant script, which means that its earliest development must be traced back at least 500 years, to the eighth century BC. It is from *Brahmi* that the scripts for the varied languages of both the Indo-Aryan family and the Dravidian family of languages came to be developed.

A useful book to read in this connection is by Steven Roger Fischer, *A History of Writing*, London: Reaktion Books, 2005, pp. 105–20.

RELEVANT QUESTIONS FOR DISCUSSION

1   In what ways is the *Arthashastra* a useful manual of political economy of ancient India?
2   Why did Ashoka inscribe his edicts on rocks and pillars but not in manuscripts? When did writing in manuscripts and books begin in India?
3   In what ways did Ashoka leave an iconic legacy for India?

Notes

1   Rawson 1977: 31–50.
2   Allen 2002: 71.
3   Drekmeier 1962: 166.
4   Raychaudhuri 1996: 262.
5   The version used for this chapter is that by Shamasastry himself, published at Mysore in 1923.
6   Shamasastry 1923: Bk 3, Ch. 20.
7   Ibid.: Bk 7, Chs. 1–3, 7.
8   Ibid.: Bk 1, Chs. 11–12; Bk 13, Ch. 3.
9   Dhar 1957: 10–12; Drekmeier 1962: 204–8.
10   Shamasastry 1923: Bk 1, Chs. 7 and 19.
11   Brown 1973: 142.
12   Ibid.: 44–5.
13   For a critique of Megasthenes' sevenfold division, see Thapar 2002: 190–92.
14   For a comparison with the recent archaeological results, consult Allchin 1995: 200–04.
15   Raychaudhuri 1996: 242–6.
16   Ibid.: 246–60.
17   Smith 1958: 110.
18   ODNB 2004, Vol. 59, 570–72; Allen 2002: 140–99.
19   'Amidst the tens of thousands of names of monarchs that crowd the columns of history, the name of Asoka shines, and shines almost alone, a star … more living men cherish his memory today than have ever heard the names of Constantine or Charlemagne': Wells 1920: Vol. 1, 212.
20   Thapar 1998: 250–66.
21   For example, translations by Thapar 1998: 250–66; Mookerji 1928: 107–207; Bhandarkar 1925: 273–337. Thapar's version is used here.

22 Thapar 1998: major rock edict 13.
23 Ibid.: pillar edict 4.
24 Ibid.: major rock edicts 3, 5 and 12; pillar edict 4.
25 Ibid.: major rock edict 8.
26 Ibid.: pillar edict 3.
27 Ibid.: major rock edict 2.
28 Ibid.: pillar edict 5 – a simple piece of safety regulation that was disregarded by commercial farming interests in Britain at the end of the twentieth century, causing much suffering to victims of BSE illness.
29 Ibid.: major rock edict 9.
30 Ibid.: major rock edict 12.
31 Ibid.: pillar edict 7.
32 Advice that we, in the twenty-first century's turmoil, need to take seriously – Dhammika: major rock edict 12.
33 Bhandarkar 1925: 107.
34 Ray *et al.* 2000: 265–6.
35 Thapar 2002: 186.
36 Shamasastry 1923: Bk 2, Ch. 24.
37 Ibid.: Bk 3, Chs. 5, 6, 7, 9, 10, 16.
38 Saletore 1973: 466–9.
39 Thapar 2002: 187.
40 Lal 1988: 33.
41 Like a 'satellite town'.
42 For a clear understanding of the urban structures in Mauryan times, see Allchin 1995: 194–209.
43 Shamasastry 1923: Bk 2, Chs. 3 and 4; Allchin 1995: 227–8.
44 Allchin 1995: 218–21.
45 Ponting 1991: 228.
46 Thapar 2002: 194–200.
47 Ibid.: 196.
48 Ibid.: 195.
49 Allchin 1995: 238–9.
50 Craven 1997: 41–2; Daheja 1997: 44–5; Smith 1958: 133–4; Allchin 1995: 238–9; Rowland 1977: 67–70.
51 Allchin 1995: 231–7.
52 Ibid.: 229–31.
53 Tomory 1989: 23.
54 Ibid.: 26–8; Rowland 1977: 63–5.
55 Tomory 1989: 165–8.

7   Diffusion and dynamism after the Mauryas

(Time-span: 185 BC to AD 320)

With the fall of the Mauryan Empire came the loss of a pan-Indian authority exercised from *Pataliputra* in *Magadha*. There now arose a number of competing power centres in different regions of India (see Map 7.1). The imperial monarchy was replaced by regional monarchies, and a centralised bureaucracy by regional bureaucracies. These changes had little effect on the continuing hold of the idea of absolutist kingship. Numerous royal eulogies, called *prasastis*, from the various regions, endowed the respective monarchs with superhuman qualities. Many regional monarchs had Central Asian origins, but they too in time conformed to the notions of kingship that had been maturing since late Vedic times and which reached their apogee in the Mauryan period. All monarchies, whether of foreign or indigenous origins, subscribed to the Brahmanic notions of caste and the fourfold *varna* system, although Buddhism provided a relatively easier route for foreigners to become adjusted to the Indian social system. The political diffusion in the post-Mauryan period and the emergence of monarchies with foreign roots, described by one historian as 'chaotic darkness',[1] might be seen as signs of regression from the heyday of Mauryan imperialism; but, in reality, both the economy and the culture showed dynamism.

One of the reasons why historians find the post-Mauryan era so absorbing is the huge scale of available evidence for research. The domestic literary evidence can be drawn from the royal inscriptions, the *shastras*, the secular literature, Buddhist religious and secular texts, and the fascinating Tamil anthologies from the south. Foreign literary sources, from China, Syria, Greece, Persia and Egypt, give credence to the political and commercial setting of this period. The clear numismatic evidence available to historians also facilitates the construction of relative chronologies. With sufficient archaeological corroboration, we can be confident that, from about 200 BC onwards, the study of Indian history takes on a definitiveness that for earlier periods often eludes us. In terms of sources, this is like a transition from the proto-historical to the historical.

New dynasties and new centres of power

The political landscape after the Mauryan collapse in 185 BC remained confused for about 200 years until the beginning of the Christian era, with a host of

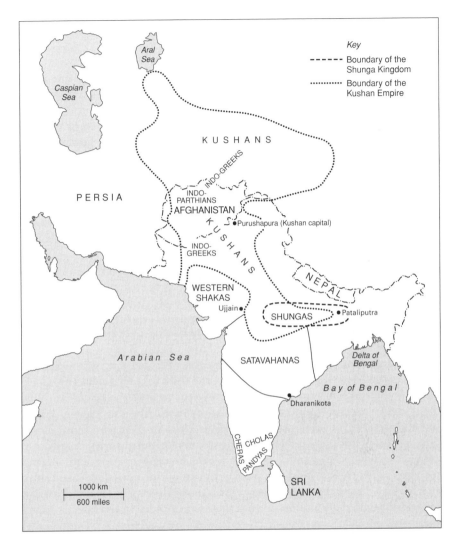

Map 7.1 Post-Mauryan kingdoms.

dynasties jostling for power. These dynasties were either native Indian or ethnically mixed, such as Indo-Greek or Indo-Scythian. During the first three centuries of the first millennium AD most of India, except for the far south, was dominated by three systems of authority: the Central Asian Kushan, the Deccan Satavahana and a branch of another Central Asian group, known as Western Shakas. Our main interest in the southern region concerns mostly the elaborate trading connections it had with different parts of the world and with the flowering of Tamil literature.

The Gangetic heartland: Shungas, Kharavela

The Shunga dynasty founded by Pushyamitra, the renegade army commander of the last Maurya, controlled the central Magadhan region for 112 years, until 73 BC. The Shungas were continually at war with their neighbours as well as more distant enemies. Their most dangerous internal enemy was Kharavela of *Kalinga*, whose deeds and activities can be studied from a classic early royal eulogy, the famous Hathigumpha inscription in an Orissan cave.[2] We learn from this inscription that Kharavela was more than a mere soldier: he was also a patron of the Jain religion. After his death in 172 BC *Kalinga*'s power waned, giving breathing space to the Shungas. Externally, however, the Shungas faced an ever-present danger from the Indo-Greek and Indo-Scythian kings and warlords of north Afghanistan and northwest India. Pushyamitra and his successors just about kept them in check, although many Mauryan-held lands were lost. Despite the distractions of warfare, the Shungas provided valuable patronage to both Buddhism and Brahmanism and also helped to create a minor architectural renaissance, which we shall touch upon later.

The northwest: Indo-Greeks, Pahlavas, Shakas

During the last two centuries before Christ much of the northwest was attacked and occupied by forces from across the border in Bactria, the part of Afghanistan that lies between the River Oxus and the Hindu Kush. Bactria, as part of the Persian conquests of Alexander the Great, had become part of the Selucid kingdom run from Syria. In the middle of the third century BC Bactria, along with another Persian province, Parthia, revolted against the Seleucids. Normally the Greek governors of Bactria were appointed by the Seleucid kings, but after their revolt they called themselves kings in their own right. These Graeco-Bactrian kings clashed with the Mauryans during their forays into northwest India. They became bolder after the Mauryan collapse and, under a monarch called Demetrius, occupied a large part of the Indus delta, Saurashtra and Kutch.[3] The Shungas were powerless against them. The Graeco-Bactrian kings belonged to various lineages, but those who invaded India and established their tiny kingdoms in parts of its northwest, particularly in *Gandhara* and Punjab, are specifically known as Indo-Greek rulers. All Greeks in India were, however, known as *Yavanas*; and the upper elite of Indians, the *brahmans*, generally held an unfavourable view of them.[4] On the other hand, those tiny territories of the Indo-Greek kings must have been lively and commercially flourishing places. A vast hoard of coins, with a mixture of Greek profiles and Indian symbols, along with interesting sculptures and some monumental remains from Taxila, Sirkap and Sirsukh, point to a rich fusion of Indian and Hellenistic influences.[5]

Both the Bactrian Greek and the Indo-Greek monarchs faced attacks, during the first century BC, from the Parthians and the Scythians. After seceding from the Seleucid kingdom, around the same time as Bactria's revolt, the Persian province of Parthia, which lay to the southeast of the Caspian Sea, went on to become the second great Persian empire (after the Achaemenid), and the power of Parthia spread east as far as the Punjab and even beyond.[6] The Indians called the Parthians Pahlavas. The Parthians themselves faced an onslaught of a Central Asian group, the Shakas (or Scythians). The latter had been facing a squeeze in their homeland near the Aral Sea from a nomadic group called Yueh-chi and had managed to escape towards eastern Iran. Eventually the Parthians tamed the Shakas and, under their leadership, directed them further east. Thus, in the first century BC, after overrunning Bactria, the Shakas moved into India too and took *Gandhara* and Punjab. A little later they penetrated the areas around Mathura, the Yamuna valley, the upper Deccan, Saurashtra and Ujjain in Malwa. In Indian history, the Shaka rulers are known as Shaka-Pahlava, meaning a mixed group of tribal Shakas and the Parthians. Effective Shaka suzerainty in India came to be exercised eventually by two authorities, respectively known as the Northern Shakas of Taxila and Mathura and the Western Shakas of Malwa and Kathiawar.[7]

From the Aral Sea to Kashi: the trans-Asiatic empire of the Kushans

Having avoided the Yueh-chi once, the Shakas came under pressure from a further Yueh-chi wave. This was because, during one of their regular bouts of nomadic warfare, the Yueh-chi in turn had suffered a defeat by a rival tribe, the Hiung-nu,[8] and been forced to move west towards Bactria around 130 BC. After overcoming the Shakas and settling down in Bactria, the Yueh-chi gradually evolved from their nomadic roots into a sedentary people.[9] They were established in five different groups, one of them being the Kuei-shuang, or Kushans.[10] Around the beginning of the Christian era the Kushans subdued the other four and assumed overall control of most of Afghanistan and eastern Iran, under their leader Kujula Kadphises. His son, Wima Kadphises, entered north India in the middle of the first century AD. All Punjab, Kashmir and the plain of the Ganges up to *Kashi* came to be Kushan-controlled. The whole of the empire, from the River Oxus to *Kashi*, was consolidated by Kanishka, who succeeded Wima.[11] There is uncertainty as to when this exactly happened and whether there was more than one Kanishka.[12] We do, however, know that he fought a number of battles, with mixed results, in order to keep his empire secure in his grasp. The Kushans maintained a powerful dominion over north India until at least AD 250; and their trans-Asian empire became one of the great conduits for India's international trade.

Kanishka, however, was more than a soldier and conventional emperor. Although personally 'cruel and temperamental',[13] he provided the framework of a firm and fair rule of law based on Buddhist precepts. He was also a great compromiser and synthesiser of different ideas. In his empire many religious traditions flourished: Persian Zoroastrian, Greek and Roman paganism, Buddhism, Chinese Confucianism, Jainism and, above all, a whole range of Vedic traditions. His coins bear their proof, because they carry images of deities from the various religions practised in his kingdom. In keeping with the broad Indian political conventions, Kanishka allowed space to differing ideas. Buddhists, however, consider Kanishka as second in importance only to Ashoka Maurya, because under his rule Buddhism had flourished as never before.[14] At the Kushana capital in *Purushapura* he built an enormous stupa, nearly 700 feet high and 300 feet in diameter, for Buddhist pilgrims and travellers crossing the empire.[15]

Under Kanishka's successors the Kushan hold over India lessened. They lost all real authority in Afghanistan, eastern Persia and Central Asia when the new powerful Sasanian dynasty, under Ardashir, seized power in Persia from the Parthians in AD 226. From then on the Kushans became the minor vassals of the new Persian Empire. In India too their authority increasingly came to be challenged by the Western Shakas and by other minor independent principalities. By the end of the third century AD a variety of tribal republics and monarchical states were reasserting themselves.

The Satavahanas of the Deccan: their prosperity and piety

The history of the lands of northern Andhra Pradesh, northern Karnataka and Maharashtra is very much a part of the history of the Deccan, which, together with the areas of the far south, makes up the great southern half of India. There arose in two particular regions of the Deccan – in northwestern Maharashtra and the Andhra region between the rivers Godavari and Krishna – a great dynasty called Satavahana (sometimes known as the Andhra dynasty). These regions had been part of the Mauryan Empire, so the dynasty arose either in the very last years of the empire or shortly after its fall.[16] The most famous of their early kings was Satakarni,[17] who ruled between about 37 and 27 BC. He is well known in history for his successful campaigns against *Kalinga* and Malwa. He gained Sanchi, the site of the great stupa, and an inscription from there refers to him as Rajan Shri Satakarni.[18] His conquest of the Godavari valley and the southern regions gained him further power and status. After his reign the Satavahana suffered a major defeat at the hands of the Western Shakas and lost their hold on Maharashtra. As the Shaka satrapies denied the Satavahana access to the western Deccan, the latter were thus forced to concentrate their energies on the eastern Deccan. This situation lasted for about a century, but eventually the Satavahanas turned the tables on the Shakas and reconquered their lost territories. Many Shaka coins found in places such as Nasik in western Maharashtra have their original Shaka images overstruck with those of the returning Satavahana monarchs.[19] Satavahana power reached its zenith during the second century AD, in the reigns of Gautamiputra (113–38) and Pulumayi II Vasisthiputra (138–70). By the time the kingdom perished in AD 236 it had been in power for more than 300 years.

The basis of Satavahana prosperity lay in agriculture and trade. The Satavahana kings were some of the greatest donors of land and land revenue to communities of Buddhist monks, the *brahmans*, and to all who wished to engage fruitfully in agricultural pursuits.[20] Merchants and traders were equally encouraged to open up new trade routes from the hinterland towards the ports. This provided a further boost to the growth of urban centres in the Deccan as a whole, but particularly the Andhra region.[21] Part of the evidence for prosperity is to be noticed in the man-made cave sites of northwest Maharashtra, which were once the centres of Buddhist religious piety. The epigraphic inscriptions retrieved from some of the caves provide us with details of religious charities and endowments made not just by the prosperous merchants or local governing elites but also by a whole variety of people belonging to various crafts and professions. Buddhism was the inspiration behind the actions of these people. Dotted all over the Satavahana Deccan were the great Buddhist monasteries which had been established by pious endowments at the significant crossing points of trading routes.[22] Into these monasteries came people from all walks of life, for peace and meditation and spiritual care, and bequeathed some of their wealth as charity to support the further material needs of these institutions. The Andhra merchants were some of the greatest donors. It is in this context of prosperity and piety that we can best appreciate the glory that was the great stupa of Amaravati, which no longer exists. This monumental structure, built by an army of labourers, masons and craftsmen who lived in the great *entrepôt* city of Dharanikota on the River Krishna,[23] was a true symbol of Buddhist piety and mercantile prosperity.

Gujarat and Malwa: the Western Shakas

Of the two Shaka branches mentioned above, the Western Shakas assumed greater dominance. While the northern branch suffered a chequered history, the western one endured until the rise of the Guptas in the fourth century AD.[24] It was under their powerful king Rudradaman I (*c.* AD 130–50) that they tightened their grip on Gujarat, Malwa and Sind. Despite the overweening power of the Satavahanas, Rudradaman found ways to co-exist with the Deccan giant. His true fame lies in the fact that he has left behind, on a rock inscription at Junagadh, a *prasasti* containing a most exquisite account of himself and of his cultural achievements and acts of valour.[25] Unlike the Ashokan edicts, which use the *Prakrit* language, the Junagadh rock inscription is in Sanskrit, which could be interpreted as Rudradaman's way of showing respect to Brahmanic Vedic culture. It must have ensured his legitimacy as a ruler, despite his Central Asian Shaka origins. The monarchs who followed Rudradaman were people of lesser stature, but they nevertheless managed to maintain hold over their territories in central India with determination and tenacity until both the Kushans and the Satavahanas, their main rivals, had perished.

The international trade of India

The beginnings of India's international trade can be noticed as early as 2500 BC, when the Harappan Civilisation traded goods with Mesopotamia and the ports of the Persian Gulf. The Vedic Age is not noted for any large-scale external commercial contacts, but from 600 BC onwards, through a strong interaction with the Achaemenid Persians and the Graeco-Macedonians, a period of great expansion in international commercial as well as cultural links set in. The links became stronger during the Mauryan period, but the really significant developments of that period were the growth in production of goods and the setting up of a sound commercial infrastructure. The post-Mauryan era is particularly well known for the range and volume of international trade that was generated; and this trade, by both land and sea, added enormously to both urban and rural prosperity. Practically no part of India was left untouched by developments resulting from increased foreign trade. Whether one examines the contents of *The Periplus of the Erythrean Sea*, an ancient guidebook for mariners, or the works of Roman historians or the *Sangam* literature of south India, or studies the ground with archaeological skills, the subject of the international trading connections of India assumes utmost importance for our understanding of the period under review here.

The infrastructure

A vital aspect of the commercial infrastructure was the guild system. During the post-Mauryan centuries the guilds came to play a crucial role in the success of both domestic and international trade. Known in India as *shreni*, the guilds can be described as associations of professional people, merchants or artisans. They acted variously as trade unions, cooperative organisations, regulatory bodies or even banks. They existed in various crafts and trades; there were, for example, guilds of potters, goldsmiths, bead and glass makers, ivory carvers, musicians and carpenters. The rules of work, the quality control over finished goods, the fixing of prices, the recruitment of labour from a specific occupational caste for a particular trade – these were all overseen by each craft guild.[26] Rich merchants and many ruling dynasties invested in the guilds, making them viable and flourishing. The guilds, in turn, provided large donations to religious foundations and monasteries. The guilds of merchants, who were known as *shreshthins*, acted also as bankers, financiers and trustees. Large sums were loaned out, bearing interest rates of between 12 and 15 per cent, with higher rates carried for the sea trade.[27] Another aspect of the commercial infrastructure was the great increase in the minting of coins during the post-Mauryan centuries. For the numismatist, the best of the early coins of India were those struck by the Indo-Greek kings and the Kushan monarchy. Through the foreign influence of the Persians, the Greeks and the Romans, the quality of Indian coins greatly improved over the older punch-marked coins. Made from gold, silver, copper or tin, the variety of coins proved especially useful for variant trading economies in different regions; and the huge quantity of local and foreign coins also made it easier for merchants to engage in forward speculation in goods and capital.

The links by road and river between the various main cities and trading towns were an essential element in the general infrastructure facilitating the volume of trade as a whole[28] (see Map 7.2). Starting with the northwest, in the centre of the Kushan territories, was Taxila, a city where the merchants of Central and South Asia exchanged their goods and the intellectuals their ideas. Taxila was joined to *Pataliputra* by a major highway; en route was Mathura, which in turn was linked to Ujjain in the Malwa region, controlled by the Western Shakas. Mathura and Ujjain linked the western Ganga valley and the lands of central India. A number of market towns were also developed in the Satavahana kingdom of the Deccan. Centres such as Nasik and Karad in Maharashtra and Nagarjunakonda in the Andhra region were all important trading centres where the farmers, pastoralists and hunter-gatherers from the hinterland congregated to sell their commodities and wares. The routes linking these places sometimes had to follow the gaps and breaks in mountains or the river valleys. All the major routes led to the five main international ports of that period, namely *Barbaricum* in the Indus delta, *Barygaza* on the Gujarat coast, *Muziris* on the Kerala coast, Arikamedu on the Coromandel coast and *Tamralipti* in the Ganges delta. These ports handled the bulk of the sea trade of India with Arabia, the Levant, the Roman Empire and Southeast Asia.[29]

The overland trade route through the Kushan territories

Since at least 600 BC the main overland trade route had run from Taxila towards West Asia and the Hellenistic world.[30] Caravans from India carried ivory, elephants, spices, cloths, salt, musk, saffron and indigo; the returning caravans brought lapis lazuli, turquoise, fine quality ceramics, wines, and gold and silver coins. The first part of the overland route was from Taxila to Begram, from where two main routes branched out: the northern route via Bactria, the Oxus, the Caspian Sea and the Caucasus to the Black sea, and the southern route via Kandahar, Herat and Ecbatana to the ports of the eastern Mediterranean. Once the Kushans came to establish their trans-Oxus empire and controlled all territory between the Aral Sea and the middle Ganga valley, a new dimension was added to the overland trade route.[31] This came to be in the form of a link to the famous Silk Road that connected China with Europe by land.[32] The Silk Road began at Lo-yang in China, progressed through Chang'an and reached Dun-huang on the eastern edge of the Taklamakan desert. From there two routes branched, one north of the desert and the other south of it, both reaching Kashgar on the western edge of the Taklamakan. From Kashgar the Silk Road entered the Central Asian and Bactrian territories of the Kushans before proceeding through the Parthian Empire towards Syria, the Levant and eventually Constantinople. Through their Kushan connections, the merchants of India could now begin to share in the handling of the products that travelled along the Silk Road, particularly the silk from China. They first did this by taking expensive gifts to the Chinese emperors.[33] At the same time, during the first and second centuries AD, Buddhist missionaries were making progress in spreading the message of the Buddha among both the Central Asians and the

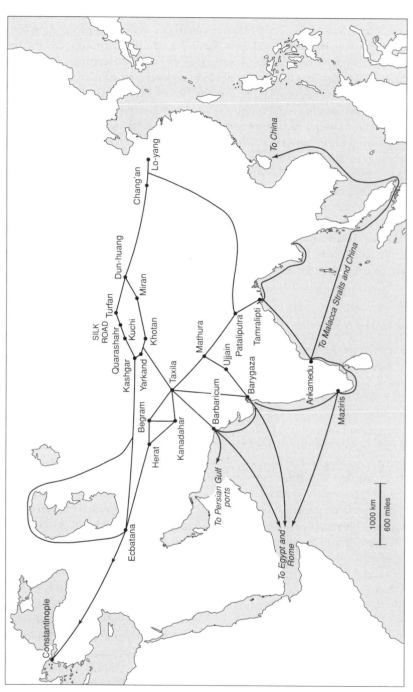

Map 7.2 Land and sea routes of ancient Indian international trade.

Chinese; and, during the period when the Kushans were dominant, Indian merchants and the Buddhist missionaries forged a powerful alliance of interests. At various junctions on both the northern and southern routes of the Silk Road, skirting the Taklamakan desert, at places such as Kashgar, Yarkand, Khotan, Miran, Kuchi, Qurashahr and Turfan, Indian merchants set up their colonies, while the missionaries established monasteries. As Buddhism spread into China, the demand for Buddhist artefacts from India underwent a manifold increase.[34] During this time the Chinese emperors were becoming concerned by the growing tensions between the Roman Empire and the Parthian Empire, resulting in Parthian impediments to the movement of goods through their territory.[35] They were therefore more than content to entrust Indian merchants with handling the silk destined for the Roman market, taking it via Taxila whence it would be dispatched southwards to the ports of *Barbaricum* and *Barygaza*, bypassing Parthian lands. Roman ships would then carry away the silk and leave behind their products such as coral, glass, silver and topaz. These, in turn, would also be handled by Indian merchants on their overland route to China. The strategic location of the Kushan state between India and China meant that the ruling nobility and the subsidiary elites were heavily involved in this trade; they too wished to partake of the share of luxury goods. However, they were not particularly interested in the handling of the trade itself; they left that to individual merchants and, probably, to the specific merchant guilds. Their benefits came in the form of imposts and levies that they charged on all movement of goods through their territory.

India and Rome

With the founding of the Roman Empire in 31 BC, India and Rome began a highly successful trading relationship that lasted for more than two centuries. The main reason was the increasing prosperity of the Roman populace and their insatiable demand for certain Indian products and those of China and Southeast Asia, which could be easily procured for them by Indian merchants. The annexation of Egypt by Rome in 31 BC was also a factor of great logistical importance, because Rome became the mistress of both the Mediterranean Sea and the Red Sea. The ports of the Red Sea, both on the Arabian and the Egyptian–Ethiopian shores, had had trading relations with India for many centuries, during the post-Alexandrine Hellenistic period and even earlier.[36] Relatively small Egyptian, Arab, Greek and Indian ships used to ply between those ports and the western Indian ones of *Barbaricum*, *Barygaza* and *Muziris*.[37] Until the first century AD foreign mariners, with perhaps the exception of the Arabs of Yemen and Hadhramaut, did not fully understand the behaviour of the Indian Ocean winds, which meant that destinations were reached after prolonged detours by ships closely hugging the Arabian and Indian coastlines. This changed after AD 45, when Hippalus, an Alexandrian, worked out the pattern of seasonal winds (the monsoon), thereby helping his fellow seamen to sail through the Arabian Sea during the right season and shortening their journey time. The trade links with south India were to be particularly strengthened by this development.

After 31 BC, the type of large vessels that used to carry Egyptian grain from Alexandria to Rome began to be built along the Red Sea ports, in order to be fitted out for trade voyages to India. They could be 180 feet in length and weigh 1,000 tons.[38] A large Roman ship, carrying from India compact and costly merchandise of silks, fine cottons, pepper, costus, nard and spikenard, and bringing to India products such as two-handled amphorae, fine ceramics, bronze vases and delicate glassware, represented a 'monumental investment'[39] by many traders. As the captains of such ships did not normally sail to the east coast ports of India, both import and export goods were loaded on to much smaller Indian ships that continually plied between the two coasts. At Arikamedu, for example, the foreign goods brought by these ships would be unloaded, and valuable spice cargoes from both India and the Indonesian spice islands, along with other Indian goods, would be loaded on to the same ships bound for *Muziris*. This was the legendary *entrepôt* trade of south India.[40] Generally speaking, the overall balance of trade between India and Rome was in the favour of India, and the Romans had to pay for the deficits in the form of bullion.[41] A large hoard of Roman coins found at Arikamedu and other places in South India, along with the archaeological remains of a Roman colony, testify to the vigour of the Indo-Roman trade. Owing to the absence of local gold coins in south India, the Roman gold and silver coins were also used as high-value currency, which would have encouraged hoarding. Only a quarter of the amount of good quality Roman coin hoards discovered in south India have been found in north India: the Kushan state issued its own gold coins, as valuable in metal terms as the Roman ones, and simply melted down the Roman coins for their metal.[42] Apart from coins, small hoards of other Roman goods, such as amphorae, bronze vessels and finer quality ceramics and potsherds, have been recovered from a variety of sites in western India, the Andhra region and the south. Much research is also directed at studying whether the excellent Red Polished Ware (RPW) pottery of western India[43] or the rouletted ware of southeastern India were imitations of Roman or Hellenistic potteries.[44] Another interesting piece of recent research concerns the role of the Indian venture capitalist in the financing of Indo-Roman trade. Until recently, it was widely assumed that the 'initiative of this long-distance sea-borne trade with west was taken by western traders, while the role of India, steeped in agriculture, was only that of the grower of some luxury and prestige commodities.'[45] This view needs to be revised in the light, firstly, of a recently discovered papyrus document detailing a loan contract between an Indian and a Roman[46] and, secondly, of the excavations in Egypt pointing to the presence there of Indian settlers and traders.[47]

New trends in Indian religions

A series of remarkable developments in the religious thinking of India took place during the post-Mauryan era. They affected both Buddhism and Vedic

Brahmanism. Within both systems particular strands of theism – belief in the existence of God with or without a belief in a special revelation – began to develop, with profound consequences for many millions of people in the sub-continent and beyond.

Mahayana *Buddhism*

Buddhism was not just the 'central public religion'[48] of India; during our period it was also assuming the status of a major world religion. A number of royal dynasties became the patrons and guardians of the religion, as can be witnessed from impressive monuments and inscriptions left behind. The monarchs of Central Asian origin were particularly attracted by its 'catholicity';[49] and the Kushan king Kanishka remains for the Buddhists even today the most cherished of monarchs, second only to Ashoka. It was the agency of the Kushan Empire that made possible the triangular commercial and cultural contacts between India, China and Central Asia and facilitated the movement of Buddhist ideas beyond the Pamirs and the Himalayas. Within India itself the religion was becoming attractive to different cults and sects. As a result of both domestic and foreign expansion and interactive encounters with beliefs inside and outside India new ideas were bound to emerge. Over many centuries the traditional Buddhist ideology had come to be crystallised into what was called the 'Three Jewels': first, the lessons to be learned from the life of the Buddha, the 'one who knows'; second, the *Dhamma*, the 'law of the cosmos ... the law of the mind, of the good life and of the spiritual path';[50] third, the austere and puritanical life in a *sangha*, the monastic community. Now, in a period of new social and historical realities, many Buddhist thinkers argued that the 'Three Jewels' approach was much too intellectual and restrictive for the masses to grasp. It was really a type of 'icy idealism',[51] quite unsuited to the needs of newer devotees subscribing to the Buddhist faith. While not repudiating the core values of the Three Jewels, they argued that the Buddha could come to life for the masses only when he was elevated to the status of a god. This deification of the Buddha and the doctrine of salvation by faith were at variance with the traditional teaching, because the Buddha had never claimed divine status. Further, he had left the endeavour of achieving bliss, or *nirvana*, to each individual through a rational understanding of his ideas and methods expounded in his Four Noble Truths and the Eightfold Path. The dissenters, however, argued that an individual needed the intercession of divine beings, the *Bodhisattvas*, who were born again and again on this earth because they were prepared to forego their own *nirvana* in order to help ordinary mortals help achieve theirs. The *Bodhisattvas* came to be arranged within the Buddhist pantheon of semi-divinities, which suggests that this new variant of Buddhism was attempting to become more attractive to local sects and cults by incorporating their gods and goddesses within the pantheon. It is also likely that another new idea, that of a saviour to come – the Buddha *Maitreya* – might have had its origins in the contacts between Buddhism and Zoroastrianism.

The latter is generally reckoned to be the first religion to develop the idea of a saviour messiah – known as *Saoshyant*.[52] The cluster of such new ideas provoked a split between the dissenters, who wanted a more inclusive and more faith-based Buddhism, to be known as *Mahayana* Buddhism, or the Great Vehicle, and the traditional elders, the *Theravadins*, who clung on to the pristine purity of ideas represented by the principle of the Three Jewels. A pejorative term, *Hinayana*, or the Lesser Vehicle, came in due course to be applied to the *Theravadin* school of thought. The final victory, ultimately, was that of the Mahayanists; their brand of Buddhism remained dominant in India until the twelfth century and, apart from Sri Lanka and Thailand, the vast majority of the Buddhist world today is *Mahayana*-oriented.

Historians of religion have argued that much of the new thinking, particularly in the *Mahayana* tradition, was really like 'old wine in new bottles', simply a reinterpretation of the traditional Buddhist viewpoints;[53] but we still need to recognise that there is a considerable literature in this period which points to dynamic and radical departures in Buddhist thinking. Some of the key *Mahayana* texts were formulated during the post-Mauryan centuries,[54] although we are uncertain about their exact dates. One particularly interesting text was the *Milindapanha*, the philosophical questions asked by the Indo-Greek king Menander to the Buddhist philosopher Nagasena. In some of his answers Nagasena laid great stress on the divinisation of the Buddha and the importance of relic worship. Another text, the *Buddhacharita*, a biography of the Buddha, composed by the renowned polymath Asvaghosha, also confirms the Mahayanist image of a divine Buddha. From an older and more traditional treatise, known as the *Mahavastu*, the Mahayanists adopted the particular styles of Buddha-worship, with copious use being made of such precious materials as gold, lapis lazuli, pearls, silver, silk, etc., as gifts for gaining merits and rewards from the Buddha. This attitude embodied 'the great influence of commerce-oriented lay worshippers on Buddhism'[55] and again demonstrated the importance of the overland trade between India and China. While the bulk of the *Theravadin* texts are in the *Pali* language, the key works of the *Mahayana* canon, made up of many different books used by different sects, were written in Sanskrit; they are known collectively as the *Vaipulyasutra*. The most important *Vaipulyasutra* is the *Saddharmapundarika* (The Lotus Sutra), a *Mahayana* text greatly revered in China and Japan. This text formulated the concept of the *Bodhisattvas* and provides elaborate details of how stupas should be designed and how the rituals of Buddha worship were to be conducted. Finally, there is the *Prajnaparamita*, a *Mahayana* philosophical text, which lists the various virtues necessary to attain the Buddha state.

Vaishnava and Shaiva traditions

The first manifestations of what we would now describe as popular Hinduism began to emerge during the post-Mauryan centuries. For more than a thousand years, until the sixth century BC, Vedic Brahmanism had been the principal religion of India. The main elements of this religion, as we have noted earlier, were the supremacy of the *Vedas*, the caste system, the sacrificial rituals for propitiating the powerful Vedic elemental gods such as Indra, Surya, Rudra, Varuna, Vayu, etc., and the monopolistic role of the *brahman* priests in the performance of all ceremonies. From the sixth century BC onwards Buddhism, Jainism and various heterodox forms of Shramanism launched a challenge to Vedic Brahmanism and gained a relatively large number of adherents. Buddhism particularly secured a powerful ascendancy during both the Mauryan and the post-Mauryan periods. However, during the post-Mauryan age, there came a certain backlash in favour of Vedic Brahmanism at some of the royal courts. What also took place was the beginning of a modified form of Vedic Brahmanism. Two very strongly theistic traditions blossomed at this time, which we call the *Vaishnava* and the *Shaiva*. They centred round three main concepts: that of a supreme deity in the form of Vishnu or Shiva; that of salvation being made possible through the supreme deity's grace; and that of attainment of that salvation by the means of intense love and devotion to the deity, the process known as *bhakti*. The two traditions did not break away from Vedic Brahmanism, but rejected some of the practices such as animal sacrifices. The *Vaishnava* form of worship at first focused on three older deities: Vasudeva, a tribal deity; Krishna, the deity of the Yadava clan; and Narayana, referred to as a deity in the *Satapatha Brahmana*.[56] All three deities eventually became identified with Vishnu, originally a Vedic god of lesser importance but now assuming a much greater status in the eyes of its followers.[57] The major strand in Vaishnavism came through those with the Vasudeva–Krishna connections, known as the *bhagvatas*.[58] Their intensely concentrated devotion to a personal lord, *Bhagavana*, attracted even some non-Indians. Their greatest spiritual and intellectual legacy to us is the world famous short dialogue between Krishna, an incarnation of Vishnu, and Arjuna, one of the five Pandava brothers, in the *Mahabharata*. Refuting such practices as withdrawal, renunciation and idle sentimentalism, Krishna enjoins Arjuna to focus his devotion upon him and fulfil his duty according to his place in society, however hard that struggle may be.

The *Shaiva* tradition rests upon the ancient deity of Shiva and upon the Mother Goddess Shakti, Shiva's consort. Shiva has an ancient pedigree in Brahmanic mythology. Some scholars have also traced this deity to the Harappan culture 'Pashupati' seal that shows a seated horned proto-Shiva figure surrounded by animals, but this is now strongly challenged by others. More convincingly, Shiva was the original god Rudra in the *Vedas*, a god who represented destructive and malignant forces of nature.[59] Rudra was known as the 'Roarer', but, like Vishnu, he too had been a marginal god in the first instance. However, from the time when he was elevated to a supreme force in one of the *Upanishads*, Shiva has been venerated by millions in India. During the period under review a definite *Shaiva* tradition emerged through the activities of sects such as Lakulin, Pashupata or Maheshvara.[60] Their intense devotion to Shiva was also emulated by great rulers such as Vima Kadphises of the Kushans, who ordered the depiction of the Shiva on his coins. The *lingam* that replaced the Shiva image in due course has been the core of intense devotion by the Shaivites throughout India.

The Dharmashastra *of Manu*

While Vaishnavism and Shaivism may have helped to access the Vedic religion to greater numbers of people, the Brahmanic thinkers nevertheless continued to reaffirm the principles of Vedic orthodoxy in much of the commentatorial literature that developed during this period. This literature was part of the great *Smriti* corpus that began with the composition of *Sutras* in the late Vedic and post-Vedic periods. It deals with a host of issues in society and life generally, with lessons and implications drawn from the *Sruti* literature. The particular component that we call the *Dharmashastras* were essentially normative texts dealing with *Dharma*, 'the whole system of Law, moral and legal, that has its foundation in the transcendent order, and the specific systems of rules and regulations under which a given individual lives.'[61] In all, nineteen *Dharmashastras*, attributed to ancient seers, have been identified,[62] but just four of them form the essential core. They are *Manavdharmashastra*, or *Manu-smriti*, *Yajnavalkyasmriti*, *Naradasmriti* (see Extract 7.1) and *Parasarasmriti*, attributed to sages Manu, Yajnavalkya, Narada and Parasara. The *Manusmriti* is the critical text for our period: it might have been composed any time between 200 BC and AD 200; the other three are later compositions, falling outside our period. Highly prescriptive and rigid in its thinking, the *Manusmriti* became the rule book for orthodox *brahmans*. Its contents, consisting of 2,684 verses divided into twelve chapters, among other things, affirm the divine right of kings; confirm and rationalise the theory of the caste system; elaborate upon and sing praises of the so-called four stages of life for Vedic followers; and express grave reservations about the constancy and capabilities of women.[63] The text was never universally followed or acclaimed by the vast majority of Indians in their history: it came to the world's attention through a late eighteenth-century translation by Sir William Jones, who mistakenly exaggerated both its antiquity and its importance. Today many of its ideas are popularised as the golden norm of classical Hindu law by Hindu universalists. They are, however, anthema to modern thinkers and particularly feminists. On caste, the *Manusmriti* emphasises the dignity of the *brahman* and casts grave aspersions over the *shudras*. At the same time, it does take notice of the fact that greater social fluidity could arise out of the union of sexes from different castes and the formation of new castes resulting therefrom. The great twentieth-century leader of the 'untouchable' communities, Dr Ambedkar, had little time and low regard for this text and condemned it outright, with much good reason.[64] On Christmas Day 1927, he and his followers burned copies of it in public.[65] While Westernised feminists feel highly affronted by the strictures on women, there may be something to be said in mitigation of the *Manusmriti*'s position. Manu wishes nothing but honour and respect to be shown to women, but does not believe that they deserve many freedoms. According to one empathetic writer, 'this contradiction is more apparent than real ... for the emphasis is not so much on the denial of any freedom to a woman as on the duty of her near ones to protect her at all costs.'[66] Although paternalistic and patronising, Manu's views are not entirely at odds with views on women held by both men and women not just in India but also in many parts of the non-Western world. Western feminism comes quite a way behind Western science and technology among their priorities.

Secular literature, sciences and the arts

A florescence of cultural creativity is distinctly noticeable during the post-Mauryan centuries. This creativity was partly an expression of the efforts and genius of the Indian people themselves, and partly the result of cross-fertilisation of ideas from different traditions and cultures. The fusion of native ideas and skills with those borrowed from Persian, Greek, Central Asian or Chinese sources gave a sharper impetus and edge to all cultural products created in India at that time. In due course, the outside world came to admire some of these products. The developments in literature, sciences and the arts will furnish us with appropriate examples of progressive creativity.

Sanskrit literature

Sanskrit was the hallowed language in which the most sacred of India's literature had been composed. Although during the age of the Buddha and under the Mauryan Empire various forms of *Prakrit* – the popular languages – came into prominence, Sanskrit always remained the language that wielded a pervasive influence. Far from being hostile to Sanskrit, the post-Mauryan monarchs, whether Indian or foreign, also provided valuable patronage; and even much of the literature of *Mahayana* Buddhism was written in Sanskrit. The most famous Buddhist writer in Sanskrit was Asvaghosha, whose life of the Buddha, the *Buddhacharita*, was an early gem of Sanskrit biographical literature and 'a work of art'.[67] In fact, during the post-Mauryan period, Sanskrit came to be recognised as the language of the educated and cultured classes, irrespective of their religion. It was the quality of language and its subtle use that preoccupied such people. The *Buddhacharita*, along with another acclaimed work, the *Mahabhashya*, by Patanjali the grammarian,[68] was admired as a fine example of Sanskrit prose literature. However, the most significant of literary developments in Sanskrit came to be expressed through poetry and drama. The poetic genre was the *kavya*, or court poetry. This poetry, in the form of either a grand narrative poem or a short lyric, described vividly such themes as nature, a love scene, a spectacle or praise for the monarch. This last function was particularly sought after by monarchs with an eye to their place in history. Thus, in the famous *prasasti* of Rudradaman, inscribed on a rock in Junagadh, referred to earlier, the king's praises are sung by the poet using various figures of speech and alliteration.[69] The *kavya* has exercised a major influence on the Indian poetic tradition generally for more than a thousand years. Parallel to it was the rise of the secular drama, the *natya*. The Indian drama tradition harked back to Vedic times and all early dramas were based on religious themes. In the new Sanskrit drama, however, the issues of morality or conduct in society were explored in plots around a hero or a heroic figure, with much use of sentiment, romance, satire or farce. They were to be more appealing to varied audiences. In the next chapter we shall refer to the contributions of India's greatest dramatist, Kalidasa; but, during our period, a most amazing textbook of dramatic criticism was produced by someone called Bharata. We know very little about him personally, but his work, the *Natyashastra*, rediscovered as late as the nineteenth century, is now considered a most compact compendium of dramaturgy, theatre, acting, costumes, make-up, dance, audience participation and theatre architecture, with pertinent advice and instruction for actors, producers and playwrights. The appropriate use of words, mimicry, gesture and posture are all, according to Bharata, necessary for the success in the performing arts, and it is only through this success that the audience's appreciation, or what is known as *rasa*, can be aroused[70] (see Extract 7.2). This notion of *rasa* (literally 'flavour', 'taste') has remained 'the most important and influential single concept of Indian criticism to this day'.[71]

Tamil literature

The Aryanisation of the Dravidian-speaking peoples during the first millennium BC had involved an increasing use of Sanskrit in the south. The Sanskritic influence is strongest in three of the southern languages: Telugu, Kannada and Malayalam. Tamil, the principal and the most ancient of the Dravidian literary languages, was also influenced by Sanskrit, but on a far smaller scale. It retained its independence and originality, particularly in its technical structure. A fuller appreciation of the political, social and cultural development of the far south can be gained only by studying the most ancient of the Tamil texts. Tamils dominated the early history of the region, and one of their major intellectual traditions was the regular gathering of a large number of poets in a *sangam*, or an academy, at which poems and stories were recited. The so-called Sangam Age lasted from approximately 500 BC to AD 500.[72] Three *sangams* were held, but the works from the first two are difficult to trace. An important grammatical work of the second *sangam*, known as *Tolkappiyam*, is an exception. It gives us, among other things, information concerning the ecology and the environment of the far south, expressed in a particular concept of a geographical habitat, known as *tinai*. A number of habitats are identified: high lands, forests, pastures, dry lands, river valleys or coastal lands. The *Tolkappiyam* tells us about the people who lived in these locales, their relationship with nature and between themselves, and their varied customs.[73] The differences, for example, in the lifestyles of people who lived in the forests and those of the river valleys are brought out by describing how large-scale cattle raids by the former on the lands of the pastoral people were carried out.[74] It is from the third *sangam* that the bulk of our literary heritage in Tamil can be drawn. Three major anthologies cover the works from this *sangam*. They are *Patthuppattu* (Ten Idylls, or short pastoral poems), *Ettuthokai* (Eight Collections) and *Padinenkilkanakku* (Eighteen Poems). Two of the Eight Collections of *Ettuthokai* are particularly valuable. One is the *Purananaru*, which contains descriptions of the life of the southern people in that period; and the other is *Kurunthokai* (*c.* AD 100) consisting of 400 verses of short love poems, between four and nine lines long, composed by 205 poets.[75] Among the Eighteen Poems of the *Padinenkilkanakku*, the eleventh, the *Kural*, laid out in 113 sections of ten couplets each, presents in verses a guide to the art of good living. The varieties of *sangam* collections also enable us to understand the differences among the people of the south. Although there was much inequality between the castes and great poverty among the lower ranked, the overall impression one has of the south is that it was suffused by a relatively peaceful and relaxed communal atmosphere. The most convincing evidence for this lies in the greater freedoms enjoyed by the female sex.

Advance in sciences

Astronomy and medicine were two of the main sciences in which steady progress was made during our period.[76] Indian interest in astronomy dated from the earliest of Vedic times, and much astronomical knowledge can be gathered from the *Samhitas*, the *Brahmanas* and *Sutra* literature. Many reflections and speculations about the sun, the moon, the earth, the planets or the eclipses were interspersed with calculations of the division of time in terms of a day, a month, seasons, solstices, equinoxes and calendars in general. Religious preoccupation and mystical interpretations, however, dominated the astronomical thinking during those centuries. It was with the beginning of the Christian era that a new turning point was reached, with a greater emphasis on a rigorous scientific method of inquiry and interpretation. There also came into use a more sophisticated system of computation, with mathematical concepts such as the integral solutions of indeterminate equations and trigonometry. The positions of the various planets were charted with greater precision, and more accurate calculations of the length of the year or of the day were recorded. The relevant literature for this information consists of a set of *siddhantas*, or the so-called final solutions, each ascribed to a particular astronomer-sage. It is believed that there were originally eighteen such *siddhantas*, but only five of them, codified in the sixth century by the great astronomer Varahamihira, are now available to us. The names of two of them, the *Romaka Siddhanta* and the *Paulisa Siddhanta*, give strong hints of the Greek and classical influences on Indian astronomy. This is a subject of intense debate, but common sense suggests that the strong commercial links of India must also have had their parallel in cultural links.[77]

Ayur-Veda, the ancient medical system of India, is today considered as one of the important branches of complementary medicine. Its relative popularity throughout the world is because of its emphasis on a more holistic approach by the physician towards illness in general (see Extract 7.3). The bulk of our knowledge of the system is drawn from the works of Charaka and Susruta, who belonged to this period. Their works constitute the standard material of *Ayur-Veda*, and have been handed down to us over the centuries in various revisions. They describe and explain fully eight branches of medical knowledge and practice: therapeutics, surgery, diseases of the sensory organs, mental illness, infant disorders, toxicology, tonics/drugs and sexual virility. The materia medica of *Ayur-Veda* was also extensive, with a variety of substances drawn from the animal, vegetable and mineral kingdoms. As with astronomy, there is debate among historians whether India contributed at all to the Greek and Hellenistic medical systems, or whether these developed independently. On balance, there is a greater likelihood of fairly strong Indian influences, in the light of the testimony from Alexander the Great's contemporaries, the accounts of Megasthenes, the export of valuable medicinal plants from India to the Mediterranean lands, and the generally more articulate and clearer instructions in Indian medical texts compared with the Greek.

Architecture and sculpture

Despite the political confusion of the post-Mauryan era, the arts developed to a remarkable degree. The stupa became the symbol of post-Mauryan architectural progress. The archetype at Sanchi is the most famous of all these structures in India, and the entire range of developments in the evolution of the stupa can be found there (see Figure 7.1). Under the Shungas the stupa of Sanchi was greatly enlarged and a terrace built around it. A stone *vedika*, or railing, encircled both the stupa and its terrace. Under the Satavahanas beautifully carved *toranas* (i.e. arched doorways) were erected, one at each of the cardinal points of the *vedika*. The art of the sculpture also took off during this confusing period. There is abundant sculptural material to analyse on the stone *vedikas* and *toranas* of the Sanchi stupa no. 2, *Bharhut* (Gajjar) (see Figures 7.2, 7.3), and the Bodhgaya

Figure 7.1 Relief from a Sanchi gateway (from Havell, op. cit., plate VD, p. 32).

Figure 7.2 A hip girdle from Bharhut Stupa (private photo, after Philip Rawson, op. cit., p. 132, by permission).

stupas. Three types of relief sculpture have been studied in great detail.[78] One is the vegetation design, consisting of lotus flowers on winding stems, trees and garlands of flowers. Another consists of individual figures, such as *yaksha* and *yakshi* (male and female semi-divine beings and life spirits) (see Figure 7.4), deities such as Indra, or soldiers. The most interesting reliefs are those of narrative tableaux depicting various scenes from the Buddha's life, such as the dream of Maya Devi, Buddha's mother, the purchase of the *Jetavana Park* or Buddha's descent from *Trayatrimsa*, and the *Jataka* legends. The sculptures of the great stupa of Amaravati are also another great artistic heritage we have received from the Satavahanas (see Extract 7.4).

Figure 7.3 A rider on the Bharhut Stupa (Pat Baker: line drawing adapted from a photo in Rawson, op. cit., p. 59).

Figure 7.4 A *yakshi* (Pat Baker: line drawing adapted from a photo in Rawson, op. cit., p. 67).

Indian art flowered during the Kushana era, with sculpture leading all other arts. The sculptures of the Buddha were most common (see Figure 7.5). Two major schools produced works of great excellence and beauty.[79] The *Gandhara* school of art was the more cosmopolitan of the two.[80] The sculptures of this school consist principally of the Buddha and the *Boddhisatva* figures that show strong Greek and Roman artistic influences on Indian themes. Some of the finest examples of *Gandhara* art are to be found in the British Museum, Peshawar Museum, Berlin Museum and Indian Museum at Calcutta. The second of the two schools was the Mathura school of art.[81] During the first three centuries of the Christian era Mathura, 50 miles southeast of Delhi on the Yamuna river, was a great hub of cultural activity. In contrast to the *Gandhara* school, a more authentically Indian artistic influence is stamped all over the art of Mathura. A whole variety of Buddha statues, in different poses and postures, all carved in the red spotted sandstone, are the distinguishing feature of this school. The portrait sculpture of rulers is also a hallmark of this style, the most famous of which is the statue of Kanishka himself. Power and authority radiate from this statue, even though its head and arms are missing (see Figure 7.6).

Figure 7.5 Buddhas in different art styles (Pat Baker: line drawings from photos in Rawson, op. cit., pp. 100–01).

Figure 7.6 Torso of King Kanishka (Pat Baker: line drawing from Rawson, op. cit., p. 143).

SELECT EXTRACTS FOR REVIEW AND REFLECTION

Extract 7.1   Wealth and morality as explained in *Naradasmriti*

The *Naradasmriti* is one of the great *Dharmashastras* of the Gupta period. Like most *Dharmashastras* it throws much light on Hindu civil and religious law. In the following passage it explains the degree of morality behind the acquisition of wealth.

Wealth is of three kinds: white, spotted and black ... White wealth is acquired by sacred knowledge, valour in arms, the practice of austerities, ... by instructing apupil, by sacrificing and by inheritance.

Spotted wealth is acquired by lending money at interest, tillage, ... by artistic performance, by servile attendance, or as a return for benefit conferred on someone.

Black wealth is acquired as a bribe, by gambling, ... by forgery, by robbery, by fraud.

Source: *Naradasmriti*, I, 44–8, trans. Julius Jolly, in Max Muller (ed.), *Sacred Books of the East*, Vol. 33, Oxford: Clarendon Press, 1889, pp. 53–4.

Extract 7.2   Four millennia of musical ancestry

In the following passage a practitioner of Indian classical music explains the development of this ancient art form.

According to Bharat every artist should create a Rasa or a mood. His nine Rasas are wonder, terror, disgust, joy, pathos, anger, love, serenity and valour. It has been said that western music describes a mood, but Indian music creates it. A Raag is a series of five or more notes on which a melody is based. Raag Basant creates joy and Raag Todi grief. Even the drum beats are used to produce a mood, e.g., the 6-beat Dadra inspires a romantic mood, while the 14-beat Dhamar creates a vigorous mood.

The whole tradition of Indian classical music has, in fact, its roots in the Hindu religion. Originally the Vedas were recited, but later they came to be chanted in three musical notes. Samveda developed to a scale of seven notes: Sa, Re, Ga, Ma, Pa, Dha, Ni [the Western major scale C–D–E–F–G–A–B]. These are compared to the cry of the peacock and the calls of the chataka bird, the goat, the crane, the cuckoo, the frog and the elephant respectively. They are said to be always of the same pitch. Later on, four flats Re, Ga, Dha, Ni and one sharp Ma were added. These twelve notes are common to both Indian and western music, but ten more notes (micro-tones) are also used in Indian music. By the end of 1000 BC the Samveda came to be sung to the scale of what we now call Raag Bageshree.

In the caste system the sub-castes produced hereditary guilds, known as Gharanas. Many Raags are produced in a variety of form, style and presentation by the Gharanas.

For further understanding, read A.H. Fox Strangways, *The Music of Hindostan*, New Delhi: Oriental Books, 1975; B. Chaitanya Deva, *Indian Music*, New Delhi: Indian Council for Cultural Relations, 1974; Reginald Massey and Jamila Massey, *The Music of India*, London: Kahn & Averill, 1986; (and in Marathi) Pandit Arvind Gajendragadkar, *Sangeet Shastrache Guide*, Pune: Mrs. K. Nitin Gogate, 1991.

Source: From a note sent to the author by Dr Mahesh Godbole, Secretary of the Indian Classical Music Society in northwest England.

Extract 7.3 Some simple advice regarding personal health

A Tamil poem of the Sangam Age (over 1,500 years ago) gives advice on the problem of overindulgence in eating, causing much suffering to the indulgent.

No need of medicine to heal your body's pain,
    if what you ate before digested well, you eat again.
Who has a body gained may long the gift retain,
    if, food digested well, in measure due he eat again.
Knowing the food digested well, when hunger prompteth thee,
    with constant care, the viands choose that well agree.
With self-denial take the well-selected meal;
    so shall thy frame no sickness feel.
On modest temperance as pleasures pure,
    so pain attends the greedy epicure.
Who largely feeds, nor measure of the fire within maintains,
    that thoughtless man shall feel unmeasured pains.

Source: *The 'Sacred' Kurral of Tiruvalluva-Nayanar*, trans. G.U. Pope, London: W.H. Allen, 1886, pp. 128–9.

Extract 7.4 The Amaravati sculptures

A priceless collection of 133 pieces of Indian sculpture from the Sata-vahana era has been exhibited at the British Museum since 1880. The sculptures are from the site of the *Mahachaitya*, or the great stupa of Amaravati, located in the lower reaches of the River Krishna in Andhra Pradesh. It was in 1816 when Colonel Colin Mackenzie, later surveyor general of India, and his staff recorded the contents and made the drawings, all of which are preserved at the India Office of the British Library. By 1880 the British Museum came to possess the larger portion of the collection, with the rest being held by the Madras Museum. The sculptures not only tell us the story of the Buddha's life, using a variety of Buddhist iconography and imagery, but they also depict the social scenes in a typically busy Indian setting. The crowds of labourers and masons and the performances of musicians and dancers are detailed, with a lively imagination, alongside men on horses, chariots and bullock carts.

Read Robert Knox, *Amaravati: Buddhist Sculpture from the Great Stupa*, London: British Museum Press, 1992.

RELEVANT QUESTIONS FOR DISCUSSION

1   How did the Kushan Empire link India with the outside world?
2   How does the Indian Ocean monsoon pattern work?
3   What could be the arguments for and against relying on the *Ayur-Veda* method and practice of medicine in the modern world?

Notes

1   Dunbar 1943: 68.
2   Thapar 2002: 212–13; Raychaudhuri 1996: 331–5, 644.
3   Narain 1957: 12–45; Frye 1996: 111–18.
4   Thapar 2002: 160.
5   For a comprehensive account of the Indo-Greek synthesis, consult Tarn 1951: 351–408.
6   Boyce 2002a.
7   Frye 1996: 121–30.
8   For their background, consult Yu 1990.
9   For a theoretical understanding of the process of sedentarisation, consult Khazanov 1984: 198–227.
10   Narain 1990: 150–76.
11   Raychaudhuri 1996: 715–32; Frye 1996: 133–50.
12   Kumar 1973: 58–77; Zevmal 1970.
13   Daniélou 2003: 130.
14   Liu 1994: 109–10, 117–18; Zelinsky 1970.
15   Kumar 1973: 97–102; Daniélou 2003: 130–31; Liu 1994: 135.
16   Raychaudhuri 1996 356–72: Allchin 1995: 279–80.
17   It should be noted that he is one of the many Satakarnis in the Satavahana dynasty of monarchs.
18   Tripathi 1999: 194; Thapar 2002: 226.

19 Thapar 2002: 226–7.
20 Ray 1986: 98–102.
21 Ibid.: 113–17, 129–32; Yazdani 1960: 138–40.
22 Ray 1986: 82–9; Yazdani 1960: 142–3.
23 Knox 1992: 9–13.
24 Raychaudhuri 1996: 446–53.
25 Ray *et al*. 2002: 327–9.
26 Saletore 1973: 528–43.
27 Thapar 2002: 252.
28 Saletore 1973: 349–60.
29 Casson 1989: 21–7.
30 Saletore 1973: 372–85.
31 Liu 1994: 2–11.
32 Ibid.: 18–22; Frye 1996: 153–7.
33 Liu 1994: 53, 77.
34 Ibid.: 88–102.
35 Ibid.: 10.
36 Tomber 2000.
37 Sidebotham 1991: 12–13.
38 Casson 1991.
39 Ibid.: 10.
40 Ibid.: 10–11; Miller 1969: 177–8.
41 Saletore 1973: 272–9; Miller 1969: 217–41.
42 Liu 1994: 10.
43 Orton 1991.
44 Begley 1991.
45 Ray *et al*. 2000: 609.
46 Ibid.: 607–9.
47 Sidebotham 1991: 23.
48 Ali 1999: 43.
49 Majumdar 1977: 166.
50 Cousins 1997: 374–8.
51 Tripathi 1999: 230.
52 Kotwal and Mistree 2002.
53 Cousins 1997: 382ff.
54 For a summary of some of the important texts, consult Liu 1994: 89–102.
55 Ibid.: 95.
56 Flood 1996: 117–27.
57 Jaiswal 1967: 1–7, 32–51.
58 Colas 2003: 229–33.
59 Flood 2003: 200–06.
60 Jash 1974: 1–17.
61 Dimock *et al*. 1974: 83.
62 Rocher 2003: 109.
63 Stein 1998: 92–5.
64 Ambedkar 1989: 100–02, 283–6.
65 Keer 1971: 100–01.
66 Embree 1992: 228.
67 Sastri 1960: 66.
68 One is not entirely sure whether Patanjali the grammarian was the same Patanjali as the composer of the Yoga Sutra.
69 Ray *et al*. 2000: 327–9.
70 Embree 1992: 264–8.
71 Dimock *et al*. 1974: 130.

72 Majumdar 1977: 193–4.
73 Gurukkal 1995: 242–4.
74 Ibid.: 252.
75 Dimock *et al.* 1974: 171.
76 Bose *et al.* 1989: 58–92; 213–35.
77 Yano 2003: 388–9.
78 Tomory 1989: 168–74; Gajjar 1971: 109–32.
79 Tomory 1989: 181–7.
80 Craven 1997: 81–102.
81 Ibid.: 102–9.

8 Stability and change under the imperial Guptas

(Time-span: AD 320 to c. 550)

In the fourth and the fifth centuries of the Christian era most of north India was ruled by monarchs of the Gupta dynasty (see Map 8.1), originally the controllers of a minor principality in the western Ganga plains. The Gupta family's fortunes rose when its third king, Chandragupta I, extended his realms into *Magadha* itself in AD 320. His acceptance among the kings and princes of the eastern Ganga basin was confirmed after he married into the Lichchhavi family, an influential republican clan on the borders of Bihar and Nepal. With Chandragupta's steady consolidation of his hold over the Magadhan heartland the Gupta principality expanded into the Gupta kingdom, and under his son and grandson the Guptas became a formidable power in north India. The extent of their lands was smaller than that of the Mauryan or future Mughal territories; nonetheless the Guptas ruled over what was essentially an empire of great majesty and consequence. Another astute marriage extended their influence further south. There ruled in the Deccan the dynasty of the Vakatakas, who had been the successors of the Satavahanas, and a politically crucial marriage alliance between a Gupta princess and the Vakataka king in the late fourth century brought the two families closer. Although the Gupta remained the senior partners, the fifth century may rightly be described as the Gupta–Vakataka Age. By the early sixth century the glory of both had faded, but a number of minor Gupta kings carried on ruling ever smaller territories right until the eighth century. We must distinguish these later, lesser, Guptas from the earlier powerful ones who are often called the imperial Guptas.

A number of early Gupta emperors of outstanding character and ability gave India two centuries of unprecedented stability. Despite much internal warfare in the early years and external threats in the last decades of the fifth century, they created a framework of peace and order for their empire that heralded much fruitful progress and activity. The beneficial effects of their benign rule and of their later subordinate partners, the Vakatakas, can be evidenced from the many achievements of that era in the varied areas of life, whether political, military, economic, social or cultural in nature. Those searching for an idyllic Hindu past of India have tended to glorify the Gupta times as the 'Golden Age' of Indian history; but there are also some who have been stern critics of such historical nostalgia.[1] Undoubtedly Gupta India was a far more

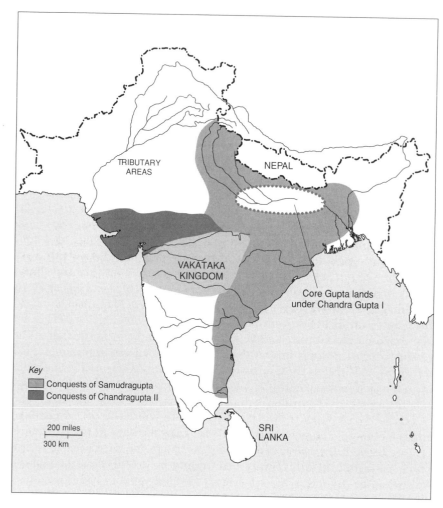

Map 8.1 Increase in Gupta territories.

desirable and creative place in which to live than the other great civilisations of that era, whether European, Chinese or Persian; but we must be careful that we do not succumb to the exaggerated notion that it was an age of well-being for all northern India's people. We need to ask critically who benefited most and who did not. Among the former were those who were most able to seize the opportunities provided by stable conditions. They were either the elites of the upper and upper middle classes of the caste pyramid or creative and gifted people. As far as the ordinary people were concerned, the reality was somewhat different. The vast majority of them lived a short life, economically precarious, and disadvantaged by social, cultural and gender inequalities. Part of the explanation for the naïve perception of the Gupta era lies in certain assumptions that are sometimes made about the post-Gupta period. These assumptions are about the consequences of regionalised and feudal politics in this period, the most negative of which is considered to be the ultimate inability of the Hindu rulers to contain the steady inroad of Muslim forces into India from the eleventh century onwards. The last three or four centuries of the first millennium AD are therefore viewed as a period of retrogression, rather than deserving to be studied and appreciated in their own context.[2]

The empire and the emperors

The imperial Guptas rightly begin with Chandragupta I, because it was he who was honoured with the title of *Maharajadhiraja*, King over Kings, whereas his father, Sri Ghatotkachagupta, and his grandfather, Sri Gupta, had carried only the title of *Maharaja*.[3] Chandragupta I's work in expanding the Gupta domain continued under his four successors, between 335 and 467. The prestige and reputation of the Guptas stood highest during these 132 years. The next eight decades saw a gradual decline in their fortunes as they faced both internal dissension and foreign invasions. The final disintegration was accompanied by the encroachment of minor tributaries and rulers on traditional Gupta-controlled lands.

Two great Guptas (335–415)

Among the many monarchs who ruled in South Asia until the end of the third century of the Christian era the names and reputations of three have withstood the test of time: Chandragupta Maurya (321 BC–298 BC), the founder of the Mauryan Empire; his grandson, Ashoka (272 BC–232 BC), who promulgated the law of *Dhamma* in that empire; and Kanishka (*c.* first–second century AD), the great Kushan king. To these three we must now add the names of two remarkable Guptas – Samudragupta and Chandragupta II – who were the best and the most sagacious of them. Their achievements define the political and social tone of India during the heyday of their rule. Samudragupta (AD 335–75) made the dynasty truly imperial. His strength and wisdom have generally been admired, but we have more definite information about him from the inscription carved on an Ashokan pillar that used to be at *Kausambi* but which is now in Allahabad.[4] This so-called Allahabad pillar lists, at length, different classes of kings subdued by Samudragupta: there were kings who were slain and their territories annexed, but there were also defeated kings who were released by the grace of Samudragupta in return for tribute, provision of military help, loyalty, granting of their daughters in marriage, etc. Frontier kings paid homage to Samudragupta and distant kings sent embassies acknowledging his suzerainty. The Gupta domain extended all the way up to the foothills of the Himalayas, ranging over the eastern Deccan and a long stretch of the eastern coastline. Samudragupta's defeat of fourteen kings of south India and his several victories led the historian Vincent Smith to describe him as the Napoleon of ancient India.[5] Unlike Napoleon, however, Samudragupta never met his Waterloo, because he refused to overextend himself. In that he showed the wisdom common to many Indian rulers. Great as were his military skills, Samudragupta was also a poet, a musician and an intellectual personality. He was honoured as a poet-king, or *kaviraja*, and he gathered about him a galaxy of poets and scholars, promoting high culture at his court. Though a Vaish-navite,[6] he showed much liberality of outlook in employing Buddhist advisers such as Vasubandhu. When Meghavarman, king of Sri Lanka (*c.* AD 350–80), sent a request for help in building a monastery at Bodh Gaya for visiting Sri Lankan monks and scholars, Samudragupta generously donated towards the construction of a building which eventually housed 1,000 of them.[7]

Under Samudragupta's son, Chandragupta II (375–415), the Gupta state became more powerful and prosperous. A spectacular conquest and a strategic matrimonial alliance were key factors. The conquest was that of the Shakas of western India. The Shakas, or the Scythians, as will be recalled, had moved into India after the collapse of the Mauryans, but by the fourth century their main power base in India was in Malwa and Saurashtra, with their capital at Ujjain. Their defeat at the hands of Chandragupta II opened the way to the Gupta control of key ports in western India, such as Broach, Cambay and Sopara, which produced greater revenues from their overseas trade.[8] The possession of Ujjain led to dominance over the internal trade routes that crossed through that great central Indian city. After his conquest of the Shakas, Chandragupta II came to be known as *Vikramaditya*, or 'Sun of Valour', a title highly esteemed in Brahmanic India. Like his grandfather, Chandragupta II was shrewd enough to understand the value of marriage alliances for enhancing the influence and dignity of his own dynasty. He himself married Kuvera-Naga, a princess from the Naga family, and thus extended his patrimony.[9] More importantly, however, he married his daughter Prabhavatigupta to King Rudrasena II of the Vakataka dynasty of Maharashtra and the western Deccan. When Rudrasena II died prematurely, Prabhavatigupta ruled as regent for her minor sons, thereby bringing the Vakatakas under Gupta influence.[10] The strength and prosperity of Chandragupta II's empire are reflected in fine gold and silver coins issued during his reign. The coins united the emperors with their far-flung subjects. Chandragupta II was also a renowned patron of art and culture. He held three courts – at *Pataliputra*, Ayodhya and Ujjain, but the one at Ujjain was particularly lustrous. It was a court where a circle of poets, commonly known as the 'Nine Gems', is said to have flourished under the patronage of Chandragupta and composed verses in his praise. The most famous of the gems was Kalidasa, the great dramatist and poet.[11]

Decentralisation and devolution of power

The honorific titles bestowed upon the Gupta emperors leave no doubt as to their belief in the Brahmanic notions of kingship.[12] The king's right was divinely ordained and was sanctified by the ceremonies that the *brahmans* performed on his behalf; but his right was only valid as long as he followed a righteous policy towards all his subjects. As the *Markandeya Purana* puts it, 'a king inaugurated in his kingdom must in the first place conciliate his subjects, without obstructing his own duty.'[13] The Gupta emperors kept to the letter and spirit of this understanding.[14] Instead of governing by absolutist principle, they followed the *rajadharma*, the duty of kings to protect their subjects and to arbitrate in disputes. They also initiated certain changes in the very style of exercise of monarchical authority. For nearly a thousand years the Indian monarchs, whether imperial or regional, had aimed at a concentration of all power in their hands. Absolutist rulers were tempted to subdue provinces and regions to their will through their bureaucracies; and the Mauryans were perhaps the greatest of centralisers. The Gupta dominions were organised on a somewhat different model, the main difference being the principle of decentralised administration.[15] The Guptas consciously devolved power on a variety of people and authorities who were then brought together in a circle of friendship and homage. Instead of bolstering a bureaucratic hierarchy, they helped to develop political hierarchies. This trend could be noticed in the power structures operating in the centuries immediately after the Mauryas, but the Guptas developed it further. To appreciate this model of decentralisation more fully it is necessary to peruse carefully the deeds of Samudragupta as narrated in the inscription of the Allahabad pillar. Samudragupta did not wish to vanquish his enemies merely for his own gratification. After defeating them he permitted most of them to keep their domains within the empire. They were to be protected by him, while he would share in their wealth. What he was developing was a form of contract between the tributary kings and himself as the overlord. This arrangement did not work for the weaker Gupta emperors of the sixth century, but during the heyday of Gupta power in the fourth and fifth centuries it functioned extremely well and helped to keep peace among the various ruling families. The post-Gupta rulers in future centuries would also, in measure of their capabilities, adopt the model of tributary rulership. Indeed, in one sense, it would be true to say that the model operated right until the end of British rule in India. After the great rebellion of 1857 the British realised that it was far better to make friends of the remaining princes of India than to subjugate them and alienate them further. They were simply following the Samudragupta principle of a network of what were called *samantas*. Over centuries the Sanskrit word *samanta*, literally meaning neighbour, has undergone many changes in its political significance; but during the Gupta period a *samanta* was coming to mean a neighbouring subsidiary ruler who was a friendly tributary of the Gupta sovereigns.

Imperial organisation

The Guptas avoided an overelaborate bureaucracy. Part of the reason for this was the decentralisation of administrative authority accompanied by land grants, carrying varied immunities and concessions, to persons and institutions. State rule was lightly exercised. At the royal palace in *Pataliputra* the monarch was advised by a council of ministers, led by the *Pradhana Mantry*, the chief minister. He headed the civil administration, but a good number of other ministers and high officials had duties related to military matters. Thus there was the minister of peace and war, the chief of police, the commander-in-chief, the chief of the palace guards, the chief of cavalry and the chief of the elephant corps. This emphasis on defence and security naturally reflected the essential concern of the central government: the maintenance of state power and the security of the people.[16] In the central secretariat each office had its own seal with which its communications were stamped for authentication. The second layer of administration dealt with the provinces, which were called *bhukti* or *desa*. A class of officers known as *kumaramatyas* headed the provincial councils.[17] The district, generally called *pradesha* or *vishaya*, and its council, headed by another group of officers, the *ayuktakas* or *vishayapatis*, were the concern of a third layer of administration. In the fourth layer were grouped the villages and towns. For each village there was a village assembly consisting of village elders, guided by a village headman.[18] In the towns there were city corporations, headed by a chairman, the *nagarashreshthin*, which consisted of many representatives of guild merchants.[19] In most town corporations there was the office of the chief scribe.[20] All substantive decisions, affecting each town or village, were taken at the local level, reflecting the decentralising policies of the state. We do not have any evidence of voting procedures, but there can be no doubt that decisions would have been arrived at after robust discussion, in the true Indian fashion. The *kumaramatyas* and the *ayuktakas* functioned as serving intermediaries between the centre and the periphery. This model of organisation was replicated in many of the lands of the *samantas*. In addition to peace with the *samantas*, the Gupta policy of general devolution of power helped, in the long run, to create layers of responsibility among the Indian people, in their villages, towns, districts and provinces. It allowed for self-governing communities to progress within the framework of their empire. The mildness of Gupta rule exerted a cohesive and beneficial effect upon the social classes of India. It was a highly pluralist world that was being created, a world in which groups of people came together to define their common interests or activities; they formed associations, solicited patronage and proceeded with creating prosperity for themselves. The Gupta state was there to guide and help, not to coerce.

Gupta power maintained intact (415–67)

From the end of the fourth century the superpower of Europe, the Roman Empire, was in great difficulties. Far from Rome, in the lands north of the Black Sea and to the northwest of the Caspian Sea, a nomadic people from Central Asia, the Huns, had established themselves in an aggressive federation. Their presence destabilised another group of people living nearby, the Goths, whose various tribes then broke through the eastern boundaries of the Roman

Empire. The empire could not be defended integrally, and in 395 it divided into western and eastern halves. The fifth century proved to be a period of horrendous difficulties for the Western Roman Empire. Alaric, the Goth leader, sacked Rome itself in 410, and the ancient provinces of Gaul, Spain and North Africa were seized by the Goths, the Franks and the Vandals. The province of Britain was also conquered, by the Angles, Saxons and Jutes. In the meantime, the Huns had moved further west, established their new head-quarters in Hungary and found a new leader in Attila. Under him in the 440s the dominance of the Huns attained its peak and, although Attila's hordes were finally defeated in the early 450s, the fate of the western empire was sealed.[21] Roman civilisation and the Pax Romana wilted away from the soil of Europe. In contrast, during this period, the Gupta state in north India main-tained its commanding position. The reign of Kumaragupta I (415–55) was a period of consolidation of the state structure, with its refined administration reaching out benevolently into the grass-roots villages of north India to ensure peace and prosperity, which came to be symbolised by the monarch's highly elegant gold and silver coins.[22] The chaos and confusion of the collapsing Roman Empire seemed far away indeed, although not for long!

The Huns who damaged Roman Europe were but one branch of the federated Hun family of the Hsiung-nu.[23] Originally migrating west from the borders of China during the first two or three centuries of the Christian era, the Hsiung-nu had divided into two branches, one moving towards the River Volga and the other towards the River Oxus. What the Volga Huns did to the Romans and Goths, the Oxus Huns were to repeat in northwest India during the late fifth and most of the sixth century. From the name of their rulers' family, the Huns of the Oxus valley came to be known as the Hephthalites, or the White Huns, as the Greeks referred to them. In India, specifically, the term *Huna* is used instead of Hun. From the Oxus valley the Huna (the White Huns) advanced towards both India and Persia, and in 460 they occupied *Gandhara*. Their advance, however, was stalled by the Gupta emperor Skandagupta (455–67), who proved to be more than a match for them. Their defeat at his hands not only gave north India another thirty years of respite from the Huna incursions but also deflected them towards launching further attacks into other parts of Eurasia.[24]

Guptas in decline (467–c. 550)

With the death of Skandagupta, in 467, the line of illustrious imperial Guptas comes to an end. From now on, until about 550, we note a succession of weak and ineffectual rulers. The liberal and benevolent polity that the Gupta state had been for nearly two centuries was now going to be a plaything for its enemies, internal and external. Despite being checked in 460, the Hunas remained the most dangerous foreign enemy. Around 500, under a leader called Toramana, they again invaded northwest India, Rajasthan and the western Ganga basin. Toramana's domain stretched from Persia to Khotan, with its capital at *Sakala*. In areas of India under his control Toramana brought much trade and encouraged groups of merchants to make donations to religious foundations,[25] and his rule was not an unmitigated disaster. In 510 he was succeeded by his son, Mihirkula, who made further and deeper inroads into Indian territory. Eventually, in 528, a powerful confederacy formed by the Gupta king Narasimha Gupta Baladitya[26] and the ruler of Malwa, Yashodharman, checked Mihirkula and forced him to take refuge in Kashmir. While Mihirkula, like his father, also gave grants and donations, most sources confirm his legendary reputation as the most aggressive Huna leader. He betrayed the ruler of Kashmir, perpetrated great massacres and visited wanton cruelties upon the Buddhists.[27] On his death in 542 north India gave a sigh of relief. The days of Huna glory were finally over by the 570s, when another group of nomadic Central Asian Turks defeated the Oxus Huns and invaded Afghanistan. Although the Hun danger had passed, the legacy of their incursions into India was bloody and tumultuous. The decentralised administration of the Gupta state could not take the strains imposed by the large-scale military counter-measures required against the Hunas. The quality of life in north India, which had attained a high level of refinement in the fourth and fifth centuries, suffered considerably in the resulting period of economic instability. While most of the Gupta revenue was drawn from land taxes, a significant part of it was obtained from India's lucrative trade, by land and sea, with West Asia, the Levant and the Mediterranean basin. The Hun incursions virtually destroyed the land trade, depriving the Guptas of valuable foreign currency; the latter were dealt a further blow when the ports of Gujarat strayed out of their control into the hands of their local rivals.[28] The sizeable diminution of their wealth is indicated by the paucity of inscriptions recording the various grants of lands and gifts traditionally conferred by them. The real death blow to the empire, however, came from the internal crisis of the Gupta dynasty: the weak and inept emperors were confronted with the assumption of their right to hereditary rule by provincial governors and imperial feudatories, and were powerless to check it. In fact, among the scanty records of the sixth century, we notice the rise of a new phenomenon: the self-asserting inscriptions issued by heads of regional families who once paid homage to the Guptas. By about 550 the empire had become a pale shadow of its former self.

Gupta society: a world in transition

Fa-hsien, a Chinese pilgrim, visited India in the early fifth century during the reign of Chandragupta II. His aim was to collect Buddhist manuscripts and relics and to seek the knowledge of Buddhism in the places of its origin. He had left China in 399, crossed the Gobi desert, the mountains of Khotan, the Pamir plateau, Swat and *Gandhara*, and stayed in India for nearly seven years, visiting such places as Peshawar, *Kanauj*, *Kashi*, *Kapilavastu*, *Kusinagar*, *Vaishali*, *Pataliputra* and several other Buddhist sites. He left India by sea from the port of *Tamralipiti*, and visited Ceylon and Indonesia on his homeward journey. Fa-hsien never had an audience with Chandragupta II, and neither was he interested in the politics of his kingdom. His main concern was Buddhism.[29] Nevertheless his recollections, which were translated by French scholars only in the nineteenth century, are worth reading from his particular viewpoint. He called India the 'Middle Kingdom', a term normally used in reference to China, and he vividly describes the free and liberal society of India that he found practically everywhere. The two particular matters that clearly impressed him were, firstly, the facilities of welfare and care for the weaker members of society and, secondly, the ordinary people going about their daily life in an atmosphere of peace and order, with little interference from the state. There was no capital punishment, and the public officers were held to be non-corrupt. People lived with moderation, abstaining from alcohol and meat-eating. Clearly Fa-hsien's portrayal of Chandragupta II's India is uncritical and adulatory, and we need to be more circumspect before accepting his observations as reliable: he only saw what he wanted to see. For example, there is evidence for the prevalence of alcohol-drinking and meat-eating.[30] Fa-hsien's work does not help us to understand some of the deeper changes that were taking place in Gupta society. The varieties of inscriptions, whether on temple walls or copper plates, are far more useful for this purpose (see Extract 8.1). From much detailed research now available, we can see that the achievements of the fourth and fifth centuries did not take place in the climate of enduring stability of Fa-hsien's imagination; there was also a considerable change coming over society. It could indeed be argued that the entire Gupta era was one of gentle transition, a transition that can be witnessed in the changes severally occurring. The age of Gupta transition acts also as a pointer to the new realities on the ground during the succeeding centuries. We select here three areas in which there were clear signs of change taking place.

Land grants and the early beginnings of feudalism

The idea of the *samanta* becomes even clearer when we examine the characteristics of the Gupta land policy. In contrast to the Mauryas, who acquired as much land as possible under their officers, the Guptas actively gave away much land in the form of land grants.[31] This practice was prevalent in its nascent form even during the early centuries of the post-Vedic era, when the kings were enjoined to give gifts to their *brahman* priests or royal officials. It became more widespread under the Satavahanas of the Deccan, the Shakas of western India and the Pallavas of south India, but the Guptas made it a substantive part of the discharge of their responsibilities. Two important types of land grants were made by them: the religious grants to *brahmans*, individually or collectively, known as *brahmadeya* grants; grants to institutions such as temples and monasteries,[32] known as *devagrahara* or *devadana*; and secular grants to crown officers, craft guilds or, on rare occasions, military commanders. The motive for the grants, particularly in the case of religious ones, was the gaining of religious merit in an age of social and moral crisis that was commented upon in the *Puranas*; however, a more pressing reason might have been the contraction of the monetary economy as a result of the shrinking of the previously very large international trade with Rome and the Levant. Land was something that technically belonged to the king, and he could dispose of it in any way he thought fit. The land grants to individual *brahmans* were more or less permanently alienated to the donees, thereby affirming their hereditary rights over the lands. No rents were charged and all revenues that could be derived from the produce of the cultivators could be retained by the new landholders. The *brahman* landlord was expected to improve his land and to contribute to rural prosperity. The cultivators became his possessions; as long as he did not wilfully mistreat them he could use their labour in any way he preferred. There is evidence that the new *brahman* owners made efforts to improve their estates.[33] Sometimes entire villages with their people were alienated by the Gupta kings either to a collectivity of *brahmans* or to the temples. The grants were rent-free, but carried an obligation to collect taxes due from the cultivators to the state. The relative lack of monetary resources would definitely explain the rationale of secular grants to officers and administrators. These land grants were in lieu of cash salaries for military and administrative service. Their privileges included also the hereditary alienation of land and rights over its produce, along with a variety of legal and administrative immunities. The various categories of cultivators were again to lose the protection of the monarch and his officials; and we can be sure that the attendant evils of forced and bonded labour would have increased considerably in these altered situations.[34]

The Gupta land grants created a class of feudatory intermediaries in the countryside. There was a limit to what the state could achieve for the countryside, but by creating layers of intermediaries the Guptas gave opportunities to various people to become proactive in the management and improvement of rural estates. While the state lost a certain amount of revenue and power, it had in the new donees a class of people who would act as its support mechanism. Some historians have described this development as a form of Indian feudalism.[35] They have recognised in it some of the features found in the full-blown feudalism of the type that was prevalent in Europe in the Middles Ages, when lord and vassal, at various levels of the social pyramid, were bound together in a chain of protection, homage and service. Other historians have raised doubts about the applicability of the European feudal model to India; and there has been a contentious debate engaged by scholarly protagonists on both sides of the argument.[36] What is indisputable is that the small-scale programme of land grants that the Guptas inherited and further encouraged became greatly accelerated in the post-Gupta centuries; and land grants created ideal conditions for some form of feudalism to flourish in India. In that sense, Indian feudalism pre-dates European feudalism. From the time of the Guptas until the mid-twentieth century feudalism remained a persistent factor in Indian political and social life.

Varying fortunes of faiths and sects

The period of Gupta transition affected the religions of India in different ways. Buddhism had been a powerful presence before the Guptas, partly owing to the favours the Buddhists had won from sympathetic monarchs. The Guptas, who were truly pluralist and broad-minded, continued with the established traditions of patronage and support to the Buddhist monasteries and institutions of learning. For most of the Gupta period Buddhism was to enjoy a healthy and robust life throughout most of India. Both the *Mahayana* and the *Theravada* schools flourished in different parts of the country; and great philosophers such as Vasubandhu, Dignaga and Dharmakirti either provided masterly expositions of the founder's teachings or expounded fresh ideas and developed new schools of thought. Some of the finest Buddhist caves of Ajanta were built under the patronage of the Vakatakas of the Deccan, the allies of the Guptas. There was, however, an ominous cloud hanging over the horizon, which was that, despite their widespread generosity, the Gupta emperors were essentially followers of the Brahmanical religion, particularly of the theistic schools of Shaivism and Vaishnavism. This meant, for the Buddhists, intense competition for monarchical patronage. They could not take for granted the quality and volume of support that they were accustomed from the previous monarchs. Shaivism and Vaishnavism were also appealing to a broader range of kings, besides the Guptas, in both north and south India; and that was bound in the long run to have a deleterious influence on Buddhist fortunes throughout the country. A much more serious and immediate danger for them in the declining decades of Gupta rule was that of the horrendous destruction wreaked on their monks and monasteries by the Hunas. What also perturbed them was the support given to the Hunas by the *Shaivite brahmans* of Kashmir, who expected to receive land grants from the Huna chief, Mihirkula.[37]

The oldest tradition in the country, Vedic Brahmanism, had been experiencing a gradual revival in the pre-Gupta centuries, but it was under Gupta patronage that it secured the opportunity to establish itself more firmly in the religious life of the people. The influence of heterodox ideas in Indian society over many hundreds of years had, however, been sufficiently strong to prevent the return of full-blooded Vedic Brahmanism. For example, one of its major planks, the highly elaborate and sometimes bizarre ritualistic sacrifices in propitiation of the old Vedic gods, was being gradually dismantled. These sacrifices incurred much expense and many resources; and even the *Dharmashastra* of Yajnavalkya recommended that an expensive sacrifice such as that of the *Ashvamedha* could only be performed when there was 'a provision for three years in one's store'.[38] There were now those who wished to modify and reform the sacrifices, while affirming their faith in the supremacy of the 'authorless and eternal'[39] *Vedas* and other essential belief systems of Vedic Brahmanism. For the *Shaivite* and *Vaishnavite* theists, neither the reformed sacrifices nor the eternal supremacy of the *Vedas* were of any consequence when compared with the power and majesty of the one supreme deity, Shiva or Vishnu. Both the theists and the reformist sacrificers, sometimes called *Smartas*, operated under the umbrella of Brahmanism, but in their own distinct ways. In both Shaivism and Vaishnavism the ceremony of the *puja*, with an image of Vishnu or Shiva as the focus of worship, superseded the Vedic sacrifice. In the matter of the conduct of worship, the orthodox Vedic Brahmanists remained wedded to the role of the priest as being central to the performance of all the rituals, while the theists greatly emphasised individual devotional worship, or *bhakti*, without the necessity of priestly intercession. In the long run, all parties eventually settled down to accepting a compromise. The upper castes continued a number of Vedic rituals short of full-blown sacrifices, along with a respect for theistic devotionalism. The mass of the people, under the influence of Shaivism and Vaishnavism, became increasingly devotional-minded in their religious attitudes.

One of the most important means by which millions of unlettered common people, and particularly women, came to be imbued with a strong passion for devotional worship was through the readings of a set of texts called the *Puranas*, composed by the learned among the *Shaivites* and the *Vaishnavites*. The *Puranas* became a primer of religious education for the masses. Written in an accessible style, and containing a mixture of morality, history, genealogy, folklore and practical wisdom, astrology, geography, medicine and countless other subjects, the eighteen major and the eighteen minor *Puranas* became the key agencies by which the *Shaivites* and the *Vaishnavites* drew the people towards them and away from both Buddhism and orthodox Vedic Brahmanism. The rationale of what we nowadays call folk Hinduism is best studied through the Puranic writings. In today's 'Indological scholarship', too, these writings 'have regained ... the central place they have always occupied in living Hinduism.'[40] While their earliest compositions might have begun in pre-Gupta times and the later works continued to be composed long after the Guptas, the *Puranas* are essentially a product of the Gupta age.[41] They are also a marker of the transition that we witness in the fourth and fifth centuries.

Caste mobility

The caste system has remained a notable feature of Indian religious and social life until the present. So it was too during the Gupta period. At the same time, we also notice some indications of mobility and fluidity affecting the system during this period. The first signs can be detected from the readings of the various *Dharmashastras* that contain ample references to the caste system. These normative sources have much to explain about the condition of the *shudras*, slaves and various categories of labourers. With increased political decentralisation, economic expansion and the liberal use of land grants, large areas of the country had become more accessible, with the result that many tribal groups who had formerly lived very isolated lives were now brought within the caste system. One might say that the detribalisation of India proceeded apace during Gupta rule. Similarly, the older foreign groups, such as the *Yavanas*, the Shakas and the Kushans, were also being acculturated into the caste hierarchy. There is also evidence that the principle of caste endogamy was not as rigidly applied as in earlier times. Both *anuloma* and *pratiloma* marriage conventions were approved and socially recognised, despite the various strictures in the *Dharmashastras*.[42] There was also a certain weakening of the links between a caste and its vocation, as instances of the *brahmans* and the *kshatriyas* following the occupations of lower classes and of *vaishyas* and the *shudras* adopting the occupations of superior classes have been recorded. In a period of mobility it was natural that some castes improved their standing, others stood still or rose marginally, and some sank in social standing. The *brahmans* maintained their status through their ability to read, write and recite; but members of lesser castes could also improve theirs by performing any type of scribal work.[43] Traditionally the *kshatriyas* were power-holders and power-brokers. However, with the rise of many non-*kshatriya* ruling houses, it came to be gradually recognised in the *Dharmashastras* that the king need not be a *kshatriya* by birth, and that the *kshatriya* status was an 'achieved, not an ascribed, rank'.[44] The *vaishyas* retained the third ritual hierarchical layer, but their influence grew with numbers of *jatis* with useful trades and occupations multiplying and flourishing. The *shudras* made a definite leap forward for themselves. The relative improvement in the status of the *shudras* in Gupta society can be evidenced by a number of developments among them. They increasingly went into farming in capacities other than labourers and turned into sharecroppers and peasants; they became craftsmen; they joined the army; and some got themselves educated.[45] They came to be granted definite legal rights that they did not previously possess. While the *Dharmashastra* of Manu adopted a harsh tone in relation to the punishments to be meted out in cases of *shudra* transgressions, the later *Dharmashastra* of *Yanavalkayasmriti* took a much more humane and pragmatic line in this matter.[46] Their forward movement, though limited in scope, was a significant marker of social mobility; but it was naturally counter-balanced by the growth of new outcaste groups, generally known as the Untouchables. The latter were assigned the most demeaning and polluting occupations, and they, along with the slaves, constituted perhaps the lowest stratum of Indian humanity. Even Fa-hsien, who showered so much praise on the India of his day, admitted that the *Chandalas* or the Untouchables had to sound a 'clapper'[47] in the streets so that the caste people would be warned of their presence, and that an upper-caste person would have to take a ritual bath in the event of close proximity with an Untouchable.[48]

The 'flowering'[49] of Gupta Classical culture

In January 2000, an international seminar was held at Tiruvanthampuram (Trivandrum), Kerala, India, to honour the 1,500th anniversary of the writing of *Aryabhatiya*, a seminal mathematical treatise by Aryabhata I, the great mathematician-astronomer of India who was born AD 476. Many Indian and international Sanskrit scholars and historians of mathematics read papers explaining Aryabhata's mathematical insights and the relevance of his work even today.[50] The time during which Aryabhata lived has been labelled by historians as the Classical period of Indian history (see Figure 8.1). The term 'Classical' implies unsurpassed intellectual and aesthetic excellence – a norm against which all other similar achievements can be judged. Although there was much creativity in India in both earlier and later times, many historians feel that the Brahmanic–Buddhist–Jainist civilisation that had been maturing for many centuries reached a particularly splendid height under the Guptas. As the Guptas were the dominant power over more than half of India, the historians talk of a Gupta Classical culture. Although this could be misleading, because Indian creativity was not confined to the peoples and territories controlled by the Guptas, there is no doubt that the liberal patronage of the Guptas and their allies for the aspiring writers, artists, poets and thinkers of all castes and creeds helped to promote excellence in general.

Mathematics and technology

Long before the Guptas came to power there had been steady progress made in Indian mathematics.[51] Such problems in mathematics as arithmetical operations, the geometry of altars, algebraic equations and the number theory had already been investigated in earlier sources such as the *Satapatha Brahmana*, the *Sulvasutras*, Jaina mathematics and the *Bakhshali Manuscript*. The Indian number system, with ten symbols representing 1 to 9 and the zero, and the

Figure 8.1 The idea of the Classical in the Indian context: dancer Vinata Godbole performing the classical dance of South India (by permission of Dr Mahesh Godbole).

decimal place-value system, were also utilised, although the earliest documented symbol for zero dates from the Gwalior inscription of the ninth century. A considerable body of astronomical knowledge, using mathematics, was additionally contained in texts called the *Siddhantas*. Indian astronomy began with the need, firstly, for accurate calendars for use in religious rituals and for predicting rainfall patterns; it developed further with the rapid expansion of Indian trade, with the charting of high seas necessitating the exact knowledge of tides and stars. Mathematical intervention was therefore crucial. However, despite such progress made before the Guptas, we do not know of any one person whom we can recognise as an iconic figure in Indian mathematics or astronomy. Aryabhata I was the first great mathematician and astronomer to whom this honour must be accorded: he lived at a time of great flux and dynamism in Indian science as a whole. Whether in medicine or metallurgy, music or mathematics, pharmacy or astronomy, new observations were being made and ideas rigorously tested, with their results codified and synthesised.[52] Aryabhata's own work was neither prolific nor exhaustive, but it was he who not only summed up, in a concise way, the precedent mathematical achievements but also provided new insights which later proved to be vital to the development of mathematics. Practically all ancient Indian mathematical and astronomical concepts were expressed in verse form, in *sutras*, in what might be termed mathematical Sanskrit. The mathematical ideas in the *Aryabhatiya* of Aryabhata I were also expressed in a *sutra* form, and only those few people closely acquainted with both Sanskrit and mathematics can decrypt the meaning of the *sutras*. Traditionally, the learned people disseminated ideas through written commentaries on the original works; and further commentaries on the commentaries were also made available[53] (see Extract 8.2). There was therefore much elitism and, perhaps, intellectual exclusivity. During the Classical period, however, owing to greater openness of outlook and exchange of ideas, schools of mathematics and astronomy began to flourish at places as far apart as *Kusumpura*, Ujjain and Mysore, where useful mathematical exchanges took place. Aryabhata himself may have been a native of Kerala, but he worked at both *Kusumpura* and Nalanda. In the *Aryabhatiya* there are four chapters, or *Padas*: *Gitika Pada, Ganita Pada, Kalakriya Pada* and *Gola Pada*. The *Ganita Pada*, consisting of thirty-three verses, is the critical mathematical text. It includes references to such concepts as squares, cubes, square-roots, cube-roots, areas of triangles, the volume of prisms, areas of circles, the volume of spheres, areas of quadrilaterals, the circumference of circles, elementary trigonometry of series-figures, triadic rules, the reduction of fractions and the theory of pulveriser. In order that mathematical information could be conveyed in poetic form, Aryabhata I developed the alphabet-numeral system of notation, by which specific numbers are allocated to specific letters of the alphabet. He provided the methods to solve simple quadratic equations, which, in the words of one historian, allowed him to earn 'for himself the credit of founding the science of Algebra'.[54] From the other *Padas* we learn about his belief that the earth was a sphere and that it rotated on its axis, and that eclipses were caused by the shadow of the earth falling on the moon. His calculations of the *pi* ratio and the length of the solar year were remarkably close to recent computations. It would be a few more centuries before the works of Aryabhata and his illustrious successor, Brahmagupta, would firstly be closely scrutinised and then approvingly appropriated for development within the Islamic mathematical tradition, which in turn eventually influenced European developments in mathematics.

Skilled craftsmen, working through their guilds, produced good quality jewellery, ivory carvings and artefacts, ceramics and textiles, but the essential technology of the Gupta period was concerned with metal work on copper and iron. A seventh-century bronze statue of the Buddha, weighing 1 ton, found in the ruins of a Buddhist monastery at Sultanganj, Bihar, in 1864, and now housed in the Birmingham Museum, is the finest example of copper metalworking that began during this period using the *cire perdue* technique, which has been described in some of the contemporary texts[55] (see Figure 8.2). The so-called Iron Pillar of Delhi, a shaft 24 feet high and weighing more than 6 tons, showing no signs of erosion or rust since about AD 400, is the best example

Figure 8.2 Sultanganj bronze Buddha (by permission of the Birmingham Museum and Art Gallery).

of iron technology in that period.[56] For many centuries, excepting China, India led the world in metal technology.

Sanskrit literature

Sanskrit literature flourished in the Gupta period. A large body of Brahmanic religious literature, whether consisting of the epics or the *shastras*, was embellished and augmented by learned commentaries and critiques. Buddhist literature was systematised, and so was Jainist knowledge. Not all Sanskrit literature was uniformly attractive or valuable, but certain works have left an indelible impression on the mind and consciousness of the outside world. For example, through the increased contacts of Classical India with the Middle East and the Levant, the collections of animal fables, such as the *Panchatantra*, and the *Hitopadesha*, or 'Book of Wise Counsels', subtly influenced medieval European literature (see Extract 8.3). A Sanskrit work that has received the unqualified praise of the literary world since the end of the eighteenth century is Kalidasa's *Shakuntala*. Kalidasa, one of the 'Nine Gems' who constituted the circle of poets in the reign of Chandragupta II, wrote three plays, but *Shakuntala* is considered his greatest work. As an admiring critic has said, 'Of the arts the best is the drama; of dramas, *Shakuntala*; of *Shakuntala*, the fourth act; of that act, the verses in which Kanva bids farewell to his adopted daughter.'[57] The falling in love of Shakuntala and King Dushyanta and the parting gift of a ring by the latter, their long separation, the curse of the sage Durvasas, Shakuntala's tender parting from Kanva and her search for Dushyanta, the story of the ring, the return of the king's memory, etc. – all these events are forthrightly unfolded as the plot progresses. Sir William Jones was the first to translate the play into English from its Bengali recension and to publish it, in 1789. The real impact of the play was felt most on a long line of German Romantics, great geniuses such as Schiller, Goethe and Herder; through their writings the glory of *Shakuntala* was laid bare before the world. Another enchanting work of classical Sanskrit literature, and now an international bestseller, is the *Kama Sutra* by Vatsyayana. Although a great textbook of erotic love, it is unfortunately much misrepresented and grossly maligned. This is partly because of the inadequate translation of its depictions into English by Sir Richard Burton, one of the reckless adventurers and philanderers of the nineteenth century. Burton's translation gave the *Kama Sutra* a reputation of being a pornographic work. The *Kama Sutra* fell victim to Burton's own infantile and orientalist fantasies; and even today the general public frankly feigns embarrassment at the mention of this powerful work. A fresh translation, along with a new psychoanalytical interpretation of the text, has recently been published, allowing us to appreciate the *Kama Sutra* for what it was intended: an account of the untainted and sublime beauty of erotic pleasure, entirely separated from the 'crude purposefulness of sexual desire'.[58] A fascinating section of the text, called 'The lifestyle of the man-about-town', gives us an insight into what it was like to be a sophisticated rich young man in the Indian urban culture of the fifth century AD.

Dissemination of knowledge: the Nalanda monastic college

The greatest of all the educational institutions of India during the second half of the first millennium was the Buddhist college at Nalanda. It first gained its status as a major centre of higher learning in the reign of Kumaragupta I (415–55), and the year 425 AD 'is the most approximate date' of its establishment.[59] For a long time before that there had existed a Buddhist monastery on the Nalanda site, and Buddhist monks were trained there. Nalanda's transformation into an academic centre was a result of several fruitfully interacting factors during the Gupta era. If one of the purposes of such a centre is to help young minds to understand, absorb, interpret and disseminate knowledge, then ancient India was uniquely the land where there was no dearth of knowledge. By the time of the Guptas, the amount of knowledge available in India, albeit mostly oral, had reached a critical mass in terms of its range and depth. The first huge area concerned the three religious systems themselves – Brahmanism, Buddhism and Jainism – and the similarities and differences between them. The second was that of philosophy and logic. Many philosophical ideas had, by now, come to be crystallised into six major schools of thought, called *darshans* or 'points of view'; and there were intense intellectual debates centred on their validity. The third area concerned grammar and epistemology. From Panini onwards we know of a number of grammarians who had been analysing, recording and classifying the vocabulary and grammar of Sanskrit; and other scholars similarly worked in the *Prakrit* languages. Besides the trinity of theology, philosophy and grammar, there existed much practical knowledge in areas as varied as medicine, music, agriculture, astronomy and mathematics. For a college or an academic institution to impart knowledge usefully it needs able and learned scholars who are not narrow or biased in outlook. At the Nalanda monastery the highest standards were set by the Buddhist scholars and managers who comported themselves like true academics. Scholars of other faiths were always made welcome and given the opportunity to introduce and discuss intellectual issues. The style of teaching was unpedantic and non-didactic. It was very much in the form of dialogue or discourse, respectfully conducted through a series of propositions about the various qualities and theories of knowledge and their refutations; and great philosophers such as Dignaga, Asanga and Vasubandhu were teaching complex ideas at Nalanda.[60] When the monastery received a large land grant, with rent eventually drawn from nearly 100 villages,[61] from the Vaishnava-oriented Kumaragupta I, its financial affairs and future became secure. It was to last until about 1205. With the range of subjects taught, the quality of the academic staff, the very high standards demanded from the students, and the great renown of the institution within and outside India – all these factors enable us to describe Nalanda as a multi-functional college. Long before the Western world came to embrace the idea of a college as an institution and as a centre of instruction from the scholars of the Islamic world,[62] everything that a college was ideally capable of was being realised at Nalanda. The size of the silent ruins of the Nalanda campus today allows us a glimpse of its glorious past.

The Vakataka achievement at Ajanta

Among the many great productions that have taken place over the years at the Royal Opera House, Covent Garden, London, perhaps the most enchanting one for connoisseurs of Indian arts must have been the Ajanta Ballet of 1923.[63] Performed by two of the twentieth century's greatest dancers, Anna Pavlova and Uday Shankar, the choreography of this ballet was based on the dance gestures of the fresco figures and images in the Ajanta caves of Maharashtra. The ballet was, in a sense, a culmination of a hundred years of the art world's fascination with the caves and their contents since they were 'rediscovered' by a hunting party of British soldiers in 1819.[64] What we see in Ajanta today is a mute but eloquent testimony to the beauty and vigour of the Buddhist art and architecture of India over a period of 700 years, between about 200 BC and AD 500. The site of Ajanta was strategically placed at the crossing of merchants' and travellers' routes that ran alongside it; and Buddhist monks and monasteries were richly supported by that merchant class. Ajanta was only one, although the most noble, of the many Buddhist caves of this period. Here, cut through the living rock of the Deccan, around the bend of the River Waghora, are twenty-nine man-made caves (see Figure 8.3, which shows twenty-eight of these), and we can see the two main features of all such caves: the *Chaityas* and the *Viharas*. The *Chaitya* caves are huge preaching halls with horseshoe-shaped windows pierced above the entrance porches. The *Viharas* were like monastic

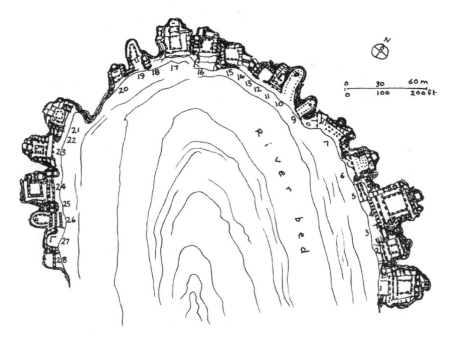

Figure 8.3 The plan of the Ajanta caves (Pat Baker: line drawing adapted from Rawson, op. cit., p. 84).

cells, sometimes two or three storeys high. The great bulk of the excavation and construction had taken place during the first phase of 400 years after 200 BC; but the most spectacularly creative portions were completed in the very short second phase of less than two decades in the second half of the fifth century AD (see Figure 8.4). This later phase coincided with the reign of the Vakataka king Harishena (460–78), the last great patron of Ajanta. The Vakatakas had been, for the most part, subsidiary feudatories of the imperial Guptas, but with the waning of Gupta power they came to enjoy a brief, if truncated, spell of true independence and expansion of their territory. It was

Figure 8.4 An Ajanta façade (from Havell, op. cit., p. 52).

indeed good fortune for Indian art that Harishena was not only wealthy but also truly dedicated to further embellishing the Buddhist art at Ajanta. New caves were hewn, and it was chiefly on his orders that the most beautiful frescos came to be created, depicting both divine and human scenes and associated legends. More than the architecture, it is the Ajanta paintings that have captured universal imagination (see Figure 8.5). These paintings, executed with masterly skill in the use of materials and colours, portray Vakataka court scenes and the *Boddhisattava* manifestation in its full glory (see Figure 8.6), along with the narration of stories from the *Jatakas*. We can confidently assert that 'the architecture, paintings and sculpture that emerged and evolved in Ajanta (in the Gupta–Vakataka Age) were to leave an impression on all subsequent Indian, Central Asian and Far Eastern Art.'[65]

Figure 8.5 Shiva and Parvati at Ajanta (from Havell, op. cit., p. 196).

Figure 8.6 Head of Bodhisattava at Ajanta (from Havell, op. cit., p. 200).

SELECT EXTRACTS FOR REVIEW AND REFLECTION

Extract 8.1   The Mandasor inscription of the silk-weavers

One of the most important developments in ancient Indian historiography
has been the opening up of studies of new areas of social and economic

life revealed by researches into a variety of inscriptions. A little-known inscription, found some years ago at a place called Dasapura, now known as Mandasor, in Madhya Pradesh, throws light on a number of themes relating to ordinary peoples' lives in Gupta India. This inscription, written in verse form on a block of stone by an unknown *brahman* poet, Vatsabhatti, celebrates the building of a temple by a guild of silk-weavers who had come to Mandasor from their homeland of Lata, between the rivers Narmada and Tapti. After invoking prayers to Surya, the sun god, the poet introduces the weavers, their history and their industriousness; he then describes the landscape of Mandasor by presenting an idealised picture of its people and houses; and lastly he eulogises the glories of the Gupta emperor Kumaragupta and the local ruler Bandhuvarman. The temple, like a glorious crest-jewel shining in white with its lofty spires, was built in the honour of Bandhuvarman in the year AD 437–8. However, The Huna aggressions of the late fifth century had a destructive effect on both the people and their buildings, and the temple had to be repaired in the year AD 473–4 when, it is thought, Vatsabhatti also composed the inscription.

Source: John F. Fleet, *Corpus Inscriptionum Indicarum: Inscriptions of the Early Guptas and their Successors*, Vol. 3, Calcutta: Government of India, 1888, texts and translations, pp. 79–88. See also A.L. Basham, 'The Mandasor Inscription of the Silk-Weavers', in B. Smith (ed.), *Essays in Gupta Culture*, New Delhi: Motilal Banarsidass, 1983, pp. 101–3.

Extract 8.2 A problem attributed to Aryabhata by Bhaskara I (*c.* AD 600), one of the most able commentators on his work

Ancient Indian mathematicians formulated their problems with a human touch, as can be shown in the following example.

Oh beautiful maiden with beaming eyes, tell me, since you understand the method of inversion, what number multiplied by 3, then increased by three-quarters of the product, then divided by 7, then diminished by one-third of the result, then multiplied by itself, then diminished by 52, whose square root is then extracted before 8 is added and then divided by 10, gives the final result of 2?

The solution offered is elegant and simple: We start with the answer 2 and work backwards. When the problem says divide by 10, we multiply by that number; when told to add 8, we subtract 8; when told to extract the square root, we take the square; and so on. It is precisely the replacement of the original operation by the inverse that gives the method its name of 'inversion'. Thus

$((2)(10)-8)^2 + 52 = 196$

$\sqrt{196} = 14$

$\dfrac{(14)(3/2)(70(4/7)}{3} = 28$ Answer

Source: A problem sent in a note to the author by Dr George Gheverghese Joseph, whose book *The Crest of the Peacock: Non-European Roots of Mathematics*, London: Penguin, 2000, contains a number of examples and problems from ancient Indian mathematics.

Extract 8.3   Doubts about the extent of influence of Indian fables on European literature

It is generally taken for granted that many European fables have their origin in Indian fables. The following passage serves as a corrective to this perception.

It would be difficult to make an exact account of the European folk tales which are truly derived from India. No two stories are precisely alike. The degree of similarity required before a particular tale can be considered genuinely derivative from another one will differ from one researcher to another. The earlier investigators of this problem in the late nineteenth century had a tendency to overstate their case. For instance, Joseph Jacobs calculated that, of the approximately 260 Aesops' fables extant in Latin, 56 had Indian counterparts ... But in 1957 Laurits Bodker, summing up the results of decades of folklore research, asserted that, of about 500 animal tales recorded from modern European oral tradition, only about 20 had close Indian counterparts. Interestingly, the count goes much higher in the case of literary fables: the Panchatantra is the most prolific source of Indian stories found in Europe.

Source: Jean W. Sedlar, *India and the Greek world*, Totowa, NJ: Rowman & Littlefield, p. 106.

RELEVANT QUESTIONS FOR DISCUSSION

1   In what ways did the Mauryan and Gupta policies differ?
2   Why has *Kama Sutra* been such a misunderstood work of literature?
3   What do the Ajanta caves reveal to us about society in ancient India?

Notes

1 Compare and contrast the works by Majumdar and Pusalker 1954, Mukerjee 1958 or Tripathi 1999 with those by Thapar 2002 or Jha 2004; but, for a concise balanced judgement, see Ray *et al*. 2000: 618–19.
2 A good example of this approach is by Tripathi 1999: 493–505.
3 Raychaudhuri 1996: 468.
4 For an understanding of the style of such imperial inscriptions as on this pillar, see Sircar 1971: 1–16.
5 Smith 1924: 306.
6 Tripathi 1999: 248.
7 Majumdar and Pusalker 1954: 11–12.
8 Majumdar 1977: 234.
9 Raychaudhuri 1996: 489–90.
10 For the background to the Vakatakas, see ibid.: 769–77.
11 Majumdar and Pusalker 1954: 19–20.
12 Thapar 2002: 290; Majumdar 1977: 414.
13 Quoted in Ray *et al*. 2000: 386.
14 Dikshitar 1993: 108–39.
15 Chattopadhyaya 1995: 314–18.
16 Dikshitar 1993: 215–26.
17 Ibid.: 239–52.
18 Ibid.: 271–8.
19 Ibid.: 265–71.
20 Schwartzberg 1992: 28.
21 For details, see Collins 1991: 45–57; Previte-Orton 1971: 45–59, 77–102.
22 Maity 1957: 165–78.
23 Schwartzberg 1992: 179–80.
24 Thapar 2002: 286.
25 For Toramana's piety, read the copper plate inscription in Ray *et al*. 2000: 615–16.
26 Raychaudhuri 1996: 518–19.
27 Jha 2004: 207; Wink 1991: 227.
28 Schwartzberg 1992: 180.
29 Liu 1994: 127–36.
30 Auboyer 2002: 195–7.
31 Maity 1957: 43–7.
32 Sharma 1959: 202–5.
33 Thapar 2002: 291–2.
34 Maity 1957: 141–54.
35 Sharma 1959: 202–33; Sharma 1985.
36 The contested views may be found in Mukhia 1981, Mukhia 1985, Sharma 1985 and Stein 1985.
37 Thapar 2002: 287.
38 Quoted in Kachroo 2000: 365.
39 Ali 1999: 45.
40 Klostermaier 1994: 94.
41 Rocher 1986: 101.
42 Trautmann 1981: 271–7.
43 Stein 1998: 99.
44 Ibid.
45 Sharma 1958: 231–8.
46 Ibid.: 268, 273.
47 Thapar 2002: 303.

48 Sharma 1958: 261–5.
49 McNeill 1967: 173.
50 Kerala Sastra Sahitya Parishad 2002.
51 Joseph 2000: 215–63.
52 Bose *et al*. 1989: 584–93.
53 To understand the general context of the mathematical work in one part of India
    – Kerala – for example, see Joseph 2002: 129–35.
54 Sarasvati 1986: 64.
55 Bose *et al*. 1989: 299.
56 Ibid.: 299–303.
57 Quoted in Rawlinson 1965: 137.
58 Doniger and Kakar 2002: xxxix.
59 Sankalia 1972: 57.
60 Ibid.: 123–6.
61 Majumdar 1977: 453.
62 Makdisi 1981: 224–80.
63 Keay 2001: 148–55.
64 Allen 2002: 128–34.
65 Sengupta 1993: 15.

9 The post-Gupta era and the rise of the south

(Time-span: c. AD 550 to 750)

With the decline and fall of the imperial Guptas came the demise of the imperial idea. It was in north India that this idea had had its greatest potency and diffusion through the great empires built over many centuries by outstanding personalities such as Chandragupta Maurya, Ashoka, Kanishka and Samudragupta; it was therefore in north India that the impact of its passing was most felt. From the middle of the sixth century onwards, large and small regional kingdoms were to dominate the north Indian political and state apparatus, and their authority was to last for several centuries. Individual kings dreamt about the attraction of pan-Indian control, and many of them, out of sheer egotism, adopted pompous titles; but just one of them, Harsha, in the seventh century, came near to realising such control, and that only for the duration of his reign. In contrast to north Indian post-imperial fragmentation, however, the south assumed greater prominence with the rise of two great kingdoms. The first was that of the Chalukyas who, following in the footsteps of the Satavahanas and the Vakatakas, established their authority in the Deccan. The second was that of the Pallavas in the far south: after a long period of acculturation and political gestation, the southern peninsula emerged from political obscurity and began to assert its influence (see Map 9.1).

Our historical knowledge of this period is dependent on a variety of interlocking interpretations drawn by historians, linguists, archaeologists and anthropologists. The historians and linguists have concentrated on numerous inscriptions that either speak for themselves or need interpreting, along with both contemporary historiographical material, such as the biography of young Harsha by Banabhatta, and later historical sources. The archaeologists have arrived late on the scene, but their research is helping to corroborate the conventional evidence; the anthropologists, bringing some of the insights gained in other regions of the world, have given us incisive interpretations of the south Indian cultures. If we are asked, however, to name one work from this period that can be said to symbolise the spirit of the age, then it has to be *Si-Yu-Ki*, the great account of India as portrayed by the famous Chinese Buddhist traveller and pilgrim Hsuan Tsang. More than any other single work by him, it is this text that today grips our imagination.[1] It contains all the rich details of life in the India of the early seventh century, and must be classed among the great geographical and social documents of the ancient world. We learn about

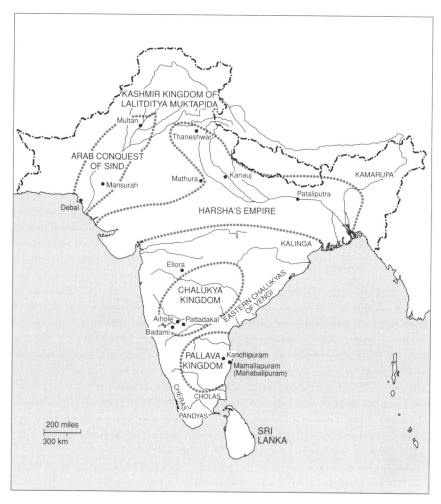

Map 9.1 Post-Gupta kingdoms and the southern states.

the conditions in several towns and villages, the social structure, the economy and character of the people of India, their different laws and punishments, their religious events and their festivals. While all the details naturally will not meet our modern criteria for historical verifiability, this book is an indispensable asset for the historians of India.

North India fractured

A number of dynasties became engaged in fierce competition for the control of north India during this period.[2] It all began in the middle of the sixth century, with the later Guptas struggling against not only the Hunas but some powerful regional families too. Independent kingdoms began to spring up in different places on the borders of the empire. Such kingdoms as *Valabhi* in Gujarat, Gauda and Vanga in Bengal and *Kamarupa* (Assam) asserted their autonomy at the margins of their empire, while the Gangetic heartland was itself subjected to undue strains. In the latter area two great dynasties were finally to supplant the weaker Guptas of the sixth century: the Pushyabhuti, based at Thaneshwar in *Sthanivishvara* (now Haryana) and the Maukhari, based at *Kanauj* (modern Kanyakubja), controlling the prime estate of north India, the *doab*, or the land between the rivers Ganga and Yamuna. A marriage alliance between the two royal houses was followed, however, by a war waged upon them by the kings of Bengal and Malwa, resulting in many tragic killings.[3] Eventually the Pushyabhuti prince Harsha became the ruler of both houses, with his capital in *Kanauj*, and controlled a substantial portion of the former Gupta territories. Although *Kanauj* now began its period of glory, it also became a bone of contention among the rival dynasties.

Harsha's kingdom

Harsha's kingdom lasted from 606 to 647. We know much about it from accounts left by two of his greatest admirers: his friend, courtier and biographer, Banabhatta, and the great Chinese traveller Hsuan Tsang. From their writings, along with his own literary works, we can discern that Harsha played three different roles: as a conqueror, an administrator and a man of intellect and culture. Leaving aside the last two roles for consideration later, we must acknowledge that Harsha was a man of power whose conquests were wide and far-reaching. After he had unified the Pushyabhutis and the Maukharis and transferred the capital to *Kanauj*, giving him the overlordship of the Maukhari domains in the central Gangetic heartlands, he went on to conquer Bengal, Bihar, Orissa, Gujarat and Punjab. Although he met defeat on the River Narmada at the hands of the Chalukyan king Pulakeshin II, he came to be recognised as the master of what was termed 'the five Indies'.[4] An inscription at Aihole in Karnataka, although outside his realm, describes him somewhat exaggeratedly as the ruler of the whole of north India.[5] On defeating his rivals he too, like the Guptas, adopted the neighbourly policy of the *samanta*. So successful was this policy that even the powerful kings of Kashmir, Nepal and Valabhi counted among his tributaries. Tai Sung, the Tang emperor of China, was particularly friendly to Harsha, owing to the latter's closeness to Hsuan Tsang and extreme generosity towards the Buddhists.[6] Shortly after Harsha's death in 647 his kingdom broke up. No one of comparable stature appeared on the scene, and the ensuing anarchy lasted for more than seven decades.

Yashovarman and Lalitditya

In the second quarter of the eighth century power in north India came to be strongly contested by two great protagonists. One was Yashovarman, who acceded to the throne of Kanauj after the post-Harshan anarchy and who ruled between about 725 and 752. Yashovarman's ambition was to conquer the whole of India, and his armies penetrated as far as Bengal. He embellished the city of *Kanauj* and established it as a symbol of his power and authority. He was a great patron of arts and letters, and at his court resided the famous playwright Bhavabhuti.[7] Yashovarman, however, faced hostility from the other protagonist, Lalitditya Muktapida, the ruler of Kashmir between about 724 and 760.[8] Much conflict resulted between them, and other parties also became involved in the fray: the Chinese, the Tibetans, the Arabs and the rising Rajput dynasty of Gurjara–Pratihara. Each of these groups had strategic agendas of their own, creating much confusion.[9] Lalitditya was able to keep Yashovarman in check and deftly negotiated his way through the north Indian political and military morass; but ultimately he perished with his army while fighting the Tibetans in Sinkiang. With the passing of both Yashovarman and Lalitditya, north India became the scene of rivalry among three great dynasties of Gurjara–Pratihara, the Palas and the Rashtrakutas. The next chapter will explore this in greater detail.

The Arab seizure of Sind

The fracturing of north India was aggravated by the Arab invasion of Sind, the first foreign intrusion into India since that of the Hunas. Both Hindus and Buddhists vied for power and influence in Sind before the Arab incursion. The Buddhist Rai dynasty ruled until 622, when Chach, the *brahman* minister of the Buddhist king, usurped the throne and imposed a tyranny. By the time his reign ended, in 666, he had alienated the varied groups of Jats, Meds and Buddhists.[10] The civil unrest worsened after Dahir, the son of Chach, became king in 679, and it was he who faced the Arab invasion in 711. Although considered to be an exceptionally difficult task to achieve, the conquest of India was one of the very early aims of the Muslim geo-political strategy. As early as 644, at the end of the caliphate of Umar, the Arabs had entered Makran on the Baluchi coast. By the time the Umayyad caliphate began under Muawiya (661), systematic Arab reconnaissance of the Sind coast was under way.[11] The Umayyads had their power centre at Damascus, but they appointed provincial governors in the areas the Arabs held or wished to hold. One such governor was Al-Hajjaj, who was based in Baghdad from 694 to 714, with his official title of 'governor of Iraq and Hind and Sind'. An opportune moment for Al-Hajjaj to attack Sind occurred when Dahir failed to respond positively to a request by him to act over an incident of piracy in which Muslim women and children had been caught up. After his lord and master in Damascus, Caliph al-Walid (705–15), had been persuaded to authorise punitive measures against Dahir, the command of an invasion force was entrusted to his young nephew Muhammad al-Qasim. A relatively small and highly mobile naval task force, equipped with some deadly siege artillery, enabled Muhammad first to take Debal, the commercial port. From there, after crossing the River Indus, he marched upon

Brahmanabad, where, in a major battle, Dahir was killed. Muhammad then married his widow, Rani Ladi. With Lower Sind taken, Muhammad moved up the Indus, towards Upper Sind, and eventually reached Multan. Sind had now definitely become part of the Umayyad-controlled Islamic Empire.

Chalukyas and Pallavas: the Deccan and the deep south

In the Deccan the two mighty kingdoms of the Satavahana and the Vakataka had exercised uninterrupted power after the Mauryas; and the monarchic tradition was set to continue with the Chalukya and Pallava dynasties. The former established a major presence during our period, while the latter assumed importance after the mid-eighth century. The Deccani kingdoms had a strong commercial tradition; during these centuries they were to become great beneficiaries of the Indian Ocean trade with the rising power of the Arabs. In the deep south of India, while the Aryanisation process over many centuries had been making a considerable social and religious impact on the life of the people, the imperial idea had not grasped the peoples' imagination, partly because of the enormous distance separating the far south from the imperial heartland in the Gangetic basin. State foundation and the rise of kingdoms in the far south came much later than in the north, but their development arose out of factors unique to southern culture and its geography. From the sixth century the southern kingdoms, drawing strength from their prosperous agrarian base, their profitable commercial links with the outside world and their powerful temple cultures, created and imprinted their own styles of authority and governance.

The Chalukyas

The Chalukyas originated from the Kadamba region of the Karnataka, which remained their main base.[12] They also pushed into the lands where the Satavahanas and the Vakatakas had once dominated. Three distinct families of the Chalukyas eventually emerged: the Early Chalukyas of Badami (525–757), the Eastern Chalukyas of Vengi (624–1020) and the Later Chalukyas of Kalyani (973–1200); in terms of relative importance, the Early Chalukyas were the most significant. Their real power began with Pulakeshin I (543–66); it reached its zenith in the reign of Pulakeshin II (609–42); and it was consolidated by strong-minded rulers such as Vikramaditya I (654–68), Vijayaditya (696–733) and Vikramaditya II (733–44). The last ruler, Kirtivarman II (744–57), was overthrown by another regional power, the Rashtrakutas. History's most famous Chalukyan monarch was Pulakeshin II. During his reign of thirty-three years he made aggressive moves against all the rulers who surrounded the Chalukyan heartland. He established suzerainty over Gujarat and Malwa, and frightened off King Harsha sufficiently for the latter to confine himself to the overlordship of the lands north of the Narmada river. He brought the Andhra region into his family's patrimony, and this eventually gave rise to the dynasty of the Eastern Chalukyas of Vengi. His great victories are honoured in the renowned Aihole *prasasti* by his court poet, Ravikirti, and inscribed on a slab of the eastern wall of the great Meguti Temple of Aihole in Karnataka.[13] The Chinese traveller Hsuan Tsang also paid tribute to his courage and valour, and said about his army that, 'if a general loses a battle they do not inflict punishment, but present him with women's clothes, and so he is driven to seek death for himself.'[14] Pulakeshin overreached himself, however, when he attacked the rising southern power of the Pallava kingdom, resulting ultimately in his defeat and death in 642.

The Pallava kingdom

From the *Sangam* literature of the Tamils we learn that, as early as the third century BC, there were three distinct kingdoms in the south of India: the Chola kingdom of the southeast coast, the Chera kingdom of the southwest coast in Kerala, and the kingdom of the Pandyas in Madurai region.[15] For many centuries just before and after the Christian era, while experiencing increasing Aryanisation, Brahmanisation and Sanskritisation, south India had also enjoyed relative prosperity through a rich base of agriculture and international trade. This can be evidenced from the *Sangam* literature.[16] The three kingdoms themselves, however, registered little impact upon the overall Indian political scene. Their territorial interests were generally parochial, except in relation to Sri Lanka, whose capture always appeared to them as a tempting prize. The political situation changed dramatically in the sixth century with the rise of the Pallava kingdom in a core region of the south called *Tondaimanadalam*, which today corresponds to the northern portion of Tamil Nadu. Kanchipuram was the main urban centre. There are two theories about the origins of the Pallavas. One is that they were the descendants of a group of Parthians from Iran; and the other describes them as the descendants of north Indian *brahman* migrants.[17] No one can be entirely certain, but, whatever their origins, it cannot be denied that they became one of the great southern regional dynasties. The dynasty dated itself as early as AD 275, but its great epoch straddled the seventh and the eighth centuries, when rulers such as Narasimhavarman I (630–68), Parameshvaravarman I (670–700) and Narasimhavarman II (695–728) left their mark on contemporary history – all dates falling within our period.

The Pallavas and Chalukyas held sway in adjacent territories. They had much in common in terms of religion, society and economy, and had many overlapping cultural traditions and rituals. Yet they were unable to live in complete peace with each other. In fact, a hundred years' war raged between them, and the inscriptions of both dynasties provide long lists of conquests by their rulers. The first round in the interminable Chalukya–Pallava conflict had gone to Pulakeshin II, whose victories are recorded in the Aihole inscription. The Pallava revenge, however, came with Narasimhavarman I's attack on Badami in 642, resulting in the death of Pulakeshin II. The Chalukyas were for a time overshadowed by the Pallavas, and their dynasty also faced a succession crisis. However, from 655 onwards, under Vikramaditya I, they commenced the second round of warfare against the Pallavas and captured their capital city, Kanchipuram. Once more, the Pallavas took their retribution. And so it went on, the Chalukya–Pallava conflict, year after year, during the late seventh and early eighth centuries. The last great attack by the Chalukyas on the Pallavas took place during the short reign of Vikramaditya II (733–44). In a major campaign of 740, Kanchipuram was again captured. As if to safeguard his reputation and the honour of his people for posterity, Vikramaditya II ordered an inscription to be carved on a pillar of the city's newly built Kailasanatha Temple, recording both his conquests and his generosity towards the people of the vanquished city. This inscription was left unerased by the Pallavas when they regained the city.[18] While on certain occasions, and particularly if the army commanders were especially cruel, this type of conflict could be very barbaric, resulting in death and destruction on a horrendous scale, it is also worth noting that most inter-Indian conflicts in this period took the form of low-intensity warfare. The final outcome of their hundred years' war, however, proved to be destructive for both the Chalukyas and the Pallavas. The former had always been the initial aggressors, and had therefore aroused the envy and hatred of many of their neighbours. By the middle of the eighth century, with their energies sapped, they became ready prey to the rising power of the Rashtrakutas. The Pallavas survived for a century more, but they too had exhausted themselves by their wars with the Chalukyas and the Pandyas of Madurai. In the ninth century they would be overwhelmed by both the Rashtrakutas and their older rivals, the Cholas.

Political and economic perspectives

Sources of royal legitimacy

Generally speaking, most Indian kingdoms of this period were hierarchical and bureaucratic states. Harsha's kingdom was a case in point. The legitimacy of the political sovereignty of his kingdom was derived from the concepts articulated in such famous texts as the *Upanishads*, the *Mahabharata*, the *Arthashastra* and the *Manusmriti*, written before the fourth century AD, or more recent texts such as *Katyayanasmriti* (*c.* AD 400–600), *Haritasmriti* (*c.* 400–700) and Kamandaki's *Niti-Sara* (*c.* 400–600), which contained useful advice on kingship.[19] Of great importance was the concept of *dharma*, the moral law. There might be different types of kings and conquerors – righteous, greedy or plain demonic – but they were all obliged to follow *dharma*. The king, however, had a powerful tool at his disposal, which was the threat of *danda*, or punishment. Both *dharma* and *danda* were the backbone of kingship, but successful kingship also depended upon the close alliance of the *brahman* and the *kshatriya*.[20] Most kings were genuinely *kshatriyas* or contrived to be so; however, the legitimacy of their power also rested on the *brahman* support mechanism.

Once secured, that power became real, and exercised through bureaucracy. The rulers could control taxation and maintain large centralised armies. The land grants, made either to the *brahmans* or to the feudal vassals, reduced overall the king's actual control over land, but did not affect his ultimate exercise of sovereignty. Thus, some of the famous rulers of our period, such as Harsha and Pulakeshin II, exercised real control through bureaucracy, even while devolving power over many of their lands to their subordinates.

Most conventional histories of south Indian kingdoms also described the kingdoms of the Pallavas and their famous successors, the Cholas, as centralised bureaucratic states, with overall supremacy vested in the king. However, this view has been countered by another argument, which holds that the south Indian kings enjoyed mostly symbolic or ritual power, legitimised by notions of *dharmic* kingship; the real power lay with the self-governing and near-autonomous peasant communities or local power structures of south India known as *nadus*.[21] Certainly, owing to the increasing level of Brahmanisation in south India, it was natural that the monarchs made available land grants to the *brahmans* and extended royal patronage to the temples; but these were in fact defence stratagems for the monarchs. Instead of calling the Pallava or Chola kingdoms bureaucratic, it is argued, an appropriate term to use would be 'segmentary', because political authority and control were highly local.[22] This particular interpretation owes its source to comparative anthropological studies of certain African peasant societies that structurally resembled the peasant communities of south India.[23] Although there is no universal agreement on this interpretation, we have here at least two different models of power and legitimacy.

The mandala and the samanta

Inter-state relations among the Indian states of that period, like those of Harsha, were organised on the principle of what is generally called a *mandala*.[24] This principle, articulated in the *Arthashastra* of Kautalya and the *Niti-sara* of Kamandaki, presupposed a circle or orbit of states around any one kingdom; the circle normally consisted of twelve states, including the dominant kingdom. Starting with the nearest state and moving outwards, the five states with shifting allegiances in front of the kingdom were presumed to be the enemy, the friend, the friend of the enemy, the friend of the friend, and the friend of the friend of the enemy. Similarly, at the rear of the kingdom, again in the order of location, would be positioned the rearward enemy, the rearward friend, the friend of the rearward enemy, and the friend of the rearward friend. Somewhere in the orbit, but fairly close to the kingdom as well as to the enemy, there was posited an intermediary state; and, finally, a neutral state was situated somewhere well beyond the territory of all the other states. Although a theoretical construct, bearing only a notional relationship to events 'on the ground', the *mandala* principle allowed 'political elites to make sense of the shifting events of their political world and to formulate theories of "diplomatic action'".[25] It was evidently enunciated on the basis of common-sense observation of the political state system in post-Vedic India. The kings were encouraged to be active participants of the *mandala* by adopting certain key strategies at appropriate times. These would include making an alliance, declaring a war, being neutral, preparing for attack without declaring a war, seeking protection from another state, or making use of a 'double policy' which was making peace with one and waging war against another. Each king had to try to secure his position in the *mandala* by adopting one or other of the six strategies. Headstrong kings, such as the great Chalukyan ruler Pulakeshin II, simply went for total domination of their *mandala* by being always aggressive or adopting aggressive stances, until in the end they dominated wholly for a while or were then themselves consumed by a great defeat, as Pulakeshin himself was. Wiser rulers, such as Harsha, followed in the footsteps of the great Gupta monarch Samudragupta, who won many conquests but never exulted over the vanquished. These rulers normally created the *samantas*, those defeated peers who continued to maintain their dignity and honour even as they became lesser tributaries paying homage to the conqueror. Harsha's *mandala* became a less intimidating circle of states for him, because it consisted of friendly *samantas* or *maha-samantas* who acknowledged him as paramount sovereign.[26]

Political accommodation within the Islamic context

The seizure of Sind by the Arabs in 711 provides an opportunity, within the period covered by this chapter, to look afresh at some of the Islamic political strategies of accommodation with contesting powers. This is important because of much misunderstanding over this aspect, resulting in needless demonisation of medieval Islamic rulers. From the second quarter of the seventh century the Arabs began a series of military campaigns that eventually established their domination over the Middle East and North Africa. A new social and cultural order, based on the principles of Islam, was forged in the conquered territories. The early Muslim philosophers and theologians conceived of the ordered world as the 'House of Islam' (*dar al-islam*), which, according to them, was their world of peace. Those who lived beyond that world lived in the 'House of War' (*dar al-harb*), or 'foreign territory'. From the earliest period of their own internal struggles within Arabia, and across many centuries, the believers battled to bring the infidels into the 'House of Islam'. Only defeats, sheer exhaustion or internal decay could stop them. From the very beginning, however, the promoters of the Islamic Empire faced a major problem, which was how to reconcile their aspirations with the realities of the world. It is important to appreciate that, however impassioned the religious rhetoric behind the projection of the Islamic Empire might have been, Muslim leaders and men of action on the ground were never entirely swayed by it and, more often than not, exercised their authority either pragmatically or rationally. For example, the arrangements and treaties made with their potential enemies created for Islamic jurists a new legal category of the 'House of Truce' (*dar al-ahd*, or *dar as-sulh*), which meant that an Islamic ruler could be reconciled to a ruler, a people or a state which was not Islamic but was at peace with him.[27] Over the question, too, of the treatment of unbelievers, the scriptural injunctions were flexibly interpreted by most Muslim rulers. Originally, the status of the 'people of the book' (*ahl al-kitab*) was granted to the Jews and the Christians, and they were therefore 'protected subjects' (*ahl adh-dhimma*). However, since the same status had been earlier granted to a people called the Sabians, most Muslim rulers appreciated that the Zoroastrians of Iran and the Hindus of India, both people with their own extensive scriptural heritages, should also qualify for that status.[28] Such flexibility was displayed by the conqueror of Sind, Muhammad al-Qasim, in his dealings with the various power groupings in that province.[29] The promoters and rulers of the Islamic Empire were also often victims of circumstances caused by internal squabbling and civil wars. These disturbances were called *fitna*, and they often resulted in horrendous dynastic and family killings. The idea of a constitutional monarchy remained an alien concept in such an atmosphere. Many a good Muslim ruler in history was a victim of *fitna*, leading to his destruction. Just four years after his conquest, Muhammad al-Qasim himself became such a victim and forfeited his life.[30] It is therefore important not to exaggerate the power of the mediaeval Islamic rulers. In the control of Sind by the Arabs for nearly four centuries we have a trenchant example of both the power and the limitations of those rulers.

Political and economic strategy behind land grants

We observed in the previous chapter that the imperial Guptas had increasingly followed the ancient practice of donating state land as grants to *brahmans* or to some of their officers. The programme of land grants accelerated during the post-Gupta centuries, and the royal dynasties saw in it a means of demonstrating their power and authority. Specific evidence is available for Harsha's land grants to *brahmans* or religious institutions from just a few inscriptions, along with the references in *Harsha-charita* or *Si-Yu-Ki*; one of his religious endowments was a donation of 100 villages of 1,000 ploughs each to *brahmans*.[31] The copper plates of the Pallava kingdom provide information on land grants in the far south. Historically, there had been a continuing argument among the political and social thinkers of India as to whether the king had the sole right of ownership of all land in his kingdom or merely the entitlement to collect taxes; the general assumption was that all waste land or uncultivated terrain was state property and kings could confer those lands upon whom they pleased.[32] During his travels through Harsha's kingdom, Hsuan Tsang observed that royal land was divided into four categories assigned to four items of expenditure, namely expenses relating to government and state worship, endowments to ministers, rewards to persons of great ability, and charity to various faiths and sects.[33] Land was generally measured in terms of ploughs, drawn by a given number of cattle, to till a certain acreage. Therefore, when the kings donated their income from land they declared the extent of arable territory in plough measures. A minor *samanta* in Harsha's time would be entitled to an average village of 1,000 plough units, or 1,333 acres of land.[34] Differential conditions applied to different beneficiaries: some were granted outright gifts with all the assets of the land, including peasants; others could enjoy the revenue but had to pay a land tax; while yet others were expected to provide a certain amount of service. Although mostly unrecorded, Harsha's secular grants provided a considerable boost to the growth of feudalism and a feudal mentality in north India. The Pallava kings of south India made substantial endowments to the *brahmans*. As mentioned above, the far south had a flourishing tradition of peasant cultivation within local autonomous units called *nadus*; but Brahmanisation also proceeded apace throughout south Indian society over many centuries, and the influence of the *brahmans* was paramount in the villages. While the Pallavas needed the *brahmans* to confirm the legitimacy of their rule through the use of rituals, they also appreciated the valuable role the latter could play in increasing land productivity. They therefore created entirely new villages called the *brahmadeya*, by granting either the entire village or parts of it to a single *brahman*, or groups of them, who not only kept the revenue arising from the labour of the peasants, but also did not pay any tax.[35] The practice of granting lands to institutions such as temples became more pronounced after the Pallavas, under the Cholas.

The state of agriculture

Despite all the political upheavals of this period, Indian agriculture remained robust and prosperous, as attested by a number of sources. For example, the late Gupta encyclopaedia and lexicon the *Amarakosha*, for example, has much information on the forests and gardens as well as trees and plants of India.[36] Another useful source is the travelogue of the Chinese pilgrim Hsuan Tsang. He mentions the cultivation of cereals such as rice and wheat, with the region of *Magadha* producing a most fragrant variety of rice called 'rice for grandees'; there were also rich and extensive orchards of delicious fruits such as mangoes, melons, plums, peaches, apricots, grapes, pomegranates, sweet oranges, apples, jackfruits and coconuts.[37] Another source, Banabhatta, mentions the fertility of the soil in Harsha's kingdom, and refers to plentiful crops of sugar cane, vines and a variety of beans. For generating greater revenue from land, the Indian kings encouraged the sciences of agriculture and animal husbandry.[38] They also asked the specialists to construct reservoirs for the regular supply of water. The state was meant to provide facilities for cattle-breeding and for controlling plant and cattle diseases. Then, as now, the more or less guaranteed and seasonally regular natural supply of water ensured a flourishing agriculture on the vast plains of north India, from Punjab down to Bengal. The one limiting factor was that, with crops grown through undemanding labour, the north Indian peasant was content with a minimal level of agricultural technology. An exception to this may be found in a dry region such as Rajasthan, where irrigation by wells and water-tanks was more common, and where evidence exists of a primitive form of technology prior to the Persian wheel.[39] With low rainfall and a relatively small volume of water carried by the southern rivers, southern agriculture required great ingenuity in the use of soil, seeds and water. From even before the *Sangam* Age the southern peasants had been experimenting with various forms of irrigation and mixed-crop farming[40] (see Extract 9.1). It was, however, during our period, under the Pallavas, that huge irrigation tanks, or man-made lakes with earthen walls, known as *eri*, were built on *eripatti*, or tank land.[41] The Pallava kingdom was constituted from twenty-four localities of *Tondaimandalam*, called *kottams*. Each *kottam* was a unique zone of agrarian, pastoral and village-based economy, supported by irrigation based on reservoirs and small lakes.[42] The advanced skills required in the building and maintenance of these tanks would have been provided by the *brahman* entrepreneurs and settlers in the *brahmadeya* villages.[43] The Pallava inscriptions provide us with details of the use and care of these earthwork tanks (see Figure 9.1), and there is evidence of sluice mechanisms being used in the Pallava irrigation schemes.[44]

New directions in India's international trade

The fall of the Western Roman Empire and the disappearance of the flourishing trade with Rome meant a certain definite decline from the end of the fourth century in the value and volume of Indian international trade.[45] One indicator of this was the paucity of metallic money from the late Gupta period onwards.[46] That was certainly a time of turbulence, but it would be wrong to assume that international trade suddenly collapsed and society relapsed into ruralism. In fact, during the two centuries under review, new prospects for long-distance trade were emerging; and then, almost until the beginning of the eleventh century, Indian international trade remained brisk and dynamic. As far as the western Indian Ocean trade was concerned, it is worth noting that the Eastern Roman Empire had not fallen to the Huns or the Goths, and the Greek and Byzantine mariners were now jointly venturing with the Ethiopian traders in activating and promoting the Indian Ocean trade.[47] Another major maritime power, in direct competition with Byzantium, was Persia. Before the rise of Islam the pagan Arabs, Persian Zoroastrians and Persian Christians had all plied the trade routes of the Arabian Sea and the Persian Gulf under Persian suzerainty. However, with the sudden emergence of Islamic power after 622 and the spectacular defeat of Persia by the Arabs in 651, the new masters of the Indian Ocean were all now Muslim. This control enabled the Muslims to link the Indian markets with the Islamic world.[48] We shall examine this Muslim commercial dominance in greater detail in the next chapter. In the eastern Indian Ocean too, great opportunities for trade were opening up for the merchants of south India. By the seventh century a number of kingdoms had

Figure 9.1 South Indian tank scene (by permission of RHPL).

been established in Southeast Asia, such as *Kambuja* and *Funnan* (Cambodia), *Champa* (Vietnam) and *Sri Vijaya* (southern peninsula of Malaysia, Java and Sumatra). There had been a strong Indian cultural and commercial influence on these kingdoms for many centuries, and during the heyday of Roman trade the Indian merchants and shippers had brought spices from there to India for transhipment to Rome in exchange for some of the Roman wares. The Pallava rulers built dockyards and developed a navy, which enabled the south Indian mariners to enjoy a near monopoly of trade until the Muslim maritime challenge in the eighth century.[49] Besides the oceanic trades, the land routes also continued to be used. According to Hsuan Tsang's testimony, the medium of exchange in trade consisted of such items as gold, silver, cowries and small pearls.[50] India–China land trade flourished in the seventh century as well as it had in the post-Mauryan centuries, and Chinese silk was always highly prized. It may be noted, however, that both the Chinese and the Indians suffered as a result of the Byzantines surreptitiously learning the art of cultivating silk-worms.[51] The land trade with Central and West Asia also continued; Banabhatta refers to fine steeds and horses from there in Harsha's stables.[52] In conclusion, we can say that there was little diminution of trade in the two post-Gupta centuries between 550 and 750.

Cross-currents of culture

The religious landscape

The most reliable information about Buddhism in our period comes from the works of Hsuan Tsang, the inveterate Chinese Buddhist traveller-monk who wandered through India for fifteen years, between 630 and 645, eight years of which he spent in Harsha's kingdom. His reputation for Buddhist learning and wisdom had brought him to the attention of Harsha, who wanted to meet him and honour him. He and Harsha very soon struck a bond of friendship. Hsuan Tsang has left us records of the grand assemblies and festivals that Harsha organised, at which Buddhism was feted and honoured.[53] What Hsuan Tsang saw in Harsha's kingdom, however, was not the whole story. In many parts of India he actually found Buddhism in great decline, and the ruins of monasteries and stupas testified to this decay. Some rulers were exceptionally harsh towards Buddhists, but in most places there was general tolerance and acceptance. The challenge to Buddhism, and Jainism too, came not so much from Vedic Brahmanism as from the two great schools of Vaishnavism and Shaivism. As we saw in the previous chapter, both these schools of thought had begun in the earlier centuries; but, during our period, their influence grew enormously in the south of India. The 'simple-hearted'[54] devotees, or *bhaktas*, sometimes known as saints, were the Shaiva *Nayanars* or Vaishnava *Alvars*. Their songs, poems and hymns, all glorifying either Vishnu or Shiva, were utilised principally in the process of weaning the south Indian masses away from the heterodoxies. The Bhakti Movement can also be seen, in that sense, as a reaction against the power structures and elites within the south Indian kingdoms, such as those of the Pallavas.[55] The religious literature that was born out of the Bhakti Movement of intense devotion and surrender to personal gods, led by the *Nayanars* and *Alvars*, lay at the heart of worship in the great temple centres of the south[56] (see Extract 9.2). An unfortunate aspect of it, however, was the growth of sectarianism and sectarian rivalry among its diverse following.[57]

Sanskrit literature

A great deal of Sanskrit literature of this period relates to the great north Indian king Harsha. We have already referred to Harsha's leadership qualities and administrative prowess, but he saw his role extending beyond the onus of waging wars and conducting affairs of state. He was a man of considerable literary talent (see Extract 9.3), as evidenced by the three Sanskrit dramas that he himself wrote. His *Ratnavali* was a masterpiece, a very standard Sanskrit drama, which dealt with the story of the marriage of King Udayana and Ratnavali, the daughter of the king of Sri Lanka. The second work, *Priyadarshika*, had a similar theme, but also contains a play within a play, which is called *garbhanka*. His third drama, *Nagananda*, deals with the themes of self-sacrifice and love. All three dramas made a contribution to the evolution and development of Sanskrit literature after Kalidasa.[58] He led the way for other Sanskrit dramatists such as Bhavabhuti and Bhatta Narayana and served as inspiration for the Pallava king Mahendravarman, who composed a farce called *Mattavilasa*. The best example of Sanskrit prose in this period comes from the pen of Bana (Banabhatta), Harsha's biographer. Bana is admired by Sanskrit scholars because of the intensity and vivaciousness in his use of language. He has a unique gift for portraying all manner of situations and circumstances in the India of his day, whether domestic or public; his eye for detail shows in his depiction of themes as varied as war, love, revenge, faith or plain daily life.[59] His biography of Harsha, the *Harsha-charita*, is what is called an *Akhyayika*, in contrast to a *katha* or a romance based on a purely poetic creation. It would not be wise to rely on it for a systematic historical account of Harsha's reign, but there is sufficient information in it for us to form a strong mental picture of the personality and character of this great king.[60] It is a very positive image that we receive, as Harsha is Bana's hero; and Bana's admiration is reflected in his prose.

Southern literary culture

Literary culture in the south was promoted in the early stage by the educational institutions and monasteries run by the Jain and Buddhist monks and scholars, many of whom specialised in Sanskrit. With the advance of Vaishnavism and Shaivism through the region, essential Brahmanical learning in Sanskrit came to be provided by an institution called a *matha*, which was like a boarding school. The Pallava kings were no mean donors to the cause of education and culture, and the city of Kanchipuram housed many educational and cultural centres. Sanskrit enjoyed royal patronage,[61] and all the early Pallava inscriptions are in that language. While the later inscriptions were in Tamil, the *prasastis* were nevertheless composed in Sanskrit. To the Pallava courts, both in this period and earlier, came famous Sanskritists such as Dignaga and Dandin, the great writer on poetics; and there can be no doubt that the Pallavas were patrons of such literati. While Sanskrit was promoted as a language of high culture, Tamil nevertheless remained the key medium of instruction in the far south. Its confidence was far greater than, for example, that of Kannada in the Chalukya kingdom, which was, at this stage, still considered a somewhat poor relation to Sanskrit. Lyric poetry and great epics were composed in Tamil. Just before our period the great epic of *Shilappadikaram*, produced by Ilango Adigal, had appeared;[62] in contrast to the earlier stories of heroic violence, it extolled the virtues of non-violence and duty. The very famous text of *Tirukkural*, composed by Tiruvalluvar, again a little before the period covered by this chapter, was also part of the rich tapestry of Tamil literature.[63] The Tamil poems were suffused with rich descriptions of both country and town and the activities and lifestyles of people engaged in different spheres of work; and it has been said that 'compared with classical Sanskrit literature, the early Tamil literature was closer to the realities of life'.[64] During the reign of the Pallavas the hymns, the devotional songs and the *mantras* chanted by the *Nayanars* and *Alvars* and their devoted followers of Vaishnavism and Shaivism were collected into a volume which came to constitute a major branch of Tamil literature. In fact, one could say that the best of Tamil literature of this period is almost wholly influenced by the religious movements in the south.

Temple architecture in the south

The great temples of India are normally classified into three styles of architecture: northern, Deccani and southern. All of them have common features such as the *vimana* (sanctuary), the *garba griha* (inner chamber for the idol), the *shikhara* (tower) and the *mandapa* (pavilion), but there are some key differences. The towers of the northern-style temples are curvilinear or bulging, while those of the southern style are pyramidical. The Deccani towers, while pyramidical, are lower than in the northern style. The southern-style temples also have extensive enclosures and great *gopurams* (gateways), while the Deccani temples are star-shaped or polygonal rather than square, as in the other two styles. It is only from the ninth century onwards that the northern-style temples develop in all their glory. In contrast to the late start of the northern style, the Deccani and the southern varieties developed during the epoch under review. The Deccani styles began with the Early Chalukyas of Badami (535–757) and developed further under the Late Chalukyas (tenth to fourteenth centuries) and the Hoysalas (twelfth to fourteenth centuries). The southern temples began with the Pallavas in our period, and reached their apogee under the Cholas (900 to 1150) and the Pandyas (1100 to 1350). The Chalukyan culture revolved around the temples, and what remains of the striking architecture of that kingdom cannot fail to impress upon us the significance of a richly endowed Brahmanic religious culture in their part of the Deccan. The main monuments are clustered around three sites in the Karnataka: Aihole, Badami and Pattadakal (see Figure 9.2). Each was the centre of royal power in its turn. Aihole was the first capital; here, for many centuries, the Chalukyan craftsmen perfected the styles of the first built temples, as distinct from those carved out of solid rock. The oldest of such temples is the Meguti Temple, built in 634, according to an inscription by the court poet Ravikirti.[65] The first dated reference to Kalidasa, the author of *Shakuntala*, as provided by Ravikirti, may also be seen in this temple. Badami was the second capital. Here there are some extraordinary temples with immensely vivacious sculptures of gods and goddesses. The Melagitti Shivalaya Temple is one of the finest examples in the seventh-century Deccani temple style. Inside a large number of many other temples can be seen the valuable inscriptions detailing the victories of a regal hero such as Pulakeshin II or treaties and relationships between the Chalukyas and their rivals, the Pallavas.

Two main centres of population, the capital city of Kanchipuram and the port city of Mamallapuram (Mahabalipuram), were at the hub of Pallava

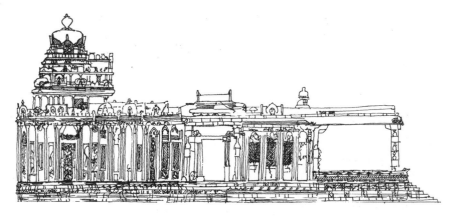

Figure 9.2 The Deccani-style temple of Pattadakal (Pat Baker: line drawing adapted from Tomory, op. cit., p. 118).

culture and influence. Kanchipuram is one of the seven sacred cities of Hinduism, dedicated to both Shiva and Vishnu, and renowned as a great seat of learning and philosophy in all Tamil Nadu. Among the great freestanding temples the Pallavas built in the city, the most beautiful are the Kailashanatha Temple and, slightly ahead of our period, the more famous Vaikuntha Perumal Temple.[66] Inscriptions narrating the history of the Pallava kings and eulogising their glories formed part of the panelled sculptures on the temple walls. At the port city of Mamallapuram are further testimonies to the Pallava contribution to culture and architecture. The Five Rathas, named after the five Pandava brothers, are miniature temples demonstrating the evolution of the southern temple style.[67] The *Mahabharata* episode of Arjuna's penance and the flowing of the River Ganga from Shiva's hair are depicted in an enormous frieze which is cut into a flat, granite rock face, 28 metres long and 12 metres high.[68] The most glorious monument of Mamallapuram is, of course, the famous Shore Temple, facing the Bay of Bengal, and renowned throughout the civilised world (see Figure 9.3).

Translations and transmission of ideas

Indian intellectual and cultural influences were felt far and wide during this period. Although clear evidence of the lines of transmission is not always easily available, we are on fairly certain ground in relation to two foreign nations: China and Persia. With the rise of the Tang dynasty in China in 618, Indo-Chinese diplomatic and cultural contacts increased apace. The Chinese monks, including Hsuan Tsang, arrived in India to learn about Buddhism; they were particularly excited by the idea of spending some time at the Buddhist educational centres such as Nalanda.[69] On the other hand, the Indian Buddhist missionaries and scholars in turn were increasingly to be seen in the principal

Figure 9.3 Shore Temple at Mamallapuram/Mahabalipuram (Pat Baker: line drawing adapted from a photo in Rawson, op. cit., p. 109).

cities of China. Learning each other's language was the great passion of the period, and Hsuan Tsang led the way in this venture. He translated seventy-four different Indian works consisting of 1,335 chapters.[70] On his return journey to China he needed twenty-two horses to carry all the manuscripts.[71] Prabhakaramitra, the great Indian scholar and professor from Nalanda, reached China in 627 and, with the help of nineteen Chinese scholars, was engaged in translating Indian Buddhist texts into Chinese.[72] Another, Bodhiruchi, went to China in 693; with the help of the Chinese board of translators, specially set up for him by the royal court, he translated fifty-three volumes of Indian texts before his death in 727.[73] Apart from Buddhism, the Chinese were interested in Indian mathematics, medicine and astronomy. A Sui dynasty catalogue of about 600 lists Chinese translations of Indian works in these three subjects.[74] Indian astronomy was also taught at an official Chinese centre for astronomical education. In both India and China, at that time, there was much mathematical work being pursued independently; but there was a good possibility of the transmission of ideas and knowledge in both directions. Their renditions were the most important means to achieving the success of the transmission.

The last great non-Islamic dynasty of Persia was that of the Sasanians. As inheritors of the famous Achaemenid dynasty, the Sasanian rulers held a high conception of their role and power. Their imperial ideology was based on the Zoroastrian doctrine that all knowledge that was useful, wise and sacred emanated from Ahura Mazda, the Lord of Wisdom; and to promote that ideology the Sasanians spared no efforts at collecting, recording and editing historical and religious texts and treatises from wherever they could be found.[75] King Shapur I inaugurated an academy of learning at Jundishapur in the third century AD, but it was another Sasanian king, Khosrau I Anushirvan, who, in the sixth century, encouraged translations of Greek, Syriac, Indian and Chinese scientific and literary works into Pahlavi (Middle Persian).[76] It was under Khosrau's patronage that his minister Burzoy travelled around India meeting learned people, one of whom introduced him to the *Panchatantra*, which he translated into Pahlavi; from then on, this book of Indian fables became highly popular through numerous translations.[77] While we lack the names of particular scholars, we can be fairly certain that a number of Indian mathematicians, astronomers and medical practitioners also went to Jundishapur to disseminate their knowledge. Reliable Arab-Islamic sources of later centuries confirmed this and noted the importance of both the Jundishapur academy and the Indian contribution there.[78] It should also be noted that the game of chess originated in India, and it moved to Iran in the seventh century.

SELECT EXTRACTS FOR REVIEW AND REFLECTION

Extract 9.1 Agricultural innovations in the Tamil country

An eminent specialist of the agricultural history of India explains the way the Tamils learned to practise agriculture in a fairly harsh natural environment.

> Technologically, two processes over the centuries formed the agrarian landscape [of the Tamil country] that we see today. On the one hand, people dug and shaped the earth to manipulate water, to put surface and sub-soil moisture to work. Tamil people built their civilization around irrigation. On the other hand, they adapted an enormous array of crops, seed varieties and cropping techniques to exploit the potentials of different soils and variable water supplies ... Irrigation has throughout Tamil history provided a proven means to raise land productivity. Not surprisingly, Tamils divided agriculture into two main categories, whose lands connote goodness and poverty, respectively.

Irrigated wet land is 'nanjai', and un-irrigated dry land is 'punjai'. Each of these two categories of cultivation supports its own staple grain – rice or millet – and, in Tamil cultural tradition, one embodies the good life, the other meagre subsistence.

Source: David Ludden, *Peasant History in South India*, Princeton, NJ: Princeton University Press, 1985.

Extract 9.2 An example of Shiva bhakti in Tamil religious literature

An Alvar, known as Appar, a great Tamil poet-saint who lived in the seventh century, has left us this powerful hymn devoted to Shiva:

We are not subject to any; we are not afraid of death; we will not suffer in hell; we live in no illusion; we feel elated; we know no ills; we bend to none; it is all one happiness for us; there is no sorrow, for we have become servants, once for all, of the independent Lord . . .

Source: Ainslee Embree, *Sources of Indian Tradition*, London: Penguin, 1992, p. 346.

Extract 9.3 Harsha's signature

A particular inscription from the early seventh century, known as the Banskhera Inscription, was issued in Harsha's name. Inscriptions with royal signatures are extremely valuable, and this has one of the very fine examples of a royal signature. The signature, MAHARAJADHIRAJASRI-HARSASYA, was prefaced by the phrase SVAHASTO MAMA ('This is my signature'). The German scholar J.G. Buhler, has said:

if Harsha really used these characters in signing all legal documents, he must have been a most accomplished person, and the cares of government and conquest of India must have left him a great deal of leisure.

A great art historian has explained thus:

It should be remembered that Harsha was an eminent poet and connoisseur . . . and his appreciation of penmanship may have led him to master the beautiful script attributed to him. The florid lines of these letters have parallels in the southern Pallava Nagari inscriptions at Mahabalipuram and in the Kailasanatha temple at Kanchipuram.

Source: Calambur Sivaramamurti, *The Art of India*, New York: Harry Abrams, 1977, pp. 61–2.

RELEVANT QUESTIONS FOR DISCUSSION

1   What are the main differences in the practice of agriculture between north India and south India?
2   Why did Vaishnavism and Shaivism put down such strong roots in south India?
3   What were the reasons for the advance of Sanskrit in southern literature?

Notes

1   The translations consulted are those by S. Beal (1884) and T. Watters (1904).
2   Majumdar and Pusalker 1954: 60–95.
3   Devahuti 1970: 56–81.
4   Beal 1884: Vol.1, 213.
5   Devahuti 1970: 93.
6   Ibid.: 207–29.
7   Majumdar and Pusalker 1954: 308.
8   Ibid.: 131–6.
9   Wink 1991: 44–5, 241ff.
10   Ibid.: 149–54.
11   Ibid.: 201–9.
12   Majumdar and Pusalker 1954: 227–54.
13   Ibid.: 407.
14   Beal 1884: Vol. 2, 256.
15   Stein 1980: 30ff.
16   For some of this evidence, see documents in Ray *et al.* 2000: 279–87.
17   Majumdar and Pusalker 1954: 255–7.
18   Keay 2000: 173–4.
19   Devahuti 1970: 111–24, 129–35.
20   Thapar 2002: 120–21, 128–9, 148–9.
21   Champakalakshmi 1995: 270–75; Champakalakshmi 1996a: 41–5; Ludden 1985: 34–6.
22   Stein 1980: 67ff.
23   Champakalakshmi 1995: 273–4.
24   For details, see Devahuti 1970: 135–41.
25   Quoted from a note sent to the author by Dr Daud Ali, University of London.
26   Devahuti 1970: 152–4.
27   Wink 1991: 197.
28   Ibid.: 192–4.
29   Ibid.
30   Ibid.: 206ff.
31   Devahuti 1970: 169.
32   Ibid.: 166.
33   Ibid.: 169.
34   Ibid.: 203.
35   Champakalakshmi 1995: 279–81; Champakalakshmi 1996a: 38–42; Thapar 2002: 387–9.
36   Majumdar and Pusalker 1954: 585–6.
37   Beal 1884: Vol. 1, 88–9.

38 Devahuti 1970: 201ff.
39 Chattopadhyaya 1994: 43–4.
40 Ray *et al*. 2000: 279–83; Ludden 1985: 18–23; Thapar 2002: 338–9.
41 Ludden 1985: 21.
42 Champakalakshmi 1995: 279–80.
43 Ludden 1985: 34–41.
44 Frasch 2006: 8.
45 Thapar 2002: 456.
46 Jha 2004: 192.
47 Wink 1991: 47.
48 Ibid.: 45–53.
49 Thapar 2002: 342.
50 Watters 1904: 178.
51 Wink 1991: 51, 221.
52 Devahuti 1970: 147.
53 Beal 1884: Vol. 1, 213–14.
54 Majumdar and Pusalker 1954: 327.
55 Flood 1996: 170.
56 Ibid.: 129–32; Champakalakshmi 1996a: 60–5.
57 Champakalakshmi 1996a: 61.
58 Sastri 1960: 107–8.
59 Cowell and Thomas (n.d.): vii–xiv; Keith 1928: 314–19, 326–30; Sastri 1960:
    134–5.
60 Singh 2003: 90–6; Pathak 1997: 30–55.
61 For an example, see Mahalingam 1969: 74.
62 Pollock 2003: 295–301.
63 Ibid.: 292–5.
64 Jha 2004: 156.
65 Sivaramamurti 1977: 484.
66 Mahalingam 1969: 139–42, 184; Sivaramamurti 1977: 508–9.
67 Craven 1997: 148–50; Sivaramamurti 1977: 513–17.
68 Craven 1997: 145–7.
69 For Hsuan Tsang's impressions of Nalanda, see Watters 1904: 165–70.
70 Majumdar and Pusalker 1954: 608.
71 Beal 1884: Vol. 1, xx.
72 Majumdar and Pusalker 1954: 609–10.
73 Ibid.: 610.
74 Joseph 2000: 19.
75 Rypka 1968: 34ff.
76 Ibid.: 6.
77 Blois 1990: 40–4, 81–2, 88; Edgerton 1965: 12.
78 Wickens 1976.

10 Regionalism and feudalism

Rajput, Pala and Rashtrakuta kingdoms

(Time-span: c. AD 750 to 1000)

The two and a half centuries of Indian history covered in this chapter were characterised by two crucial developments that led to profound consequences for the succeeding 800 years of history. Firstly, India became increasingly regionalised. Between the mid-eighth century and the end of the tenth century we see the growth of a number of regional kingdoms, of which some demonstrated unique features of state formation. Secondly, the regionalised society became highly feudal. Feudalism would long remain a persistent factor in the shaping of Indian society and its mindset, although its characteristics would undergo much transformation in succeeding centuries. The political economy of the kingdoms was substantially feudal; and, despite various dissenting views among historians, the inscriptions provide strong evidence of the way feudalism linked the state and its economy. The political narrative of this period is dominated by struggles among three particularly powerful regional kingdoms for control of the core territory of *Madhyadesha*. There were conflicts in the south too, but it would not be until the next two centuries that the southern story would become especially significant, with the rise of the Chola kingdom. Regional kingdoms served as the geographical bases of regional cultures and languages, and the literary culture of our period begins to show signs of a distinction between Sanskritic elitism and the regional literary styles. Some of the finest religious architecture of India was conceived and completed during this period.

Three regional kingdoms

Of the many kingdoms of our period, three may be classified as metropolitan in terms of their size, strength and capacity: the Gurjara–Pratihara kingdom in Rajasthan and *Madhyadesha*, the Bengal kingdom of the Palas, and the Rashtrakuta kingdom of the Deccan. Each of these kingdoms was more or less equally matched, but each was also weakened by internecine warfare over primacy in *Madhyadesha* (see Map 10.1).

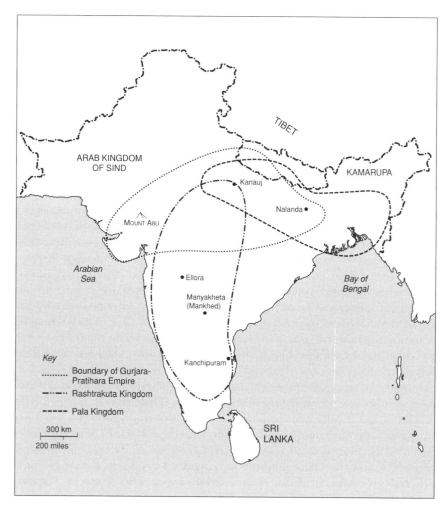

Map 10.1   The struggle for Kanauj among the three titans.

The Gurjara–Pratihara kingdom in Madhyadesha

From the middle of the eighth century the dominance over *Madhyadesha* became the ambition of two particular clans among a tribal people in Rajasthan, known as the Gurjara and the Pratihara. They were both part of a larger federation of tribes, some of which later came to be known as the Rajputs (see Figure 10.1). There has been much controversy about the origin of the Rajputs, as to whether they were the descendants of the indigenous inhabitants of India or of the Central Asian Hunas (the White Huns) who had attacked northwest India during the later Gupta period.[1] It is difficult to arrive at a firm conclusion;

but what we do know for certain is that the various Rajasthani tribes, including the Gurjara and the Pratihara, who were originally a nomadic and pastoral people, underwent a major social transformation between the late sixth and the ninth centuries AD. A process of assimilation into the Aryan Hindu fold gathered strength at this time throughout north India, and the Pratiharas particularly vaunted their martial qualities, in order to be recognised as the *kshatriya* Rajputs.[2] With their enhanced status, the Gurjara–Pratihara made a significantly tactical move by transferring their capital from Bhilmal in Rajasthan to *Kanauj* in *Madhyadesha*, a move made as a result of the latter being perceived as both a spiritual and a geo-political heartland. It also became clear that whoever held the city of *Kanauj* would enjoy a pre-eminence over north India. From this city it was easier to subdue most of the Ganga valley. The control of this fertile and resource-rich region, with its busy water transport system and considerable trade, has throughout history been essential for raising revenue for all Indian rulers. Under Harsha (606–47) *Kanauj* had gained metropolitan status as both an imperial seat and a centre of north India's finest culture; but its star shone brightest after the Gurjara–Pratihara made it their capital in 815 and held a brilliant court there, becoming the envy of their neighbours. A ninth-century Persian traveller, Abu Zayd of Siraf, wrote of numerous *brahman* 'poets, astronomers, philosophers and diviners' in *Kanauj*[3] (see Extract 10.1). Honouring their earlier commitment to defend India against the Arabs, the Gurjara–Pratihara put strong pressures on Sind; in a contemporary Arab account from 851 about the greatest of the Pratihara kings, Raja Mihir Bhoja, we read that 'among the princes of India there is no greater foe of the Muslim faith than he [Bhoja]'; but there 'is no country in India more safe from robbers'.[4] In his tenth-century description of the land of *al-Jurz* (the Arabic name for Gujarat, part of the Pratihara kingdom) the Baghdad Arab writer Al-Masudi also expressed the Arabs' concern about the hostility of the Pratihara towards them.[5] He, however, exaggerated their strength, because the military realities on the ground were exceedingly complex. The Arabs were not the only enemy that the Pratihara had to deal with. Their two Indian rivals, the Pala and the Rashtrakuta, were far more dangerous, and did their utmost to deny them the monopoly of power in *Madhyadesha*. They did not succeed, however, because in the late eighth and ninth centuries six of the ablest Pratihara monarchs, particularly Bhoja (840–85), fought them to a standstill.

The Pala kingdom of Bengal and beyond

Bengal played a leading role in Indian politics between the eighth and the eleventh centuries.[6] This was the age of the famous Pala dynasty, some of whose rulers were the ablest in ancient India. For nearly a century after Harsha's death in 647, Bengal had been subject to much interference and disruption by its near and farther neighbours. The respite came in 765 with the election by the people of an able leader, Gopala, who was neither a *brahman* nor a *kshatriya*. The dynasty prospered under Gopala's successors, Dharamapala and Devapala.

Figure 10.1   The Rajput stronghold of Jaisalmer (by permission of RHPL).

The Palas realised the importance of *Madhyadesha* in the Indian political world, and fought hard to gain power and influence there. Their main rivals, of course, were the Gurjara–Pratihara and the Rashtrakuta, although with the latter there were useful marriage alliances. In the triangular contest over *Madhyadesha* and *Kanauj*, all three dynasties ultimately exhausted themselves. However, the fact that the Palas were ever-present, asserting their right to reorder affairs to their advantage, meant that Bengal was no longer on the margins of the Indian polity. Over different periods of time, the dynasty also ruled over Bihar, Orissa and Assam. The Bengal kingdom's reputation reached beyond the boundaries of India, into Nepal and Tibet and, above all, towards Southeast Asia, in Java, Sumatra and the Malay peninsula ruled by the Shailendra dynasty.

Commerce and religion linked the fortunes of Bengal, Tibet and Nepal. There was also the desire for territorial power. The Palas were forced to pay attention to their northern frontier by keeping a wary eye on Tibetan aspirations. Nepal was the principal bone of contention between Tibet and Bengal. From the seventh century onwards the Tibetan resurgence had begun to over-awe Nepal; and for nearly two centuries Nepal remained within the political shadow of Tibet.[7] At the same time, Nepal could not escape the Sanskritic influences and Buddhist missionary work that continued to arrive from Bengal. Through Nepal also ran a major trade route between Tibet and Bengal. Although Nepal herself broke loose from Tibetan hegemony in 879, the general Tibetan domination was a fact of life that the Palas could not ignore.

While Tibet maintained very close commercial and Buddhist links with Bengal, on a number of occasions her armies invaded Bengal and posed a major threat to the Pala supremacy. Some of the Tibetan sources, in fact, talk of a kingdom extending from Mongolia down to the mouth of the Ganga.[8] It may be surmised that the Tibetans ultimately contributed to the collapse of the Palas.

Bengal's relations with Assam and Burma too were complex. Assam was known as *Kamarupa* or *Pragjyotisha*. Here there were many Mongoloid-featured people, who had migrated from such areas as Nagaland and Burma, and between 350 and 800 two Mongoloid dynasties ruled over Assam. However, just as in Bengal, the Sanskritisation process had been under way throughout the first millennium of the Christian era. Assamese monarchs had dominated Bengal until Dharamapala reversed the situation and extended the Pala suzerainty in Assam.[9] The key factor that made Assam a vital area for the Pala monarchs was its strategic position, lying on the main trade routes between Bengal and China and between Bengal and Burma. Assam was the entry point into the northeast then, and is so today. The great Arab geographers of the Middle Ages have described at length the extensive trade network of Bengal with Burma.[10] A continual supply of gold and silver facilitated commerce greatly. The extensive silver mines of Burma were particularly crucial, and the River Irrawaddy was a major transport waterway. The commodities from Bengal included aloe-wood, pottery, rice and both fine and coarse textiles. Among cultural influences from Bengal were particular architectural forms, sculptures and *Tantric* forms of Buddhism. Both Bengal and Burma strengthened their ties further when new challenges arose from the Cholas.[11] Pala suzerainty in Bengal and eastern India lasted until the end of the eleventh century, when they were succeeded by the Senas, who, in turn, lost out to the Turkish Khaljis in the thirteenth century.

The majesty of the Rashtrakuta in the Deccan

The word 'Rashtrakuta' means 'peaks among kingdoms'. It was used as an epithet for a dynasty of rulers who carried the Sanskrit title of *Vallabha-Raja* and who ruled from their capital at *Mankir*, or *Manyakheta*, now called Malkhed, southeast of Sholapur in Maharashtra. The title of *Vallabha* meant 'beloved'. It was from a Prakrit term, *Ballaha-Raya*, that the Arabs came to call the Rashtrakutas *Al-Ballahara*; and in Arab historical sources the Rashtrakuta kings were thus known.[12] The dynasty was founded by Dantidurga, who called himself *Prithvi-Vallabha*, 'the beloved lord of the earth', but it truly prospered under his successors. It lasted until the end of the tenth century and produced some of the most outstanding monarchs of India: Krishna I (760–75), Dhruva (780–93), Govinda III (793–814), Amoghavarsha I (814–80), Indra III (914–28) and Krishna III (939–67).[13] The Arab travellers of the ninth and tenth centuries have left us vivid accounts of the wealth and glory of the Al-Ballahara. According to Al-Masudi (d. 956) and Ibn Khordadbih (d. 912), most of the kings of Hindustan turned their faces towards the Ballahara king while they were praying, and they prostrated themselves before his ambassadors. The Rashtrakuta king was the King of kings who possessed the mightiest of armies and whose domains extended from Konkan to Sind.[14] Another Muslim writer, Al-Idrisi, talks of a large kingdom, with vast stretches of cultivated lands, abundant commerce and plentiful resources, resulting in huge wealth and revenue.[15] And this was the Indian kingdom that was to be most hospitable to the Arab merchants. The Rashtrakuta controlled the Deccan vigorously, but the north and the south had to be fought over continually. The main aim, in all northern campaigns, was the capture of *Kanauj*, which was finally achieved in the early tenth century by Indra III. In the south the enemy was the Chola kingdom, whose rulers were crushingly defeated in the middle of the tenth century. Despite these victories, the Rashtrakuta confronted the same challenges that all Deccan monarchs always faced: they had to be careful to balance their gains in the north with the possible losses in the south if they tarried overlong in the north, and vice versa. Continual fighting drained their resources; and, in the eleventh century, they were overthrown by a feudatory who established a new dynasty, known as the Western Chalukyas of Kalyani.

Political economy in the feudal era

The debate on feudalism

Karl Marx described feudalism as the pre-capitalist stage of development in the social and economic history of Europe. It was a stage in which the mode of agricultural production was based on the relationship between the lord and the peasantry. In this relationship the peasants owed the lord labour service for being allowed to till the soil and eke out a subsistence living. They also had to accept extensive judicial powers over their lives as a measure of protection by the lord. Historians have also debated over feudalism as a method of maintaining order at a time, particularly between the tenth and the fourteenth centuries in Western Europe, when public institutions were in a state of crisis and flux. In that situation private relationships had become crucial; and one of the key manifestations of this relationship was the arrangement by which a tributary lord attached himself to a liege lord for protection through homage, tribute and military service. Whichever way feudalism may be understood, it was essentially 'a system based primarily on the exploitation of the peasantry', as Frank Williamson, a dedicated communist thinker of recent years, has put it.[16] One of the noted social features of any system of exploitation is the obsequious-ness shown by the humble towards their superiors. The distinguished twentieth century historian R.S. Sharma has argued that the political, social and economic development of India during the period examined here can be characterised as feudal too.[17] He sees the subservience of the lower classes of people and their servile mentality arising out of the oppression of their superiors. He has based his argument on the evidence, as he saw it, of manifestations resulting from the widespread disruption in the post-Gupta period, such as the loss of public revenues through the decline of trade and debased coinage, the issuing of land grants (fiefs) by monarchs to their subordinates, the subjugation of the peasantry by landed intermediaries, and the rise of religious devotional movements emphasising loyalty and reverence in general. The fact that the *Puranas* contain descriptions of the general disorientation within contemporary society, leading to the breakdown of old loyalties and certainties, has also been used as an argument to support the feudal thesis. In opposition to Sharma, it has been contended that, far from being an age of political decentralisation, the post-Gupta period in fact witnessed a growth in state power through a continual series of state formations in the form of new regional kingdoms. The land grants were not a sign of the sovereign's weakness, but a method of legitimising his authority; and a question may also be posed as to whether the land grants could be said to be responsible for the increase in the oppression of the peasantry, when in fact the peasant subjugations increased from the thirteenth century onwards under the Delhi Sultanate, which made comparatively few land concessions. The point about the decline of trade and coinage is also fiercely contested.[18]

While the counter-arguments against the feudal thesis are increasingly being articulated on the basis of new research, there is still a core of evidence that lends support to the essentials of Sharma's analysis. Land was the critical resource for the potentates of a pre-modern society. Other resources included control over manufacturing and trade, but they could not match in importance the land factor. The inscriptions from our period contain many references to grants of land from the monarch to his subjects and their emergent issues. The king parcelled out lands to groups of people for different reasons – either to the *brahmans* or to royal officers and bureaucrats – and with the land concessions went the attachment of the rights of land revenue. Many of the grantees of land acquired a range of fiscal and judicial rights over taxes and rents; and most often the contracts stipulated that they could collect revenues and rents from the peasants but were not obliged to pay taxes themselves.[19] At a higher level of decision-making, large grants of land were conferred by monarchs to dynastic collaterals for maintaining princes within the orbit of their influence. The subordinate princes, as feudatories, bore certain responsibilities, for example to raise levies for the king's armies, to consent to marriage alliances, or to attend court with appropriate pomp and pageantry. The king assured for himself a continuing check on these feudatories by creating titular posts as indicants of their place and status in the overall scheme of things. Of course, the feudatory princes became all-powerful in their own domains, enjoying luxurious lifestyles in their palaces and castles. They, too, in turn, created a subordinate layer of lesser feudatories; and in this way the feudal structure and power spread from our period onwards.[20] The magnificence of the famed courts of the Indian *maharajas* of later centuries derived directly from the feudal princely courts of this earlier period (see Figure 10.2).

Figure 10.2 An Indian maharaja of modern times (by permission of RHPL).

Kingdom formation and dynastic legitimation: the northern context

A great variety of regional kingdoms flourished in this era. They arose for a number of reasons.[21] Quite often, those whose ancestors had originally received land grants from a previous ruler broke loose from the existing kingdom and formed new polities. Again, as utility lands were being increasingly wrested from forested terrain, new territories emerged under new names, with local chieftains sometimes assuming a dominant role and, sometimes, forming alliances with existing kingdoms. The forest dwellers, who normally lived in a pre-state situation, were being increasingly drawn into the processes of state formation through interaction with the sedentary peasant societies, thereby fostering a new state. Once a kinship group or a clan acquired power over a defined territory and control over the economic resources of that region, then it was not too difficult for its power-holders to initiate the process of forming a new state. In practically all the states the caste system was to retain its grip wherever Brahmanic influence remained pervasive.[22] This meant that the kingdom model, based on the girder of the *brahman–kshatriya* alliance, became the standard for all states. The boundaries of kingdoms never remained static, because the ambitions of their rulers led to either the expansion or the diminution of their territories, depending upon their capabilities. Nevertheless there was an enduring association of a particular kingdom with a distinct geographical or cultural zone. The dynasties that controlled them had, in some cases, a long and distinguished lineage; but a majority emerged out of their feudatory status.[23] It is of course a mistake to assume the continuity of a kingdom merely because a branch lineage bearing the name of the original royal family appears in its genealogical records. The family name Chalukya, for example, was applied to three sets of dynasties; but it would be far fetched to imagine that the Chalukyas of the eleventh century were the controllers of the same territory ruled by the Western Chalukyas of the seventh and eighth centuries.

Each new dynasty wished to acquire full legitimacy in the eyes of the others. The case of the Gurajara–Pratihara provides a good example of the extraordinary lengths taken to achieve this. Originally a nomadic and pastoral people, the Gurjara consciously underwent a major social transformation between the late sixth and the ninth centuries by assimilating into the Aryan fold, relinquishing pastoralism and taking up agriculture. The Pratihara became specialised in military skills, and demonstrated their prowess by keeping a wary check on the Arabs who had captured Sind in 711. They became the dominant partner. To call themselves *kshatriya*, they first underwent, in 747, a major purification ceremony before a great sacrificial fire on Mount Abu, in the presence of *sadhus*. This made them 'fire-born' *kshatriya* Rajputs.[24] The Pratihara status among the monarchs of north India rose greatly from then on. The symbolic ceremony on Mount Abu was only one of the ways of legitimising their power and social status. Another was keeping a record for posterity. This was achieved by claiming genealogical links with the most ancient recorded *kshatriya* families, forging marriage links with the existing members of such families, granting lands to the *brahmans* as an act of piety, and registering such facts in *vamshavalis*, which were the histories of ruling families, or the *charitas*, which were eulogies of particular kings. It could be said that, to a certain extent, the genealogical pedigrees thus constructed by the Pratihara were purposefully fabricated, intended to enhance their royal status and obliterate their own pastoral and nomadic origins from popular memory.[25]

The Arab mercantile impact

A distinct imperial Arab Muslim identity had been built up by the Umayyad dynasty which ruled the extensive Islamic Empire between 661 and 750. Under the Umayyads, Arabic became the standard language of administration and a uniform Islamic coinage was instituted. From their capital in Damascus, the Umayyads encouraged trade and enterprise throughout the Islamic world.[26] With the capture of Sind in 711 the Arabs gained a most valuable piece of Indian territory. Sind had become extremely rich through its trading networks, and, although initially the Arab invaders had raided its vast treasures of gold and silver, they ensured that the commercial edge of the province was not blunted. The Umayyads lost power to the Abbasids in 750, and Baghdad became the new metropolis of the Islamic world. As the centre of Islamic power shifted from Syria to Iraq the Perso/Arabian Gulf became the vital trade artery in the Islamic empire.[27] Since the Islamic Empire also enjoyed a full monopoly over the Red Sea and the Arabian Sea routes and a near monopoly in the Mediterranean, the Muslim merchants came to control most of the world trade of that era.[28] An integrated Islamic trading system was being created which would shape the global economy almost until the end of the Middle Ages.[29] The products of India were in great demand throughout the Islamic world; and although India imported certain specialised commodities the general balance of trade was tipped in her favour, which meant that she received large quantities of gold and silver bullion from the Muslim merchants. The gold *dinar* and the silver *dirhem* were the dominant currencies in the Abbasid Empire. The main lands on both sides of the Gulf, Arabia and Persia, were Abbasid-controlled; and from the ports of the Gulf the Arab and Persian seamen and merchants took passage to various Indian ports. Whether Arab or Persian, the Muslim travellers and traders were to be found in small settlements all along the coast. Sind was already Arab-controlled, so the Muslim influence could spread more easily. It was from Sind also that many important Indian intellectual influences flowed towards the Islamic world.[30] The ports of Gujarat contained many Muslim settlers; and both the Rashtrakuta and the local Gujarati rulers not only facilitated their trade but also provided them with hospitality, if for no other reason than their own interest in securing a share of the mercantile profits. The Rashtrakuta kingdom produced teak wood in quantity that the Arabs needed for shipbuilding.[31] Further south, on the Malabar coast, in the kingdom of Kerala, Muslim traders continued the same trade once handled by Romans and Persians. Clusters of Muslims were established in Sri Lanka and on both the Coromandel and Bengal coasts. Until about 1000, with the exception of Sind, the Indian interaction with the Arabs was confined to the sphere of mercantile trade within the coastal ports. And, with the exception of Kerala, there were hardly any Arabs in the Indian hinterland. Thus, the Arab impact upon India could not but be marginal, which meant that there had not existed any general sense of grievance against the Muslims in this period.

Commerce and urbanisation

One of the key arguments used for characterising our period as feudal has traditionally been the notion of commercial decline and deurbanisation. The historic towns and cities that had developed during the second phase of Indian urbanisation, between the sixth century BC and the fourth century AD, appeared to have lost their vitality and importance from the Gupta period onwards. The principal reason for this was considered to be the drying up of the profitable Indian trade with Rome and the extreme dearth of coinage. Hiuen Tsang's observations of urban decay during his travels in the seventh century are generally cited as evidence of the increase in ruralisation.[32] More recent research casts doubt upon the validity of this theory of decay. It is no longer believed that the Roman trade was so fundamental to the well-being of the country that its disappearance led to an irreparable commercial decline. Commerce never really died out; it merely changed its orientation. As was referred to earlier, as well as in the previous chapter, the great appetite for Indian goods in the Islamic markets and the Arab mercantile role in satiating it meant that the traditional Indian exports did not cease. The Chinese market remained buoyant too. There was no shortage of coins because all payments continued to be made in gold and silver specie. Since, at this time, agricultural production generally expanded as a result of the opening up of new lands, partly through land grants and the drafting in of the newly constituted peasant labour, there was ample surplus for external trade. The epigraphic information concerning the mercantile classes, market centres, interest rates, merchant associations and the rates of levies and cesses belies greatly the notion of commercial wane.[33]

Even if we accept that the volume of trade could not have declined in our period, and that its value might in fact have increased, the issue of urban decay cannot be easily ignored. Whatever little that archaeology has yielded us from the post-Gupta sites has indeed confirmed a marked decay in urban architecture, particularly in north India. The historic cities of the earlier second phase, having grown from an epicentre, were located in the older imperial territories. They were centres of political power or of Buddhist patronage, with deep hinterlands and situated along the main trade routes. With the fading away of the imperial idea, the decline of Buddhism, the growing importance of the coastal areas and the opening up of new hinterlands in different regional kingdoms, it was inevitable that the older cities would suffer decay. But this decay was not a reflection of a malady affecting the very idea of urbanism in general; it really was confined to the historic cities, such as *Pataliputra* and Taxila; and it did not prevent a new phase of urbanisation in our period. In fact, it is this third phase of Indian urbanisation, along with the incorporation of subsequent Islamic notions of urbanism, that gave rise to the pre-modern towns and cities of the Indian sub-continent (see Map 10.2). The absence of archaeological confirmation is amply compensated by numerous regional inscriptional records. They point to a methodology that gives us fresh insights into the new phase of urbanism.[34] We discover that the hierarchy of settlements,

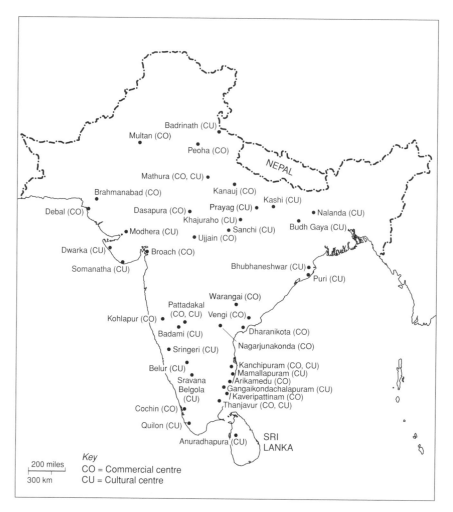

Map 10.2 Important commercial and cultural centres between *c.* 900 and AD 1200.

as symbolised by such terms as *grama*, *pura*, *nagara* or *mahanagara*, that we examined in Chapter 5 for example, did not change substantially; and the Indians of this period were perfectly aware of the differences in urban scale of, say, a *pura* settlement and a *nagara*. Secondly, the details specified in the charters of land grants give us a spatial context of the land that was being gifted: whether it was a purely rural space or a mixed rural–urban one. In the case of the latter, it would include such features as a market exchange point, residential quarters or manufacturing units. If these predominated in a kingdom's land grants, then that would allow us to determine the scale of urbanism. Thirdly, the records tell us about the various types of exchanges and, indeed, guilds of merchants and craftsmen. The market exchange in north India was generally called a *hatta*, and in the south it was the *nagaram*. The presence of market exchanges implied an urban population density, and exchanges could meaningfully continue trade only in the context of urban centres. Both barter and money were in common use. Fairs too could only be held in some sort of urban centres, however small.[35] Fourthly, the inscriptions give us copious information about places of pilgrimage and the temples. Our period is profuse with the northern- and southern-style regional temples; and royal patronages were continually creating new sacred spaces that drew in people from the hinterlands. People generally like to live near a great cathedral, a mosque or a temple, and so it was in this period too; the sacred spaces also represented the continuity of an older tradition of sacred towns from the very early centuries of the second phase of Indian urbanisation.[36] In conclusion, therefore, we can say that, although the older towns and cities declined, the newer ones always arose, and some of these were to become even more bustling and busy during the following six centuries of the Sultanate and Mogul eras.

Cultural highlights of the age

Shankara, the master philosopher of India

A unique intellectual tradition that guided the philosophers of ancient India consisted of providing commentaries and reflections upon the *Vedas* and other Vedic knowledge. Unlike some of our modern intellectuals, ancient Indian thinkers were never obsessive about their own original insights or contributions; rather they took pride in the fact that they were privileged to comment upon the thoughts of the earlier texts.[37] The commentaries became the vehicles through which, in time, philosophical ideas came to be articulated and gained maturity. The ideas came to be grouped into several schools that dealt with such philosophical concepts as epistemology, logic, perception, inference, ontology, causation or human nature. Six formal schools of thought eventually came to be recognised: *Nyaya*, concerned with right reasoning and logic (see Extract 10.2); *Vaisheshika*, or atomism, concerned with the method of dealing with particular matters; *Mimamsa*, concerned with knowledge proceeding from Vedic exegesis; *Samkhya*, a dualistic philosophy concerned with theory of knowledge and the evolution of the cosmos; Yoga, or practice; and *Vedanta*, a metaphysical philosophy which considered itself to be the essence, or 'end', of the *Veda* and focused its exegesis on the *Upanishads*.[38]

Shankara, or Shankaracharya, perhaps the subtlest Indian thinker of the ancient world, is considered the greatest exponent of the monist strand of the *Vedanta* school.[39] *Monism* is the doctrine of ultimate principle or being (*Brahman*), which denies any duality of matter and mind.[40] The ideas of the *Vedanta* school were derived from the great commentary on the *Upanishads*, which was the *Brahma Sutra* of Badarayana (fifth century BC).[41] Shankara, according to traditional dating, is said to have lived between about 788 and 822 and wrote a massive commentary in his *Brahmasutra Bhashya* on Badrayana's work. He argued that there was only one non-dual reality (*Advaita Vedanta*); that the world was a product of illusion and false appearances, in the way that ignorant or gullible people mistake a snake for a rope; that the individual Self can realise the ultimate reality, or *Brahman*, through the path of knowledge; and that it is only when the Self has realised the *Brahman* that the ultimate goal of human life is reached.[42] This purist position stands in contrast to the qualified non-dualism (*Vishisht Advaita*) or dualism (*Dvaita*) stated by later philosophers such as Ramanuja and Madhava. Shankara's purist position has attracted most westernised Indians, and in modern times its popularity has been enhanced by such figures as Sri Ramakrishna, Swami Vivekananda, Swami Prabhavananda, Gerald Heard and Christopher Isherwood, who have all promoted the *Vedanta* school and its ideas.[43] Despite the rigour of his intellectual position, Shankara was a man who reached out to all groups of people. Although brought up within the *Shaivite* atmosphere of a *brahman* family of Kerala, he influenced the *Vaishnavites* too.[44] He respected both Buddhists and Jains, although he rejected their heterodox ideas and regarded 'Buddhism as Hinduism's chief enemy'.[45] He travelled the length and breadth of India, engaged in lively debates with thinkers from other schools, and made it his mission to educate the *brahman* priests into strict monism. Perhaps imitating the Buddhists, he also founded four great monasteries, at Badrinath in the north, Sringeri in the south, Puri in the east, and Dwarka in the west, places still revered by Hindu pilgrims.[46]

Piety, art and wealth at Ellora

The most concrete expression of Rashtrakuta grandeur that may be physically witnessed is the world heritage site of the Kailashanatha Temple in Ellora, Maharashtra. This great Hindu temple, dedicated to Shiva, and representing his mountain fortress, Kailasha, is the world's largest single free-standing structure, carved out of living rock, and covering an area more widespread than the Parthenon of Athens. The distinguished art historian Percy Brown has described it as 'the most stupendous single work of art ever executed in India'[47] (see Figure 10.3). His wonderment is perfectly understandable, for there is nothing in all of Hindu religious art that can compare with the monumentality of Kailashanatha. It is only one of the thirty-four rock-carved cave temples of Ellora. Half of them are Hindu caves, twelve are Buddhist and five are Jain. Kailashanatha is cave number 16, the best known and most visited. A large number of the cave temples were built in the eighth and the ninth centuries AD, a time of Rashtrakuta power and dominance in the Deccan. All the great symbols of Hindu religion and religiosity are represented in the images of the temple,[48] and, for this, nearly 3 million cubic metres of rock had to be excavated from the cliff – a stupendous effort.[49] The temple, which is still standing, and protected by UNESCO funds,[50] is a tribute to both the vision and the imagination of the Rashtrakuta king Krishna I, his chief builder and the craftsmanship of masons and labourers of the eighth century.

Figure 10.3 Tourist Sam Badni on the upper gallery of Ellora (private family photo).

Language and literature

Sanskrit continued, during this period, to be the language of courtly, refined and elite literature. Irrespective of regions, there was much royal patronage of Sanskrit poets and dramatists. The latter experimented with a new style of writing, called *Champu*, a mixture of prose and verse, particularly popular with monarchs, whose praises were sung sometimes in a sycophantic manner.[51]

Unfortunately, much of the secular literature was far too stylised, pedantic or didactic, and lacked 'specificity with details of time, place and person',[52] thus betraying a distinct lack of originality (see Extract 10.3). There was, however, an important exception, which was in the area of poetic theory. A number of literary critics had, in the past, explored the characteristics of Sanskrit poetry in terms of figures of speech, style or sheer aesthetic pleasure. In the ninth century, however, a critic known as Anandavardhana analysed a new element in poetry, which he termed *Dhvani* or suggestiveness. In his famous work *Dhvanyaloka*, he stated that all poetic work is endowed with three powers: that of denoting in a factual way, of implying something obliquely, or by suggesting an imaginative vista.[53] His work was further refined by the Kashmiri philosopher Abhinavagupta (975–1025); and the *Dhvani* theory of suggestiveness was recognised by the distinguished French critic Jacques Lacan as particularly valuable for his work in psychoanalysis.[54]

Some innovative work apart, there were ominous signs for the future of Sanskrit in our period. Just as at one time *Prakrit* languages such as Pali, Sauraseni, Magadhi and Maharashtri acquired their own autonomy, so after the *Prakrits* a new phase set in along the development of Indian languages, called *Apabrahmasha*.[55] The term signified decadence born out of change. Those Sanskrit authors for whom the language was so perfect and so well defined viewed any change in its usage as a decline in standards. And yet it was through the medium of the *Apabrahmasha* languages that the various regional languages of India evolved their own literatures. While voluminous literature had of course existed in Sanskrit, Prakrit and Tamil, the development of other regional literatures took place over a period of nearly 700 years after the eighth century AD. During the time-span of this chapter it was a Dravidian regional language, Kannada/Kanarese, which first acquired a literature of its own. It borrowed heavily in style and form from Sanskrit, but it was distinct in its own right, exploring themes and issues within the social and political parameters of Karnataka. The first great literary figure in Kannada was the Rashtrakuta king Amoghavarsha (AD 814–80), who wrote an important manual of poetic theory, *Kavirajamarga*, in which he laid down certain critical tests, with examples, by which the greatness of a poem could be judged.[56]

Pala patronage of Buddhism

The Palas were strongly Buddhist; and one might say that under their patronage Buddhism obtained its last chance to retain its influence in India before a newly resurgent Hinduism finally crushed it. Buddhist institutions and endowments proliferated under Dharamapala, Devapala and other Palas. Buddhist scholars, travellers and visitors came from all the places where the Buddha was revered: Sind, Kashmir, Ceylon and Nepal within the sub-continent; Burma, Laos and the Indonesian islands; and China and Tibet. King Dharamapala continued to support the great Buddhist monastic and educational institute at Nalanda, while building another centre of higher learning at Vikramshila on the banks of the Ganga in Bihar.[57] While to this latter centre came many Tibetan scholars, Nalanda continued to attract monks and students from Southeast Asia.[58]

The most important power in Southeast Asia during the heyday of the Palas was that of the Shailendra dynasty, which ruled over the Malay peninsula and the Indonesian archipelago, including Sumatra, Java, Bali and Borneo. The Shailendras were the followers of *Mahayana* Buddhism and derived their religious inspiration from Bengal, which was then the chief centre of the *Mahayana* and *Tantric* traditions. They had extensive diplomatic relations with the Palas, and there was much cultural traffic between Pala Bengal and the Shailendra Empire. The most important symbol in stone of the cosmic system of *Mahayana* Buddhism is the great temple of Borobudur in Java. Apart from Buddhism, the Southeast Asians generally borrowed many elements of Indian culture. However, they did so in a proactive manner rather than as passive colonial subjects. Using their own originality and genius, they changed it sufficiently to make it a natural part of their landscape, environment and personality.[59] This is the reason why Indian cultural imprints and forms which still exist there are not regarded by the populace as an alien cultural burden. They adhere to this particular heritage with pride because it has become an integral part of their native cultures.

Indian scientific influence at Baghdad

The most important centre of intellectual life in the Islamic world during this period was Baghdad. The Abbasid rulers of that city soon realised that their people had only a rudimentary knowledge of such sciences as astronomy, mathematics and medicine. They looked to India and Persia for enlightenment. Two independent Arab writers, Ibn al-Adami and Abu Mashar, have recorded the visit of Kanaka, an Indian astronomer-mathematician and diplomat from Sind, at the court of the Caliph Al-Mansur (754–75). With his curiosity in Indian astronomy and mathematics greatly aroused by the visitor, the caliph ordered two scholars, Ibrahim al-Fazari and Yaqub ibn Tariq, to translate the two critical works of Brahmagupta (late sixth century), *Brahmasphutasiddhanta* and *Khandakhadyaka*. Through the resulting Arabic translations, known as *Sindhind* and *Arkand*, the knowledge of Indian numerals passed on to the Islamic world[60] (see Figure 10.4). Similarly, the Persian astronomical tables, known as *Zig-I shahriyarr*, which were influenced by Indian astronomy, were translated into Arabic under the title of *Zijashshahriyar*.[61] The ninth-century scholar al-Khwarizmi learnt Sanskrit and explained to his readers the Indian system of notation, and through his work the internationalisation of the Indian number system began.[62] Another scholar from the same century, al-Kindi, wrote four books on Indian numerals. Indian medical methods and drugs were also in great demand in the Islamic world. A large number of Sanskrit medical, pharmacological and toxicological texts were translated into Arabic under the patronage of Khalid, the *vizier* of Al-Mansur. Khalid was the son of a chief

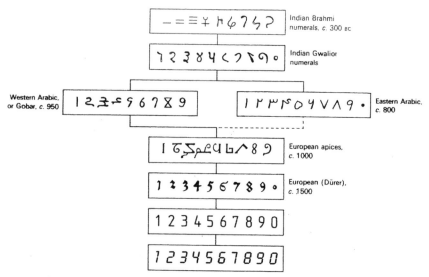

The evolution of present-day numerals (after Open University, 1976, p. 53).

Figure 10.4   The Gwalior numerals (by permission of Dr George Joseph).

priest of a Buddhist monastery in Balkh. Some of his family were killed when the Arabs captured Balkh; others, including Khalid, survived by converting to Islam. They were to be known as the Barmakis of Baghdad, who were fascinated by new ideas from India.[63] Indian medical knowledge was given a further boost under the caliph Harun ar-Rashid (788–809), who ordered the translation of *Susruta Samhita* into Arabic. A great Arabic medical text of the late ninth and tenth centuries, *Kitab al-hawi*, translated into Latin as late as the thirteenth century and known as *Liber continens*, was written by al-Razi, or Rhazes (865–925), who embodied much Indian knowledge in that work.

Welcoming the adherents of non-Indic faiths

By the year 1000, in addition to the Hindus, Buddhists and Jains, the adherents of four Middle Eastern faiths had settled in diverse parts of India. The Arab Muslims were the largest group, and, excepting their conquest of Sind, they took up trading and maritime occupations. They had few inhibitions about arranging temporary marriages (*muta*) with Indian women;[64] and, although initially they did not go out of their way to convert the Indians, they made sure that their offspring considered themselves Muslim. Perhaps the first authentic group of Indian Muslims were the Mapillas of Kerala, descendants of the Arab merchants and Keralan women from marine and fishing castes. The steady process of Brahmanisation in Kerala was, at that time, leading to an increasing emphasis within the Hindu population on purification rites and caste rituals, resulting in the exclusion of the majority from maritime activities. This gave the Mapillas a unique opportunity to control harbours and long-distance shipping routes. The profits they made not only yielded tax revenues for the Hindu kings of Kerala, but also helped them to carve out a distinct place for themselves within Keralan society[65] (see Extract 10.4).

Kerala was also the place where a visible Christian presence had been evident for several hundred years. According to a commonly held Keralan tradition, the earliest Christian church was established by St Thomas, the apostle of Christ, in AD 52.[66] Doubts felt by the Western Christians about this claim have centred upon two issues: the lack of written testimony and the hazards of long sea journeys. Modern historical research into the many oral traditions within the Kerala church has put the first doubt to rest. Also, since Roman and Egyptian ships were trading regularly with Kerala in the first century AD, there was no reason why St Thomas could not have travelled on one of those ships. The Kerala church had no direct contacts with Rome; in fact, from the fourth century onwards, its main link with the Christian world was through the merchants and immigrants who came to Kerala in Persian trading ships. Many of them were West Asian and Levantine Nestorian Christians who owed allegiance to the Persian state, and whose prelates and bishops lived in the Persian Empire of the Sasanians. Their liturgy was in the Syriac language, a variant of Aramaic, the language of Christ and his apostles.[67] It is through this Levantine connection that the St Thomas church came to be known as the Syrian church.[68] While these Christian immigrants helped to familiarise the Syrian church with the various revisionist dogmas of Christianity that were convulsing Europe and the Middle East during the first Christian millennium, the essential strength of the church lay in the numbers of converted natives. A regular series of conversions of some of the most high-caste and influential *brahman* families of Kerala not only provided numerical strength but also helped to Indianise this church in a way realised by no other Christian church in India.[69] In the period covered by this chapter, the most reliable documentary evidence of the influence of the St Thomas church comes from three inscriptions on the so-called Tarisapalli Copper Plates of the year 849. The inscriptions record a set of privileges granted to the Syrian church at Quilon by the then local ruler, placing the Christians on an equal footing with the Hindus of Kerala.[70]

As with the Christians, it was again Kerala that was the main hosting society for the followers of yet another Middle Eastern faith: Judaism. The Keralan hospitality went back, according to Indian and Jewish traditions, to 1000 BC, when King Solomon's fleet was supposed to have traded in Indian waters.[71] The Jews were in Kerala at the time of Christ; and, again according to tradition, thousands of Jews landed at *Muziris* after the destruction of the second temple of Jerusalem by the Romans in AD 70. The most substantial Jewish migration to Kerala, however, came about through the agency of the Islamic Empire from the eighth century onwards.[72] Jewish traders and entrepreneurs, whether domiciled in Damascus, Baghdad or Cairo, facilitated a huge amount of commerce within that empire.[73] Their agents and mariners also came to Kerala, where many later settled, seeking goods produced in south India and Southeast Asia, in exchange for some of the luxury products from other parts of the empire. The Chera rulers of Kerala appreciated the financial gains and economic activity generated by the Jews: the Jewish Copper Plate of the year 1000 carries a number of inscriptions which list the various privileges and gifts granted by a local ruler, Bhaskara Ravi Varmana, to the Jewish community leader, Joseph Rabban.[74]

With the introduction of Islam in Persia after the Arab victory there in 641, the state religion of Zoroastrianism was left rudderless. While the mass of the Persian people abandoned their Zoroastrian faith for Islam out of both fear and expediency, substantial numbers of staunch Zoroastrians continued to survive there during the next few centuries. Their position fluctuated between extreme vulnerability and insecure co-existence with the Muslims.[75] According to a tradition recorded in India in the sixteenth century, a band of these Zoroastrians, from the Khorasan province of Iran (i.e. Parthia), landed on the Gujarat coast near Sanjan as refugees in 716. It is, however, more likely that they came as late as 936, when they were welcomed by a local ruler, Jadi Rana, who, most probably, was a feudatory of the Rashtrakuta king.[76] The Parsis, as they have come to be called by the Gujaratis, have lived in India ever since as a minuscule but distinct faith community.

SELECT EXTRACTS FOR REVIEW AND REFLECTION

Extract 10.1   The promotion of scholarship and scholarly exchanges

From the advice given to his monarch by a great poet and *pandit*, Rajashekhara, who was based at the Gurjara–Pratihara court of King Mahendrapala, we can surmise that cultural activities were held in high esteem in the India of the ninth century AD.

A king should find an 'Association of Poets'. He should have a hall for the examination of poetical works. The scholars at his court should be satisfied and maintained at his court. Deserving people should be awarded rewards.

Exceptionally good poems or their authors should be properly honoured. A king should make arrangements for establishing contacts with scholars coming from other lands, and show honour to them as long as they stay in his dominions.

Source: *Kavyamimamsa*, by Rajashekhara, quoted from B.N. Sharma, *Social and Cultural History of North India, c. 1000–1200 AD*, New Delhi: Abhinav Publications, 1972.

Extract 10.2 The idea of debate in the Nyaya tradition

In the following passage, by a contemporary philosopher, we are introduced to the rational and logical way of conducting a debate proposed a long time ago in ancient India.

What counts as winning a debate? If the debate is a victory at-any-cost-sort, and a debater wins when his opponent is lost for words or confused or hesitant, then the best and the most rational way to proceed would be to employ such tricks as play on the opponents' weaknesses, like speaking very quickly or using convoluted examples of referring to doctrines of which one suspects one's opponent is ignorant. In the other sort of debate, the truth-directed sort, 'winning' is a matter of persuading one's opponent, and also an impartial audience, that one's thesis is true, and the rational debater must find some other methods. Nothing is more persuasive than an argument backed up by well-chosen examples and illustrations. And so, when the Naiyayikas come to codify the form of rational debating demonstration, the citation of examples was given at least as much prominence as the citation of reasons.

Source: Jonardon Ganeri, *Philosophy in Classical India: The Proper Work of Reason*, London: Routledge, 2001, p. 28.

Extract 10.3 The imperfections of Sanskrit

The great historian D.D. Kosambi explains some of the deficiencies of Sanskrit which need to be taken into account by uncritical admirers and promoters of the language.

Even at its best, [Sanskrit] does not give the depth, simplicity of expression, the grandeur of spirit, the real greatness of humanity that one finds in the Pali Dhammapada, the Divina Commedia, or Pilgrim's Progress. It is the literature of and for a class, not a people. ... The language suffered from its long, monopolistic association with a class that had no direct interest in technique, manual operations, trade agreements, contracts or surveys. ... There is no Sanskrit word of any use to the blacksmith, potter, carpenter, weaver, ploughman ... The distinction between Sanskrit and Arabic in this respect should also be considered. Arab works on medicine, geography, mathematics, astronomy, practical sciences were precise enough to be used in their day from Oxford to Malaya ... The 'Arab' literati were not primarily a disdainful priest-caste.

Source: D.D. Kosambi, *An Introduction to the Study of Indian History*, Bombay: Popular Prakashan, 1975, pp. 283–5.

Extract 10.4 The status of the Mapillas

The Mapillas are the Muslims of north Kerala. The Zamorin [king] of Calicut [a port city of north Kerala], one of the chief patrons of the Arabian trade, is said to have directed that in every family of fishermen in his dominion, at least one male member should be brought up as a Muslim in order that there would be enough locals to man the Arabian ships. ... The Mapillas were very wealthy and owned large tracts of land. The lower classes were fishermen, labourers and petty cultivators. The Mapillas seem to have been considered 'honorary Nayars' since they were granted several privileges within the caste system. They dressed like Nayars and partly adopted their matrilineal system. Lower caste converts could overcome several of their traditional disabilities through conversion, which encouraged the process.

Source: Prema Kurien, 'Colonialism and Ethnogenesis: A study of Kerala, India', *Theory and Society*, Vol. 23, No. 3, June 1994, pp. 385–417; read also Stephen Frederick Dale, *Islamic Society on the South Asian Frontier: The Mapillas of Malabar*, Oxford: Clarendon Press, 1980.

RELEVANT QUESTIONS FOR DISCUSSION

1   Why do many modern Indian historians terminate the ancient period around the eighth century AD?
2   Is the emphasis placed on feudalism a reflection of some Indian historians' propensity to draw parallels with European history or their leanings towards Marxism?
3   For what reasons have the Jews left India in the modern period, while the Christians have held out?

Notes

1 Thapar 2002: 418–21; Chattopadhyaya 1994: 57–64.
2 Thapar 2002: 418–21; Wink 1991: 281–3.
3 Wink 1991: 290.
4 Cited in Majumdar and Pusalker 1955: 32.
5 Wink 1991: 285.
6 Ibid.: 254–77.
7 Ibid.: 258–9.
8 Ibid.: 266.
9 Ibid.: 259–60.
10 Ibid.: 273–4.
11 Ibid.: 275–6.

12 Ibid.: 303.
13 Altekar 1955.
14 Wink 1991: 304–5.
15 Ibid.: 306n.
16 Williamson 1999: 85.
17 For a succinct summary of Sharma's views, consult Chattopadhyaya 1994: 7–14; Chattopadhyaya 1995: 319–25; Ray *et al.* 2000: 624–8; Thapar 2002: 442–52; Shrimali 2001: 1–5.
18 For a summary of views opposed to Sharma, consult Wink 1991: 219–24; Chattopadhyaya 1995: 325–31; Chattopadhyaya 1994: 14–17.
19 Sharma 1985; Sharma 2001: Ch. 3.
20 Thapar 2002: 444–5; Ray *et al.* 2000: 465; Ali 2006; Kondo 2002.
21 Chattopadhyaya 1995: 332–5; Chattopadhyaya 1994: 17ff; Ludden 2002: 47–50.
22 Ghoshal 1955: 231–9.
23 Thapar 2002: 444–5.
24 Wink 1991: 277–81, 291–3.
25 Ibid.: 282–3.
26 Risso 1995: 14–15.
27 Ibid.: 15–16; Wink 1991: 53ff.
28 Wink 1991: 65–86.
29 Ibid.: 10–12.
30 Joseph 2000: 306.
31 Wink 1991: 306.
32 Chattopadhyaya 1994: 150–52.
33 Ibid.: 131–47.
34 Ibid.: 162–5.
35 Ibid.: 172–8.
36 Stein 1998: 123–5.
37 Hayes 2000: 387.
38 Clear 2000; Hinnells and Sharpe 1972: 42–51.
39 Fort 2000.
40 Gupta 1995: 215–16.
41 Pereira 1995.
42 Flood 1996: 239–43; Sen 1961: 82–4; Gupta 1995: 214–19.
43 Phillips 2000; Isherwood 1952: ix–xiv; Isherwood 1965: 112; Heard 1952; Swami Prabhavananda 1952; Mahadevan 1952.
44 Ludden 2002: 55–6.
45 Sastri 1960: 428.
46 Flood 1996: 92; Sen 1961: 67–8.
47 Cited in Sengupta 1993: 21.
48 Tomory 1989: 211–14.
49 Sengupta 1993: 19.
50 Nicholas 2003: 122.
51 Devasthali 1955: 187–8.
52 Dimock *et al.* 1974: 11.
53 Devasthali 1995: 192–3; Pollock 2003: 44; Dimock *et al.* 1974: 136–43.
54 Pandit 1996.
55 Pollock 2003: 61–75; Dimock *et al.* 1974: 12–13; Jain 1955: 212–19.
56 Nagaraj 2003; Iyengar 1955: 219–26.
57 Samaddar 1922: 119–41.
58 Thapar 2002: 409; Stein 1998: 127–8.
59 Stein 1998: 127–8.
60 Bose *et al.* 1989: 48–9, 134, 210–11; Majumdar and Pusalker 1955: 448–9.
61 Bose *et al.* 1989: 134.

62 Ibid.: 211–12.
63 Ibid.: 586–7; Majumdar and Pusalker 1955: 450.
64 Wink 1991: 71.
65 Ibid.: 71–8.
66 Menon 1990: 34–7.
67 In the fourth century the merchant Thomas Cana emigrated from Syria, leading out some 400 families to establish the Kerala Nestorian church.
68 Menon 1990: 58–61.
69 Joseph 2003: 19–20; 27–8.
70 Menon 1990: 61–3; Ray *et al.* 2000: 504–5.
71 Menon 1990: 64.
72 Wink 1991: 86–104.
73 Goitein 1973: 3–21, 175–91.
74 Menon 1990: 65–8; Wink 1991: 100; Ray *et al.* 2000: 485–6.
75 Boyce 2002b.
76 Mistree 2002: 413–14.

11 Chola domination in the south and Turco-Afghan plunder in the north

(Time-span: c. AD 1000 to 1200)

The eleventh and twelfth centuries witnessed a massive ransacking of north Indian wealth by Turco-Afghan warriors and marauders. The small Rajput kingdoms, successors to the mighty Gurjara–Pratihara kingdom of the two earlier centuries, were in a constant state of insecurity engendered by this rising menace. The raids were, in one sense, a curtain raiser to what was to happen in AD 1206. In that year Qutb-ud-din Aybak, a slave general, established his own slave dynasty at Delhi, where he constructed the famous Qutb mosque and minar. His was the first of the five dynasties that are collectively known as the Delhi Sultanate (1206–1526). The 1206 victory of the Turco-Afghans was to presage nearly 600 years of Muslim political authority and influence over a large part of India, and the Muslims, like the Arabs previously, also pulled India into the economic constellation of the Islamic world up until the coming of the European powers. Yet while the Turkish plunder of the north was at its height, the south flourished under the great Hindu Chola dynasty; when the Cholas declined other Hindu kingdoms such as the Hoysala and Vijayanagara took their place. While the fabulous wealth of the north Indian cities and temples was being drained away to Afghanistan, south Indian wealth was at the same time increasing phenomenally through the commercial and maritime endeavours of the Cholas. South India remained obstinately Hindu, even while Muslim power and authority were spreading there through the future centuries. This is just one example of the complex plurality of India that makes nonsense of periodising Indian history on the basis of religion (see Map 11.1).

The source material for the history of the two centuries lies in thousands of inscriptions relating to the Cholas and other smaller kingdoms. Contemporary historical biographies, chronicles and *vamshavalis*, or historical records of dynastic genealogies, are also sources of much useful information to students of this period. Arabic and Persian records provide many details about the Turks' domination and the Islamic influences. There is no shortage of material for primary researchers and scholars to probe and analyse, and new interpretations are always forthcoming as more material is closely studied. There are also two very important contemporary accounts that are particularly instructive in their different ways. One is the historical survey of Kashmir, the *Rajatarangini*, written by Kalhana, who attempted to provide a systematic historical study of

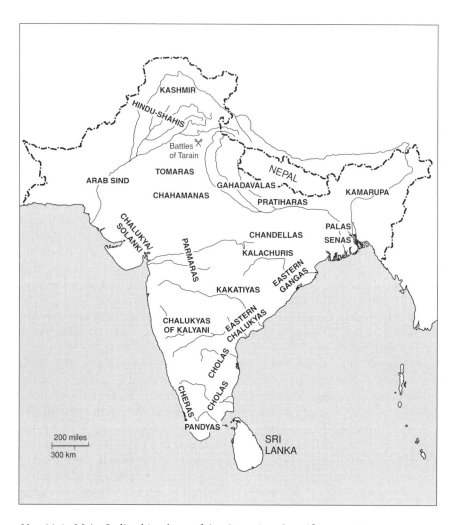

Map 11.1   Major Indian kingdoms of the eleventh and twelfth centuries.

a regional kingdom. Balanced and readable, it comes nearest to our modern perspectives on historical writing. The other, from among the many foreign sources of information, is the most useful and penetrating account of India by the Central Asian scholar Al-Biruni, who accompanied Mahmud of Ghazni and spent ten years in India.

State and society under the Cholas

The eastern seaboard of southern India is known as the Coromandel coast, the term derived from the *Cola-Mandalam*. On this coast and in its fertile hinterland a Tamil-speaking people, the Cholas, established a south Indian state with a particular identity and style of governance for nearly three centuries. Although mentioned, along with the Pandyas and the Cheras, in the *Sangam* literature of the Tamils dating back to the beginning of the Christian era, the Cholas emerged as a substantial power only in the late ninth century when they defeated the Pallavas. By the early tenth century the Cholas ruled practically the whole of the far south, excepting the Chera kingdom in Kerala. One of the important reasons for their ascendancy was the prosperity of their agriculture, based on the technology of efficient sluices in irrigating the land.[1] Their supremacy, however, came to be resented by the Rashtrakuta, who inflicted a crushing defeat on them in 949. The rest of the tenth century saw the Cholas in a state of steady decline, and it seemed that they were past their peak.[2] The picture, however, changed dramatically with the accession of a dynamic king, Rajaraja I, in 985.

Three great Chola kings

Rajaraja I (985–1012) was the first great leader of the Cholas. Under him they adopted a highly aggressive posture against their smaller neighbours such as the Pandyas, the Cheras and the rulers of Sri Lanka, basically for economic reasons. Rajaraja also attacked the Chalukyas of Kalyani, who had supplanted the Rashtrakuta in the Deccan. History, however, would have been less than kind to him if bloody warfare had been his sole achievement. In fact, he is considered as a king who solidified Chola identity through an elaborate royal administration and bureaucracy, along with the promotion of the cult of god-king at an iconic temple that he built at Thanjavur.[3] His son, Rajendra I (1012–44), was equally dynamic. It was in his reign that Chola imperialism asserted itself powerfully. All of Sri Lanka was conquered, and control in south India was consolidated more fully than before. It was the north, however, that particularly fascinated Rajendra. The lure of the lands of *Aryavarta*, and the powerful symbolism of the holy River Ganga, meant that Rajendra, a great southern ruler, had to tame the north to become a universal ruler. His territorial ambition rashly led him to send an expedition to the Pala kingdom of Bengal; and, although it did not really gain him any material benefits, he nevertheless turned it into a symbolic triumph by ordering his commanders to bring back jars of water from the River Ganga, so that he could claim token ownership of the ancient land of Aryavarta. At Gangaikondacholapuram he built a magnificent temple, surrounded by a huge lake, called *Chola-Ganga*. Rajendra also sent a naval expedition to the kingdom of *Sri Vijaya* (southern Malay peninsula, Java and Sumatra) to protect the existing India–China trade route across the Malay Straits.[4] The Chola rulers continued to enjoy the gains made under Rajaraja I and Rajendra I, and in the reign of Kulottunga I (1070–1118) the Chola kingdom reached new heights of prosperity and maturity. The kingdom became the symbol of southern classicism, and the cultural levels achieved at that time became the benchmarks for southern culture in general.

The Chola kingdom survived for about a hundred years after 1118; but from the early thirteenth century onwards it came under great pressure from not only the new Deccan kingdom of the Hoysalas but, more severely, from its older rivals, the Pandyas of Madurai.[5]

Royal authority and local autonomy in a regional kingdom: the Chola model

By any criterion, the Chola kingdom of the eleventh century was one of the great political structures of India, if not the world. The organisation of that kingdom was based on sound principles of administration and management, the evidence for which lies in detailed inscriptions and revenue records. A valuable set of inscriptions, discovered as late as 1905, and consisting of 816 lines of writing on thirty-one sheets of copper bound together, along with a seal-ring, is the so-called Order (or *sasanam*) of King Rajendra I. The purpose of this copper plate was to record the transfer of a grant to *brahmans* in a particular village to the temple itself. However, the recording of the event is perhaps not as important as the eulogy to the Chola rulers and the articulation of Chola grandeur; it expresses the belief that the space the Cholas ruled was the 'sphere of a world ruler'.[6] All the early historical studies came to the conclusion that the success of the kingdom lay in the exercise of powerful royal authority through a firm bureaucracy.[7] The monarchs of the calibre of Rajaraja I and Rajendra I provided the role models for royal authority in action.

This particular understanding of the Chola royal authority came to be challenged, in time, by what has come to be known as the segmentary state theory, proposed by a group of American historians led by Burton Stein, whose research interests lay in comparative studies of rural societies. We have already referred to this theory in relation to the Pallavas, but it is necessary to restate some of its positions because the Cholas more or less continued the traditions of the Pallavas. The segmentary state theory argued that in the feudal world of the eleventh century the Chola king did not truly exercise political sovereignty throughout his kingdom; his real political power was confined to the central core area, while in all the outer areas the king exercised only ritual or symbolic authority. True power actually lay with the assemblies of agricultural micro-regions called *nadus* (referred to in the previous chapter) or with the *brahman* lords and local chiefs who had received land grants from the king for varied reasons. The king did not control a central system of taxation or a central army. If he wished to raise resources, more often than not, the Chola king launched plunder raids on the neighbouring states. It was further argued that both the Pallavas and the Cholas built temples as a means of reaffirming their ritual sovereignty in the peripheral areas; the sponsoring of temples was a way of keeping the *brahman* elites compliant, thus preventing any disruption to their nominal authority.[8]

Further extensive research in Tamil records has, in turn, led a more recent group of historians to challenge the ideas of the segmentary state theory. The notion that the Chola kings held merely ritual sovereignty outside their core area of *Cholamandalam* is rejected on the grounds that they in fact made subtle use of the existing institutions to integrate their kingdom rather than allow the institutions to go their own way. These institutions were, respectively, the *brahmadeya*, the *nagaram* and the temple.[9] None of them was permitted to displace the *nadu*, which remained the basic agricultural unit; but the *nadu*'s power was significantly moderated by them. Through their land grants to the *brahmans*, the Chola kings extensively encouraged the creation of *brahmadeyas*,[10] which had the potential for raising agricultural productivity and the general income of the kingdom. The *brahmadeya* elites were also to be the eyes and ears of the king. The *nagaram* was the market centre and a place where powerful commercial organisations and merchant guilds,[11] such as a body called Ayyavole 500, operated (see Extract 11.1); the kings realised that they too were creators of wealth, and ensured that the *nadu* assemblies did not in any way hinder their work. Since a *nagaram* might serve a number of *nadus*, no one particular *nadu* could impose arbitrary levies on the merchants. The temple, the third institution, was more than a place of worship for the Chola kings.[12] It held great commercial and economic advantage for them. Vast donations were made to the temple by rich and poor, and huge quantities of foodstuffs were moved into the temple precincts from the hinterland. The temple could thus act as a threshold for the king's intervention in the countryside. The temple, with its iconography and its sacred space for the *Shivalingam*, for example, was the central arena where the king, through his enormous powers of patronage, could demonstrate more than ritual sovereignty. Chola centralism also effectively institutionalised the various religious cults associated with the popular *bhakti* movement in south India, and temple patronage was a key element in this aspect of the imperium.[13] The temple proclaimed to the world the Chola state's ideology.[14] Additionally, the Chola kings did not permit the *nadus* to remain stationary and unchanging. The *nadus* were not just places where all property was to be communally held. Various types of private ownership were being encouraged by the royal officials. Continual reorganisations, mergers and rationalisations were effected, and larger revenue or political units, called *valanadu*, *periyanadu* or *tanyiur*, were being created for the purpose of defining and redefining agricultural regions and revenue organisation by the will of a royal authority.[15] Once again the central bureaucracy was gaining ascendancy over the local rights of the *nadus*. With three different versions of the nature of Chola authority that we have summarised, no wonder this kingdom continues to fascinate the modern-day students of history.

The international context of Chola commercial prosperity

The ancient maritime commerce of south India was profoundly affected by two economically significant developments in the eleventh century. One was the displacement, within the Islamic economic world, of the Abbasid Empire based in Baghdad by the Fatimids of Egypt based in Cairo. In consequence, the trading links between the ports of the Persian Gulf and the once Rashtrakuta-controlled ports of western India became severed. Under the Fatimids the trade with the Red Sea ports provided greater incentive to the merchants of the far south of India.[16] The Keralan coast was thereby set to gain at the expense of the Karnataka coast. The Chola king Rajaraja I's expansionist hold over Sri Lanka, the Maldive Islands and the Chera kingdom of Kerala was part of the ongoing effort by the Cholas to ensure that their merchants were not disadvantaged. The second critical economic development was the enormous commercial opening up of China under the Sung dynasty. At that time China was undergoing a profound economic transformation.[17] She was several centuries ahead of any other part of the world in the fields of steel manufacture, the armaments sector, transportation networks and techniques, the management of credits and finance, and specialisation of production. Hundreds of Chinese commodities were entering the international market owing to the rapid expansion of her merchant marine under the Sungs. The rise of the prosperous consumer society in China led to huge amounts of imports from India, such as raw cotton and manufactured textiles (in which China was, at this stage, far behind India), spices and drugs, ivory, amber, coral, rhinoceros horn, aromatics and perfumes; it resulted in China running up a large balance of trade deficit. To a considerable extent, the Indian merchants' prosperity depended upon the goodwill of the rulers of *Sri Vijaya*, a Malay kingdom that straddled the Malay peninsula and the Indonesian island of Sumatra and controlled the Malacca Straits. This key waterway passage is today one of the most important international shipping lanes, as it was in the eleventh century. The Indian merchant marine used this waterway to shorten the journey from the southern ports of India to China. In order to increase their share of the profits from the India–China trade and its customs dues, etc., the *Sri Vijaya* authorities decided that all ships had to terminate their journeys in the straits and that their middlemen would trans-ship the goods to their respective destinations. This was much too irksome for the merchant organisations in the Chola state, and Rajendra I decided to use his substantial naval force to punish *Sri Vijaya*. There was no imperial motive for this; it was solely a matter of safeguarding the shipping lane for the Chola-sponsored merchant fleet. The close relationship between the Chola state and the merchants' organisations depended upon sufficiently assured royal protection.[18]

Turco-Afghan incursions into north India

We have referred, in the two previous chapters, to both the Arab invasion of Sind and the Arab mercantile presence on the west coast of India. The Muslim influence in India between about 700 and 1000 was limited and not particularly resented. During the next two centuries, however, we see the beginnings of the fear and paranoia engendered within the Indian psyche by the emergence of a new type of Muslim migrant: the nomadic Turco-Afghan warrior. Before we examine his impact let us first briefly review the north Indian political scene as it existed around the year AD 1000.

Regional kingdoms of north India

Nearly twenty north Indian regional kingdoms were in existence during this period, but a few of them deserve to be especially noted. They may be grouped as follows. Of the two substantial Himalayan kingdoms of Kashmir and Nepal, Kashmir was more important than the latter, and, as outlined in Chapter 9, its famous earlier leader, Lalitditya Muktapida, had briefly wielded power over *Madhyadesha* and *Kanauj* in the eighth century. It occupied, as it still does today, a highly strategic geographical zone that acted as a link route between India and the surrounding countries of Tibet, Nepal, China and Central Asia; and it also lay along one of the great trade routes between these countries.[19] Nepal had been intermittently in contact with India since before the Mauryan times, but was greatly affected by stressful relations between Bengal and Tibet.[20] Next, we have a group of Rajput kingdoms. In addition to the Gurjara–Pratihara, a number of Rajput dynastic kingdoms were spread out across the northern plains and the central regions.[21] In *Madhyadeha* and surrounding areas such as Bundelkhand, the successors to the Gurjara–Pratiharas were the dynasties of the Gahadavalas, Kalachuris and Chandellas. The last-mentioned was particularly lustrous in its glory. A tour around the Khajuraho temples, built under the patronage of the Chandellas, should be enough to dispel any notion that a small Indian kingdom in this period lacked wealth or flair. Further west, there was another cluster of four Rajput kingdoms, including those of the Chahamanas or the Chauhanas of eastern Rajasthan, the Tomaras of the Delhi region, the Parmaras of Malwa and western Madhya Pradesh, and the Chalukyas (not to be confused with the Deccan Chalukyas) or Solankis of Gujarat. The Chahamanas were the final bulwarks of defence against the Ghurid invaders, and the tragic fate of their brave king, Prithviraja Chauhan, evokes great emotion among many Indians. Still further to the west, there was the kingdom of Sind, occupied by the Arabs since 711; but in the northwest and along the frontier area, and earlier extending deep into Afghanistan, there was also a small kingdom of the so-called Hindu Shahis. Originally they had been the rulers of Kabul and the surrounding area where there were many Buddhists too. It needs to be remembered that both Brahmanism and Buddhism had a strong presence in Afghanistan before Islam. By the time of the Islamic penetration of Afghanistan, the Hindu Shahi rulers had transferred to the Punjab; they were the first of the Indian rulers to be destroyed by the Gaznavid conquerors. At the opposite end of the map, in Bengal, the great Pala dynasty was nearing its end by the middle of the eleventh century; and from 1080 onwards the Sena dynasty was to control Bengal. Further to the northeast there existed the Assamese kingdom of *Kamarupa*, which, like Nepal, had not only come under the influence of Brahmanism and Aryanisation but was also facing pressures from the rulers of Bengal.[22]

The background to the Turco-Afghans

After having defeated the Sasanians the Arab armies sped towards the northern and northeastern frontiers of Iran. Beyond these frontiers lay the terrain of the nomadic Turkic-speaking tribes of Central Asia, which had, throughout their history, faced constant harrying over land and land rights from their various neighbours and enemy confederations and, above all, from the Mongols. Migrating into Iran and Afghanistan had been their traditional response; however, after these countries came under the control of the Abbasid rulers of Baghdad from the mid-eighth century onwards, these migrants came to be seen in a different light.[23] The Abbasids and their client rulers saw in them a ready supply of 'slave' soldiers for their armies. Bought as children, they were given military training for service initially against the Mongols but also against other enemies of the Islamic Empire. They were taught the skills of archery and horsemanship. Although remaining slaves, they could rapidly rise within the ranks of the army, suffering little in the way of racial discrimination. Since they had embraced Islam, their status was higher than that of slaves, but they could not easily leave the army. They won rapid recognition in the Islamic Empire; in time, they became as ardent defenders of Islam as the Arabs had been earlier. At the same time, however, there was the danger that the various groups of these soldiers would complot in rebellions against the Abbasid caliphs, thereby gravely weakening the integrity of the Islamic Empire.

Mahmud of Ghazni's raids

A hundred miles southwest of Kabul there lie today the ruins of Ghazni, which, in the tenth century, had been a part of the Samanid Empire of Iran. In 933, a Turkish slave of the Samanids, Alptigin, in the rebellious way many slave soldiers behaved, seized the lands around the town and established a small kingdom there. In turn, another risen slave, Sabuktigin, who served in Alptigin's army, instead of rebelling against his master, contrived to marry his daughter. On the death in 977 of his father-in-law and master, Sabuktigin became the king of Ghazni, while continuing to offer nominal allegiance to the Samanids. Thus was established the Ghaznavid dynasty, which lasted from 977 to 1186.[24] Sabuktigin's major military achievement was to weaken the Indian kingdom of the Hindu Shahis, who controlled the lands east of Kabul, including the Punjab. By the time he died, in 997, he had exposed the vulnerability of the kings of northwest India. His son, Mahmud, who ruled from 997 to 1030, pressed his advantage further against the Hindu Shahis, whose ruler, Jayapala, preferred suicide by self-immolation rather than humiliating subjection by paying a ransom to Mahmud. With Jayapala's demise, Mahmud's confidence grew, and for the next quarter century he launched seventeen separate raids deep into northwestern and northern India. Neither the Gurjara–Pratihara nor the other Rajput kingdoms deterred Mahmud, partly because his strategy was simply to carry out lightning raids on cities, temples and monasteries rather than engage the Indian forces in set-piece battles. The bulky Indian armies, more accustomed to conventional static warfare, were no match for Mahmud's mobile horsemen recruited from among the varied Turkic and Afghan ethnic groups. Mahmud avoided the temptation of permanent conquests even after he had taken the city of *Kanauj*, the capital of the Pratihara kingdom, in 1019. He was focused, basically, on ensuring a secure position for his city of Ghazni within the nomadic milieu that he knew best, which was the Turco-Afghan political and social world; his raids into India were just a means to achieving this end. The transfer of Indian wealth to the treasury of Ghazni was Mahmud's key motive, because only with money could he continue to secure the support for the Ghaznavids among the chiefs and warlords. Some of his ill-gotten wealth was spent on a spate of constructions in Ghazni, with the building of libraries, mosques and palaces. Most of the bullion was minted down for the purpose of financing more trade.[25] The Indians had accrued their wealth through centuries of profitable trade balances with other countries; but this wealth was now scattered in West Asia. The economic damage for India was limited, because Indian international trade continued to be buoyant. Mahmud's Islamic iconoclasm that was given vent in his plunder of temples was, however, something that is still alive in Indian memories.

The Ghurid conquest of north India

The Ghaznavid raids did not cease after Mahmud's death in 1030. The economy of Ghazni depended upon the continuous supply of funds from India, and it became ever more necessary to attack the wealthy cities of *Madhyadesha*, such as *Kanauj* and Benares.[26] Although Ghazni itself faced a major challenge in the mid-twelfth century from the nearby province of Ghur, the Indian vulnerability to Turco-Afghan attacks remained constant. Situated between Ghazni and Herat, the territory of Ghur was ruled by a local Iranian/Tajik family of Shansabanis, who, though initially subordinate to the Ghaznavids, began to encroach upon Ghazni from the 1150s onwards. By 1186 their control over the city was complete when two brothers in the family, Ghiyasuddin Muhammad and Muzuddin Muhammad, seized all power there.[27] By agreement within the family, Muzuddin became the king of Ghazni – in the Indian context, he is generally known as Muhammad Ghuri. The financial depredation of the Indian lands was a temptation that Muhammad Ghuri could not resist; however, his ambition was not just to raid, but also to annex lands. He evolved new military strategies and introduced a number of innovations in the army.[28] The cavalry, with their well-mounted archers, was widely introduced. The army recruited from a broader range of ethnic groups with military skills, such as the Damghanis of northern Iran, the Tajiks, and the Seljuq and Ghuzz Turks. Two separate units, the advance guards and the reserve forces, were formed in every Ghurid army. The slave soldiers were granted the highest privileges in Muhammad's army, as their military prowess was recognised. Muhammad also decided to streamline the procedures for the procurement of foodstuffs by attaching officially recognised grain dealers and pastoralists, later known as *banjaras*, who, with their massive bullock carts, ensured steady supplies for his mobile forces.[29] With his preparations complete, Muhammad Ghuri launched a massive attack, through the Punjab, into the territories of the Chahamana kingdom in 1191, but was repulsed with great losses by its ruler, Prithviraja Chauhan. It is remembered as the first battle of Tarain. The second battle of Tarain was fought the very next year, but this time Prithviraja and his army were completely overwhelmed by the Ghurid forces. Prithviraja was taken prisoner and executed. Many reasons have been advanced for the latter's defeat,[30] but a few need to be especially noted. Prithviraja was a traditional Rajput ruler, steeped in the heroic traditions of his people and dependent upon the feudal levies;[31] but these were notoriously unreliable in comparison with the permanently committed centralised Turkish standing armies.[32] The Indian forces had huge numbers of poorly armed and poorly positioned infantrymen who just could not withstand the cavalry charges of the Turco-Afghans.[33] Prithviraja had asked for help from the other Rajput rulers, but none of them felt particularly threatened from across the border at the time and thus failed to come to his assistance, betraying a grave lack of foresight and reliable military intelligence. And at least one Rajput ruler – Jayachandra of *Kanauj* – was so jealous of Prithviraja that he is even supposed to have invited and encouraged Muhammad Ghuri.[34] If Prithviraja had followed up his first victory by pursuing Muhammad, the latter might have been sufficiently intimidated not to return; but Prithviraja's complacency and inaction led to his undoing at the second crucial battle. After Prithviraja there was no credible north Indian ruler who could withstand the Ghurids. The Ganga valley and *Madhyadesha* fell into Turco-Afghan hands within a few years; and the smaller kingdoms of the Ghadavalas and Chandellas lost all real authority in the province (see Map 11.2). Between 1197 and 1205 a non-slave commander of the Ghurid army, Bakhtiyar Khalji, conquered Bihar and Bengal. Although Muhammad Ghuri himself was assassinated in 1206, probably for Islamic sectarian reasons, the Turco-Afghan hold over north India could not be shaken. It was just as well for the slave captains of Muhammad Ghuri, because in Ghur itself a new Iranian power of the Khwarizm Shah was coming to the fore. With Ghur fallen, what remained to the Ghurid slave generals was the north Indian heartland that they had conquered. In 1206 Qutb-ud-din Aybak, Muhammad Ghuri's faithful slave general, became the first king of the slave dynasty and inaugurated the Delhi Sultanate (1206–1526).

Evaluating the Turkish impact

The Central Asian Turks were a people whose nomadism was to dominate the socio-cultural milieu of the Islamic Empire and the Middle East in general.[35] The trend towards nomadism was further accelerated when the greatest of all the nomads of Inner Asia, the Mongols, swooped down upon the Islamic Empire and crushed the Abbasids forever. Baghdad, the queen of Islamic cities,

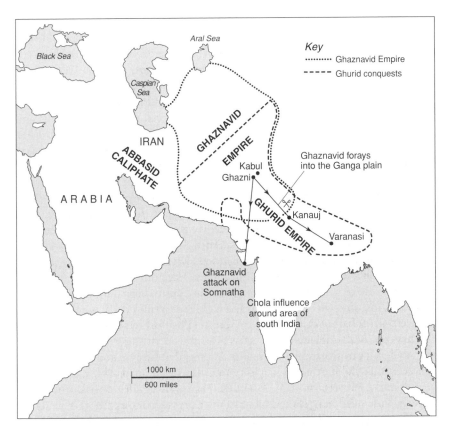

Map 11.2 Turco-Afghan intrusion into India.

was destroyed in 1258, with vast numbers of her people being put to death. A number of factors, however, prevented the triumph of nomadism in India.[36] Here, firstly, the Indian peasantry remained the foundation of the sedentary lifestyle, and the attacking Turco-Afghans learnt to respect the immutable ways of the peasants and their toil on the land. Secondly, the invaders came to appreciate the rich variety of Indian trades, crafts and occupations, only made possible by complex networks of kinship and caste arrangements so unique to India. While militarily triumphant, the Turco-Afghans nevertheless had to make compromises with Indian realities, and over time they became integrated in Indian society. Through their Delhi Sultanate they were eventually to become the greatest bulwark in the defence of India against the Mongols.[37]

Over the sensitive issue of religion, the picture is mixed for the eleventh and twelfth centuries. Muslims generally have a proclivity to convert the non-Muslim, but in those two centuries there was hardly any conversion by the Turco-Afghans. Whatever conversion was taking place was in the marginal areas such as the Malabar coast or Sind, and that was mostly undertaken by the

Arabs. The Turco-Afghans did, however, indulge in a great deal of Islamic iconoclasm. The example was set by Mahmud of Ghazni, whose greatest act of destruction was the breaking of the sacred idols of the Brahamanic/Hindu faith at the Somanatha Temple on the Gujarat coast. Where Mahmud had led, his successors followed; and, during the two centuries, the great temples of Mathura, *Kanauj* and Benares were destroyed. It is interesting to note that after the consolidation of Turco-Afghan rule in 1206 there were hardly any great Hindu temples built in north India; most of the temple building was carried on in the south.[38] The irreligious behaviour of Mahmud and other Turco-Afghan rulers might have been due in part to their own misplaced understanding of the Islamic faith, in the manner of zealots in all religions, but also in part from their desire to please the fanatics within the Islamic clerical establishment. Their actions were neither harshly criticised nor critically scrutinised in any of the Indian writings in the centuries that followed;[39] but they must have been remembered sufficiently well, with the memories of their misdeeds passed on among the succeeding generations of *brahmans* and *kshatriyas*, for a deep well of resentment to arise in their hearts. The British imperialists of the nineteenth century, ever searching for reasons to justify their own rule over India, were not above instigating anti-Muslim sentiment whenever it suited them,[40] and this has had its perverse effects within modern India. With the growth of a strong Hindu identity since the mid-nineteenth century, one of the negative effects has been the nurturing of a historical myth that all India's misfortunes began with Mahmud of Ghazni and his successors. It needs pointing out that Indian kings themselves drained away much of their wealth and resources in many a pointless struggle against one another; that they too destroyed temples and monasteries during their own bouts of sectarian hatreds; and that, while he might have been an anti-Indian iconoclast, Mahmud was certainly not an ethnic cleanser of Indians. His raids had hardly any effect, one way or the other, on Indian demography.[41] And he also pursued his Muslim enemies in the same vengeful manner, either because he considered them to be too powerful or because they were Shiite, the sect that he, as a Sunni, opposed. It is also worth pointing out that, despite a very long period of Muslim authority in India, Islam had managed to convert only a third of the sub-continent's population by the twentieth century; furthermore, vast numbers of Muslim converts were actually drawn from the marginalised and disenfranchised groups, such as forest tribes, pastoral groups and the untouchables, who had remained outside the Hindu religious and social system.

Fortunes of three Indic religions

India had, by now, become a multi-faith country. Seven of today's world religions – Hinduism, Buddhism, Jainism, Christianity, Islam, Judaism and Zoroastrianism – had generally secure footholds in the land. By far the largest number of people would have been the adherents of Hinduism, although it is most unlikely that they would have described themselves by the term Hindu.[42]

This was a term that came into popular usage from about the thirteenth or fourteenth century onwards, and, although its origins are to be found in the ancient Persian geographical references to the land that lay east of the River Indus, it was the Muslims who gave it wide circulation when they used it as a blanket term to describe those whom they considered to be idol worshippers.[43] These so-called idol worshippers would, most probably, have described themselves by either their own caste and *jati* term or a faith term such as *Vaishnava* or *Shaivite*. Buddhists, Jains and various groups of heretics from the Brahmanic fold were generally called the *Shramanas*.

Diversity within Hinduism

Three broad strands had shaped Hinduism before it encountered Islam and post-Enlightenment Europe. The oldest, Vedic Brahmanism, almost 3,000 years old by this period, had developed a most amazing framework of beliefs and practices, and it commanded at best the nominal loyalty of the vast majority of the people for many centuries. They were guided by the *brahman* priests, who inculcated into them such ideas as the supremacy of the *Vedas*, sacrifices to the Vedic gods, the caste system, the rituals of the 'rites of passage', and the divine right of the monarchy to rule benevolently. In addition to the *Vedas*, commentaries such as the *Brahmanas* and the *Upanishads*, the epics of *Ramayana* and *Mahabharata*, the *Dharma Shastras* and the *Dharma Sutras*, and the six schools of philosophy which taught such subjects as logic, cosmology, causation, atheism and the idea of the self – all these were contained within the philosophical, intellectual and theological framework of Vedic Brahmanism. The second strand developed from the fifth century AD onwards, when a new fervour came to permeate the spiritual aspirations of the people. This was the *bhakti* movement, springing from the Puranic religion formed around the *Vaishnava* and *Shaivite* traditions, which demanded from their followers intense devotion to personal gods such as Vishnu or Shiva. Led by the *Alvar* and *Nayanar* saints and poets, the *bhakti* movement swept through India like a whirlwind in the later centuries of the first millennium AD and was to remain a potent force for centuries into the next millennium. Vedic Brahmanism was not displaced, but it was heavily challenged by the Puranic religion; and it was the genius of such philosophers as Shankaracharya (788–822), Ramanuja (1017–1137) and, a little later, Madhava (1197–1276), that they attempted to bridge the differences between the two strands and not precipitate a destructive separation between them. Royal power in the regional kingdoms navigated skilfully between upholding the core values of the older strand while supporting the devotionalists, who represented the growing popular forces of the time. The role of the temples, which were the symbols of royal patronage, was particularly critical in accommodating the two strands.[44] It was in this same spirit of understanding and reconciliation that the third strand, that of the local cults, also became part of the developmental process of Hinduism. With the formation of new regional kingdoms and the opening up of hitherto inaccessible territories, remote groups of people were newly being brought into the Brahmanic fold. Many of these people followed inchoate beliefs and practices that existed at the village level, often involving goddess worship, animal sacrifice and animism. Vedic Brahmanism, being the repository of the conservative tradition, naturally remained cautious in its approach to cults; but the Puranic religion learnt to embrace them and assimilate their deities into the Hindu fold.[45] The most powerful cults, known as Devi or Shakti, were those that worshipped the Mother Goddess and her super-power for doing good or evil to the world.[46] In the Hindu pantheon the goddess Uma, or Parvati, was the Mother Goddess showing her beneficent nature, while as Durga, Kali or Shitala she assumed her demonic form.[47] The female gender is also accorded much strength and respect in the various *Tantric* cults, based on magic and mystical formulas, although some of their practices include 'elements of sexual perversion'.[48] As many non-caste and lower caste people followed the cults, it was vital to incorporate at least some of their beliefs into the Hindu practice. Hence we see, during the eleventh and twelfth centuries, a great increase in image worship and the individual worship of a deity in their human aspect. The mythologies of deities also came to be popularised through the regional languages and oral recitations.[49]

The caste system

The caste system became entrenched during this period, both among the Rajput kingdoms of the north and in the Chola kingdom. There were, however, some essential differences. In the north the idea of ritual ranking, with its neat categorisation of society into four *varnas*, of the *brahmans*, *kshatriyas*, *vaishyas* and *shudras*, was generally accepted, although there was a great degree of manoeuvring by certain groups wanting a higher status for themselves. Just as the Gurjara–Pratihara had been interested in status-seeking (Chapter 10), many intermediate groups desired a *kshatriya* status; and the presence of terms denoting various titles in the inscriptions of kingdoms, such as *ranaka* and *thakkura*, illustrates the nature of caste hierarchy.[50] Even among the *brahmans* there were demarcations. Thus, the Kanyakubja (*Kanauj*) *brahmans* were considered the most learned and most devout of their caste, while the untutored *brahmans* elsewhere, performing lower grade rituals in temples, were granted little esteem. Among the intermediate groups were various categories of merchants, artisans or even semi-professional people such as scribes. The various grades of scribes, for example, came to be collectively known as the *kayastha* caste.[51] All sought higher ritual status. With the increasing complexity of society and the growth of multifarious occupations, each *varna* contained many people who were involved in tasks that were far removed from the prescribed function of a *varna* member. The occupational groups, the *jatis*, nevertheless strove to ensure for themselves as high a place as they could secure within the *varna* framework. The *jati* formation was a tolerable process while the general Brahmanic society remained manageably small in terms of aggregate numbers;

but it became far more complicated when, with the opening up of new lands for the expansion of agriculture, large groups of non-caste people were being exposed to Brahmanisation and Aryanisation. The result was that more and more such people, consigned to the lowest occupations, swelled the ranks of the *shudra* caste. Thereupon began a major shuffle within the *shudra* ranks; the more dynamic of them came to be known as *sat-shudras* or pure *shudras*, whose members were quite often upper level merchants and peasant landowners, while those who performed the most menial and servile jobs, such as scavenging, or who were employed as bonded labour, were beyond the pale and became part of the untouchable groups. Their large numbers ensured the relative comfort of all those above them, and this helped to give feudalism a strong lease of life.[52] In the final analysis, feudalism was, and remains, an oppressive system of exploitation.

It is inadvisable to apprehend the caste system in the Tamil kingdoms of the south through the prism of the northern model. Although the historic roots of the caste system were perhaps in the north, some of the earliest *Sangam* literature of the south also mentions features of the caste system. Originally, in the south, there were agriculturists, pastoralists and hunters, but they did not see themselves partitioned into *varnas*.[53] From about the later centuries of the first millennium BC, when the northern *brahmans* began to settle in the south and disseminate the Aryan and Sanskritic culture, with the idea of caste implicit therein, we can see the faint beginnings of an incipient caste system taking shape. All through the first millennium AD the kings of south India, whether Pallavas, Pandyas, Cheras or Cholas, encouraged and supported the *brahmans* in order to gain enduring legitimacy for themselves. They conferred increasingly large land grants to the *brahmadeyas*, or to the temples, which were the *devadanas*. The *brahmadeyas* and the temples perforce became the main centres around which the southern model of the caste system would evolve and be established.[54] This model possessed its own distinctive characteristics. It conceived of society as being made up of two segments: the *brahmans* and the rest, collectively called *shudras*. Being far more numerous than the *brahmans*, the *shudras* contained diverse groups of non-*brahman* people. The most dominant and the wealthiest of these groups, known as the *vellalars*, was made up of prosperous landowners and rich farmers. Having no choice, the *brahmans* accepted the *vellalars* almost as equals. The members of both groups shared their responsibilities as managers and functionaries of the temples whose substantial resources and assets they oversaw. The non-*vellalar shudras* followed a host of occupations, ranging from various trades and crafts to the most menial tasks. With the increasing complexity and mobility of the southern society in general and the emergence of new trades, the non-*vellalar shudras* could no longer be treated as a homogeneous group. Instead of being given a traditional *varna* ranking after the northern model, the south Indians newly devised a twofold division called the Right Hand and the Left Hand, known as *valangai* and *idangai*.[55] The idea of the left/right caste divisions originally began with the description of units in the Chola armies, but later on became marked by occupational status. The Right Hand came to contain relatively more superior occupational groups than the Left Hand. It used to be believed that the Right Hand groups were those who were involved in stable agricultural occupations and the Left Hand groups were mostly different types of artisans, but this would be to oversimplify the purpose of the division. This division should be seen as a particular form of cultural tool to resolve the problem of status or ranking in a complex situation where different groups of people – newly emergent Sanskritised hill people, forest people and tribals, craftsmen and merchants, traders and pedlars – competed for space and position within the social system. In the south Indian model of the Cholas, therefore, we had the *brahmans*, the *vellalars*, and the Right Hand and the Left Hand groups. It might be thought that this was a more rational and less oppressive system, but, alas, it was not to be. There were always to be some groups of people whose status could not be assigned even to the extreme left of the Left Hand, because these were the people whose oppression was a *sine qua non* for the comfort and prosperity of the society above them;[56] and these people, in the south Indian context, were the *paraiya*, the lowliest of the low – truly pariahs – those who were not only untouchable but unworthy of approach. As far as oppression was concerned, the south Indian model was no different from the northern one. It was only in 1924 that the issues raised by the famous Vaikkom Satyagraha, over the question of temple entry for the untouchables of the south, gave impetus to initiate serious discourse on this subject among the thinking people of both north and south India.[57]

Decline of Buddhism: some explanations

In the centuries under review here there were still a substantial number of Buddhists in the northeast and northwest, along with some of their large monasteries and monastic sites. The close of this period signalled the swift demise of Buddhism. Among a number of lines of argument advanced by historians for this sudden decline, four need to be looked at more closely. Firstly, it has been argued that the Buddhist laity had lost its passion and lacked any sense of organisation. Each person, according to the Buddha, had to undertake his or her own journey towards salvation, and no amount of sacrifices or rituals could help towards reaching that final goal. As it was, this was not easy advice to follow; but its simplicity had made Buddhism popular both among the poor and the socially and commercially mobile people during the earlier centuries. The laity, however, could hardly be expected to retain that sense of loyalty to the Buddha's pristine message in an age when the ideologically revived Brahmanism, with its myriad rituals and caste etiquettes, could more easily draw the Indian masses into its embrace. Besides, the Buddhists themselves had increasingly become highly attracted towards the *Tantric* practices that were being incorporated particularly into the *Mahayana* form. Fewer and fewer Indians were being convinced of the distinctness of

Buddhism. A church without laity is like a university without a student body; and with the rapid dissolution of its laity the Buddhist church in India soon became an empty shell.[58] Secondly, it has been argued that Indian Buddhism lacked the political skills of survival in a changing environment. The *sanghas*, the communities of monks, had been obliged to maintain a puritanical lifestyle, although dependent for sustenance on the laity. In the age of benevolence of rulers such as Ashoka and Kanishka the *sanghas* could continue with their traditional calling. However, all institutions need sound political 'antennae' if they wish to maintain their position. Unfortunately, the Buddhist *sanghas* lacked any sense of the shifting winds of politics. Many of their monasteries were situated along the trade routes rather than close to the cities, where political news travels faster.[59] All this mattered little wherever the local ruler was sympathetic to the Buddhists. After the fifth century AD, more often than not, the rulers favoured Brahmanism or its offspring, *Shaivism* or *Vaishnavism*.[60] Thirdly, it has been argued that, in an age of Buddhist decadence, the flexible and tolerant broad church that was Hinduism offered a real home for the assimilation of Buddhists. There was supposed to be no harassment or persecution of the Buddhists. After all, the Buddha himself was incorporated into the Hindu pantheon of gods.[61] This is a somewhat questionable proposition, because it was not unknown for Buddhists to be persecuted by kings inclining towards *Shaivism* and *Vaishnavism*.[62] In a number of *Puranas* too the persecution of many non-Brahmanic groups, including Buddhists, is considered as praiseworthy.[63] We can only guess why it should be that the history of Buddhism in India can be studied solely with the help of Brahmanic or foreign sources, such as Tibetan, Sri Lankan or Nepali; it must be because there are hardly any original surviving Buddhist documents from the Indian mainland.[64] Of course, many valuable manuscripts would have been taken away by the fervent and devoted Chinese and Tibetan travellers, but a good number must have been destroyed in the Brahmanic persecutions or the Turkish attacks on the monasteries. From the ninth century onwards the Buddhists themselves began to rationalise their assets, and they transferred their most important manuscripts and treasures to larger monasteries.[65] One particular dynasty, the Palas of Bengal, showed exceptional favours to the Buddhists, and with their help great monastic institutions such as Nalanda and Vikramashila were enabled to continue. Finally, there is an argument that the Buddhist demise was the result of the cruelty and rapacity of the Turks who raided India in the eleventh and twelfth centuries and started ruling north India from the thirteenth century onwards. This is true as far as the wealthy monasteries such as Nalanda were concerned, because all aggressors, past and present, have the pillaging instinct in them; but it is far from the truth if it is implied that the Turks carried out genocidal massacres of the Buddhist populace at large. They did not, and did not need to, because the relatively few Buddhists who were left in India at the end of our period posed no particular threat to them.[66] Buddhism had been dying in India long before the advent of the Turks.

The resilience of the Jains

The Jains did not suffer the same fate as the Buddhists. Their numbers might not have been large, but they were able to preserve and maintain their religious identity. A number of reasons might explain their survival instinct. They were a highly literate trading community, with a finely developed sense of business enterprise, which was valued by monarchs who appreciated the commercial gains.[67] They maintained a strong theological discipline among themselves; and much of their asceticism and orthodoxy came to be admired by the Hindus. While keeping close to the Hindu doctrine of salvation, they rejected any notion of adopting theistic ideas of *Shaivism* and *Vaishnavism*, which helped them to preserve their distinctness. Laity and monks monitored each other closely.[68] While the Buddhist laity was losing its fervour, the Jain fold took upon itself the task of upholding the values and rituals of their religion. Unlike the Buddhist monk, the Jain did not spend most of his time in monastic establishments. The Jain monks were expected to mix with the general public and be truly wandering mendicants. By the eleventh and twelfth centuries the Jains had only a limited foothold in the Gangetic basin, but they were reasonably secure in Rajasthan, Gujarat and Karnataka. In Rajasthan and Gujarat they suffered persecution at the hands of the Turks, but nevertheless survived and continued to flourish in business and banking. In Gujarat particularly the twelfth century was a golden age for the community. A great Jain intellectual, Hemchandra, provided a powerful impetus to the growth and development of the Gujarati language through his numerous writings.[69] In Karnataka it was their involvement with the Arab mercantile trade that won the Jains favourable royal patronage. In the long run, however, their influence in Karnataka waned during our period owing to the rise of the *Lingayat* sect of the *Virashaivas*, led by a saint known as Basav. The *Lingayats* were extremely anti-Jain.[70] Occasionally, the Jains also came under severe persecution at the hands of the *Shaivites*. The Chola rulers in the deep south were *Shaivites*, but supported the Jains, probably because the latter were important benefactors of the merchant guilds, such as the Ayyavole 500, that were based in the *nagarams*.[71]

Literature and great temples

Three literary masterpieces

The evolution of Indian languages and literatures in the eleventh and twelfth centuries continued along the same routes marked out in the previous two or three centuries. Sanskrit was cherished as a language of perfection and purity by those with facility in it. For the masses, however, it remained a highly elitist language. Good literature could also be written in Prakrit and *Apabrahamasha*, according to the Jain polymath Hemchandra.[72] Regional languages such as Tamil and Kannada flourished, and Telugu and Gujarati evolved in this period. The great writers commanded royal patronage and found favour at various courts. They wrote poems, histories, dictionaries, grammars, plays and manuals of science and medicine. It is difficult to be excited by the intellectual rigour or the originality of these numerous and voluminous works; but there are three particular gems that stand head and shoulders above these works and have been esteemed by posterity. The first is the great Sanskrit lyrical poem *Gita Govinda*, written by Jayadeva, the court poet at the court of Lakshmansena, the Sena king of Bengal (1178–1205). This poem, combining words and music, has become one of the great sources of religious inspiration in both medieval and contemporary *Vaishnavism*, and millions of people in Bengal and Orissa have, over the last 800 years, sung the songs embedded in the poem in their homes and at the great *Vashnavite* fairs and festivals. Described as 'a dramatic, lyrical poem',[73] the *Gita Govinda* celebrates the passion of Krishna, the 'cosmic cowherd lover',[74] for Radha, the *gopi*, and it deals with the concept of love by exploring what might be called 'sacred profanities',[75] in the same way as the artwork of the temples of Khajurao may be said to fuse eroticism with religious experience.[76] It uses all the techniques of good poetry that were known in India: alliteration, lyricism, and grace of image for effect. In later centuries it inspired the Bengali saint Chaitanya and the artists of the *Kangra* and *Pahari* schools of painting.

The second great work of our period was the *Rajatarangini*, 'River of Kings', a historical account of Kashmir written, in Sanskrit, by Kalhana, a Kashmiri poet-courtier of the twelfth century (see Extract 11.2). Using diverse sources of evidence, such as royal eulogies, coins, land grant records and temple inscriptions, Kalhana wrote 7,826 verses in eight books. While the author does not strictly follow the modern historical method and quite often beautifies or idealises the past, the *Rajatarangini* does provide us with a credible history of Kashmir, particularly in its last five books.[77] The general depiction through the narrative is one of gradual decline, as the virtuous kings of the beginning give way to wicked kings whose courts are filled with corruption as part of the decline of the *Kali Yuga*. As a backcloth to its history, however, Kalhana does provide a sound ecological and environmental perspective of the Kashmir of his day.[78]

The third great and immortal work of this period is the famous account of India, *Kitab fi Tahqiqi ma li-l Hind*, written in Arabic by an Iranian scholar, scientist and traveller, Al-Biruni, who came to India with Mahmud of Ghazni in 1017 and who stayed on until 1030. Mahmud of Ghazni may have a bad reputation, but the Ghaznavids were not uncultured. Great poets and writers such as Masud Razi, Masud Sa'ad Salman and Data Ganj Baksh flourished under them, and Lahore was the centre of many cultural activities.[79] Al-Biruni was a true intellectual. During his thirteen years in India he mastered Sanskrit and went on to study all the religious, philosophical, scientific and mathematical literatures of India. He had a great respect for much of the Indian knowledge, particularly the mathematical and astronomical knowledge, although he had harsh words to say about some of the Indian intellectuals' lack of critical scrutiny (see Extract 11.3). He was also a keen observer of the Indian social scene, and wrote about the innumerable customs and traditions of the Hindus. Although he was a devout Muslim he did not disparage the Hindus; but he did point out some of their traits that he, arguably, considered to be inferior. He thought them arrogant and intellectually lazy.[80] He blamed both Hindus and Muslims for their inability to empathise with each other;[81] and, although he had been favoured by Mahmud of Ghazni to accompany him, he was bold enough to write that Mahmud's raids were nothing short of barbaric.[82] When one compares Al-Biruni's work with that of some nineteenth-century British commentators of India, such as James Mill, for example, one is struck by the detached and independent outlook of the Iranian scholar in contrast to the blatant racism that perverted the minds of so many nineteenth-century British and European historians and intellectuals.[83]

The glory of Indian temples

Notwithstanding the iconoclasm of Mahmud of Ghazni and other Turco-Afghans, the eleventh and twelfth centuries were a period of remarkable progress in temple building in different parts of India. We have already referred to the three Indian temple styles – northern, southern and Deccani – in Chapter 9. The temples were constructed under the supervision of the *sutradharas*, the architects, who designed religious precincts in strict accordance with the geometrical rules laid down in the ancient *Shilpashastras*.[84] The architecture of the northern-style temples reached its culmination and maturity at this time, and the finest examples from the eleventh and twelfth centuries can be seen at four site complexes. The largest concentration of such temples is to be found at Bhubhaneshwar, in Orissa, dating from the seventh to the thirteenth centuries. The most famous of these temples, from the eleventh century, is the Lingaraja, whose architecture is characterised by motifs of human, animal and vegetable life-forms and by lofty spires[85] (see Figure 11.1). Another great complex of northern temples has been left to posterity by the Chandella rulers of Bundel-khand at Khajuraho in Madhya Pradesh (see Figure 11.2). The largest, and sculpturally the most notable, of the nearly twenty temples in the area is the Khandariya Mahadeva, which enthrals the eye with its fine statuary and decoration.[86] Owing to their distance and remoteness, the Orissa and Khajuraho temples might have escaped despoliation by the Turks. This was not the case of the Rajasthan and Gujarat sites, where the Turks did cause much damage.[87] Nevertheless we still have some fine examples from both areas to enrich our senses. The most exquisite Rajasthani examples are the Dilwara Jain temples on Mount Abu, especially the Vimala Vasahi, which was built in the eleventh century by Vimala Shah, a wealthy Jain merchant, and dedicated to the first *Tirthankara*. With its forty-eight pillars in the main hall and a richly carved dome of eleven rings, the Vimala Vasahi is a remarkable showpiece of Jain religious philanthropy.[88] The carving in this temple is that of the Solanki style, named after the dynasty that ruled both Gujarat and Rajasthan in the eleventh and twelfth centuries. The best surviving example of the Solanki temples on

Figure 11.1 Temple styles of Bhubhaneshwar (Pat Baker: line drawing adapted from a photo in Rawson, op. cit., p. 112).

the Gujarat site is the *Surya* temple at Modhera, the beauty of which so moved an art historian that he called its creator 'a weaver of dreams'.[89] Rich and refined Solanki carving is one of the key features of this beautiful sandstone temple sited beside a stepped tank.

It was mentioned in Chapter 9 that the southern-style temples began with the Pallavas in the seventh and eighth centuries; however, they reached their apogee under the Cholas in the eleventh century and under the Pandyas in the thirteenth and fourteenth centuries. The two most iconic temples, within the period under review, are those at Thanjavur and Gangaikondacholapuram. The first, the Brihadiswara Temple, built by Rajaraja I, in the Chola capital of Thanjavur (Tanjore), is one of the grandest Hindu temples of India (see Figure 11.3). With its 62 metre high *vimana*, a dome carved from an 80 ton block of granite and, mounted on the tower, the innumerable carvings of dancers along with the sculptures of Shiva, Vishnu and Durga, and a gigantic *Nandi* bull guarding the entrance, this World Heritage Site temple is expressive of Chola religious piety at its best. Among the many buildings within the temple complex were housing blocks for nearly 400 *devadasis*, or temple dancers, who,

Figure 11.2 Temple scene from Khajuraho (by permission of RHPL).

along with the priests and the musicians, were an integral part of the Chola temple community.[90] Modelled on this temple was the second temple, built by Rajaraja's son, Rajendra I, to commemorate his expedition to the sacred River Ganga and its water that was brought all the way from Bengal. This too is an extremely large site, 100 metres long and 40 metres wide. Its *mandapa* (assembly hall) and the sanctuary inside the compound were raised on a high platform, while its *vimana* soars 55 metres into the sky. It too contains a fabulous array of sculptures.[91] The Chola artists specialised in both stone and metallic sculptures, and the most prominent figure portrayed was the god Shiva. The world-famous graceful bronze sculpture of *Shiva Nataraja*, from Tiruvalangadu, has been described by the French sculptor Rodin as 'the most perfect representation of rhythmic movement in art'.[92]

The chief feature of the Deccani-style temples, found mostly in Karnataka from the time of the early Chalukyas of Badami in the seventh and eighth centuries, was the enormous polygonal, star-shaped base on which the temple structure stood. This style continued to evolve under the later Chalukyas of Kalyani and the Hoysalas. The best examples of the Deccani style during the

Figure 11.3 Brihadisawara Temple at Thanjavur (Pat Baker: line drawing adapted from a photo in Rawson, op. cit., p. 110).

eleventh and twelfth centuries are to be found at Belur and Halebid. The temples, small but 'superbly conceived',[93] were built to supplicate the gods for victory in battles. The Hoysaleswara Temple in Halebid, begun in the twelfth century, took more than a hundred years to complete; but the richness of its frieze carvings, and particularly that of a line of 650 elephants, and of the various jewels and ornaments worn by gods and goddesses provide ample evidence of the skills of the builders and sculptors of the Deccan.[94]

SELECT EXTRACTS FOR REVIEW AND REFLECTION

Extract 11.1 The guild of Ayyavole 500

The Ayyavole 500 was one of the main south Indian guilds of merchants who were the controllers of the Chola overseas trade. They dealt in a variety of commodities sought by foreign merchants; and their influence throughout south India was wide ranging. Some of the guild's activities are described in the following passage:

> The chief source of information on Ayyavole ... is the corpus of inscriptions [which] are generally recorded on stone and also occasionally on copper plates ... and often located in or near temples and are intended as records of the taxes in cash and in kind levied for the benefit of the temple, from merchant groups and from townspeople, on commodities produced in the area, or on goods in transit. Occasionally they recorded public services in villages or urban areas which are initiated or maintained by merchants. And on a few occasions they record details of what appears to be an agreement between ruler and merchant, demarcating merchant townships, or in one case, a contractual agreement recording trading rights granted to a group of foreign traders, as well as to local trade groups.

As with most Indian inscriptions, the charter generally began with a eulogy to the ruler, known as the *parasasti*; its usefulness is explained thus:

> Both from the standardised phrases and from the newer interpretations one obtains indications of intricate factors such as the relationship of merchants with the state or ruler, or the position of the guild to other corporate bodies, or the religious affiliation of its members at a particular time and place.

Source: Meera Abraham, *Two Medieval Merchant Guilds of South India*, New Delhi: Manohar, 1988, pp. 3–4; also check pp. 156–81.

Extract 11.2 Kalhana as a historian

Although Kalhana cannot be considered as a historian in the modern sense, his *Rajatarangini* does provide evidence that he had a certain definite sense of what a good historian should or should not be. In his opinion, as the following passages show, a historian must have a vision; he must be impartial; he should present his version of the story from his own perspective; and he must be able to synthesise a number of previous accounts into a coherent whole.

> If the poet did not see in his mind's eye the existences which he is to reveal to all men, what other indication would there be of his possessing divine intuition?

> That noble-minded poet is alone worthy of praise whose word, like that of a judge, keeps free from love or hatred in relating the facts of the past.

If I narrate again the subject matter of tales which others have treated, still the virtuous ought not to turn their faces from me without hearing my reasons.

What is the skill required in order that men of a later time should supplement the narrative of events in the works of those who died after composing each the history of those kings whose contemporaries they were? Hence my endeavour is to give a connected account where the narrative of past events has become fragmentary in many respects.

Source: M.A. Stein, *Kalhana's Rajatarangini*, New Delhi: Motilal Banasi-dass, [1900] 1961, Book 1: 5, 7, 8, 10. Read also A.L. Basham, *Studies in Indian History and Culture*, Calcutta: Sambodhi, 1964, pp. 45–56.

Extract 11.3 Al-Biruni's assessment of the Indian intellectual scene

Among the many subjects pertaining to India that Al-Biruni writes about, his views on Indian mathematics and astronomy are quite critical. Although the Arabs had received many useful mathematical concepts from the Indians, Al-Biruni is not too impressed, but he also suggests some reasons for this state of affairs:

I can only compare their mathematical and astronomical literature ... to a mixture of pearl shells and sour dates, or of pearls and dung, or of costly crystals and common pebbles. Both kinds of things are equal in the eyes (of the Hindus), since they cannot raise themselves to the methods of a strictly scientific deduction.

He provides three interesting reasons for this dismal state of affairs. Firstly:

The Indian scribes are careless, and do not take pains to produce correct and well-collated copies. In consequence, the highest results of the author's mental development are lost by their negligence, and his book becomes already in the first or second copy so full of faults, that the text appears something entirely new, which neither a scholar nor one familiar with the subject, whether Hindu or Muslim, could any longer understand.

Secondly:

Mahmud [of Ghazni] utterly ruined the prosperity of the country ... the Hindus became like the atoms of dust scattered in all directions ... This is the reason, too, why Hindu sciences have retired far away from those parts of the country conquered by us, and have fled to places which our hand cannot yet reach, to Kashmir, Benares, and other places. And there the antagonism between them and all foreigners receives more and more nourishment both from political and religious sources.

Thirdly:

Folly is an illness for which there is no medicine, and the Hindus believe that there is no country but theirs, no nation like theirs, no king like theirs, no religion like theirs, no science like theirs.

Source: E. Sachau, *Alberuni's India*, Vol. 1, London: Trubner, pp. 18, 22, 25.

RELEVANT QUESTIONS FOR DISCUSSION

1   Why are the Cholas considered a great monarchy?
2   Is it time for modern Indians to lay aside the hatreds caused by the iconoclasm of Mahmud of Ghazni and some of his successors, and to move on?
3   Why is Buddhism reviving in India once again?

Notes

1 Frasch 2006: 2.
2 Satianathaier 1957: 252–5.
3 Champakalakshmi 1996a: 425–37.
4 Sastri 1977: 183–4.
5 Thapar 2002: 367–8; Majumdar 1977: 409–13.
6 Ali 2000: 206.
7 Champakalakshmi 1995: 271, 294–6; Wink 1991: 315.
8 Wink 1991: 315–19; Champakalakshmi 1995: 272ff.
9 Champakalakshmi 1995: 279–85, 288–90; Hall 2001.
10 Champakalakshmi 2001a.
11 Champakalakshmi 2001b.
12 Champakalakshmi 1995: 281–5.
13 Champakalakshmi 1996b.
14 Champakalakshmi 1996a: 425–37.
15 Champakalakshmi 2001a: 68–84.
16 Wink 1991: 56; Wink 1997: 18–23.
17 Wink 1991: 327–34.
18 Ibid.: 322–3; Champakalakshmi 1995: 289–90.
19 Majumdar 1977: 260–63, 354–64; Wink 1991: 231–54.

20 Wink 1991: 258–9; Majumdar 1977: 351–4.
21 Majumdar 1977: 288–304, 312–43.
22 Wink 1991: 259–60, 273.
23 Wink 1997: 67ff.
24 Ibid.: 112–35.
25 Ibid.: 125.
26 Ibid.: 131–5.
27 Ibid.: 135–49.
28 Ibid.: 137–41.
29 Ibid.: 142; Thapar 2002: 459.
30 D'Souza 2004: 26–30; Ikram 1964: 41–2.
31 Wink 1997: 172–5.
32 Stein 1998: 136–7.
33 Wink 1997: 87–110.
34 Daniélou 2003: 200.
35 Wink 1997: 8–23.
36 Ibid.: 3–4.
37 Daniélou 2003: 203–5; Stein 1998: 138.
38 Wink 1997: 294.
39 Thapar 2002: 430.
40 Ibid.: 431.
41 Wink 1997: 4.
42 Thapar 2002: 438–41.
43 Wink 1997: 328.
44 Stein 1998: 122–3; Thapar 2002: 356–7.
45 Jha 2004: 205.
46 Flood 1996: 174–97; Hinnells and Sharpe 1972: 52–4.
47 Flood 1996: 193–5.
48 Sen 1961: 70.
49 Thapar 2002: 483–4.
50 Ibid.: 462–3.
51 Jha 2004: 196–8.
52 Chattopadhyaya 1995: 330.
53 Gurukkal 1995: 245.
54 Champakalakshmi 1995: 279–85.
55 Ibid.: 285–8; Thapar 2002: 389–91.
56 'One half of the world must sweat and groan, that the other half may live!'
57 Joseph 2003: 19, 158–82.
58 Wink 1997: 335ff.
59 Ibid.: 343.
60 Omvedt 2003: 172–4.
61 Majumdar 1977: 429.
62 Wink 1997: 310–11; Omvedt 2003: 169–70.
63 Omvedt 2003: 169.
64 Ibid.: 165–7.
65 Wink 1997: 343.
66 Omvedt 2003: 174–81.
67 Thapar 2002: 461; Wink 1997: 273.
68 Wink 1997: 352.
69 Yashaschandra 2003: 567ff; Wink 1997: 354–5.
70 Jha 2004: 207–8.
71 Heitzman 2001: 128; Champakalakshmi 1995: 289–90; Champakalakshmi 2001b.
72 Pollock 2003: 567.

73 Miller 1977: 17.
74 Ibid.: 9.
75 Siegel 1978: 1–13.
76 Desai 1975: 188, 191–5.
77 Singh 2003: 113–22.
78 Thapar 2002: 415–16.
79 Ikram 1964: 33–6.
80 Ibid.: 26–8; Sachau 1888: Vol. 1, 18.
81 Dani 1973: 1–2, 5–6.
82 Sachau 1888: Vol. 1, 22.
83 For an enlightened discussion on this issue, see Sen 2005: 142–50.
84 Ray *et al.* 2000: 537–9; Thapar 2002: 476.
85 Tomory 1989: 92, 95.
86 Desai 1975: 135–7; Tomory 1989: 102–6.
87 Tomory 1989: 106–8.
88 Marett 1985: 70–71; Tomory 1989: 107, 206–7.
89 Cited in Nicholson 1993: 163.
90 Bradnock and Bradnock 1998: 812; Thapar 2002: 358, 391–2.
91 Bradnock and Bradnock 1998: 808.
92 Cited in Tomory 1989: 231.
93 Bradnock and Bradnock 1998: 972.
94 Evans 1997: 195–211; Thapar 2002: 403; Tomory 1989: 123, 216.

Afterword
India post-AD 1200

The resilience of Indian civilisation is legendary. Developed during the eight millennia of its evolution, the accumulated wisdom and complex character of this mature land helped India to absorb the best of foreign influences after patient revaluation, and ultimately to assimilate these within her own enriched persona.

Between 1200 and 1526 India was convulsed by the successive Turco-Afghan invasions; and yet, despite the unpredictability of their military stormings, it was an *Indo-Islamic* civilisation that was born from this uneasy gestation. This synthesis of the Hindu and Muslim cultures and traditions, matured by some generations of enlightened souls, resulted in the blossoming of Sikhism, the rejuvenation of the Sufi schools from Central Asia and the creation from the vigorous blend of Arabo-Persian and Hindi tongues of the widely spoken Urdu language – a powerful literary force. That this wonderful fusion of cultures is today the object of ruinous deconstructions by uninformed and myopic revisionists and pseudo-nationalists is something which is to be deplored – they go against the very spirit of civilisation, a concept which ancient India itself had so long striven to formulate.

Under the Moguls (1526–1707 – formally continuing until 1858) the culture of India reached new heights in literature, arts and aesthetics. The Mogul-era paintings, architecture, gardens and cuisine have been universally admired until today. Islamic kings did not, as a rule, mete out uniformly penal treatment to the Hindus. Some fanatical advisers did endeavour to set their masters against their toleration of non-Islamic cultural manifestations, but the Islamic rulers generally drew a sharp distinction between their personal faith and their public responsibility as monarchs of all India. Hindu culture and social values retained their energy and vitality even under the most anti-Hindu Islamic kings.

Under British rule (1757–1947) India's resources were drained away in order to augment the wealth of Britain. The Indian middle classes who had initially accepted and adapted several Western-imposed notions of civilisation quickly realised the naked truth behind that colonialism. English education, along with new political and legal ideas from the West, and faster communications and media outlets gave Indians the tools to resist colonialism. The resistance lasted for over a hundred years, but the iconic leadership of Gandhi prepared the stage for an independent, free India. The tragedy of the 1947 partition, however, caused a dark shadow over the future of the sub-continent.

Some six decades have elapsed since independence. There are no external enemies threatening the countries of the sub-continent, but there remains a corrosive sickness within the south Asian people. At the heart of their malaise lie their own mutual fear and irrational suspicions. Their resultant inability to dispel such nightmarish chimeras means, in turn, a continuing failure to alleviate the deep rooted poverty of the majority populations and to obtain acceptable standards of living. This still hampers the full development of the sub-continental countries and delays the fulfilment of their great destinies.

Glossary of Indic terms

The following list is only a selection of Indic terms most frequently used in the book. All others have been explained within the text.

Aryan	An Indo-European-speaking group of people who came to India soon after 2000 BC
atman	Soul
Bhagavan	God
Bodhisattava	An incarnation of Buddha before his birth, symbolising Compassion
brahman	A member of the highest caste (priests and teachers)
chakravartin	A strong, peaceful universal king
dana	Gift
dharma	Religious duty
Dravidian	A group of four southern languages of India: Tamil, Kannada, Telugu and Malayalam
ghats	The embankments of the River Ganga at Varanasi/Benares
Hindutva	The ideology of Hindu religious nationalism
jana	People
kshatriya	A member of the warrior/bureaucratic caste (second in ritual ranking)
maha	Great
mahajanapada	A great kingdom
Mahayana	The great vehicle; an important school of Buddhism
nadu	A local peasant community in south India
nagara	Town
nirvana	Release from the cycle of rebirth
Pali	The language in which the early Buddhist Canon was recorded
pandit	A learned man
pradesh	Province
Prakrit	A name given to many non-standard vernacular languages, as distinct from the highly literary and refined language of Sanskrit

prasasti	A royal eulogy
raga	Indian musical mode or scale
raja	King (*maharaja* = great king)
rasa	Essence, or flavour, as in drama or music
rajdhani	Capital city
sangam	A literary festival; an academy of learning in the south Indian literary context
sangha	An assembly; a Buddhist monastic community
Sanskrit	One of the oldest of the Indo-European languages; a language of refined culture in ancient India
Shaivite	A follower of the god Shiva
shastra	A text of learning
shudra	A member of the lowest caste (fourth in ritual ranking)
stupa	A Buddhist building housing the Buddha's relics
tirthankara	A founding teacher of the Jain faith
Vaishnavite	A follower of the god Vishnu
vaishya	A member of the trading caste (third in ritual ranking)
varna	Colour; used in the ritual ranking of castes
Veda	Truth, as expressed in the four *Vedas*
Vedanta	Final consummation of the *Veda*, as expressed in the philosophy of monism of Shankara
Yavana	A Greek or a Macedonian; or an outcaste foreigner

Glossary of selected ancient Indic place-names

Aryavarta	Indo-Gangetic plains of north India which the Aryans colonised
Barygaza	Port of Broach in Gujarat
Bharat	India – the supporters of the Hindutva movement strongly champion the term *Bharat* instead of India
Dakshinapatha	Lands south of the Vindhya mountains
Gandhara	The town in the northwest, known to the Persians and the Greeks, and famous for Gandhara sculptures
Indraprashtha	Delhi
Jambudvipa	The Indian sub-continent
Kalinga	Orissa
Kanauj	Kanyakubja in the Gangetic plain
Kashi	Benares/Varanasi
Madhyadesha	Western Gangetic basin
Magadha	Area covered by modern Bihar
Meru	A mythical mountain in the Himalayas
Muziris	Cochin
Pataliputra	Patna
Pracya	Eastern India
Praticya	Northwestern India
Prayag	Allahabad
Purushapura	Peshawar
Sakala	Sialkot
Sapta Sindhava	Punjab
Saraswati	Ancient river of the Indus basin, now dried up
Sindhu	River Indus
Sthanivishwara	Haryana State
Uttarapatha	Northern India

Classification of ancient Indian texts by subjects

The Four Vedas (Chapter 4)

1 *Rig-Veda*
2 *Sama-Veda*
3 *Yajur-Veda*
4 *Atharva-Veda*

Other Vedic and post-Vedic religious literature (Chapters 4 and 8)

5 *Brahmanas* (*Aitreya*, *Jaiminiya*, *Taittiriya*, *Satapatha*)
6 *Aranyakas*
7 *Upanishads*
8 *Vedangas*
9 *Upavedas*
10 *Bhagvad Gita* (part of the epic *Mahabharata*)
11 *Puranas*
12 *Vaishnava* and *Shaivite* hymns

Dharmashastras and Dharmasutras (religio-legal works) (Chapter 7)

13 *Manusmriti*
14 *Yajnavalkyasmriti*
15 *Naradsmriti*
16 *Parasarasmriti*
17 *Katyayanasmriti*

Epics (Chapter 5)

18 *Mahabharata*
19 *Ramayana*

Early Buddhist texts (Chapter 5)

20 *Tripitaka*
21 *Vinayapitaka*
22 *Nikayas*
23 *Dipavamsa*
24 *Milindapanha*
25 *Jatakas*

Mahayana Buddhist texts (Chapter 7)

26 *Mahavagga*
27 *Suttapitaka*
28 *Abbidhammapitaka*
29 *Upanga*
30 *Mahavastu*
31 *Vaipulyasutra*
32 *Suddharmapundarika*
33 *Prajnaparamita*
34 *Mahabhashya*

Jain texts (Chapter 5)

35 *Agam Texts*
36 *Chadasutra*
37 *Nandisutra*
38 *Anuyogadvara*
39 *Surya Prajnapti*
40 *Jambudwipa Prajnapti*
41 *Tamdulu Veyaliya*
42 *Prakirnakas*

Mathematical and astronomical texts (Chapters 4, 7, 8, 9, 10)

43 *Taittiriya Brahmana*
44 *Satapatha Brahmana*
45 *Jyotisha Vedanga*
46 *Sulbasutra*
47 *Romaka Siddhanta*
48 *Paulisa Siddhanta*
49 *Bakshali Manuscript*
50 *Aryabhatiya*
51 *Brahmasphutasiddhanta*
52 *Khandakhadyaka*
53 *Gwalior Inscription*

Grammars and lexicons (Chapters 5, 9)

Literature, arts and aesthetics (in Sanskrit) (Chapters 7, 8, 9, 10, 11)

Tamil literature (Chapters 7, 9)

Medical knowledge (Chapter 7)

History and biography (Chapters 7, 9, 11)

86   *Buddha-charita*
87   *Harsha-charita*
88   *Rajatarangini*

Political economy (Chapters 6, 9)

89   *Arthashastra*
90   *Haritasmriti*
91   *Nitisara*

Architecture

92   *Silpashastra* (Chapter 11)

Philosophy (Chapters 4, 10)

93   *Upanishads*
94   *Brahmasutra*
95   *Brahmasutra Bhashya*

Contemporary foreign accounts (Chapters 6, 9, 11)

96   *Indica*
97   *Si-Yu-Ki*
98   *Kitab fi Tahqiqi ma li-l Hind*

Select inscriptions (Chapters 6, 7, 8, 9, 11)

99   Major rock edicts of Ashoka
100   Minor rock edicts of Ashoka
101   Pillar Edicts of Ashoka
102   Hathigumpha Inscription of Kharavela
103   Junagadh Rock Inscription of Rudradaman
104   Allahabad Pillar Inscription of Samudragupta
105   Mandasor Inscription
106   Aihole Inscription of Pulakeshin II
107   Sasanam of Rajendra I

Bibliography

Abraham, M. (1988) *Two Medieval Merchant Guilds of South India*, New Delhi: Manohar.

Agrawal, D.P. and Sood, R.K. (1982) 'Ecological Factors and the Harappan Civilization', pp. 223–31, in G. Possehl (ed.), *Harappan Civilization: A Contemporary Perspective*, Warminster: Aris & Phillips.

Ali, D. (1999) 'The Hindu World', pp. 34–53, in N. Smart (ed.), *Atlas of the World's Religions*, Oxford: Oxford University Press.

Ali, D. (2000) 'Royal Eulogy as World History: Re-thinking Copper-Plate Inscriptions in Cola World', pp. 165–229, in R. Inden *et al.*, *Querying the Medieval: Texts and the History of Practices in South Asia*, Oxford: Oxford University Press.

Ali, D. (2006) 'Feudalism', pp. 70–74, in S. Wolpert (ed.), *Encyclopedia of India*, Vol. 2, New York: Thomson Gale.

Allchin, B. (1984) 'The Harappan Environment', pp. 445–54, in B.B. Lal and S.P. Gupta (eds), *Frontiers of the Indus Civilisation: Sir Mortimer Wheeler Commemoration Volume*, New Delhi: Indian Archaeological Society.

Allchin, B. and Allchin, R. (1982) *The Birth of Indian Civilization*, Cambridge: Cambridge University Press.

Allchin, F.R. (1961) 'Ideas of History in Indian Archaeological Writing: A Preliminary Study', pp. 241–59, in C.H. Philips (ed.), *Historians of India, Pakistan and Ceylon*, London: Oxford University Press.

Allchin, F.R. (1982) 'The Legacy of the Indus Civilization', pp. 325–33, in G. Possehl (ed.), *Harappan Civilization: A Contemporary Perspective*, Warminster: Aris & Phillips.

Allchin, F.R. (ed.) (1995) *The Archaeology of Early Historic South Asia: The Emergence of Cities and States*, Cambridge: Cambridge University Press.

Allen, C. (2002) *The Buddha and the Sahibs*, London: John Murray.

Altekar, A.S. (1955) 'The Rashtrakuta Empire', pp. 1–18, in R.C. Majumdar and A.D. Pusalker (eds), *The Age of Imperial Kanauj*, Bombay: Bharatiya Vidya Bhavan.

Ambedkar, B. (1989) *Writings and Speeches*, Vol. 5, Bombay: Education Department, Government of Maharashtra.

Associated Press (2006) 'Ancient Axe Casts Light on North–South Divide', *The Guardian*, 2 May, p. 20.

Auboyer, J. (2002) *Daily Life in Ancient India, from 200 BC to 700 AD*, London: Phoenix Press.

Bahn, P (ed.) (1996) *The Cambridge Illustrated History of Archaeology*, Cambridge: Cambridge University Press.

Bala, M. (2004) 'Kalibangan: Its Periods and Antiquities', pp. 34–43, in D.K. Chakrabarti (ed.), *Indus Civilization Sites in India: New Discoveries*, Mumbai: Marg.

Basham, A.L. (1954) *The Wonder that was India*, London: Sidgwick & Jackson.

Basham, A.L. (1964) *Studies in Indian History and Culture*, Calcutta: Sambodhi.

Basham, A.L. (ed.) (1975) *A Cultural History of India*, Oxford: Clarendon Press.

Basham, A.L. (1983) 'The Mandasor Inscription of the Silk-Weavers', pp. 101–3, in B. Smith (ed.), *Essays in Gupta Culture*, Delhi: Motilal Banarsidass.

Beal, S., trans. (1884) Si-Yu-Ki: Buddhist Records of the Western World, 2 vols, London: Trubner.

Begley, V. (1991) 'Ceramic Evidence for Pre-Periplus Trade on the Indian Coast', pp. 157–96, in V. Begley and R. de Puma (eds), *Rome and India*, Madison: University of Wisconsin Press.

Bhan, S. (2002) 'Aryanisation of the Indus Civilization', pp. 41–55, in K. Panikkar *et al.* (eds), *The Making of History: Essays Presented to Irfan Habib*, London: Anthem Press.

Bhandarkar, D.R. (1925) *Asoka*, Calcutta: University of Calcutta Press.

Bhardwaj, S.M. (1973) *Hindu Places of Pilgrimage in India*, Berkeley: University of California Press.

Blois, F. de (1990) *Burzoy's Voyage to India and the Origin of the Book of Kalilah wa Dimnah*, London: Royal Asiatic Society.

Borza, E. (ed.) (1974) *The Impact of Alexander the Great*, Hiusdale, IL: Dryden Press.

Bose, D.M. *et al.* (1989) *A Concise History of Science in India*, New Delhi: Indian National Science Academy.

Bosworth, A.B. (1995) *A Historical Commentary on Arrian's History of Alexander*, Vol. 2, Oxford: Oxford University Press.

Bosworth A.B. (1996) *Alexander and the East: The Tragedy of Triumph*, Oxford: Clarendon Press.

Boyce, M. (1984) *Zoroastrianism*, Manchester: Manchester University Press.

Boyce, M. (2002a) 'The Parthians: Defenders of the Land and Faith', pp. 99–115, in P. Godrej and F.P. Mistree (eds), *A Zoroastrian Tapestry: Art, Religion and Culture*, Ahmedabad: Mapin.

Boyce, M. (2002b) 'Zoroastrianism in Iran after the Arab Conquest', pp. 229–45, in P. Godrej and F.P. Mistree (eds), *A Zoroastrian Tapestry: Art, Religion and Culture*, Ahmedabad: Mapin.

Boyce, M. (2002c) 'The Teachings of Zoroaster', pp. 19–27, in P. Godrej and F.P. Mistree (eds), *A Zoroastrian Tapestry: Art, Religion and Culture*, Ahmedabad: Mapin.

Bradnock, R. and Bradnock, R. (1998) *India Handbook*, Bath: Footprint Handbooks.

Breckenridge, C. and Veer, P. (eds) (1993) *Orientalism and the Post-Colonial Predicament: Perspectives on South Asia*, Philadelphia: University of Pennsylvania Press.

Briant, P. (1996) *Alexander the Great: The Heroic Ideal*, London: Thames & Hudson.

Bright, W. (ed.) (1992) *International Encyclopaedia of Linguistics*, Vol. 2, Oxford: Oxford University Press.

Brockington, J. (1984) *Righteous Rama: The Evolution of an Epic*, Oxford: Oxford University Press.

Brockington, J. (1998) *The Sanskrit Epics*, Leiden: Brill.

Brown, T.S. (1973) *The Greek Historians*, Lexington, MA: D.C. Heath.

Cardona, G. (1976) *Panini: A Survey of Research*, The Hague: Mouton.

Casson, L. (1989) *The Periplus Maris Erythraei*, Princeton, NJ: Princeton University Press.

Casson, L. (1991) 'Ancient Naval Technology and the Route to India', pp. 8–11, in V. Begley and R. de Puma (eds), *Rome and India*, Madison: University of Wisconsin Press.

Chakrabarti, D.K. (1998) *The Archaeology of Ancient Indian Cities*, Delhi: Oxford University Press.

Chakrabarti, D.K. (1999) *India, An Archaeological History: Palaeolithic Beginnings to Early Historic Foundations*, New Delhi: Oxford University Press.

Chakrabarti, D.K. (ed.) (2004) *Indus Civilization Sites in India: New Discoveries*, Mumbai: Marg.

Chakravarti, R. (ed.) (2001) *Trade in Early India*, New Delhi: Oxford University Press.

Champakalakshmi, R. (1995) 'State and Economy: South India *c.* AD 400–1300', pp. 266–308, in R. Thapar (ed.), *Recent Perspectives of Early Indian History*, Bombay: Popular Prakashan.

Champakalakshmi, R. (1996a) *Trade, Ideology and Urbanisation – South India 300 BC to AD 1300*, Oxford: Oxford University Press.

Champakalakshmi, R. (1996b) 'From Devotion and Dissent to Dominance: The Bhakti of the Tamil Alwars and Nayanars', pp. 135–63, in R. Champakalakshmi and S. Gopal (eds), *Tradition, Dissent and Ideology*, Oxford: Oxford University Press.

Champakalakshmi, R. (2001a) 'Reappraisal of a Brahmanic Institution: The Brahmadeya and its Ramifications in Early Medieval South India', pp. 59–84, in K. Hall (ed.), *Structure and Society in Early South India: Essays in Honour of Noboru Karashima*, New Delhi: Oxford University Press.

Champakalakshmi, R. (2001b) 'The Medieval South Indian Guilds: Their Role in Trade and Urbanisation', pp. 326–43, in R. Chakravarti (ed.), *Trade in Early India*, New Delhi: Oxford University Press.

Champakalakshmi, R. and Gopal, S. (eds) (1996) *Tradition, Dissent and Ideology*, Oxford: Oxford University Press.

Chandra, A.N. (1980) *The Rig-Vedic Culture and the Indus Civilisation*, Calcutta: Ratna Prakashan.

Chattopadhyaya, B. (1994) *The Making of early Medieval India*, Oxford: Oxford University Press.

Chattopadhyaya, B. (1995) 'State and Economy in North India: Fourth Century to Twelfth Century', pp. 309–46, in R. Thapar (ed.), *Recent Perspectives of Early Indian History*, Bombay: Popular Prakashan.

Chattopadhyaya, S. (1974) *Achaemenids and India*, Delhi: Munshiram Manoharlal.

CHOI (1970) *Cultural Heritage of India*, Calcutta: Ramakrishna Mission Institute of Culture.

Claessen, H.J.M and Skalnik, P. (eds) (1978) *The Early State*, The Hague: Mouton.

Clear, E.H. (2000) 'Hindu Philosophy', pp. 353–4, in *Concise Routledge Encyclopedia of Philosophy*, London: Routledge.

Clive, J. and Pinney, T. (eds) (1972) *Thomas Babington Macaulay: Selected Writings*, Chicago: University of Chicago Press.

Cohen, R. (1978) 'State Origins: A Re-appraisal', pp. 31–75, in H.J.M. Claessen and P. Skalnik (eds), *The Early State*, The Hague: Mouton.

Colas, G. (2003) 'History of Vaisnava Traditions: An Esquisse', pp. 229–70, in G. Flood (ed.), *The Blackwell Companion to Hinduism*, Oxford: Blackwell.

Collins, R. (1991) *Early Medieval Europe 300–1000*, London: Macmillan.

Coningham, R. (2005) 'South Asia: From Early Villages to Buddhism', pp. 518–51, in C. Scarre (ed.), *The Human Past: World Prehistory and the Development of Human Societies*, London: Thames & Hudson.

Conze, E. (1993) *A Short History of Buddhism*, Oxford: Oneworld.

Cook, J.M. (1983) *The Persian Empire*, London: J.M. Dent.

Cousins, L.S. (1997) 'Buddhism', pp. 369–444, in J.R. Hinnells (ed.), *A Handbook of Living Religions*, London: Blackwell.

Cowell, E.B. and Thomas, F.W. (n.d.) The Harsa-Charita of Bana, Delhi: Motilal Banarsidass.

Craven, R. (1997) *Indian Art*, London: Thames & Hudson.

Crystal, D. (1997) *The Cambridge Encyclopaedia of Language*, Cambridge: Cambridge University Press.

Cunningham, A. ([1872/3] 1979) ' Harappa', pp. 102–4, in G. Possehl (ed.), *Ancient Cities of the Indus*, New Delhi: Vikas.

Daheja, V. (1997) *Indian Art*, London: Phaidon.

Dale, S.F. (1980) *Islamic Society on the South Asian Frontier: The Mapillas of Malabar*, Oxford: Clarendon Press.

Dales, G.F. ([1964] 1979) 'The Mythical Massacre of Mohenjo Daro', pp. 293–6, in G. Possehl (ed.), *Ancient Cities of the Indus*, New Delhi: Vikas.

Dales, G.F. ([1966] 1979) 'The Decline of the Harappans', pp. 307–12, in G. Possehl (ed.), *Ancient Cities of the Indus*, New Delhi: Vikas.

Dales, G.F. ([1968] 1979) 'Of Dice and Men', pp. 138–44, in G. Possehl (ed.), *Ancient Cities of the Indus*, New Delhi: Vikas.

Dange, S.S. (2002) 'Zoroastrianism and Hinduism: The RigVeda and the Avesta', pp. 185–91, in P. Godrej and F.P. Mistree (eds), *A Zoroastrian Tapestry: Art, Religion and Culture*, Ahmedabad: Mapin.

Dani, A.H. (1973) *Alberuni's Indica: A Record of the Cultural History of South Asia about AD 1030*. Islamabad: University of Islamabad Press.

Dani, A.H. (1986) *The Historic City of Taxila*, Paris: UNESCO.

Daniélou, A. (2003) *A Brief History of India*, trans. K. Hurry, Vermont: Inner Traditions.

Das Gupta, R.K. (1961) 'Macaulay's Writings on India', pp. 230–40, in C.H. Philips (ed.), *Historians of India, Pakistan and Ceylon*, London: Oxford University Press.

Date, G.T. (1929) *The Art of War in Ancient India*, Oxford: Oxford University Press.

Desai, D. (1975) *Erotic Sculpture of India: A Socio-Cultural Study*, New Delhi: Tata McGraw-Hill.

Devahuti, D. (1970) Harsha: A Political Study, Oxford: Oxford University Press.

Devasthali, G.V. (1955) 'Language and Literature: Sanskrit', pp. 177–206, in R.C. Majumdar and A.D. Pusalker (eds), *The Age of Imperial Kanauj*, Bombay: Bharatiya Vidya Bhavan.

Dhammika, S. (n.d.) 'The Edicts of King Ashoka', www.birminghambuddhistvihara. org/Asoka's%20Dhamma.html.

Dhar, S. (1957) Chanakya and Arthasastra, Bangalore: Indian Institute of World Culture.

Diamond, J. (1998) *Guns, Germs and Steel: A Short History of Everybody for the Last 13,000 Years*, London: Vintage.

Dikshitar, V.R. (1993) *The Gupta Polity*, Delhi: Motilal Banarsidass.

Dimock, E.C. *et al.* (eds) (1974) *The Literatures of India: An Introduction*, Chicago: University of Chicago Press.

Dolcini, D. and Freschi, F. (eds) (1999) *Tessitori and Rajasthan: Proceedings of the International Conference at Bikaner, 1996*, Udine: Societa Indologica.

Doniger, W. and Kakar, S. (2002) *Kamasutra*, Oxford: Oxford University Press.

Drekmeier, C. (1962) *Kingship and Community in Early India*, Stanford, CA: Stanford University Press.

D'Souza, E. (2004) *Medieval India*, Mumbai: Manan Prakashan.

Dunbar, G. (1943) *A History of India from the Earliest Times to the Present Day*, London: Nicholson & Watson.

Edgerton, F. (1965) *The Panchatantra*, London: Allen & Unwin.

Elst, K. (2005/2006) 'The Merits of Lord Macaulay', http://koenraadelst.bharatvani. org/articles/hinduism/macaulay.html.

Embree, A. (ed.) (1992) *Sources of Indian Tradition*, London: Penguin.

Erdosy, G. (ed.) (1995a) *The Indo-Aryans of Ancient South Asia: Language, Material Culture and Ethnicity*, Berlin: Walter de Gruyter.

Erdosy, G. (1995b) 'City States of North India and Pakistan at the Time of the Buddha', pp. 99–122, in F.R. Allchin (ed.), *The Archaeology of Early Historic South Asia: The Emergence of Cities and States*, Cambridge: Cambridge University Press.

Evans, K. (1997) *Epic Narratives in the Hoysala Temples*, Leiden: Brill.

Fagan, B. (1999) *World Prehistory: A Brief Introduction*, New York: Longman.

Fairservis, W., Jr. (1971) *The Roots of Ancient India: The Archaeology of Early Indian Civilization*, London: Allen & Unwin.

Fischer, S.R. (2005) *A History of Writing*, London: Reaktion Books.

Flood, G. (1996) *An Introduction to Hinduism*, Cambridge: Cambridge University Press.

Flood, G. (ed.) (2003) *The Blackwell Companion to Hinduism*, Oxford: Blackwell.

Fort, A.O. (2000) 'Sankara', p. 792, in *Concise Routledge Encyclopedia of Philosophy*, London: Routledge.

Francfort, H.P. (1984) ' The Harappan Settlement of Shortughai', pp. 301–10, in B.B. Lal and S.P. Gupta (eds), *Frontiers of the Indus Civilisation: Sir Mortimer Wheeler Commemoration Volume*, New Delhi: Indian Archaeological Society.

Frasch, T (2006) 'Engineering Expansion: Technological Progress in the Early States of South and Southeast Asia', unpublished paper based on a research project on 'Irrigation, Labour and the State in Early India' at Manchester Metropolitan University, 2003–4.

Frawley, D. and Rajaram, N.S. (1995) *Vedic Aryans and the Origins of Civilization: A Literary and Scientific Perspective*, Quebec: World Heritage Press.

Frye, R.N. (1996) *The Heritage of Central Asia: From Antiquity to the Turkish Expansion*, Princeton, NJ: Marcus Weiner.

Fryer, P. (1984) *Staying Power: The History of Black People in Britain*, London: Pluto Press.

Gadd, C.J. and Smith, S. ([1924] 1979) 'The New Links between the Indian and Babylonian Civilizations', pp. 109–10, in G. Possehl (ed.), *Ancient Cities of the Indus*, New Delhi: Vikas.

Gafurov, B. *et al.* (eds) (1970) *Kushan Studies in the USSR*, Calcutta: Indian Studies Past and Present.

Gajjar, I.N. (1971) *Ancient Indian Art and the West: A Study of Parallels, Continuity and Symbolism from Proto-Historic to Early Buddhist Times*, Bombay: D.B. Taraporevala.

Gamkrelidze, T.V. and Ivanov. V.V. (1990) 'The Early History of Indo-European Languages', pp. 82–90, in *Scientific American*, March.

Gandhi, M.K. (1940) *An Autobiography, or The Story of my Experiments with Truth*, Ahmedabad: Navajivan.

Ganeri, J. (2001) *Philosophy in Classical India: The Proper Work of Reason*, London: Routledge.

Ghosh, A. (1982) 'Deurbanization of the Harappan Civilization', pp. 321–4, in G. Possehl (ed.), *Harappan Civilization: A Contemporary Perspective*, Warminster: Aris & Phillips.

Ghoshal, U.N. (1955) 'Political Theory, Administrative Organisation, Law and Legal Institutions', pp. 231–55, in R.C. Majumdar and A.D. Pusalker (eds), *The Age of Imperial Kanauj*, Bombay: Bharatiya Vidya Bhavan.

Godrej, P. and Mistree, F.P. (eds) (2002) *A Zoroastrian Tapestry: Art, Religion and Culture*, Ahmedabad: Mapin.

Goitein, S.D. (1973) *Letters of Medieval Jewish Traders*, Princeton, NJ: Princeton University Press.

Goodall, D. (1996) *Hindu Scriptures*, London: Phoenix.

Griffith, R.T.H. (1920) *The Hymns of the RigVeda*, 2 vols, Benares: E.J. Lazarus.

Gupta, B. (1995) 'Shankara', pp. 214–19, in I.P. McGreal (ed.), *Great Thinkers of the Eastern World*, New York: HarperCollins.

Gurukkal, R. (1995) 'The Beginnings of the Historic Period: The Tamil South', pp. 237–65, in R. Thapar (ed.), *Recent Perspectives of Early Indian History*, Bombay: Popular Prakashan.

Hall, K. (2001) 'Merchants, Rulers and Priests in an Early South Indian Sacred Centre: Cidambaram in the Age of the Colas', pp. 85–116, in K. Hall (ed.), *Structure and Society in Early South India: Essays in Honour of Noboru Karashima*, New Delhi: Oxford University Press.

Havell, E.B. (1920) *A Handbook of Indian Art*, London: John Murray.

Hayes, R.P. (2000) 'Indian and Tibetan Philosophy', pp. 387–91, in *Concise Routledge Encyclopedia of Philosophy*, London: Routledge.

Heard, G. (1952) 'Vedanta and Western History', pp. 1–11, in C. Isherwood (ed.), *Vedanta for Modern Man*, London: Allen & Unwin.

Heitzman, J. (2001) 'Urbanisation and Political Economy in Early South India: Kancipuram during the Cola Period', pp. 117–56, in K. Hall (ed.), *Structure and Society in Early South India: Essays in Honour of Noboru Karashima*, New Delhi: Oxford University Press.

Herodotus (1972) *The Histories*, London: Penguin.

Heskel, D.L. (1984) 'Iran–Indus Valley Connections: A Revaluation', pp. 333–46, in B.B. Lal and S.P. Gupta (eds), *Frontiers of the Indus Civilisation: Sir Mortimer Wheeler Commemoration Volume*, New Delhi: Indian Archaeological Society.

Hinnells, J.R. (1985) *Persian Mythology*, London: Newnes.

Hinnells, J.R. (ed.) (1997) *A Handbook of Living Religions*, London: Blackwell.

Hinnells, J.R. and Sharpe, E. (1972) *Hinduism*, London: Oriel Press.

Ikram, S. (1964) *Muslim Civilization in India*, New York: Columbia University Press.

Inden, R. *et al.* (2000) *Querying the Medieval: Texts and the History of Practices in South Asia*, Oxford: Oxford University Press.

Isherwood, C. (ed.) (1952) *Vedanta for Modern Man*, London: Allen & Unwin.

Isherwood, C. (1965) *Ramakrishna and his Disciples*, London: Methuen.

Iyengar, K.R.S. (1955) 'Dravidian Languages and Literature', pp. 219–30, in R.C. Majumdar and A.D. Pusalker (ed.), *The Age of Imperial Kanauj*, Bombay: Bharatiya Vidya Bhavan.

Jaggi, O.P. (1969) *History of Science and Technology in India*, Vol. 1: *Dawn of Indian Technology: Pre- and Proto-Historic Period*, Delhi: Atma Ram.

Jain, H.L. (1955) 'Apabrahmasha Language and Literature', pp. 212–19, in R.C. Majumdar and A.D. Pusalker (eds), *The Age of Imperial Kanauj*, Bombay: Bharatiya Vidya Bhavan.

Jain, S. (2004) 'Telling the True Story of History: Genetic Tests against the Fictional Aryan Race', 9 June, www.geocities.com/dipalsarvesh/genes.html.

Jaiswal, S. (1967) *The Origin and Development of Vaisnavism*, New Delhi: Munshiram Manoharlal.

Jamison, S. (1996) *Sacrificed Wife, Sacrificer's Wife: Women, Ritual and Hospitality in Ancient India*, Oxford: Oxford University Press.

Jamkhedkar, A. (2002) 'Parsi and Hindu Sacraments', pp. 193–7, in P. Godrej and F.P. Mistree (eds) *A Zoroastrian Tapestry: Art, Religion and Culture*, Ahmedabad: Mapin.

Jarrige, J.F. (1982) 'Excavations at Mehrgarh: Their Significance for Understanding the Background of the Harappan Civilization', pp. 79–84, in G. Possehl (ed.), *Harappan Civilization: A Contemporary Perspective*, Warminster: Aris & Phillips.

Jarrige, J.F and Meadow, R.H. (1980) 'The Antecedents of Civilization in the Indus Valley', pp. 102–10, in *Scientific American*, Vol. 243.

Jash, P. (1974) *History of Saivism*, Calcutta: Roy & Chaudhury.

Jha, D.N. (2004) *Early India: A Concise History*, New Delhi: Manohar.

Johnson, G. (1996) *Cultural Atlas of India*, New York: Facts on File.

Jong, A. de (2002) 'Zoroastrianism and the Greeks', pp. 65–81, in P. Godrej and F. P. Mistree (eds), *A Zoroastrian Tapestry: Art, Religion and Culture*, Ahmedabad: Mapin.

Joseph, G.G. (1996) *Geometry of Vedic Altars*, www.leonet.it/culture/nexus/96/joseph. html.

Joseph, G.G. (2000) *The Crest of the Peacock: Non-European Roots of Mathematics*, London: Penguin.

Joseph, G.G. (2002) 'Infinite Series in Kerala: Background and Motivation', in Kerala Sastra Sahitya Parishad, *Proceedings of the International Seminar and Colloquium on 1500 years of Aryabhateeyam, 2002*, Kochi.

Joseph, G.G. (2003) *George Joseph: The Life and Times of a Kerala Christian Nationalist*, Hyderabad: Orient Longman.

Jyotsna, M. (2000) *Distinctive Beads in Ancient India*, Oxford: Archaeopress.

Kachroo, V. (2000) *Ancient India*, New Delhi: Har-Anand.

Kak, S. (n.d.) 'Edmund Leach on Racism and Indology', www.omilosmeleton.gr/ english/skak.html.

Katre, S.M. (1987) *Astadhyayi of Panini*, Austin: University of Texas Press.

Keay, J. (2000) *India: A History*, London: HarperCollins.

Keay, J. (2001) *India Discovered: The Recovery of a Lost Civilization*, London: HarperCollins.

Keer, D. (1971) *Ambedkar: Life and Mission*, Bombay: Popular Prakashan.

Keith, A.B. (1928) A History of Sanskrit Literature, Oxford: Oxford University Press.

Kenoyer, J.M. (1998) *Ancient Cities of the Indus Valley Civilization*, Oxford: Oxford University Press.

Kerala Sastra Sahitya Parishad (2002) *Proceedings of the International Seminar and Colloquium on 1500 years of Aryabhateeyam, 2002*, Kochi.

Khan, F.A. (1964) *The Indus Valley and Early Iran*, Karachi: Pakistan Ministry of Education.

Khazanov, A.M. (1984) *Nomads and the Outside World*, Cambridge: Cambridge University Press.

Khazanov, A.M. and Wink, A. (eds) (2001) *Nomads in the Sedentary World*, London: Curzon Press.

Klein, R.G. (2005) 'Hominin Dispersals in the Old World', pp. 84–123, in C. Scarre (ed.), *The Human Past: World Prehistory and the Development of Human Societies*, London: Thames & Hudson.

Klostermaier, K. (1984) *Mythologies and Philosophies of Salvation in the Theistic Traditions of India*, Waterloo, Ontario: Wilfrid Laurier University Press.

Klostermaier, K. (1994) *A Survey of Hinduism*, Albany: State University of New York Press.

Knox, R. (1992) *Amaravati: Buddhist Sculpture from the Great Stupa*, London: British Museum Press.

Kochhar, R. (2000) *The Vedic People: Their History and Geography*, Hyderabad: Orient Longman.

Kondo, S. (2002) 'Feudal Social Formation in Indian History', pp. 56–77, in K.N. Panikkar *et al.* (eds), *The Making of History: Essays Presented to Irfan Habib*, London: Anthem Press.

Kosambi, D.D. (1965) *The Culture and Civilisation of Ancient India in Historical Outline*, 2nd edn, London: Routledge & Kegan Paul.

Kosambi, D.D. (1975) *An Introduction to the Study of Indian History*, Bombay: Popular Prakashan.

Kotwal, F. and Mistree, K. (2002) 'Protecting the Physical World', pp. 337–65, in P. Godrej and F.P. Mistree (eds), *A Zoroastrian Tapestry: Art, Religion and Culture*, Ahmedabad: Mapin.

Kramrisch, S. (1959) 'Traditions of the Indian Craftsman', pp. 18–24, in M. Singer (ed.), *Traditional India: Structure and Change*, Philadelphia: American Folklore Society.

Kulke, H. and Rothermund, D. (1990) *A History of India*, London: Routledge & Kegan Paul.

Kumar, B. (1973) *The Early Kusanas*, New Delhi: Sterling.

Lal, B.B. and Gupta, S.P. (eds) (1984) *Frontiers of the Indus Civilisation: Sir Mortimer Wheeler Commemoration Volume*, New Delhi: Indian Archaeological Society.

Lal, D. (1988) *Hindu Equilibrium: Cultural Stability and Economic Stagnation*, Vol. 1, Oxford: Oxford University Press.

Lamb, H. (1959) 'The Indian Merchant', pp. 25–34, in M. Singer (ed.), *Traditional India: Structure and Change*, Philadelphia: American Folklore Society.

Lamberg-Karlovsky, C.C. ([1972] 1979) 'Trade Mechanisms in Indus–Mesopotamian Interrelations', pp. 130–37, in G. Possehl (ed.), *Ancient Cities of the Indus*, New Delhi: Vikas.

Leshnik, L. ([1968] 1979) 'The Harappan "Port" at Lothal: Another View', pp. 203–11, in G. Possehl (ed.), *Ancient Cities of the Indus*, New Delhi: Vikas.

Liu, X. (1994) *Ancient India and Ancient China: Trade and Religious Exchanges, AD 1–600*, Oxford: Oxford University Press.

Ludden, D. (1985) *Peasant History in South India*, Princeton, NJ: Princeton University Press.

Ludden, D. (2002) *India and South Asia*, Oxford: Oneworld.

McCrindle, J.W. ([1896] 1969) *The Invasion of India by Alexander the Great, as described by Arrian, Q. Curtius, Diodoros, Plutarch and Justin*, New York: Barnes & Noble.

McCrindle, J.W. ([1901] 1971) *Ancient India as described in Classical Literature*, Amsterdam: Philo Press.

McGreal, I.P. (ed.) (1995) *Great Thinkers of the Eastern World*, New York: HarperCollins.

Mackay, E. (1948) *Early Indus Civilization*, London: Luzac.

McMahon, B. (2006) 'Long in the Tooth: Skeletons Reveal Secrets of 9000 year old Dentistry', p. 17, in *The Guardian*, 18 April.

McNeill, W. (1967) *A World History*, Oxford: Oxford University Press.

Mahadevan, T.M.P (1952) 'Western Vedanta', pp. 15–19, in C. Isherwood (ed.), *Vedanta for Modern Man*, London: Allen & Unwin.

Mahalingam, T.V. (1969) *Kanchipuram in Early South Indian History*, London: Asia Publishing House.

Mainkar, V.B. (1984) 'Metrology in the Indus Civilization', pp. 141–51, in B.B. Lal and S. P. Gupta (eds), *Frontiers of the Indus Civilisation: Sir Mortimer Wheeler Commemoration Volume*, New Delhi: Indian Archaeological Society.

Maity, S.K. (1957) *Economic Life of North India in the Gupta Period*, Calcutta: World Press.

Majumdar, R.C. (1961a) 'Ideas of History in Sanskrit Literature', pp. 13–28, in C.H. Philips (ed.), *Historians of India, Pakistan and Ceylon*, London: Oxford University Press.

Majumdar, R.C. (1961b) 'Nationalist Historians', pp. 416–28, in C.H. Philips (ed.), *Historians of India, Pakistan and Ceylon*, London: Oxford University Press.

Majumdar, R.C. (1977) *Ancient India*, Delhi: Motilal Banarsidass.

Majumdar, R.C. and Pusalker, A.D. (eds) (1954) *The Classical Age*, Bombay: Bharatiya Vidya Bhavan.

Majumdar , R.C. and Pusalker, A.D. (eds) (1955) *The Age of Imperial Kanauj*, Bombay: Bharatiya Vidya Bhavan.

Majumdar, R.C. and Pusalker, A.D. (eds) (1957) *The Struggle for Empire*, Bombay: Bharatiya Vidya Bhavan.

Makdisi, G. (1981) *The Rise of Colleges: Institutions of Learning in Islam and the West*, Edinburgh: Edinburgh University Press.

Mallory, J.P. (1989) *In Search of the Indo-Europeans*, London: Thames & Hudson.

Marett, P. (1985) *Jainism Explained*, London: Jain Samaj.

Marr, J.R. (1975) 'The Early Dravidians', pp. 30–37, in A.L. Basham (ed.), *A Cultural History of India*, Oxford: Clarendon Press.

Marshall, J. ([1923/4] 1979) 'Harappa and Mohenjo Daro', pp. 181–6, in G. Possehl (ed.), *Ancient Cities of the Indus*, New Delhi: Vikas.

Marshall, J. ([1924] 1979) 'First Light on a Long-Forgotten Civilization', pp. 105–7, in G. Possehl (ed.), *Ancient Cities of the Indus*, New Delhi: Vikas.

Marshall, J. (ed.) (1931), *Mohenjo Daro and the Indus Civilization*, Vol. 1, London: Arthur Probsthain.

Melling, D. (1993) 'Indian Philosophy before the Greeks', Nehru Lecture, delivered at Manchester Metropolitan University, 3 December.

Menon, A.S. (1990) *Kerala History and its Makers*, Madras: S. Viswanathan.

Miller, B.S. (1977) *Love Song of the Dark Lord: Jayadeva's Gita Govinda*, New York: Columbia University Press.

Miller, J.I. (1969) *Spice Trade of the Roman Empire*, Oxford: Oxford University Press.

Mishra, M. (2004) *The Aryans and Vedic Culture*, Delhi: Shipra.

Mistree, K. (2002) 'Parsi Arrivals and Early Settlements in India', pp. 411–33, in P. Godrej and F.P. Mistree (eds), *A Zoroastrian Tapestry: Art, Religion and Culture*, Ahmedabad: Mapin.

Mookerji, R. (1928) *Asoka*, London: Macmillan.

Mukerjee, R. (1958) *A History of Indian Civilisation*, Vol. 1, Bombay: Hind Kitabs.

Mukherji, R. (1989) *Hindu Civilisation*, Bombay: Bharatiya Vidya Bhavan.

Mukhia, H. (1981) 'Was There Feudalism in Indian History?', pp. 273–310, in *Journal of Peasant Studies*, Vol. 8, No. 3, April.

Mukhia, H. (1985) 'Peasant Production and Medieval Indian Society', pp. 228–51, in *Journal of Peasant Studies*, Vol. 12, Nos. 2–3, Jan–April.

Nagaraj, D.R. (2003) 'Critical Tensions in the History of Kannada Literary Culture', pp. 323–9, in S. Pollock (ed.), Literary Cultures in History: Reconstructions from South Asia, Berkeley: University of California Press.

Nagaraja Rao, M.S. (ed.) (1981) *Madhu: Recent Researches in Indian Archaeology and Art History*, Delhi: Agam Kala Prakashan.

Narain, A.K. (1957) *The Indo-Greeks*, Oxford: Oxford University Press.

Narain, A.K. (1974) 'Alexander and India', in E. Borza (ed.), *The Impact of Alexander the Great*, Hiusdale, IL: Dryden Press.

Narain, A.K. (1990) 'Indo-Europeans in Inner Asia', pp. 151–76, in D. Sinor (ed.), *The Cambridge History of Early Inner Asia*, Cambridge: Cambridge University Press.

Narasimhiah, B (1981) 'Pre-Neolithic and Neolithic Cultures in Tamil Nadu', pp. 19–22, in M.S. Nagaraja Rao (ed.), *Madhu: Recent Researches in Indian Archaeology and Art History*, Delhi: Agam Kala Prakashan.

Nicholas, R.W. (2003) *Indian History: Ancient and Medieval*, New Delhi: Encyclopaedia Britannica.

Nicholson, L. (1993) *India Companion*, London: Vermilion.

ODNB (2004) *Oxford Dictionary of National Biography*, Vols. 45 and 59, Oxford: Oxford University Press.

Omvedt, G. (2003) *Buddhism in India: Challenging Brahmanism and Caste*, New Delhi: Sage.

Oppenheim, A.L. ([1954] 1979) 'The Seafaring Merchants of Ur', pp. 155–63, in G. Possehl (ed.), *Ancient Cities of the Indus*, New Delhi: Vikas.

Orton, N.P. (1991) 'Red Polished Ware in Gujarat: A Catalogue of Twelve Sites', pp. 46–81, in V. Begley and R. de Puma (eds), *Rome and India*, Madison: University of Wisconsin Press.

Pande, B.M. (1982) 'History of Research on the Harappan Culture', pp. 395–403, in G. Possehl (ed.), *Harappan Civilization: A Contemporary Perspective*, Warminster: Aris & Phillips.

Pandit, L. (1996) 'Dhvani and the "Full Word": Suggestion and Signification from Abhinavagupta to Jacques Lacan', *College Literature* [West Chester University, Pennsylvania], February 1996, www.findarticles.com/p/articles/mi_qa3709/is_199602/ai_n8752166.

Panikkar, K.N. *et al.* (eds) (2002) *The Making of History: Essays Presented to Irfan Habib*, London: Anthem Press.

Parpola, A. (2006) 'Vedic Aryan India', pp. 211–15, in S. Wolpert (ed.), *Encyclopedia of India*, Vol. 4, New York: Thomson Gale.

Pathak, V.S. (1997) *Ancient Historians of India*, Gorakhpur: Purva Samsthana.

Patil, P. (2004) *Myths and Traditions in India: A Fusion of the Past and the Present*, New Delhi: BPI India.

Pereira, J. (1995) 'Badarayana', pp. 170–74, in I.P. McGreal (ed.), *Great Thinkers of the Eastern World*, New York: HarperCollins.

Pettitt, P. (2005) 'The Rise of Modern Humans', pp. 124–73, in C. Scarre (ed.), *The Human Past: World Prehistory and the Development of Human Societies*, London: Thames & Hudson.

Philips, C.H. (1961) 'James Mill, Mountstuart Elphinstone, and the History of India', pp. 217–29, in C.H. Philips (ed.), *Historians of India, Pakistan and Ceylon*, London: Oxford University Press.

Phillips, S.H. (2000) 'Vedanta', pp. 913–14, in *Concise Routledge Encyclopedia of Philosophy*, London: Routledge.

Pollock, S. (ed.) (2003) Literary Cultures in History: Reconstructions from South Asia, Berkeley: University of California Press.

Ponting, C. (1991) *A Green History of the World*, London: Penguin.

Possehl, G. ([1976] 1979) 'Lothal: A Gateway Settlement of the Harappan Civilization', pp. 212–18, in G. Possehl (ed.), *Ancient Cities of the Indus*, New Delhi: Vikas.

Possehl, G. (ed.) (1982) *Harappan Civilization: A Contemporary Perspective*, Warminster: Aris & Phillips.

Possehl, G. (1999) *The Indus Age: The Beginnings*, Philadelphia: University of Pennsylvania Press.

Previte-Orton, C. (1971) *The Shorter Cambridge Medieval History*, Vol. 1, Cambridge: Cambridge University Press.

Prinja, N. (ed.) (1996) *Explaining Hindu Dharma: A Guide for Teachers*, Norwich: Religious and Moral Education Press.

Puri, B. (1963) *India in Classical Greek Writings*, Ahmedabad: New Order.

Raikes, R.L. ([1964] 1979) 'The End of the Ancient Cities of the Indus', pp. 297–306, in G. Possehl (ed.), *Ancient Cities of the Indus*, New Delhi: Vikas.

Ramesh, R. (2006) 'A Tale of Two Indias', pp. 10–13, in *The Guardian G2*, 5 April.

Rao, S.R. ([1968] 1979) 'Contacts between Lothal and Susa', pp. 174–5, in G. Possehl (ed.), *Ancient Cities of the Indus*, New Delhi: Vikas.

Rapson, E.J. (ed.) (1922) *Cambridge History of India*, Vol. 1, Cambridge: Cambridge University Press.

Ratnagar, S. (1995) 'Archaeological Perspectives on early Indian Societies', pp. 1–52, in R. Thapar (ed.), *Recent Perspectives of Early Indian History*, Bombay: Popular Prakashan.

Rawlinson, H.G. (1965) *India: A Short Cultural History*, London: Cresset Press.

Rawson P. (1977) *Indian Asia*, London: Elsevier-Phaidon.

Ray, H. (1986) *Monastery and Guild: Commerce under the Satavahanas*, Oxford: Oxford University Press.

Ray, N. *et al.* (eds) (2000) *A Sourcebook of Indian Civilisation*, Hyderabad: Orient Longman.

Raychaudhuri, H. (1996) *Political History of Ancient India*, Delhi: Oxford University Press.

Renfrew, C. (1987) *Archaeology and Language: The Puzzle of Indo-European Origins*, London: Penguin.

Renfrew, C. and Bahn, P. (eds) (2000) *Archaeology: Theories, Methods and Practice*, London: Thames & Hudson.

Riencourt, A. de (1986) *The Soul of India*, London: Honeyglen.

Risso, P. (1995) *Merchants and Faith: Muslim Commerce and Culture in the Indian Ocean*, Boulder, CO: Westview Press.

Rocher, L. (1986) *The Puranas*, Wiesbaden: Otto Harrassowitz.

Rocher, L. (2003) 'The Dharmasastras', pp. 102–15, in G. Flood (ed.), *The Blackwell Companion to Hinduism*, Oxford: Blackwell.

Rocher, R. (1993) 'British Orientalism in the 18th Century: The Dialectics of Knowledge and Government', pp. 215–49, in C. Breckenridge and P. Veer (eds) *Orientalism and the Post-Colonial Predicament: Perspectives on South Asia*, Philadelphia: University of Pennsylvania Press.

Roebuck, V. (2000) *The Upanisads*, London: Penguin.

Rowland, B. (1977) *The Pelican History of Art*, London: Penguin.

Rypka, J. (1968) History of Iranian Literature, Dordrecht: D. Reidel.

Sachau, E. (1888) *Alberuni's India*, Vols. 1 & 2, London: Trubner.

Said, E. (1994) *Culture and Imperialism*, London: Vintage.

Saletore, R.N. (1973) *Early Indian Economic History*, London: Curzon Press.

Samaddar, J.N. (1922) *The Glories of Magadha*, Patna: Patna University Press.

Sankalia, H.D. (1972) *The University of Nalanda*, Delhi: Oriental.

Sarasvati, S. (1986) *A Critical Study of Brahmagupta and his Works*, Delhi: Govindram Haranand.

Sarkar. J.C. (1928) *Some Aspects of the Earliest Social History of India*, London: Oxford University Press.

Sastri, G. (1960) *A Concise History of Classical Sanskrit*, Oxford: Oxford University Press.

Sastri, K.N. (1957) *New Light on the Indus Civilization*, Vol. 1, Delhi: Atma Ram.

Sastri, K.N. (1965) *New Light on the Indus Civilization*, Vol. 2, Delhi: Atma Ram.

Sastri, N. (1977) *A History of South India*, Madras: Oxford University Press.

Satianathaier, R. (1957) 'The Cholas', pp. 234–55, in R.C. Majumdar and A.D. Pusalker, (eds), *The Struggle for Empire*, Bombay: Bharatiya Vidya Bhavan.

Savory, R.M. (ed.) (1976) *An Introduction to Islamic Civilization*, Cambridge: Cambridge University Press.

Scarre, C. (ed.) (2005) *The Human Past: World Prehistory and the Development of Human Societies*, London: Thames & Hudson.

Schwartzberg, J. (1992) *A Historical Atlas of South Asia*, Oxford: Oxford University Press.

Sen, A. (2005) *The Argumentative Indian: Writings on Indian History, Culture and Identity*, London: Allen Lane.

Sen, K.M. (1961) *Hinduism*, London: Penguin.

Seneviratne, S. (1978) 'The Mauryan State', pp. 381–402, in H.J.M. Claessen and P. Skalnik (eds), *The Early State*, The Hague: Mouton.

Sengupta, P. (1950) *Everyday Life in Ancient India*, Oxford, Oxford University Press.

Sengupta, R. (1993) *Ajanta and Ellora: Our World in Colour*, Hong Kong: The Guidebook Company.

Shamasastry, R. (trans.) (1923) *Arthasastra*, Mysore: Wesleyan Mission Press.

Sharma, B.N. (1972) *Social and Cultural History of North India* c. *1000–1200 AD*, New Delhi: Abhinav.

Sharma, J.P. (1968) *Republics in Ancient India*, Leiden: Brill.

Sharma, R.N. (1977) *Brahmins through the Ages*, Delhi: Ajanta.

Sharma, R.S. (1958) *Sudras in Ancient India*, Delhi: Motilal Banarsidass.

Sharma, R.S. (1959) *Aspects of Political Ideas and Institutions in Ancient India*, Delhi: Motilal Banarsidass.

Sharma, R.S. (1985) 'How Feudal was Indian Feudalism?', pp. 19–43, in *Journal of Peasant Studies*, Vol. 12, Nos. 2–3, Jan–April.

Sharma, R.S. (2001) *Early Medieval Indian Society: A Study in Feudalisation*, Hyderabad: Orient Longman.

Shrimali, K.M. (2001) 'Medievalism Defined', in *Frontline* [magazine of the newspaper *Hindu*], 18, June–July.

Sidebotham, S.E. (1991) 'Ports of the Red Sea and Arabia–India Trade', pp. 12–38, in V. Begley and R. de Puma (eds), *Rome and India*, Madison: University of Wisconsin Press

Siegel, L. (1978) *Sacred and Profane Dimensions of Love in Indian Traditions as Exemplified in the Gita Govinda*, Delhi: Oxford University Press.

Singer, M. (ed.) (1959) *Traditional India: Structure and Change*, Philadelphia: American Folklore Society.

Singh, G.P. (2003) *Ancient Indian Historiography: Sources and Interpretations*, New Delhi: D.K. Printworld.

Singh, S.D. (1965) *Ancient Indian Warfare, with special reference to the Vedic Period*, Leiden: Brill.

Sinor, D. (ed.) (1990) *The Cambridge History of Early Inner Asia*, Cambridge: Cambridge University Press.

Sircar, D.C. (1971) *Studies in the Geography of Ancient and Medieval India*, Delhi: Motilal Banarsidass.

Sivaramamurti, C. (1977) The Art of India, New York: Harry Abrams.

Smart, N. (ed.) (1999) *Atlas of the World's Religions*, Oxford: Oxford University Press.

Smith, B. (1983) *Essays in Gupta Culture*, Delhi: Motilal Banarsidass.

Smith, V. (1909) *Asoka*, Oxford: Oxford University Press.

Smith, V. (1924) *Early History of India, from 600 BC to the Muhammadan Conquest*, Oxford: Oxford University Press.

Smith, V. (1958) *The Oxford History of India*, 3rd edn, rev. P. Spear, Oxford: Oxford University Press.

Soundararajan, K.V. (1981) 'In Quest of Man: Anthropological Bias in Archaeology', pp. 3–7, in M.S. Nagaraja Rao (ed.), *Madhu: Recent Researches in Indian Archaeology and Art History*, Delhi: Agam Kala Prakashan.

Southworth, F.C. (1995) 'Reconstructing Social Contact from Language: Indo-Aryan and Dravidian Pre-History', pp. 258–77, in G. Erdosy (ed.), *The Indo-Aryans of Ancient South Asia: Language, Material Culture and Ethnicity*, Berlin: Walter de Gruyter.

Spellman. J.W. (1964) *Political Theory of Ancient India: A Study of Kingship from the Earliest Times to c. AD 300*, London: Oxford University Press.

Srivastava, K.M. (1984) 'The Myth of Aryan Invasion of Harappan Towns', pp. 437–43, in B.B. Lal and S.P. Gupta (eds), *Frontiers of the Indus Civilisation: Sir Mortimer Wheeler Commemoration Volume*, New Delhi: Indian Archaeological Society.

Stadter, P.A. (1980) *Arrian of Nicomedia*, Chapel Hill: University of North Carolina Press.

Stein, B. (1980) Peasant State and Society in Medieval South India, Oxford: Oxford University Press.

Stein, B. (1985) 'Politics, Peasants and the Deconstruction of Feudalism in Medieval India', pp. 228–51, in *Journal of Peasant Studies*, Vol. 12, Nos. 2–3, Jan–April.

Stein, B. (1998) *A History of India*, Oxford: Blackwell.

Stein, M.A. ([1900] 1961) *Kalhana's Rajatarangini*, Vols. 1 & 2, Delhi: Motilal Banarsidass.

Swami Prabhavananda (1952) 'Is Vedanta for the West?', pp. 12–14, in C. Isherwood (ed.), *Vedanta for Modern Man*, London: Allen & Unwin.

Tarn, W.W. (1951) *The Greeks in Bactria and India*, Cambridge: Cambridge University Press.

Tattersall, I. (1997) 'Out of Africa Again … and Again?', pp. 60–67, in *Scientific American*, Vol. 276.

Thapar, B.K. (1984) 'Six Decades of the Indus Studies', pp. 1–25, in B.B. Lal and S.P. Gupta (eds), *Frontiers of the Indus Civilisation: Sir Mortimer Wheeler Commemoration Volume*, New Delhi: Indian Archaeological Society.

Thapar, R. (1993) *Interpreting Early India*, Oxford: Oxford University Press.

Thapar, R. (1995) 'The First Millennium BC in Northern India', pp. 80–141, in R. Thapar (ed.), *Recent Perspectives of Early Indian History*, Bombay: Popular Prakashan.

Thapar, R. (1998) *Asoka and the Decline of the Mauryas*, Oxford: Oxford University Press.

Thapar, R. (2002) *Early India: From the Origins to AD 1300*, London: Allen Lane.

Time-Life Books (1994) *Ancient India: Land of Mystery*, Alexandria, VA: Time-Life Books.

Tomber, R. (2000) 'Indo-Roman Trade: Ceramic Evidence from Egypt', pp. 624–31, in *Antiquity*, 74 (285), September.

Tomory, E. (1989) *A History of Fine Arts in India and the West*, Hyderabad: Orient Longman.

Toth, N. and Schick, K. (2005) 'African Origins', pp. 46–83, in C. Scarre (ed.), *The Human Past: World Prehistory and the Development of Human Societies*, London: Thames & Hudson.

Trautmann, T. (1971) *Kautiliya and the Arthasastra*, Leiden: Brill.

Trautmann, T. (1981) *Dravidian Kinship*, Cambridge: Cambridge University Press.

Trautmann, T. (1997) *Aryans and British India*, Berkeley: University of California Press.

Tripathi, R. (1999) *History of Ancient India*, Delhi: Motilal Banarsidass.

Venkat, K. (n.d.) 'A Critical review of Romila Thapar's "Early India, from the Origins to AD 1300"', www.bharatvani.org/RomilaThapar-EarlyIndia.html.

Vivekananda Kendra Prakashan (1980) *Imprints of Indian Thought and Culture Abroad*, Madras: Jupiter Press.

Walker. B. (1968) *The Hindu World*, Vols. 1 & 2, London: Allen & Unwin.

Warder, A.K. (2002) *Indian Buddhism*, Delhi: Motilal Banarsidass.

Watters, T. (1904) On Yuan Chwang's Travels in India, 629–645 AD, London: Royal Asiatic Society.

Wells, H.G. (1920) *The Outline of History*, 2 vols, London: Waverley.

Wells, S. (2003) *The Journey of Man: A Genetic Odyssey*, New York: Random House.

Wheeler, M ([1947] 1979) 'Harappan Chronology and the Rig Veda', pp. 289–92, in G. Possehl (ed.), *Ancient Cities of the Indus*, New Delhi: Vikas.

Wheeler, M. (1955) *Still Digging*, New York: E.P. Dutton.

Wheeler, M. (1966) *Civilization of the Indus Valley and Beyond*, London: Thames & Hudson.

Wickens, G.M. (1976) 'The Middle East as a World Centre of Science and Medicine', pp. 111–19, in R.M. Savory (ed.) *An Introduction to Islamic Civilization*, Cambridge: Cambridge University Press.

Williamson, F. (1999) Marx and the Millennium: A Short Guide to the Universe, Ceredigion: Owain Hammond.

Wink, A. (1991) *Al-Hind: The Making of the Indo-Islamic World*, Vol. 1: *Early Medieval India and the Expansion of Islam, 7th to 11th centuries*, Leiden: Brill.

Wink, A. (1997) *Al-Hind: The Making of the Indo-Islamic World*, Vol. II: *The Slave Kings and the Islamic Conquest 11th to 13th centuries*, Leiden: Brill.

Wink, A. (2001) 'India and the Turko-Mongol Frontier', pp. 211–33, in A.M. Khazanov and A. Wink (eds), *Nomads in the Sedentary World*, London: Curzon Press.

Witzel, M. (1995) 'RigVedic history: Poets, Chieftains and Polities', pp. 307–52, in G. Erdosy (ed.), *The Indo-Aryans of Ancient South Asia: Language, Material Culture and Ethnicity*, Berlin: Walter de Gruyter.

Witzel, M. (2006) 'Languages and Scripts of India', pp. 50–56, in S. Wolpert (ed.), *Encyclopedia of India*, Vol. 3, New York: Thomson Gale.

Witzel, M. and Farmer, S (2000) 'Horseplay in Harappa', in *Frontline* [magazine of the newspaper *Hindu*], 20, 30 Sept–13 Oct.

Wolpert, S. (ed.) (2006) *Encyclopedia of India*, 4 vols, New York: Thomson Gale.

Yano, M. (2003) 'Calendar, Astrology and Astronomy', in G. Flood (ed.), *The Blackwell Companion to Hinduism*, Oxford: Blackwell.

Yashaschandra, S. (2003) 'From Hemacandra to Hind Swaraj', pp. 567–611, in S. Pollock (ed.), Literary Cultures in History: Reconstructions from South Asia, Berkeley: University of California Press.

Yazdani, G. (1960) *The Early History of the Deccan*, Vol. 1, Hyderabad: Oxford University Press & Government of Andhra Pradesh.

Yu, Y.-S. (1990) 'The Hsiung-nu', pp. 118–49, in D. Sinor (ed.), *The Cambridge History of Early Inner Asia*, Cambridge: Cambridge University Press.

Zelinsky, A.N. (1970) 'Kushans and Mahayana', pp. 156–7, in B. Gafurov *et al.* (eds), *Kushan Studies in the USSR*, Calcutta: Indian Studies Past and Present.

Zevmal, E.V. (1970) 'Kaniska's Dates', pp. 152–5, in B. Gafurov *et al.* (eds), *Kushan Studies in the USSR*, Calcutta: Indian Studies Past and Present.

Index

0799 151